THE FORGING OF THE UNION
1781–1789

The
New American Nation Series

EDITED BY

HENRY STEELE COMMAGER

AND

RICHARD B. MORRIS

THE FORGING OF
THE UNION
1781 ★ 1789

RICHARD B. MORRIS

ILLUSTRATED

1817

HARPER & ROW, PUBLISHERS, New York
Cambridge, Philadelphia, San Francisco, Washington
London, Mexico City, São Paulo, Singapore, Sydney

FIRST EDITION

Designer: Sidney Feinberg

Copy editor: Ann Adelman

Indexer: Maro Riofrancos

Library of Congress Cataloging-in-Publication Data

Morris, Richard Brandon, 1904–
  The forging of the Union, 1781–1789.

  (The New American Nation series)
  Bibliography: p.
  Includes index.
  1. United States—Politics and government—1783–1789.
2. United States—Constitutional history. 3. United
States—Constitution. I. Title. II. Series.
E303.M884 1987   973.3   86-46091
ISBN 0-06-015733-X
ISBN 0-06-091424-6 (pbk.)   87 88 89 90 91 HC 10 9 8 7 6 5 4 3 2 1
                                 87 88 89 90 91 HC 10 9 8 7 6 5 4 3 2 1

CASS CANFIELD
In Memoriam

Contents

Illustrations

*These photographs, grouped in a separate section,
will be found following page 114*

These photographs, grouped in a separate section, will be found following page 242

Preface

IN June of 1785, shortly after arriving in Paris as America's minister to France, Thomas Jefferson urged James Monroe to take a trip to Europe. "It will make you adore your own country," he urged, "its climate, its equality, liberty, laws, people, and manners. My God! How little do my countrymen know what precious blessings they are in possession of, and which no other people on earth enjoy!"

Jefferson was speaking in comparative terms, of course. When he had left his native land, the postwar depression had by no means run its course. The Congress under the Confederation, lacking both power and energy, was still attempting unavailingly to resolve crucial issues both foreign and domestic, and the majority of America's rapidly growing population—blacks, poor whites, Indians, and women—possessed few of the "precious blessings" to which Jefferson alluded.

A very different comment was elicited a little over a year later by George Washington: "I predict," he warned, "the worst consequences from a half-starved, limping government, always moving upon crutches and tottering at every step." Other nationalist statesmen of the stamp of James Madison, Alexander Hamilton, and John Jay would have emphatically endorsed the General's further observation: "I do not conceive we can long exist as a nation without having lodged somewhere a power which will pervade the whole

Union in as energetic a manner as the authority of the State government extends over the several states."

Washington's opinion of the necessity of a more effective union found dissenters among the ranks of state political leaders and other Antifederalists. Rather, did the latter subscribe to the judgment of New York's governor, George Clinton, that the calling of the Federal Convention in Philadelphia was "calculated to impress the people with an idea of evils which do not exist."

In sum, whether judging the Confederation period from the vantage point of Europe or of America, whether possessed of the cosmopolitan vision of nationalist-minded statesmen or seen in a narrower and more parochial focus, the years 1781 to 1789 were perceived very differently, and these differences have divided historians down to the present day. On balance one must concede that the burgeoning sense of American nationality, both culturally and politically, was an essential prelude to the establishment of the federal government. Crowded with critical events and culminating in crucial decisions, the Confederation years had their severe shortcomings and failed initiatives, to be sure. However, these very same years witnessed the states putting their written constitutions to the test, while a Congress, circumscribed though it was by the Articles of Confederation, created a notable plan for the settling and government of the West.

Debates raged during these years over the critical issue of how best the American people could bolster their central government. Grave doubts were entertained whether a central government could effectually extend its rule over an immense expanse of territory and remain a republic, faithful to the great principles for which the American Revolution was fought. Would not so strong a central structure fatally weaken the sovereignty of the states and threaten civil liberties? Would it not perpetuate a government by the elite to the detriment of the common people?

The statesmen of that day, a collection of dedicated and creative figures, wrestled with these central issues and argued them at length both in print and in the forums provided by the Federal Convention and the state ratifying conventions that followed. Seemingly intractable problems were resolved by combining audacious initiatives with a series of compromises deemed necessary to forge a union, preserve the states, and guarantee the people's liberties.

Reexamined in these pages, the Confederation interlude proved an extraordinary, if brief, period of trial and experimentation. Prior to the adoption of the federal Constitution, misgivings were widespread as to whether an American union could survive, whether republican values could be perpetuated, whether a strengthened central government could be trusted with the power to deal as an equal with the great states of Europe, whether its creation would bring prosperity to a nation wracked by depression, would allay sectional tensions and silence secessionist murmurings. The inauguration of a creative constitutional era which endowed a federal republic with powers necessary to promote the general welfare and secure the blessings of liberty held out the prospect of resolving these questions, of confounding the doubters, and placing the national interest on a durable foundation.

In the preparation of this volume the author needs acknowledge a number of weighty debts: first of all, to the co-editor of the New American Nation series, a former colleague and ever close associate, Henry Steele Commager, who has mingled patience, discerning judgment, and encouragement in the right proportions at every stage of the enterprise; to the late Cass Canfield, editor and dear friend, whose enthusiasm and unstinting support contributed so much to the initiation of this volume and to the series which he persuaded his firm to undertake; for helpfulness at every turn my sincere appreciation to the Associate Editor of the Papers of John Jay, Ene Sirvet, as well as to another Jay Papers associate, Richard B. Bernstein of the New York bar, whose close knowledge of discrete sources and relevant monographic items proved most suggestive; and to my wife, Berenice Robinson Morris, whose literary criticisms have been invaluable. Margaret C. M. Christman of The National Portrait Gallery, Smithsonian Institution, and Cynthia Harrison, managing editor of *this Constitution,* were most helpful in locating illustrative material. Recognition is due as well to Project '87—a joint enterprise of the American Historical Association and the American Political Science Association—whose knowledgeable colleagues and stimulating conferences over the past decade with their focus on constitutional issues have provided numerous insights and points of departure for this writer.

The John Simon Guggenheim Memorial Foundation generously provided the support essential to completing this enterprise. Chapter III was written at the Villa Serbelloni in Bellagio, for whose gracious hospitality I am indebted to the Rockefeller Foundation.

*   *   *   *

   The Forging of the Union, 1781–1789 constitutes a volume in the New American Nation Series, a comprehensive and cooperative study of the area now embraced in the United States from the days of discovery to our own age. While the focus of the present volume is, as the title suggests, on the events leading toward the adoption of the Constitution, it has a much wider orbit. The subsequent course of constitutional development is surveyed in four other volumes in this series: the period from 1789 to 1835, from the Jay court through Marshall, to be treated in a forthcoming volume by Richard E. Ellis. Professors Harold M. Hyman and William M. Wiecek in *Equal Justice Under Law* examine the critical constitutional years, 1835 to 1877; Loren P. Beth has explored the subject from 1877 to 1917; while Paul L. Murphy has taken the story down through the Warren court.

                                        RICHARD B. MORRIS
Columbia University

CHAPTER 1

A People, Independent
and at Peace

The Wounds of War

THE great news traveled slowly. It was not until November 22, 1783, two years and three days after the British had laid down their arms at Yorktown, that John Thaxter, Jr., private secretary to peace commissioner John Adams, reached Philadelphia with a copy of the Definitive Treaty between Great Britain and the United States recognizing America's independence. State delegates to Congress, at the summons of President Thomas Mifflin of Pennsylvania, headed toward the Annapolis State House where Congress was assembling. They proceeded at their customary sluggish gait, further slowed by winter travel. Nine states were needed for ratification of a treaty, and one state was still missing.

Finally on January 13, 1784, Richard Beresford, a delegate from South Carolina and convalescing from a long illness, managed to make his appearance. The true hero of the moment, Beresford provided the necessary vote, and Congress proceeded to ratify the treaty the following day. Only six weeks remained to exchange formal ratifications according to the treaty's terms, and three separate agents were chosen to engage separate passage to Europe, each with a copy of the ratification. The British proved not at all sticky about the delay, and, when Colonel Josiah Harmar reached Paris first, Benjamin Franklin and John Jay for the United States and David Hartley for Great Britain exchanged ratifications on May 12.

True, fighting had ceased for some two years, but now the war was officially at an end.[1]

For almost a whole decade a state of war had existed on the lands bordering the North Atlantic coast, and for most of those years men had bled and died. A countryside had been devastated, cities burned and trashed, and families left to their own resources. From Burgoyne's path of burning and desolation in the north country to Waxhaws and Eutaw Springs, from the climactic victory at Yorktown to that nameless field in South Carolina where the gallant John Laurens had fallen a victim of partisan warfare that had continued for months after Cornwallis's surrender, the war had inflicted immense human and property losses. The war had ended, too, on other continents and on the high seas where fighting had spread, as France and then Spain joined the war against England, and the Dutch were forced into it as well. But in America the scars were not easily erased, not all the wounded completely healed, nor could families too quickly forget the tragedy of a civil war fought by a divided people for independence from a great world empire.

Perhaps nowhere on the North American main were the wounds of war more visible than in New York City, soon to be the seat of Congress under the Confederation. On November 25, 1783, the British and Hessian troops—some six thousand who stayed until the end—in addition to the many thousands of despondent Loyalists, who had already begun their exodus from the city months before, evacuated the city.[2] It was a cheerless parting, no formal surrender or even the lowering of the British colors, which had to be removed from a greased flagpole on the Battery and the American flag raised in their place.[3] Attainted, their property forfeited, or fearful of reprisals from returning Patriots, the Loyalists left with bitterness in their hearts toward the insurgents and with grave doubts about the wisdom of the British government's strategy in fighting the lost cause. One of the wealthiest, William Bayard, was clear about his feelings. "The Rebels, for I shall never call them anything else—have confiscated every shilling of my valuable property in this Country and passed an Act of Attainder against my person, so that I am now going off in a manner of a Beggar to my children and Friends in old England."[4] Fortunately for Bayard and many other Loyalists, the British government proved generous in settling their claims and making it possible for them to start a new life in Nova Scotia,

Canada, or England, while a select group of Loyalists managed to ride out the storm and build solid new careers in New York, Philadelphia, and elsewhere in the States.

The wounds of war were shared by distressed and impoverished Loyalists and by British troops as well. When the latter disembarked in England at a variety of harbors, the thinness of their ranks must have provoked some comment on the costs of the war. Fraser's Highlanders, who left England in 1776 two thousand strong, returned from New York with but three hundred men, and the thousand men of the Twentieth Regiment were reduced to some hundred and ten.[5]

In turn, a skeleton force of picked Continental troops, a mere eight hundred, made their entry into the city on Evacuation Day, moved down the Bowery in martial order, to be warmly greeted by large crowds of returned Patriots at Queen (Pearl) and Wall streets. The Battery was the scene of the formal occupation, the flag-raising, and the thirteen-gun salute. Later in the day Governor George Clinton gave a public dinner at Fraunces Tavern, located at the corner of Queen and Broad streets, an event followed a week afterwards at the same location by Washington's farewell to his officers. Toasting them with a glass of wine, he said, "I cannot come to each of you but should be obliged if each of you will come and take me by the hand." He then embraced each officer in turn.[6] Following this final gathering, Washington walked to Whitehall where a boat waited to ferry him to New Jersey. Thence he proceeded to Annapolis, where he resigned his commission in a brief but eloquent address, and returned to his plantation at Mount Vernon.

The returning Patriots, a ragged lot, were confronted by the spectacle of a city in ruins. The great fire of '76, quickly following the occupation of the British Army after Washington's miraculous escape from Brooklyn Heights, cut a swath up both sides of Broadway to Rector Street, a tragic sight enhanced by a second fire two years later, which reduced the lower part of the city to a charred wreck. "The skeletons of the remaining walls cast their grim shadows upon the pavement, imparting an unearthly aspect to the street. The semicircular front of old Trinity still reared its ghastly head, and seemed to deepen while it hallowed the solitude of the surrounding graves," was the way one resident remembered it.[7] Canvas roofs covered ruined buildings and served as temporary housing for the impoverished and even disreputable elements, earning the name of "Canvas Town." Everywhere lay filth, dirt, and rubbish, testimony to how thoroughly the town had been trashed in the years of military occupation.

A city so completely unprepared for the mass arrivals of Patriot families who had fled from it in 1776 suffered a degree of poverty in the winter of 1783–84 it had never before experienced. Almost a thousand families were reported by the newspapers in 1784 to be on relief rolls. The almshouse was jammed beyond capacity, and Mayor Varnum was moved to express concern about "an idle and profligate banditti" and other "abandoned Vagrants and prostitutes" who were guilty of "shameful Enormities."[8]

New York City's experience was by no means unique. Port cities and inland villages had been put to the torch. The British Navy had burnt Falmouth (now Portland, Maine), given an artillery drubbing to Bristol, Rhode Island. As late as 1788, Brissot de Warville saw vestiges of the deliberate burning of handsome Patriot residences in Fairfield, Connecticut, at the behest of Tory Governor Tryon,[9] while New London and Groton still bore the scars of raids.

Frontier outposts, scenes of Indian warfare, like Cherry Valley and German Flats in New York and the Wyoming Valley of Pennsylvania, bore devastating testimony to some of the ugliest engagements of the war. Areas where war raged back and forth over the long years suffered the most. Despite the injunctions of both Howe and Cornwallis against plundering by their troops, New York and New Jersey proved fair game for Hessians and Redcoats. Pillaging was ruefully conceded by British and Hessian officers, while at the behest of Congress long and detailed lists of depredations allegedly committed by enemy forces were prepared.[10]

True, looting was not limited to one side, and the misbehavior of American troops embittered many patriotic civilians as well as Loyalist victims of "foraging," a word often synonymous with plundering.[11] If Westchester County, Princeton, Woodbridge, Newark, Bergen, and Elizabethtown suffered heavily from military incursions on both sides,[12] the South was not spared. Scenes of pillage and looting were still visible at war's end. Henry Laurens found his Charleston residence pillaged, and his plantation wrecked, with damages estimated at £30,000.[13] Eliza Lucas Pinckney has left us a graphic account of looting and pillaging of plantations by British troops, of days spent in anxiety and nights "wearisome and painful." The fire in 1778 which enveloped a considerable part of Charleston contributed to the wartime losses suffered by the principal Southern city to be occupied by the British. The deprivations of the aged and other civilians during the British occupation provided a topic of incessant conversation in the years that followed the British withdrawal from the South. Francis Marion, coming up after a Tarleton raid, told of finding "women and children" sitting "in the Open air round a fire without a blanket or any Cloathing but what they had on."[14] In their northern progress the Redcoats slashed through Wilmington, North Carolina, and the Cape Fear region, while tidewater Virginia between the York and James was ravished of slaves and livestock.

Ugly stories of rape by British and Hessian troops were given credence, if not always verified. In 1779 depositions were collected from women victims at Fairfield and New Haven, as well as in New Jersey and adjacent Staten Island. Lord Rawdon, a cavalry commander, dismissed such incidents with ill-disguised male chauvinism. "The fair nymphs of this isle [Staten Island] are in wonderful tribulation," he reported, adding: "as girls cannot step into the bushes to pluck a rose without running the most imminent risk of being ravished," with the result that "we have the most entertaining courts-martial every day." Depositions were also collected by the Continental Congress of multiple rapes of young girls in New Jersey.[15]

Although abroad on a diplomatic mission for the greater part of the war, old Benjamin Franklin was as well informed about war atrocities, real and fictitious, as anyone who had suffered scalping in the Northern forests or felt the cold steel of Banastre Tarleton's bayonets. At a critical moment in the preliminary peace negotiations when the British were insistent on compensation to the Loyalists for their losses, Franklin pulled a paper out of his pocket which was in fact a memorandum addressed to his good friend Richard Oswald, peace commissioner of the opposite side. Reading through his bifocal lenses he insisted that

if a reconciliation was intended, no mention should be made in our negotiations of those people [i.e., the Loyalists]; for they having done infinite mischief to our properties, by wantonly burning and destroying farm houses, villages, and towns, if compensation for their losses were insisted on, we should certainly exhibit against it an account of all the ravages they had committed, which would necessarily recall to view scenes of barbarity, that must inflame. Instead of conciliating, they tend to perpetuate an enmity that we all profess a desire of extinguishing.

Then the old doctor proceeded to itemize wanton acts committed not only by the Loyalists but by British troops—listing towns and villages, he added, "besides near a hundred and fifty miles of well settled country laid waste; every house and barn burnt, and many hundred of farmers, with their wives and children, butchered and scalped." Toward the close of the negotiations he came up with a new demand for reparations, citing a variety of atrocities, including the rifling of his own library in Philadelphia, and Henry Laurens reminded the negotiators of the plundering of Negroes and plate from the Carolinas. According to Shelburne's later recollection, Franklin threatened to sell the German prisoners unless the Negroes were restored or paid for.[16] Franklin was bluffing, of course, but he sent chills up and down the spines of the British Cabinet members, who made strenuous efforts to stiffen the terms their conciliatory negotiator was ready to concede.

Perhaps fortunately for history there were no reparations and no war guilt clause, but a number of provisions of the treaty concerning the treatment of Loyalists and British creditors plagued diplomatic negotiations between the former colonies and the mother country for another twenty years.

All the wounds to America's land and resources were not war-inflicted. Fortuitously, the prospects of expansion into vast new and largely virgin lands made possible by the Peace of 1783 (albeit migrants into the Southwest had preceded that diplomatic triumph by some decades) came at a critical time for American farming, forestry, and hunting. By the time of the Revolution the forested portion of lands in the seaboard colonies had been drastically reduced. Fast disappearing were such animals as the beaver, bear, deer, porcupine, and wolf. Fish in traditional waters were far less plentiful, and birds like eagles, pigeons, heathcotes, turkeys, and swans were disappearing. Writing three quarters of a century after the American Revolution, Henry David Thoreau contrasted the land and wildlife he saw round about him with what had been described in 1633 by William Wood in his *New England Prospect,* and concluded, "I cannot but feel as if I lived in a tamed, and, as it were, emasculated country," where nature was "maimed and imperfect."[17]

Conceding that the ecological changes had not been as severe in 1783 as in the 1850s, when Thoreau was writing, it is all too evident that they had been under way since the first white settlers came to the New World and for a long time before. What contemporaries observed in the 1780s was that, while the landscape was altered, human development had greatly progressed. What they were comparing, of course, was the Indian's role as clearer of the forests and in subsistence culture to the relatively prosperous commercial farming of the white settlers.

That achievement had come at a great cost to the ecological systems of the older settled areas. Aside from deforestation, to which the Indians had heavily contributed by burning forests to clear land for agriculture and facilitate hunting, the white European settlers' use of maize as a staple crop in New England because of its high yield, and of tobacco cultivation in the upper South, contributed enormously to soil exhaustion. Similarly, by allowing livestock to wander about the land, the farmers, in areas where this practice was prevalent, lost one of the principal sources of fertilizer in Europe—animal manure, a failure in America which adversely affected not only cropland but meadows and pastures as well, despite the use of fish as a substitute fertilizer. By the Confederation years, the building of dams for mills and the initiation of canal projects prevented both the smaller fish like alewives, a fish of the herring family, and larger fish as well from returning upstream, emptying whole rivers of products like salmon.

People in farming areas, who represented some 95 percent of the total population in 1790, were victimized by more obvious disasters. By the end of the eighteenth century the Hessian fly had brought a virtual end to wheat raising in Connecticut, and New England wheat production would never recover. New Jersey's wheatlands were similarly blighted. What the Hessian fly did not accomplish a fungus, black stem rust, provided in additional devastation, destroying the leaves of wheat plants before they had a chance to produce seed.

Industrialization also had ecological consequences. Iron furnaces in New England, the Middle Colonies, and Virginia raised the fuel consumption of these regions appreciably, as they required the burning of excessive amounts of charcoal, which in turn could only be obtained by burning still more excessive piles of wood. In New Jersey, the Union furnace, after exhausting a forest of twenty thousand acres in a dozen years, had to be abandoned.[18] Thus, local deforestation could be directly attributed to the expanding iron industry, while the spread of tanneries encouraged the cutting of oak and hemlock for their tanbark.

Hence, the opening to the inhabitants of the original thirteen states of unsettled lands in northern New England and beyond the Piedmont in the South, as well as the later population of the fertile lands of the Old Northwest, injected a new note of optimism for the occupations of farming and hunting, seemingly holding out boundless opportunities for merchants and skilled artisans.

The lessons of the ecological dangers wrought by European settlement, farming methods, and industrialization should have sounded a note of caution. As Carl Sauer remarks, America had "not yet learned the difference between yield and loot," or as a recent ecological observer has put it, "ecological abundance and economic prodigality went hand in hand; the people of plenty were a people of waste."[19] As long as land was cheap and available, why conserve? The decline of the soil was a price pioneers were prepared to pay so long as they were ready to move to new virgin lands and so long as these were available on relatively easy terms. The story should have been learned by 1783. But it had to be relearned in virtually every generation thereafter down to the Dust Bowl, acid rain, and nuclear radiation, and at the expense of the earth, its priceless but limited resources, and all its inhabitants.

Wounds there were, physical as well as psychological, but time and industry would heal them, restore ravaged towns and countryside, and get the American people to move from the tasks of war to the work of peace. Franklin, still overseas, quite judiciously summed up the situation in America after the war:

> The Truth is, that though there are in that Country few People so miserable as the Poor of Europe, there are also very few that in Europe would be called rich. It is rather a general happy mediocrity that prevails. There are few great Proprietors of the Soil and few Tenants; most People cultivate

their own Lands, or follow some Handicraft or Merchandise; very few [are] rich enough to live idly upon Their Rents or Incomes. . . . Of civil Offices, or Employments, there are few, no superfluous Ones, as in Europe; and it is a Rule established in some of the States, that no Office should be so profitable as to make it desirable.[20]

True, some recent historians might challenge the notion of this "happy mediocrity," of the lack of poverty, or of Franklin's failure to mention the importance of slave labor, which gave an aristocratic complexion to the Southern plantation scene. But for much of America, for the penniless returning soldiers, Franklin's was the kind of country they found—a land where big business had not yet established a firm foothold, a country basically agricultural, where land in freehold tenure was preferred and almost everywhere available (save for a few pockets of tenancy in the Hudson Valley and the Chesapeake), and where the vast territories acquired by the Peace of 1783 widened the horizons for the average man and woman beyond the limits of pre-Revolutionary years.

By no stretch of the imagination could one call America in 1783 an egalitarian society (and this book will treat this subject at some length), but reforming idealism was heading the nation in that direction, swiftly for some, haltingly for others. There were church establishments, but their impact was attenuated by the increasing multiplicity of sects and the growing climate of freedom of conscience and disestablishment. Deference still existed, but it lacked any legal or institutional base. Exclusive elites could no longer control politics in a society where 50 to 80 percent of the adult white male population were enfranchised. Above all inequalities there was slavery, but even here the momentum for outright or gradual abolition was under way in the North. Abuses of power were checked by state constitutional structures, by enumerated bills of rights in some states, and by systems of representative government. A slow, if tortuous reform of the law was also under way, and, while large sections of the population—blacks, white indentured servants, Indians, women, and minors—benefited marginally, if at all, by these reforms, the white male freeholding citizenry shared opportunities for advancement unparalleled in any corner of the inhabited globe.

Freehold tenure and seemingly limitless possibilities for acquiring land held forth by the victorious treaty proved a magnet for

European peasantry. Surely this was no *ancien régime,* and prospects for social mobility seemed boundless. As one historian has penetratingly observed, "The Revolution transformed America, not apocalyptically (there was no need or desire for that) but incrementally, and it has continued to radiate out into the ever-recurring evils of a dynamic, fiercely ambitious, ruthlessly creative, tense, and violent society because, despite the evident obstacles to fulfillment, its goals have always, in some significant degree, seemed realistic."[21]

The Prize of War

Suffering and loss were the toll of war. The constructive fact was that a world war had ended. From the first successful revolution of modern times of colonies against a mother country, a new nation had emerged. Tom Paine could exult in a closing "Crisis" paper written April 19, 1783: "The times that tried men's souls are over and the greatest and completest revolution the world ever knew gloriously and happily accomplished." With his accustomed rhetorical enthusiasm Paine may have given the impression that all the aims of the Revolution had been accomplished, which was far from true, but immense opportunities lay ahead, and the prize of the war was commanding.

Aside from the acknowledgment of independence, with its freedom from colonial subordination, the Definitive Treaty more than doubled the territory of the United States. In effect, it now was the largest republic in territorial extent since the Roman Republic which failed to survive Julius Caesar.

The treaty acknowledged as American territory huge belts of unoccupied land stretching from the eastern coast of Maine to the Great Lakes, southward to the borders of Spanish Florida, and from the Atlantic to the Mississippi. Almost all of northern New England invited occupancy, its only settled areas extending perhaps forty miles up the valleys of the Kennebec and Penobscot rivers, and in Vermont habitations stretched on thin strips along the Connecticut River and the eastern shore of Lake Champlain. New York beckoned New Englanders in the forested areas north of the Mohawk River, while the upper three fifths of Pennsylvania were virtually uninhabited, to say nothing of the wooded lands of Ohio and Indiana. The western frontier of Virginia, the greatest state then in population and in extent of territory, was largely unsettled, as were modern West Virginia and Kentucky. Most of the western fifth of North Carolina invited occupancy, although some clearings had already been made in the Watauga River Valley. The unsettled backcountry of Georgia, three hundred miles wide, stretched to the Mississippi, a huge area more than four hundred miles in length at the northern end and nearly six hundred at the southern.[22]

Over these lands, states with charters to the "South Sea," native-born Americans, newly arrived immigrants, and covetous speculators pressed claims and occupancy with a rapidity beyond the expectation of most of the Founding Fathers, and in the process exacerbated conflicts with the Indians who occupied scattered stretches west of the Appalachians. The utilization and ownership of the West would be a preoccupation both of Congress and the states for many years to come, but despite sectional differences, state boundary disputes, mountain barriers, and congressional oversight, the territorial gains won at the peace held out the promise of phenomenal growth for the nation in the decades ahead.

The question was insistent. Could so vast a territory, one divided by two utterly diverse labor systems, be manageable and lasting under a republican form of government, one pursuing elective instead of hereditary principles of choosing leaders, with authority divided between a Congress, technically responsible for war and peace and foreign affairs but limited in its internal authority, and thirteen states tenacious in retaining their sovereignty over most domestic matters? Contemporary examples offered little guidance. The United Provinces which had secured its independence from Spain had formed a Union of Utrecht of 1579, but was in fact a loose confederacy soon ruled by hereditary stadholders, and the Swiss Confederation with its atypical cantonal arrangements and its oligarchic control claimed long precedence as republics. Neither provided a model for this New World nation so vast in territorial extent. The Italian city states were republican in form, but in fact miniature oligarchies. What was now being created was new on the face of the earth.

European observers were generally pessimistic about America's future as a united republic. Josiah Tucker, dean of Gloucester, and a noted political economist, scoffed at the idea of America's potential for grandeur. American diversity of interests, manners, and government could not be bridged, and the citizens' distrust of one another would keep them divided, he prophesied. Other European America-watchers waited impatiently for the new nation to fall apart. The Comte de Vergennes, France's magisterial foreign minister, who scarcely relished America's vast territorial and fisheries' gains at the peace table, observed in 1784 that "the American Confederation has a great tendency toward dissolution," while Frederick the Great predicted that "little by little, colony by colony, province by province Americans would rejoin England and their former footing." Turgot, the French financier and professed friend of America, failed to see the emergence of a "general union of the states," a coalition, "a melting of all the parts together." Rather, he perceived "only an aggregation of parts, always too separate and preserving a tendency to division," nor more than "a copy of the Dutch Republic."[23] Even Tocqueville, writing many years later, but at a time when the American republic was much more sharply divided over the slavery issue than in 1783, expressed his doubts about the duration of a government called upon to hold together forty different peoples disseminated over a territory equal in extent to one half of Europe.[24]

Rising American statesmen shared some of this concern, but the American people and prospective European immigrants saw only opportunity and success where wiser heads saw perils and failure. While they were not privy to the correspondence of the Abbé Galiani, many self-confident Americans would have applauded the sentiments he expressed. As early as May 1776, he had predicted the fall of Europe and the transmigration to America, where lay their fortunes. "Do not buy your house in Chausée d'Antin," he advised one female correspondent. "Buy it in Philadelphia. My misfortune is that there are no abbeys in America."[25]

The Peopling of the New Nation

The six years from the end of the war to the inauguration of the new federal government under the Constitution were marked by a rebound and exceptionally rapid growth of the American population. Estimates placed the population of the United States in 1775 at 2,600,000.[26] Over the eight war years, population, according to the more liberal congressional estimate, dropped to 2,389,300, hardly surprising in view of the war's casualties, the temporary break-up of family life, and the vast exodus of Loyalists and blacks. Then the tide turned. A compounded annual rate of growth of 3.5 percent took place, the highest in American history from 1783 to 1870.[27] The increase may be attributed in no small part to a combination of renewed family life, early marriages, large families, and a surge of immigration which had been curtailed during the war years. The 1790 census reveals that the population had grown to 3,929,625, and that 62.9 percent of the families of the free inhabitants numbered three or more children, with an average of 490 white persons under sixteen years of age to every 1,000 white inhabitants. Out of the total population, blacks numbered 697,624, of whom 59,557 were free blacks. The Southern states, counting their heavier black population, contained a much larger proportion of the nation's inhabitants than they would in the decades ahead. According to the 1790 census, the Southern states had 48.5 percent of the population, with the remainder almost evenly divided between New England and the Middle States.[28]

The Americans of the years of the Confederation were a rural people. Almost 95 percent dwelt on farms or inhabited villages and small towns. On the other hand, although larger towns claiming 2,500 or more inhabitants constituted a mere 5.4 percent of the population, their importance is belied by the statistics. Philadelphia, the nation's capital during most of the years of the Revolution, grew from 30,000 in 1776 to 42,000 (including its suburbs) in 1790; New York, the nation's capital for most of the Confederation years, from 22,000 to 33,000, to which one must add 800 residents of Harlem. Contrariwise, Boston and Charleston expanded more slowly—the former from 16,000 to 18,000; the latter from 14,000 to 16,000. Of the Southern towns, Baltimore scored the greatest gain, more than doubling its numbers from the start of the Revolution to the first federal census, when it boasted 12,500 inhabitants. Urbanization would accelerate in the decades ahead, but the larger towns of the Confederation exercised an influence in commerce, finance, and politics far out of proportion to their numbers and played an exceptional role during the battle over the ratification of the federal Constitution.

While the rates of infant mortality were shockingly high and children's diseases like measles took a heavy toll, those who lived to maturity had almost as good a prospect of longevity as do people today and generally enjoyed a longer life than the average European. The Founding Fathers themselves comprised a respectable number of octogenarians.[29]

"Irregular" though the immigration data prior to 1819 may well be, one can hardly contest the fact that the ever-increasing inflow from Europe and Africa accounted significantly for the noteworthy population expansion in that very brief period between 1783 and 1789. Some immigrants lingered in the coastal ports but the majority seems to have spread into the interior. An impressive segment, perhaps as many as 12,500 German mercenaries, did not avail themselves of the opportunity to join the British and Hessian armies and return to their homes. They seem to have spread out from Baltimore into Virginia and the Carolina mountains and the trans-Allegheny settlements, but, above all, in the German settlements of Pennsylvania.[30]

A heavy majority, however, still came from the British Isles, including Scotch-Irish and Irish, with France adding a small portion. These were largely the hungry, unemployed, and landless, and America beckoned them. "It is our business," said John Adams, "to render our country an asylum, worthy to receive all who may fly to it." While Great Britain attempted to control the exodus of skilled workers and enacted a statute in 1785 prohibiting persons from selling their future service for passage to America, these laws were honored in the breach.[31] During these years it is estimated that redemptioners arriving in Pennsylvania alone from the British Isles and Germany numbered at least 25,000.

After the signing of the Preliminary Peace on November 30, 1782, the British and American participants rode out to Passy together to celebrate the event. There they were joined by some French guests, one of whom took occasion to rub salt into the wounds. Turning to the British, he harped on the theme of "the growing greatness of America," and predicted that "the Thirteen United States would form the greatest empire in the world."

"Yes, sir," Caleb Whitefoord, Richard Oswald's secretary, replied, "and they will *all* speak English; every one of 'em."[32]

Whitefoord's prediction was substantially true, with noteworthy exceptions, and it stood firm for a long, long time. One might have questioned whether, had the United States succeeded in winning

French-speaking Canada at the peace, it would have been possible to have created an effective federal union. That task was much easier in a nation which at the start was overwhelmingly Protestant and English-speaking. Indeed, the problem of creating a union with French-speaking inhabitants of the Roman Catholic faith might have strained the resources of statesmen to the breaking point. Fortunately the United States did not have to wrestle with the almost insuperable problem of the new Third World states today, the problem of building a nation in confrontation with dense and ancient cultural, racial, local, and linguistic differences—problems which are as much cultural as they are political and economic.[33]

Others viewed America not as a land of ex-Britishers but saw it through a kaleidoscope as a nation with people of multicolored coats representing diverse national origins. Tom Paine in his *Common Sense* remarked that America is not a child of England, but of Europe. That New World champion, the French settler Hector St. John de Crèvecoeur, who served for a time in the Confederation's years as a French consul, was inspired to write a tract entitled *Letters From an American Farmer,* a book widely circulated in England, Ireland, and France between 1782 and 1785. Therein he answers the question, "Whence came these people?" "They are," he tells us, "a mixture of English, Scotch, Irish, French, Dutch, Germans, and Swedes. From this promiscuous breed that race now called Americans have arisen." Crèvecoeur finds that "in this great American asylum the poor of Europe have by some means met together," and as a result of various causes, "individuals of all nations are melted into a new race of man, whose labors and posterity will one day cause great changes in the world." Crèvecoeur provides eloquent testimony to the impression that America and the Americans made on foreigners in the Age of Revolution—an America so different from Europe by reason of its intermixture of stocks from so many lands and the greater opportunity for upward mobility that he saw it held out to the poor immigrant.[34] To Crèvecoeur, the Americanization of the European immigrant did not offer insuperable obstacles. "What attachment can a poor European have for a country where he had nothing? The knowledge of the language, and love of a few kindred as poor as himself, were the only cords that tied him; his country is now that which gives him land, bread, protection and consequence. *Ubi panis, ibi patria,* is the motto of all emigrants."[35]

Since the original settlers (the aborigines and Afro-Americans, of course, excepted) came from England, and the English language, institutions, and legal system in somewhat modified form generally prevailed, it is perhaps understandable that the non-English elements in the colonial population have not generally been given their due. The historian George Bancroft stated that in 1776 only one fifth of the American people had for their mother tongue some language other than English. His rough estimate did not range too far from the statistics culled by the Bureau of the Census, basing its findings on the names of heads of families appearing in the census of 1790. That report put the English and Welsh stock as amounting to 82.1 percent of the population at that time. This overestimate served as the historical basis for the restrictive immigration legislation enacted in post–World War I years. That same tabulation credited the Scots and Irish component at 8.9 percent in 1790 and the German, 5.6 percent.

More recent research and analysis have resulted in sharply downgrading the English component of the population. A report on national and linguistic stocks made for the American Historical Association in 1931 took into account the Anglicizing of nomenclature by immigrants which normally takes place one or two generations after arrival in this country. In numerous cases national origins can no longer be definitively determined because it is impossible to differentiate British from non-British names. For instance, it is a problem to determine who were the Germans among persons with the name of Roads, because the German *Roth* is so inextricably confused with variants of the British Rhodes. Nor is it possible to distinguish between the German *Scherer* and the Scots Shearer. The German *Koehler* fused with the British Collier and *Huber* often became Hoover. Taking nomenclature changes into account, the 1931 report assigned to the English stock a figure of 60.1 percent, to the Scots, 6.6, to the Irish, including both northern and southern Ireland, 7.8, to the Germans, 7.0, the Dutch, 2.6, the French, 1.5, and the Swedes, .03 percent.[36]

The 1931 report is not regarded as the last word, but has been the subject of more recent critical analysis, with the general consensus being that a somewhat more generous proportion of the population was actually of non-English origin, with the Scots and Scotch-Irish amounting to almost 16 percent and the Germans closer to 9 percent, among other minorities.[37]

Difficulties in disentangling national origins and calculating the diverse contributions of the various national stocks must be laid at the doors of both ethnic historians and genealogists. Too often the story of national stocks has been overlaid with a veil of filiopietism and chauvinism, and grotesquely exaggerated claims have been made for groups or personages of non-English origin. Still, immigrants from the European continent contributed their share of participation in the cause of the American Revolution, but no ethnic group supported the cause of independence with unanimity. It was, after all, a civil war, which divided the Scotch-Irish, for example. On Pennsylvania's frontier they bitterly resented England's efforts to present further settlements in the interior and displayed little sympathy for the tolerant Indian policies of the proprietary government. On the other hand, on the Carolina frontier, the Scotch-Irish often sided with the Crown and disputed the dominance of the rebel elite of the Tidewater settlements. In the Mohawk Valley the Germans took up arms against unpopular Tory landlords, while in the Hudson Valley Dutch or English tenants could be found aligned against Whig manor lords. The Germans on the Georgia frontier were unwilling to risk losing the protection of British arms against the Indians, while those who lived in isolated communities or belonged to pacifist sects sought simply to remain neutral—a troublesome role in a civil war. Generalizations about ethnic loyalties do not come easily, but the weight of evidence suggests that descendants of original immigrant generations usually took the Patriot side; the more recent immigrants were more insecure and likely to be more supportive of the Crown. Let us not, of course, forget Tom Paine, Alexander Hamilton, James Wilson, Aedanus Burke of South Carolina, Thomas Burke of North Carolina, and William Paterson of New Jersey—all relatively newcomers, who enthusiastically espoused the Revolutionary cause, and there were many other exceptions to these generalizations.

Then, too, there was a heavy exodus of English-speaking inhabitants. Between 80,000 and 100,000 Loyalists left during or at the close of the Revolution. While many of the well-to-do made their way to England, a much larger number sought refuge in territories that would be merged into Canada. Nova Scotia found temporary haven for 28,000, some of whom dispersed from there in search of cheaper lands in Cape Breton, Prince Edward Island, and the St. John's Valley. Others moved into Quebec and pushed westward.

Scottish Highlanders from New York's Mohawk Valley, who had fought on the British side, established Glengarry County in Ontario. Other ethnic groups, including some Scots Presbyterians, some Dutch, and some Germans, were rewarded with Canadian lands after fighting on the Crown side. They founded homogeneous ethnic communities along the St. Lawrence River and Lake Ontario. The exodus of so large a number of American Loyalists helped set different patterns for Canada and the United States, the exiles more conservative and consistently anti-American. The failure of the United States to acquire Canada, an effort never strenuously pressed, kept America from confronting the perils of bilingualism and Protestant-Catholic divisions while it was seeking to shape a national political and cultural consensus.

English America was in fact a mosaic of peoples. The Dutch language, though long abandoned in what was once New Amsterdam, survived in the Haarlem and Hudson valleys as far north as Albany for several post-Revolutionary generations. As late as 1841, church services were delivered in Dutch in the Hudson Valley. Clinging to their language and traditions, the Germans kept largely to themselves. In the region between the Lehigh and the Susquehannah they constituted a cultural island cut off from the mainstream of the English-speaking population. With their own printing presses and newspapers, their own German-language schools, and a vernacular that was a corruption of German and English and popularly called "Pennsylvania Dutch," they posed a problem to leaders of public opinion. Even the printed German was described by one traveler from the homeland as "sorrowful examples of the miserably deformed speech of our American fellow countrymen." The same observer was moved to exclaim that "it was hardly to be expected that the German language, even at its worst degenerated, could ever have gone to ruin and oblivion with quite such rapidity."[38]

German cultural isolation posed a threat to leaders of public opinion. Even so broad-minded a liberal as Benjamin Franklin was moved to express reservations. "Few of their children in the country know English," he remarked. "They import many books from Germany. The signs in our streets [Philadelphia] have inscriptions in both languages, and some places only in German. . . . Unless the stream of importation could be turned from this to other colonies . . . they will soon so outnumber us that all the advantages we will have will in my opinion not be able to preserve our language." At a later date Thomas Jefferson, another advocate of assimilation, wished to discourage foreigners from "settling together in large numbers, wherein, as in our German settlements, they preserve for a long time their own language, habits, and principles of government, and that they should distribute themselves among the natives for quicker amalgamation."[39]

Ethnically it would be correct to speak of the people of Scottish origin as non-English immigrants. Varying dialects were spoken in the Lowlands and the Highlanders continued to speak Gaelic after coming to America. The French offered far less resistance to assimilation than did the Germans and the Scots. They came to all the colonies spurred by the persecutions that followed the revocation of the Edict of Nantes in 1685, and long bore the scars of harried years, from which numbers escaped to England or America.

Despite the rapid progress of American nationalism the postwar influx of European immigrants did not yet spark a nativist movement, although scattered opposition could be found in the press and some criticism was expressed by public figures. One parochial versifier condemned the arrival of *"convict rogues and refugees,"* who would contaminate Americans:

> Let *Dutchmen* come and drain our bogs,
> Let *Frenchmen* come and feast on frogs,
> Let *Jews* among you toil and sweat,
> Let stout *Hibernians* children get.

Then an even more spiteful stanza:

> The eggs are citizens if you please,
> The rotten ones are *refugees*.
> A single rotten egg shall spoil
> The largest custard you can boil.[40]

To some uptight republicans, anything foreign—people, goods, especially luxury items, high fashion, loose morals, and aristocracy—were perils to be avoided in building a virtuous society.

At the Philadelphia Convention the Framers took care to narrow the orbit of alien influence in American politics by limiting the access of foreign-born Americans to elective federal offices. To qualify for office, representatives and senators had to be citizens for at least seven to nine years, respectively, while no immigrant naturalized after the adoption of the Constitution was eligible for the offices of President or Vice President.

The Progress of "Americanization"

It was not these pockets of linguistic isolation that concerned America's political and cultural leaders. Rather, did they recognize the need to nurture a distinctive non-British culture—in short, to "Americanize" the American people, as John Jay described the process at a somewhat later date,[41] thereby coining a new verb. What Jay had in mind was that it was fortunate that the new United States, sans Canada, did not have to grapple with a bilingual problem or have to absorb in one gulp a sizable non-Protestant people. In his second *Federalist* he said it more felicitously, by exaggerating the homogeneity of the population:

. . . Providence has been pleased to give this one connected country, to one united people, a people descended from the same ancestors, speaking the same language, professing the same religion, attached to the same principles of government, very similar in their manners and customs, and who, by their joint counsels, arms, and efforts, fighting side by side throughout a long and bloody war, have nobly established their general Liberty and Independence.[42]

By war's end, as the leaders and shapers of public opinion saw it, America had to resolve serious cultural problems whose resolution was a prerequisite to its becoming a nation. The first problem was to overcome the provincial and sectional attachments which kept people from thinking and behaving as Americans, instead of as Yankees, or Yorkers, or Virginians. The notion that loyalty to the nation should transcend state bonds was a revolutionary concept which was embraced with enthusiasm by nationalist-minded statesmen, young Hamilton to cite one of the very first. In a series of "Continentalist" letters published in 1782, he declared: "there is something noble and magnificent in the perspective of a great Federal Republic, closely linked in the pursuit of a common interest, tranquil and prosperous at home, respectable abroad. But there is something proportionably diminutive and contemptible in the prospect of a number of petty states, with the appearance only of union, jarring, jealous, and perverse, without any determined direction, fluctuating and unhappy at home, weak and insignificant by their dissensions in the eyes of other nations." In sum, "think continentally," Hamilton counseled the new nation.[43]

Perhaps Hamilton excepted, John Jay stands out as the foremost proponent of centralization and subordination of the states as essential to the building of an American nation. Writing John Lowell in 1785, he remarked: "It is my first wish to see the United States assume and merit the character of one great nation, whose territory is divided into different States merely for more convenient government and the more easy and prompt administration of justice, just as our several States are divided into counties and townships for the like purpose."[44] Jay in these observations was not only thinking of what he considered a constitutional shift toward centralization but the building of a more united American nation with a distinctive non-European character.

The evacuation of the British troops from the seaport towns sparked the process of Americanizing the population. Its fulfillment was a fervent wish of General Washington. "We have now a National character to establish; and it is of the utmost importance to stamp favourable impressions upon it; let justice be then one of its characteristics, and gratitude another."[45] This new force, love of country, superimposed upon but not displacing ties of affection to one's own state, was best epitomized by Washington when he chose the vehicle of his first inaugural address to speak of "my country whose voice I can never hear but with veneration and love." By that date, when the President alluded to "my country" he did not mean Virginia.

The process of Americanization in a way started with the first settlement at Jamestown, but it was accelerated in part by geographic separation from the mother country and in Revolutionary and post-Revolutionary years by political and ideological differences with the British government and people.

In the great procession held in New York City on July 23, 1788, to celebrate the ratification of the Constitution, a band of linguistic nationalists marched with the New York Philological Society, dressed uniformly in black. Among them one would recognize Noah Webster, the lexicographer, and William Dunlap, painter and playwright, and the secretary of the society held a scroll "containing the principles of a *Federal* language." Noah Webster's conspicuous part in the procession was indeed appropriate since no one was more assiduous than he in contributing system and uniformity to the "American" language. The Connecticut lexicographer and committed Federalist, Webster gave up the law to promote the American-English language, a project which he felt it to be his patriotic as well as scholarly duty to carry out. His first effort was an elementary speller prepared in 1782 and published the next year at Hartford as the first part of *A Grammatical Institute of the English Language.* Webster completed the *Institute* with a grammar in 1785 for the use of schoolchildren. Known to generations as the *Blue-backed Speller,* it was both an American product and a fantastic publishing success. Some 60 million copies were estimated to have been sold within a century of its first appearance. The *Blue-backed Speller* helped standardize spelling in America, and to a lesser degree pronunciation, along lines differing from prevailing fashion in England. His *Reader* was patriotic enough to justify *American* in its title.

Noah Webster wrote an essay in 1789 arguing for the American version of the English language with its own spelling. The author argued that "a chief advantage of this reform in these states would be that it would make a difference between the English spelling and the American." He expressed confidence that "such an event is of vast political consequence," for "*a national language* is a band of *national union,*" urging that every means be employed "to render the people of this country *national* and to inspire them with the pride of national character."[46] Perhaps Webster found his long-range goal somewhat too radical for the tastes of his contemporaries, for his *American Dictionary of the English Language,* published in 1828 and representing a quarter century of hard labor and the last major dictionary ever compiled by a single individual, did not live up to the sweeping changes he had earlier predicted. He did drop the *u* from such words as *colour, mould,* and *honour,* and changed the *-re* to *-er* in words of French origin, such as *centre* and *theatre.* He also dropped the superfluous *e,* as in *ax* instead of *axe* and the *k,* as in *music* instead of *musick,* along with the double consonant in *traveler* instead of *traveller,* or spelt more phonetically, as in *plow* instead of *plough.* However, his initiation in later editions of *iz* for *is* and *wurd* for *word* never gained acceptance. Still, Webster did not hesitate to include "Americanisms" which he deemed worthy, while seeking at the same time to restore "the English language in its purity" by purging it of eighteenth-century innovations. In sum, Webster had caught in his linguistic net merely a small fraction of distinctive Americanisms in a language which to this day has continued to absorb regional and folk culture, and to demonstrate its adaptability to industrialization, mechanization, and the colloquialisms of a "People's English."[47]

"At no time did Literature make so rapid a progress in America as since the peace," reported the *Massachusetts Centinel* in 1785.[48] "It must afford pleasure to every son of science, that our swords are beaten into ploughshares, and that the torch of Learning now shines with such lustre in this western hemisphere." True, no Voltaire, no Goethe emerged, but a lively press poured forth a flood of newspapers, magazines, and books, and native writers were encouraged to create and to criticize.

Newspapers now flourished as never before. Take New York City as an example. By the time of the Constitution the city's readership enjoyed the advantages of seeing a newspaper almost daily. The Antifederalist Thomas Greenleaf issued his *Independent Journal* on Wednesdays and Saturdays. The *Packet,* edited by Samuel and John Loudon, came off the press on Tuesdays, and Francis Childs, a protégé of both Franklin and Jay, put out the *Advertiser* on Thursdays. By penny-press standards of the next century, circulation may have been limited, but one way or another every reader in town could be reached promptly. Whether one subscribed to the newspapers or read them in the taverns or coffeehouses, a concerned citizenry could keep abreast of the volume of criticism and defense of state governments, of Congress, and of the proposed Constitution, for these newspapers proved hospitable to a high level of political discourse. In the other major cities the newspaper press flourished as well as in New York. Boston boasted a consecutive run during these years of at least three newspapers, not to speak of Isaiah Thomas's extraordinary success with the *Massachusetts Spy,* which he had removed to Worcester at the start of hostilities. In addition to a German-language paper published by Michael Steiner, Philadelphia was served by at least four newspapers that had virtually unbroken runs during these years, while Charleston, South Carolina's, *Gazette,* under slightly varying titles competed with the *City Gazette* and the *Columbian Herald.*[49]

Perhaps more significant in terms of a native literary culture was the boom in magazine publishing during these postwar years. The driving force in this area was an Irish émigré named Matthew Carey, who started *The Columbian Magazine* in Philadelphia in 1786 and within less than a year *The American Museum*. Washington encouraged Carey in the belief that these vehicles fostered republicanism by disseminating knowledge, and were "more happily calculated than any other, to preserve the liberty, stimulate the industry, and meliorate the knowledge of an enlightened and free People."[50] Embellished with engravings by Carey's partner, James Trenchard, these two magazines put into print some of the best thinking in America about invention, architecture, and horticulture, published American music and even native poetry, both past and contemporary, along with selections from Goethe's *Werther,* a sensitive and sorrowful tale which proved a literary sensation in the America of the 1780s.

When John Adams remarked in 1786 that "the Muses have crossed the Atlantic,"[51] he indubitably reflected his nationalist bias, but his claims could be supported by the emergence of relatively mature and extensive literary works by American writers inspired by the unfolding postwar scene. True, the gifted black woman poet Phillis Wheatley would die in 1784 at the age of thirty, leaving as one of her last poems a paean in favor of *Liberty and Peace.* Works of fiction, whose plots frequently drew upon Revolutionary War themes, appealed to readers who had long been entertained by Richardson and other English authors. But significant novels did not emerge for another decade, when they were to come from the pens of Charles Brockden Brown and Hugh Henry Brackenridge.

In the Confederation years, the showpiece of the new literary nationalism proved to be the epic poem. Timothy Dwight's *The Conquest of Canaan,* written during the war and frequently revised, but not published until 1785, proved to be a prolix and even bombastic work which appealed to its readership as an allegory in the Miltonic manner, in which the wars of the Israelites and their leaders in battle bore striking analogies to the late war in America, with Washington represented by Joshua. What made the epic especially distinctive was its attempt to depict an ideal American character embodying benevolence and courage, combining democratic aspirations with virtue.

Poets inevitably were drawn to the American character and felt obliged to warn their readers to shun luxury and abhor the depravities of Europe. Some were aroused by the sense of crisis that the Federalist leadership perceived in the late 1780s. Notable among the latter were the "Hartford Wits," that talented team made up of Joel Barlow, John Trumbull, and David Humphreys, who began the *Anarchiad*, in 1786, a medley of poetry, songs, doggerel, and patriotic odes issued in twelve numbers between October 1786 and September 1787. Sparked by Shays' Rebellion in Massachusetts, the *Anarchiad* depicted the ravages of anarchy, warned the public of the dangers of mobbism, and denounced paper money and similar palliatives.

Of all the epic poems, Joel Barlow's *The Vision of Columbus* still seems to be both the most ambitious and the most creative product of a forceful imagination. Surveying American history from Columbus and the Indians to contemporary times, it closes with a plea for humanity united in peace, a social order transcending national lines and based on a social compact—in short, a radical outlook of the world, one tinged with deistic pacifism.[52]

When John Trumbull told his father that he planned to go to England to study painting, the latter, who preferred a legal career for his son, pointedly reminded him: "You appear to have forgotten, sir, that *Connecticut is not Athens.*" Edmund Burke reiterated the advice. Study architecture, he advised young Trumbull. America needs public buildings, not paintings.[53] Trumbull would not be dissuaded. Pursuing his studies at the London studio of the celebrated American expatriate Benjamin West, whose protégés included such talented young Americans as the master portraitist Gilbert Stuart, the versatile William Dunlap, and the still more youthful Robert Fulton, Trumbull succeeded in perpetuating on canvas the glorious moments of American history. Already a mythical generation of Revolutionary War heroes, they were the subject of a great series of historical canvases, beginning with *Bunker's Hill* and *The Death of Montgomery.* Trumbull felt obliged to preserve the record of an incomparable group of leaders, who, as he put it, "once wielded the arms of their Country with such effect" and now in peacetime "could also guide her Councels with great Dignity," and to "write, *in my language,* the History of our Country." Already back in America Charles Willson Peale, soldier-painter, radical Whig politician, and promoter, who many years before had studied in

London, had begun preserving on canvas a galaxy of war heroes and Founding Fathers, and made his creations available to a public visiting his Philadelphia gallery. Nor did he miss playing a role in commemorating the great postwar moments, the designing of floats for celebrations of the coming of peace, the ratification of the Constitution, and Washington's inaugural journey, for which he designed a special arch. Most popular of his paintings were perhaps his portraits of Washington at Trenton and Valley Forge.[54]

Enjoying a spirited revival from wartime restrictions on theatrical performances, productions chiefly confined to the zones of British occupation or to entertaining the French military forces, the repertoire of dramatic productions in leading towns still reflected the rich English heritage of Restoration plays and, of course, Shakespeare, and they were produced largely by itinerant troupes like that of David Douglass and the numerous progeny of Lewis Hallam. The longtime Puritan antipathy to the stage now found nurture in stout republicans who viewed the stage as a sign of luxury and depravity contaminating republican virtue. Others refused to accept the arguments stemming from a cultural parochialism bolstered by an exaggerated sense of virtue. "Have Shakespeare and Johnson written to be admired by all Europe, and forgotten or neglected by the Philadelphians?" one proponent of the drama asked, while another deplored the fact that "genius meets with so little encouragement in a land of liberty." In a spirited debate over a proposal to impose a heavy fine on theatrical productions, the Pennsylvania legislature was split between the interior legislators (strongly Antifederalist) and the cosmopolitans from Philadelphia. American artists had to study abroad without encouragement at home, it was pointed out. "Are we to be forever indebted to other nations for genius, wit and refinement?" asked George Clymer, a Signer of the Declaration and a friend of Franklin. But the anti-theater bill passed and the professional theater was closed down; yet probably in deference to the coming Constitutional Convention the law was not to take effect until August 31, 1787, and it would be repealed in 1789.

Despite these discouragements, the New York theater, successfully resisting those who would shut it down, flourished in its John Street home, and even played host to the first significant American drama by a war veteran and New England lawyer named Royall Tyler. *The Contrast,* first performed on April 16, 1787, hardly a month before the opening of the federal Convention, transformed what might have been a conventional sentimental comedy into a satire on the debate between Virtue and Luxury, American simplicity against European affectation. As one commentator has observed, *The Contrast* proves to be "as much a work of social and cultural history as it is a play," adding, "No other writer of the eighteenth century gave Americans so perfect a glass of their existence." Accordingly, it deserves a place beside epics like *The Vision of Columbus* and the broad canvasses of Trumbull, while anticipating the cosmopolitan detachment and faint cynicism of a Washington Irving.[55]

In 1788 Daniel Read, the Massachusetts composer and publisher of *The American Singing Book* some three years earlier, included in his pages "American masters" whom he deemed worthy to be placed side by side with "the best . . . European masters." Considering that the European masters of those years included the younger Bachs, Haydn, and Mozart, it would seem clear that an American inferiority complex in music did not emerge as early as the years of the Confederation. From psalm singing to sea chanties, to tavern songs and Afro-American plantation songs, there had always existed a powerful amateur music tradition in America. That music could not be impervious to European influence. European music had been introduced by the German Dunkers, who had organized the Ephrata Cloister, some fifty miles west of Philadelphia, while the Moravians had founded the first singstunde at Bethlehem, Pennsylvania, in the early 1740s. Concerts, ballad operas, and musical societies had been flourishing before the Revolution, and Handel's *Messiah* had been performed at New York's Trinity Church prior to the war.

There had, in short, been a happy mixture of European music and musicians, supported by the importation of a variety of musical instruments before the founding of the new nation. What was especially fortunate for America, where the creative arts often suffered a low regard, was the interest and patronage of men of national standing like Benjamin Franklin, Thomas Jefferson, and Francis Hopkinson. Something of a music critic himself as well as a music lover, Franklin built an improved version of the "glass harmonica," for which instrument Mozart and Beethoven later would compose works. Jefferson, who took the violin seriously, albeit his accomplishments on that instrument have received a varying range of appraisals, encouraged composers and instrumentalists, while Francis Hopkinson, a Signer of the Declaration, may well be regarded as the first of a line of amateur composers. His charming and witty songs include "My Days Have Been so Wondrous Free" (a setting to Thomas Parnell's "Love and Innocence") and "The Battle of the Kegs," although his own claim to being "the first native of the United States who has produced a Musical Composition"[56] may be somewhat extravagant.

But it was William Billings's "Chester" which proved to be the most enduring of the Revolutionary War songs. That New England part-time tanner who reformed New England psalm singing had struck the right note, combining patriotism with religious fervor, and his stanzas still stir listeners today:

> Let tyrants shake their iron rod,
> The foe come on with mighty stride,
> And slavery clank her galling chains,
> Our troops advance with martial noise.

> We fear them not. We trust in God.
> Their veterans flee before our youth.
> New England's God forever reigns,
> And generals yield to beardless boys.

A composition of forty-five anthems—brief solo passages for any and all of the four voices, alternating with the full chorus—Billings's "Be Glad Then America" was his most grandiose example.

Other American self-taught innovators and imitators like Daniel Read and Timothy Swan notwithstanding, the coming of peace brought a flood of talented European musicians to America, and they played a notable role in raising the level of musical life. George Washington's diary reveals that on July 12, 1787, he attended a concert given by Alexander Reinagle, a British-born émigré musician, accomplished pianist, and gifted composer of sonatas for that instrument.[57] Raynor Taylor, a famous Scottish organist, shortly followed his student Reinagle to America. Among the Europeans who stayed on in America after the war was the Hessian corporal Philip Pfeil (or Phile), a versatile musician and composer, who would write the tune for the "President's March," played for the first time when President-elect Washington crossed the Delaware to Trenton in 1789 en route to his inauguration in New York. It became the tune for "Hail Columbia," the famous patriotic song written by Joseph Hopkinson, son of the Signer-composer, and an instant success.[58]

American society in the formative years of the Revolutionary generation offered some extraordinary paradoxes. Perhaps the greatest was the willingness of a society founded on freedom to harbor the system of slavery. Still another was the way in which a nation of deep religiosity could enthusiastically embrace a civil religion originating in the Enlightenment and based on morality and public virtue. True, in postwar years religion flourished, church membership grew, and Protestant sects multiplied. From the Christian orthodoxy of a John Jay, a Benjamin Rush, or a David Rittenhouse to the deism of a Franklin or a Jefferson, one finds a pluralistic society well established by the 1780s, with most deists evincing little difficulty in reconciling their private skepticism with public orthodoxy.[59]

Such a society would beget religious toleration for its very survival. Virginia's Statute of Religious Liberty and New York's Constitution of 1777 bear witness to the growing acceptance of toleration. In addition, and as a consequence of rapid Americanization, it was to be expected that churches of European origin and even control, notably the Anglicans and certain dissenting Protestant sects, would form national churches and sever the ties abroad. And that is precisely what occurred. One could also anticipate that in states where religious pluralism governed, church establishment would be terminated. James Madison's historic "Memorial and Remonstrance" broke the ground in Virginia, but in seven other states the Church of England would be disestablished by 1790.

Unique among the nations of the world was the federal Constitution in its deliberate omission of a requirement of a religious test for qualifying for public office, while the First Amendment, originally drafted by Madison as a prohibition on the states as well as the federal government—a provision somewhat mysteriously lost in committees—forbade Congress from making any law establishing religion or preventing the free exercise thereof. Significantly, this first article among the Bill of Rights (originally the third), along with nine others, was quickly ratified by a nation deeply committed to religious values.

True, a religious revival had preceded the American Revolution, and a second one, even more sweeping in character, would grip the nation within a decade after the founding of the federal government; but the appearance of the latter coincided with deistic and rational currents and advances in science,[60] and in America toleration would prove the rule, not the exception.

In his first inaugural Thomas Jefferson epitomized this profession of faith of the American people in civil religion, in a people and a government guided by morality and virtue. Jefferson's profession of faith:

Kindly separated by nature and a wide ocean from the exterminating havoc of one-quarter of the globe, too high-minded to endure the degradations of the others, possessing a chosen country with room enough for our descendants to the thousandth and thousandth generation; entertaining a due right to the use of our own facilities, to the acquisition of our own industry, to honor and confidence from our fellow citizens, resulting not from birth, but from our actions and sense of them; enlightened by a benign religion, professed, indeed, and practiced in various forms, yet all of them inculcating honesty, truth, temperance, gratitude and the love of man, acknowledging and adoring an overruling providence which by all its dispensations proves that it delights in the happiness of man and his greater happiness hereafter—with all these blessings, what more is necessary to make a happy and a prosperous people?

Still one thing more the President added: "a wise and frugal Government," which "shall not take from the mouth of labor the bread that it has earned. This is the sum of good government, and this is necessary to close the circle of our felicities."[61]

Politically retrospective overtones notwithstanding, the third President reminded his fellow citizens of the republican values cherished in the past and by implication exhorted them to stand fast against a rising tide of individualism and acquisitiveness.

CHAPTER 2

The Military-Fiscal Complex:
The Army, the Creditors, and the Nation

WITH the evacuation by the British Army according to its own deliberate timetable, Americans looked forward with equanimity to the inevitable dissolution of the Continental Army as well as the navy, which in the last year of the war had virtually disintegrated. The war had been under the civilian control of Congress, regardless of its competence, and people expected that peacetime would maintain the status quo. A dislike of Old World militarism had been deeply rooted in the colonies. For nine long years of the French and Indian War British troops had been quartered on colonial soil. With the end of that conflict, the colonists assumed that these troops would be withdrawn. In fact, the reverse took place.[1] George Grenville decided to maintain a standing army of ten thousand troops in the colonies, Major-General Thomas Gage was made commander-in-chief, and New York the military capital. Gage governed a vast area extending from Newfoundland to the Floridas and from Bermuda to the Great Lakes and the Mississippi. To his office came reports on every outbreak of violence whether by Indians or American colonists and on every incident of resistance.

It was logical that resentment against the military would be most sharply felt in the colony which had been the headquarters of the British Army. The two quartering acts of 1765 and 1766 were resisted by the New York Assembly, which refused to comply fully until June of 1767. Tension and open conflicts between the soldiery and New York's inhabitants were not infrequent, and were reflected in other colonies as well. In 1768, Governor William Pitkin of Connecticut asserted that the maintenance of British troops produced uneasiness among the people, impaired their morals, and hindered their industry. Benjamin Franklin took a high stand in 1770 when he asserted that the keeping of a standing army in America without the consent of the assemblies "is not agreeable to the Constitution."

In New York the tension led to a clash between the Sons of Liberty and British soldiers on Golden Hill early in 1770. In less than two months after the flareup, with British troops shipped to Boston, there occurred the so-called Boston Massacre, an incident which Paul Revere's engraving made out as a cold-blooded butchery. In America the effect of the latter incident was to arouse anew the tension against Britain and to confirm Americans in their distrust of standing armies. The First Continental Congress in 1774 in its Declaration and Resolves denounced the keeping of a standing army in the colonial towns in peacetime, and the Declaration of Independence charged the king with having "affected to render the Military independent of and superior to the Civil Power," a theme that Thomas Jefferson had previously stressed in his notable tract *A Summary View of the Rights of British America.*[2] "Instead of subjecting the military to the civil power," Jefferson charged, "his majesty has expressly made the civil subordinate to the military."

Despite the experience with the militia in the Intercolonial Wars and in the American Revolution and the low opinion of them held by military experts, the states clung tenaciously to their militia systems. The traditional standing of the Minute Men–militia concept would be reflected in later years in Madison's second article of the Bill of Rights: "A well regulated Militia, being necessary to the security of a free State, the right of the people to keep and bear Arms, shall not be infringed."

From this phrasing it seems to many to be perfectly clear that the Second Amendment was intended to protect the right of the states to use their militia to check by physical force any unconstitutional usurpation of authority, rather than of the ordinary person to carry a gun or other lethal weapons. Indeed, Maryland and Virginia had such provisions in their constitutions when the Constitutional Convention met in Philadelphia, and the issue was raised in the ratifying conventions.[3]

The Emergence of the Continental Army

In a war for national independence, with battle lines rapidly shifting from state to state, a Continental Army soon proved to be an absolute necessity for the effective conduct of the war. In the face of deep and pervasive sentiment against standing armies, Congress authorized such a force in May 1775 with George Washington designated commander-in-chief. Thenceforward Washington, his staff, and the special administrative departments involved concluded that the Continentals, committed for longer service, should replace the largely untrained citizen militia. "They come in you Cannot tell where," Washington wrote of the militia, charging the state bodies with consuming the Continental Army's provisions, exhausting its stores, while deserting "at the critical moment."[4]

For the officers of the Continental Army, committed as they were for the duration of the war, the service provided them with a national outlook, one not necessarily shared with the populace, and brought them face to face with the deficiencies of the operation of the government under the Articles of Confederation. Within their ranks lay the corpus of future constitutionalists and Federalists.[5]

Outside the officers' corps, the rank and file of private and noncommissioned officers hardly lived up to the characteristic generalities of a "citizen army." They were able-bodied young men in their late teens and early twenties, usually unmarried and poor. But they chose above all the military service instead of favoring the more rewarding careers offered by privateering, farm labor, brief service as a militia substitute, or opportunities as civilian profiteers. Faced with the ever-present threat of death from combat or disease in military service, they may not have fought out of a profound understanding of the political issues at stake, but one cannot fairly discount their patriotic motives as some recent writers have done.[6]

As the war drew to a slow termination, two questions involving the military were insistently raised: Could a nation devoid of a national army and navy enforce its newly made peace treaty, including a defense of its boundaries; and could it discharge its obligations to the officer corps and the body of common soldiers shortly to disband? These questions were ominously linked to the fiscal conditions of the nation and to the claims of its various creditors, foreign and domestic. To comprehend the complexities of the problem and the close links being forged between the public creditors and the military, one needs consider the situation prior to the appointment of Robert Morris to the powerful office of Superintendent of Finance, a post to which Congress named him on February 20, 1781. The circumstances Morris would confront were directly related to the limited constitutional powers that Congress possessed and the devices it employed to operate under such restrictions.

Financing the War

That Continental outlook which many of the army officers shared with their commander-in-chief raised among the people of the states the specter of consolidation. The people were unprepared to replace the old British Empire against which they had rebelled with a strong central government over themselves or to confer upon Congress the power to levy taxes when such a power as exercised by Parliament had proved to be a precipitating cause of the war itself. Lacking the power to tax, but faced with the huge fiscal problems of running a lengthy war, Congress had no recourse but to juggle its financial affairs.

First Congress turned to the printing press, authorizing eleven emissions of Continental currency. When it stopped the presses in 1780, $241,550,000 had been issued.[7] Paper money would not bring war materiel from abroad, where foreign sellers demanded specie or trade goods. Initially, France and Spain provided subsidies,[8] not directly since both nations were still technically neutral, but through the Farmers General, a consortium of wealthy individuals responsible for the collection of taxes in France. Once France entered the war, Louis XVI provided the United States with a series of direct loans totaling 18 million livres; then in 1782 he negotiated a loan for the United States of 6 million livres in Holland, and advanced a final loan to the United States in 1783 of 6 million livres. A modest loan of $174,011.12 was grudgingly advanced by Spain in 1782, and the next year John Adams negotiated a loan of 5 million guilders (2 million Spanish milled dollars) from several banking firms. These loans were to be repaid at interest ranging from 4 to 5 percent and at various dates beginning in 1785 and ending in 1791.[9]

Throughout the war, at least until 1781, Congress had continued its financial sleight-of-hand operations. Aside from Continental currency, its main sources of revenue had been loans from foreign governments or foreign banking consortia and domestic loans. On the domestic front Congress opened up a Continental Loan Office in each state, issuing loan office certificates in rapidly depreciating Continental dollars. As these certificates proved increasingly unattractive, Congress authorized the acceptance of state paper money in payment of such certificates,[10] while paying off the certificates at a low rate of interest with bills of exchange drawn on creditors in France, a highly speculative procedure which caused America's commissioners abroad no end of embarrassment,[11] and later with paper money, with the rates rising more than seven-fold between 1778 and the close of the loans in 1781.

As each domestic program failed in turn, Congress began issuing certificates for such departments as the Quartermaster and Commissary to cover purchases of war materiel, food, and horses. In fact, such items were largely impressed from civilians, an unpopular program attacked as "legal robbery qualified by a promissory note."[12] These certificates bore no interest and declined in value as inflation spiraled.

The rapid depreciation of Continental paper presented Congress with a formidable crisis as early as 1779. On May 10 of that year Washington warned John Jay, then president of Congress, "on the state of our currency," pointedly remarking "that a wagon-load of money will scarcely purchase a wagon-load of provisions," and asked whether anything was being initiated "to restore the credit of our currency."[13] Congress and its president responded. Congress coupled the placing of a ceiling of $200 million on emissions of bills of credit,[14] with a Circular Letter from President Jay calling on the states to pay their requisitions, a request that closed on an eloquent passage:

Let it never be said that America had no sooner become independent than she became insolvent, or that her infant glories and growing fame were obscured and tarnished by broken contracts and violated faith, in the very hour when all the nations of the earth were admiring and almost adoring the splendor of her rising.[15]

Fortunately for Jay, he was dispatched abroad and missed most of the domestic chaos over fiscal obligations, but he was in Spain long enough to find himself obliged to protest overdue bills because of lack of funds.[16]

In short, any attempt by Congress to restore the standing of its currency was undercut by massive quantities of certificates or promissory notes issued to underwrite the expenses of the war. By 1781 approximately $226 million in currency, from which Congress had derived a real income of over $40 million in specie, had shrunk to almost nothing. As money depreciated in the hands of the public, the decline in value of the Continental paper amounted to a national tax on behalf of the war effort.[17] Thus, while currency and certificates were considered the "common debt" of the Revolution, "loan office certificates" were preferred securities and received the most favorable treatment within Congress's means. Such certificates, it should be borne in mind, were held mostly in the commercial states by merchants and other monied investors.[18] As Continental paper vanished in value, the delegates in Congress virtually threw up their hands and looked to the states for the support of the war,[19] including obligations to pay the army for both arrears in salary as well as current service. Some nine states paid soldiers "military" or "depreciation" certificates, which in most cases stood out as the largest portion of state debts after the Revolution.

In March 1780, Congress came up with a new plan. It reevaluated the "old" Continental currency at forty to one in specie, a rate considerably above its current value, and called upon the states to tax this money out of existence at the rate of $15 million per month. Bills of new emission, jointly guaranteed by Congress and the states, were to draw 5 percent interest payable in bills of exchange, which by request of Congress were to be accepted as legal tender by the states. This great stroke of repudiation elicited surprisingly little adverse comment, for as John Adams put it to the Comte de Vergennes, "the public has its rights as well as individuals."[20] The states responded to the dire emergency, accepting and eventually paying out some $37 million.[21]

One must not assume that the public was passive about the depreciation of paper or indifferent to spiraling inflation. Almost from the start of the war attempts were made by regional conventions, by state statutes, or by adoption of resolutions in county conventions and town meetings to halt inflation. In addition, local committees had been set up to regulate prices, fees, or services in special callings with the purpose of stopping an inflation spiral in the absence of effective controls by Congress. The first two conventions were called at the initiative of Massachusetts, the first meeting at Providence at the close of 1776 and the second at Springfield in July of '77. The Providence convention evoked a spirited debate in Congress. Opponents felt that the business of price regulation was "continental" and required the approval of Congress. While not explicitly endorsing the convention's results, Congress referred "the propriety of adopting similar Measures" to the "serious Consideration" of the other states, and called two meetings, one at York, Pennsylvania, for commissioners from New York, New Jersey, Pennsylvania, Delaware, Maryland, and Virginia, and another at Charleston for commissioners from North and South Carolina and Georgia. The York convention was hopelessly divided, and contented itself with sending copies of the proceedings to Congress and the states represented. There is no record of a meeting at Charleston. Nevertheless, despite criticism in high places, these early conventions were clearly representative of a substantial body of public opinion which favored curbs on all sorts of profiteering and sought to keep a lid on prices under wartime conditions.

With the precipitate decline in the value of money the Massachusetts legislature found it necessary to revise the schedule it had earlier enacted, and authorized towns to choose committees annually to aid in its enforcement. The action by Massachusetts stirred dissatisfaction in neighboring states which had been parties to the Providence convention, and, aside from revising prices upward, the Continental Congress issued a call for three interstate conventions: one for South Carolina and Georgia to meet at Charleston in February 1778; another for North Carolina, Virginia, and Maryland to meet at Fredericksburg, Virginia, in January of that year, and still a third, comprising the remaining eight Northern states, to meet at New Haven, Connecticut. The New Haven meeting, the only one of the three actually held, resulted in the addition of a group of the Middle States to the numbers enacting wage and price codes, but the resolves of that convention met a mingled reception. New Hampshire, Massachusetts, and Rhode Island took no action, while Connecticut, New York, New Jersey, and Pennsylvania enacted laws establishing wage and price schedules in close conformity with the New Haven proposals. Congress, after due deliberation, decided to step in and advised the states to repeal the New Haven schedule, a recommendation that was promptly carried out.

However, in defiance of both Congress and the compliant state legislatures, town meetings and county and regional conventions proceeded to revive wage and price regulations with considerable éclat, a reflection on the catastrophic decline of paper money and the widespread disillusionment with Congress's ability to stabilize the currency. In this grass-roots movement the Massachusetts towns assumed leadership, but New Hampshire, Rhode Island, New York, New Jersey, Pennsylvania, and Delaware set up sweeping price and wage schedules. A tidal wave swept the Northern and Middle States. In October 1779 commissioners from the New England states and New York, meeting at Hartford, found it incumbent upon themselves to defend price regulation to protect the poor and counteract further depreciation of the currency. Congress, in response, recommended that a general limitation be enacted throughout the states, holding prices for farm products, wages for common labor, tradesmen, and mechanics, and various services to a maximum of "twentyfold of the prices current through the various seasons of the year 1774."[22] States as far south as Maryland fell in line, as the drama of futility was drawing to a close and despite regional meetings that continued to be held. Although both economic and constitutional arguments were raised against proponents of regulation, there was also fear on the part of its opponents of the example being set by the states acting in combination. Later New England conventions in 1780 and 1781, while not attempting to enforce further price codes, did make important recommendations of an economic nature and advocated a stronger federal government.[23] The Articles of Confederation, soon to go into effect, contained a prohibition of such combinations between states, and Hamilton and Madison opposed them, "not as absolute violations of the Confederacy," but as leading ultimately to them and "in the meantime exciting pernicious jealousies."[24]

Nevertheless, the convention idea survived within the states even though the original objectives were no longer determining. Local conventions within the counties in such states as Massachusetts continued to grapple with economic and social grievances, and, as we shall see, Shays' Rebellion can trace its lineage to a long line of county meetings starting in Revolutionary days. At the same time, the path to the Constitutional Convention of 1787 was actually paved by the interstate conventions on economic affairs, most notable being the last at Annapolis, to be more fully treated in its proper place.

From the failure of these state, county, and town experiments in price and wage regulation to have a realistic relation to currency depreciation, two consequences followed. First, public opinion burgeoned for the creation of a strong federal government, which could act across state lines and provide a uniform currency; and secondly, sentiment among men who would later serve as delegates to the Constitutional Convention crystallized in favor of laissez-faire policies in the internal economic life of the nation.[25]

Depreciation and insolvency rocked the ruling radical party in Congress, with the legislatures of states like Massachusetts, Pennsylvania, and Virginia choosing new, more nationalistic-minded congressional delegates. In fact, both the Northern and Southern delegations took on a more conservative coloration. Young Alexander Hamilton, a nationalist to the core, knew what had to be done —the adoption of a sweeping fiscal program along national lines. In a lengthy letter to a fellow conservative, James Duane, dated September 3, 1780, he set forth his plan: he would give Congress "powers competent to the public exigencies." Either one could resume and exercise the "discretionary powers" with which he felt Congress had been vested "for the Safety of the States," or call "the sooner, the better" a convention of all the states to correct the defects in Congress's powers, including vesting in Congress "the whole, or a part of the unoccupied lands to provide a fund "for the arrangements of finances." More sweeping was his insistence that the Confederation "should give Congress complete sovereignty, except as to that part of internal police which relates to the rights of property and life among individuals, and to raising money by internal taxes." Otherwise he proposed that the Confederation be assured "a stable foundation" for its finances by being given "perpetual revenues, such as a land tax, poll tax, duties on trade and the unlocated lands."

As a further recommendation Hamilton would substitute single department heads, including that of finance, for the current performance of executive functions by committee. Additionally, he recommended the placing of the Continental officers upon half pay for life as "a great stroke of policy . . . binding them to the service by substantial ties." A final point in the Hamilton program was setting up a bank "on the joint credit of the public and of individuals," a step that would tie the "moneyed men" to the government.[26]

Eventually most of these measures would be adopted, some very shortly, some not until the establishment of the federal government under the new Constitution, when Hamilton himself was the directing hand in national finance. To initiate some of these steps, however, was to be the task to which the prestigious merchant-financier Robert Morris would dedicate himself upon his taking office as Superintendent of Finance in 1781. With the witty, urbane, and sometimes indiscreet Gouverneur Morris as his assistant, Robert Morris proposed, as had Hamilton before him, that the entire public debt be settled upon Congress (a program ardently promoted by the nationalists and just as fiercely opposed by states' righters who opted for continued emissions of paper money by the states). Morris further proposed that Congress be given the power to levy and collect taxes, a power which it lacked under the Articles of Confederation.[27] Finally, Morris proposed the chartering of a national bank, the Bank of North America, a request with which Congress complied before the year's end.[28] The Bank, for whose support Morris drew upon the bulk of the recent French loans and to which he himself heavily subscribed, opened its doors in January 1782. It served the nation usefully by holding government funds, making loans to the government, and discounting its notes. Hopefully Morris expected that the Bank's circulating notes would provide a medium of exchange for the entire nation. In fact, the Bank's capitalization proved too small to achieve the last design. In addition to this and other measures taken by Morris, timely subsidies from France and French backing for a large Dutch loan enabled him to make some progress toward returning the country to a specie basis by the end of the year.

It was expected of a Necker in France or a Morris in America that the person who directed a nation's finances would use every device to make his performance look good, whether by prudent fiscal management or by juggling accounts. As a start, Morris introduced drastic economies in fiscal administration, substituting the contract system for the wasteful operations of regimental commissaries, which he abolished. By sleight of hand he was enabled to finance the Yorktown campaign. His beginnings were indeed auspicious.

Looking toward a balanced budget as the foundation of public credit, Morris ruled that current revenue must be applied to current expenses and that the public debt be paid over a lengthened period. To put pressure on the creditors and the army, he discontinued all interest payments on loan certificates, obligations now assumed by the several states,[29] and in effect stopped paying the army; payments to the army by the states were no longer authorized by Congress. During 1781 and 1782 the soldiers and officers received virtually nothing, and not until the moment of their discharge in 1783 did Morris feel obliged to pay them anything. These claims, he insisted, must come out of requisitions, paid into the common treasury, and since the states were delinquent in complying, the troops could not get paid.

Had Morris made these decisions for the purpose of stirring up the public creditors to take action jointly with the army in protest against an impotent Congress, they were surely well conceived. Congress was now bombarded by public creditors from Philadelphia; in New York and Albany, meetings of public creditors held in September 1782 proposed a convention in their state to take some form of uniform action with creditors from other parts of the country.

These pressures left Congress no alternative but to propose a federal impost payable in specie in lieu of the traditional system of requisition on the states. The impost would amount to a duty of 5 percent on goods imported into the country, the money to be used to discharge foreign loans. At Morris's prompting, Congress called upon the states for an immediate decision. Here is where Morris's scheme went awry. Rhode Island, where recent elections had brought the "country party" to power, rejected the impost, and Virginia soon followed. To the chagrin of Morris and his nationalist friends in Congress, that unanimous consent was not obtained then, nor at any later time under the old Congress.

Rhode Island's rejection strengthened the forces in the nationalist camp. Writing on February 23, 1783, from the army camp at Newburgh, Major Samuel Shaw, later to be America's first consul at

Canton, questioned whether his country possessed a system "adequate to the government and prosperity of this rising empire," adding:

No money, no funds, and what is worse, no disposition in the people to establish funds, the certain consequence of which must be the death of public credit. It is astonishing with how much obstinacy the State of Rhode Island has opposed the impost, and by its non-concurrence defeated a measure which seemed so essential to the public welfare. That the smallest State in the union should thus counteract and annul the proceedings of the other twelve argues an awful defect in the Confederation. Unless there be a power vested in some supreme head, sufficient to enforce a compliance with such regulations as are evidently calculated for the general good, adieu to all government,—I mean that species of it which alone deserves the name. Thirteen wheels require a steady and powerful regulator to keep them in good order, and prevent the machine from becoming useless. The prospect of peace makes a politician of the soldier. We are thirteen States, and *a hoop to the barrel* is the prevailing sentiment.[30]

Already on January 24, 1783, Morris, in despair and with mortification, tendered his resignation to Congress, a calculated move, as we shall see. "To increase our debts while prospects of paying them diminish does not consist with my ideas of integrity," he asserted. "I must therefore quit a situation which becomes utterly insupportable."[31] Despite violent abuse heaped upon him by the press, Morris was prevailed upon by Congress to retain his office until the army was paid and disbanded. A timely loan from the Dutch obtained by John Adams enabled Morris to function in office, and it was not until September 1784 that he managed to extricate himself from affairs of state. Thereafter he devoted himself to advancing his own business fortunes, a subject he had never neglected while on public business. Henceforward he continued to support the nationalist cause and to seek a more powerful central government.[32]

The public creditors had voiced loud cries of alarm. Now it was the turn of the embittered army, whose main force was encamped at Newburgh on the Hudson. Although men and officers of all ranks had suffered cruelly and even unfairly (as Morris continued to reimburse administrative personnel while ignoring the army), it was the officers who now seized the initiative in venturing a protest, seemingly conspiratorial on its face, inflammatory in its content, and potentially dangerous in its ultimate objective.

Much of the background of the so-called Newburgh Conspiracy is in unrecorded conversations about which historians are reduced to conjecture. More substantial evidence can be culled from the correspondence of the major civilian figures involved, notably Robert and Gouverneur Morris and Alexander Hamilton, and from sketchy memoirs. The army, on the verge of disbanding, fearful that, with war ending, it would be cheated of its due, commanded a measure of justice and sympathy, even if the tactics of its self-appointed spokesmen proved extremely imprudent. Nor is it likely that events could have proceeded to such lengths without the silent approval from some, or at least one, high-ranking officer in the Continental Army and the backstairs encouragement of the Superintendent of Finance, his associate Gouverneur Morris, with some equivocal support from Washington's confidant, Alexander Hamilton.[33]

It started innocently enough. In the last week of December 1782, Major General Alexander McDougall, a man of impeccable credentials as an early Patriot and the officer Washington chose to command West Point after Arnold's treason, joined two fellow officers, Colonels John Brooks and Matthias Ogden, in a ride to Philadelphia. They had been chosen at a meeting of the officers to carry a petition to Congress from the army at Newburgh. The petition pointed out that "our private accounts are at an end," and that neither officers nor men had been paid for some time. Reminding Congress of the action it took in 1780 to provide officers with half-pay pensions, the delegation proposed to commute that pension to some equivalent lump-sum payment. While the proposal seemed modest, the petition closed on a thinly veiled warning: "Any further experiments on their [the army's] patience may have fatal consequences." The army's situation, McDougall declared, would "make a wise man mad."[34]

What appears to have stiffened the resolve of the Newburgh delegation was the reported advice of General Arthur St. Clair, urging them to warn Congress that unless immediate action were taken, that harried legislative body could expect "a convulsion of the most dreadful nature and consequence."[35] In view of Morris's intransigent stand, the Newburgh delegation warned the Committee of the States that they could expect "at least a mutiny" from the men, despite the prudent conduct of the officers.[36]

In response, Hamilton, Madison, and John Rutledge were named to draft a report on the army's claims and on the monetary resources that Morris regarded as being at the disposal of the Confederation. Morris picked this moment of anxious debate to tender his resignation. Congress's response to the triple threat posed by the army delegation, the impost rejection, and the resignation was to leave the issue of present and past pay to Morris's discretion, along with a promise to make every effort to obtain from the states monies adequate to the funding of the whole debt of the United States.[37] Still, the central purpose of the army delegation—the commutation of half pay to an outright grant—was sidetracked.

With news of peace expected momentarily and the commutation issue still up in the air, Colonel Brooks left Philadelphia on February 8, carrying a letter from Gouverneur Morris to General Henry Knox personally pleading for a union of the officers with other public creditors to enact permanent taxes.[38] What did Hamilton really want? Apparently a declaration by the army that it would not disband, one which might convey overtones of a military takeover. Whether or not Hamilton realized the consequences of his suggestion, it offered a small extremist group at Newburgh, disillusioned with Washington's leadership, the occasion to rally around Horatio Gates, whose Saratoga laurels had been badly tarnished by his wretched Southern campaign. This clearly would not have been to Hamilton's liking, since Hamilton and his father-in-law General Philip Schuyler were sworn enemies of Gates and of any survivors of the old and discredited Conway Cabal. The resolve of the army delegation was further stiffened by a visit to Robert and Gouverneur Morris, where they were informed that the states of Rhode Island and Virginia had just killed the impost, thereby destroying the army's last hope. The Morrises urged the McDougall group to petition Congress and let them know that their plans were no idle threats. "The army have swords in their hands," Gouverneur Morris told Hamilton. "I am glad to see things in their present train." As though to precipitate more forceful action on the part of the military, Robert Morris added to the general consternation by informing a Committee of the States that, in view of the rejection of the impost, he could not advance a shilling to the army or even a promise to pay "unless certain funds should be previously established."[39]

The army officers could still count on powerful friends in Congress. Madison and Hamilton joined forces. Considering that Congress had agreed to pay the officers half pay for life two years before, the Virginian found their proposal both reasonable and even modest, and warned that "any further experiments on the army's patience may have fatal effects." Madison could not forbear reminding Congress that the failure of the impost revealed a serious defect in the Articles of Confederation which required unanimous consent of the states to levy and collect a tax. That provision must be changed and very speedily, he urged. In support of Madison, Hamilton now proposed to Congress that the army's claims be made the basis for forcing a national fund upon the states. Hamilton, never the soul of discretion, advocated his plan by remarking that the lack of energy on the part of the federal government was an argument in support of the expediency of introducing "the influence of officers deriving their emoluments from and consequently interested in supporting the power of Congress." Madison, in his notes, took exception to Hamilton's remark, characterizing it as "imprudent and injurious to the cause which it was meant to serve," and pointing out that the army influence "was the very source of jealousy which rendered the States averse to a revenue under the collection as well as the appropriation of Congress." Madison then observed: "All the members of Congress who concurred in any degree with the states in the jealousy smiled at the disclosure,"[40] and were heard privately to remark that "Mr. Hamilton had let out the secret."

Congress, oppressed, as Madison recorded it, with "an anxiety" that had been "scarcely felt in any period of the revolution,"[41] continued debating the need to set up a permanent fund to deal with such emergencies as back pay due the army. According to his own notes, Madison joined Hamilton and some other delegates in a lengthy private conversation held at the home of Thomas FitzSimons, an Irish-born Philadelphia merchant and delegate to Congress, who had already been involved in setting up Robert Morris's Bank of North America. In this session Hamilton took center stage. Warning that he was "certain" that the army had "secretly determined" not to lay down their arms until the issue of their back pay was satisfactorily resolved, he expressed his private fears that the discontented officers might turn to Gates instead of Washington.

To prevent such an eventuality, or, as some historians would have it, to sound out Washington about his willingness to take the lead, Hamilton decided to tip Washington off about what was transpiring. Writing to the General sometime before the middle of February 1783, Hamilton explained the army's situation and cautioned about the difficulty of keeping "a *complaining* and *suffering army* within the bounds of moderation." Despite rumors in the army that Washington was not prepared to espouse the army's cause "with sufficient warmth," Hamilton advised that this "falsehood" must be laid to rest and that the General seize the initiative "to moderate the pretensions of the army and make their conduct correspond with their duty."[42]

The General, who could be both inscrutable and taciturn, took almost three weeks to reply to Hamilton's urgent letter. While seeming to evade Hamilton's request for his active intercession and leadership of the army's cause, Washington reassured Hamilton that he supported the army's "just claims" and felt that they would not exceed "the bounds of reason and moderation." Nor did he believe that the "old leaven"—meaning the anti-Washington cabal —was again "beginning to work."[43]

While Hamilton was having second thoughts about an aroused army that might result in Washington's loss of influence both with the officers and Congress, the Morrises seemed to take the situation in stride. Reporting on his meeting with McDougall to John Jay, then a peace commissioner in Paris, Gouverneur Morris wrote in a ciphered dispatch: "The army have swords in their hands. I am glad to see Things in their present Train. Depend on it, good will arise from the Situation in which we are hastening," a sentence not in cipher. Then, in a revealingly nonchalant aside, reverting to cipher, he added:

Although I think it probable that much of Convulsion will ensue, yet it must terminate in giving the Government that Power without which Government is but a Name. Government in America is not possessed of it, but the People are well prepared. Wearied with the War, their Acquiescence may be depended on with absolute Certainty, and you and I, my Friend, know by Experience that when a few Men of sense and spirit get together and declare that they are the Authority, such few as are of a different opinion may easily be convinced of their Mistake by that powerful Argument the Halter.

The implications were even stronger than anything McDougall had dared to say, but it is clear that when Gouverneur Morris was talking about "the People," he meant a small nationalist elite, whom he was too cautious to name. Again in cipher: "When I look round for the actors—let us change the subject."[44]

What shook Washington from his noncommittal stance was a visit to Philadelphia paid by Colonel Walter Stewart, now inspector of the Northern Army and a former Gates aide. Returning to headquarters from Philadelphia, Stewart reported to his friends that Congress planned to dissolve the army in the near future and argued that the army officers should take action to ensure that Congress would fulfill the promises it had made. Stewart had a long talk with Gates, and the information he conveyed seems to have been the signal for which Gates or his supporters were waiting. The Gates clique numbered John Armstrong, Jr., Timothy Pickering, along with Stewart among others.

Events moved swiftly—and to a powerful and unanticipated climax. First, a call was anonymously issued for a meeting on Monday, March 10. The call was accompanied by the first of the so-called Newburgh Addresses, penned by Major Armstrong. Inflammatory, even mutinous in tone, half-baked in reasoning, this first Address reminded its readers of the nation's ingratitude to the men who had placed it "in the chain of independency." Dropping the "milk and water style" of their past petitions to Congress, the Address denounced Washington by implication for his past "moderation" and urged that a tough and final memorial be sent to Congress. If rejected, the army was advised "to retire to some unsettled country, smile in their turn, and mock when their [Congress's] fear cometh on."[45]

Deeply aroused at long last to the dangerous implications of the activities going on behind his back, Washington let an impatient Hamilton know that he was determined to hold the army "within the bounds of reason and moderation."[46] Acting swiftly, he issued general orders objecting to the Address and condemned its call to a meeting as "disorderly" and "irregular." Instead, he summoned the officers to a meeting on that Saturday to discuss McDougall's report from Philadelphia. His strategy worked, calling forth a second Address from the Gates faction accepting the commander-in-chief's alternate date, asserting that the solemnity of his order had "sanctified" their appeal, and craftily implying that Washington's language had made him a party to the complaint.[47]

Saturday, March 15, 1783, marked one of the turning points in the history of the newly independent nation. There was something forbidding about the leaden clouds which hung heavy and dark over a late wintry landscape, with snow still visible on the mountaintops. The weather hardly lightened the spirits of the officers from every unit stationed at Newburgh, who filed up the sloping hill to the newly constructed meeting house that Washington had ordered built to encourage "sociability" among the officers of different states. Gates, whom Washington had shrewdly named to chair the meeting, could hardly refuse his superior's request to address the assemblage. Washington's remarks and behavior on that occasion are now part of the great legends of Revolutionary days.

The General took the offensive from the start, attacked Armstrong's first Address, its motives, its appeal to "feelings and occasions," and went so far as to accuse it of "insidious purposes." Imagine, he asked, for the army not only to leave their wives and children but to desert their country "in the extremist hour of her distress!" Could it contemplate anything so "shocking" as to turn its swords against Congress, "plotting the ruin of both and sowing seeds of discord" and separation "between military and civil. My God!" Washington exclaimed, "What can this writer have in view?" He is neither a friend of the army nor of the country, rather, "an insidious foe."

Taking a more constructive line, the General assured his officers that Congress might move slowly but that it would ultimately justify the army's faith. His formal speech ended with "a final appeal to reason and virtue."[48] He then turned to a letter from Joseph Jones as proof of Congress's decent intentions. He paused, fumbled in his vest, found the pair of spectacles that Dr. Rittenhouse had sent him in February, and putting them on, observed, "I have grown gray in the service of my country and now feel myself growing blind."[49]

The assemblage sat stunned. The simple dramatic gesture broke the tension and cleared the hostile atmosphere. Some officers openly wept. "There was something so natural, so unaffected in this appeal," Major Samuel Show entered the event in his journal, "as rendered it superior to the most studied oratory. It forced its way to the heart, and you might see sensibility moisten every eye."[50]

With the climactic conclusion, Washington departed, and Gates's plan, if we can fairly attribute it to him, collapsed. After Washington withdrew, the officers unanimously declared their "abhorrence" and "disdain" of the "infamous propositions" and disavowed "the secret attempt of some unknown persons" to subvert "all discipline and good order."[51]

Washington appeared to have acted spontaneously, but, as one interpreter sees it, the whole affair was carefully stage-managed by his loyal supporters, Putnam, Knox, and David Humphreys.[52] What made the action of the commander-in-chief so bizarre was that he had made an appearance "not at the head of his troops, but as it were in opposition to them; and for a dreadful moment the interests of the army and General seemed to be in competition." An observer at the occasion continued, "he spoke—every doubt was dispelled, and the tide of patriotism rolled in again in its united course."[53]

Once more the ball was in Congress's court, and the delegates put pressure on the lone malcontent in their midst, Eliphalet Dyer of Connecticut, to agree to the passage of a recommendation of five years' full pay to all officers in lieu of pension; the officers from any state line, acting collectively, might elect to receive payments from their state. Otherwise they would receive federal securities.[54] Because difficulties proved formidable in the way of officers applying to the states, the effect, as one historian correctly views it, was to add the commuted pensions to the growing corpus of the federal debt and to unite the officers with the public creditors. Since under Morris's direction the other debts of the army were also converted into federal securities, the army debt passed to the federal government.[55] Recommendations of Congress for back pay were implemented by a new impost amendment, a bundle of compromises limited to twenty-five years, with revenue restricted to paying debts and enforcement left to the states.[56] That, too, failed of unanimous passage. Meantime, Morris managed to dig up enough cash to pay the army a month's pay at the rate of 50 cents a month for privates and notes for officers for three months' pay.[57]

One may sum up the affair by observing that Washington knew the score and understood that Robert and Gouverneur Morris, as prime instigators, would in terms of power have been the principal beneficiaries of the movement. Hamilton conceded that the nationalist politicians in Philadelphia were supportive. So cleverly were the moves made, and with such circumspection, that those who pieced the story together, Hamilton shrewdly concluded, could have difficulty "supporting their insinuations by a single fact."[58] The General never publicly placed the blame on any one because, in a state where the civilian authority had maintained its supremacy over the military, any public awareness of the high standing of the civilian leadership engaged in flirtations with a military coup might have served as a dangerous example for the future. In fact, the civilian leadership never really wanted a *coup d'état*. That would have meant supplanting Washington. Gates would have been the last man they would have chosen. And so, by unspoken agreement, the origins and objectives of the so-called Newburgh Conspiracy remain clouded in the mists of history.

One might have thought that the country would have been contented that the real dangers of a *coup d'état* were eliminated by the simple promise of Congress to commute the half-pay pension to Continental officers to full pay for five years. Instead, the decision was greeted by a storm of dissent, notably among New Englanders distinctly prone to indict the proposal as laying the seeds of an aristocracy.

Unhappily for the military's case, and shortly before the disbanding of the Continental Army, two events occurred which strengthened antimilitary sentiment. On June 21, 1783, mutinous soldiers from the third Pennsylvania regiment, joined by the Philadelphia militia, clamoring for back pay, surrounded the State House in Philadelphia where Congress was in session. They poked their muskets through the windows at such celebrities as James Madison and Alexander Hamilton, and demanded immediate satisfaction of their grievances. Rather than remain besieged by a segment of their own army, and outraged by the admission of John Dickinson, president of the state's Executive Council, that he could not count on his own militia to protect the delegates, conduct which Hamilton labeled "to the last degree weak and disgusting," the delegates quit the building,[59] encountering no more than "mock obstruction" by the mutineers. Their flight to Princeton was an undignified display, but prudence dictated that they conduct their business in greater safety. There they reconvened on June 26, sitting from that date until December at Nassau Hall.[60] The delegates' next move was to be to Annapolis, where Congress would ratify the Definitive Treaty of

Peace on January 17, 1784, before making its final moves as the old Continental Congress, first to Trenton and then to New York.

It was at this most unfortuitous conjunction of events, while Congress was in flight from a disgruntled soldiery, that a group of officers, men who had formed lasting friendships together, formed themselves into the Society of the Cincinnati at the suggestion of General Henry Knox. The Society, named in honor of Cincinnatus, the Roman dictator who returned to the plow, was headed by none other than General Washington. The ostensible purpose of the organization was to raise a fund for widows and children of those slain in the Revolutionary War. In addition to its beneficent goals, it also had a political side, as one of its aims was to promote a closer union among the states. Only Continental officers were eligible, and by descent their eldest sons, or if a direct descent failed, collateral descendants could join. The order was divided into state societies, with a branch in France which was closed down during the French Revolution.

Although accorded considerable respect in some circles,[61] the aristocratic tone of the Society's objectives, coming at a time when primogeniture was rapidly being abolished in virtually every state, provided a special target for criticism. Many leading Americans, including the New Englander Elbridge Gerry, joined the popular opposition in assailing the order. John Jay, reporting to his friend Gerry about sentiment in France, stated that "some of our best Friends think the order of Cincinnatus will eventually divide us into two mighty factions." He then went on to criticize Louis XVI for giving permission to French officers to wear the badge of the order "without having requested the opinion of Congress."[62] The heaviest broadsides were fired by an Irish-born jurist, legislator, and later Antifederalist, Aedanus Burke of South Carolina, who warned that, if unchecked, the Society would divide the country into two classes, the patricians and the rabble. Burke labeled the Society "an hereditary peerage," and as such contrary to the Articles of Confederation, the sixth article of which banned granting of titles of nobility by either Congress or the states. But since the membership was self-chosen, the relevance of Burke's reference is not clear. Burke went on to denounce the Society as "planted in a hot, fiery ambition," which would one day "undermine the Constitution and destroy civil liberty," and to predict that within one generation the order would be established "immoveably" and lead to the assertion of arbitrary power based on heredity, a power that no descendant was likely to renounce.[63]

Burke's pamphlet quickly reached the furthest corners of the Confederation. In remote portions of New England town meetings and county conventions, joined by one state legislature after another, proceeded to denounce the Society.[64] In France, Benjamin Franklin, who scoffed at the Cincinnati as "hereditary knights," turned Burke's pamphlet over to Mirabeau to translate into French. Soon to be a Revolutionary protagonist in his own land, Mirabeau issued his own adaptation and amplification of Burke's indictment. Therein he warned that, while monarchies might need an aristocracy, such a "body" was antipathetical to the republican spirit and to the American state constitutions and bills of rights which asserted the equality of all citizens.[65] The relative quiescence of the Society did not calm the fears of Dr. Benjamin Rush. While the Constitutional Convention had hardly begun its sessions, he expressed the fear that the Society held the potential for another Newburgh affair and would not hesitate to use force, if necessary, to secure the adoption of the Constitution when that instrument was finally hammered out.[66] He could hardly have known that the final version of the Constitution, in Article I, section 9, contained the provision: "No Title of Nobility shall be granted by the United States."

Retrospectively, the anxieties aroused both in France and America over the Order of the Cincinnati seem all out of scale with that society's aims and capacities. Bowing to the almost universal clamor, the order promptly abolished its original rules by which membership passed only to the oldest male descendants, at least in some of the states, and placed the funds of the state societies in the keeping of the state legislatures. The order still functions, but has yet to prove a threat to the people's liberties.

With the nation in the grip of antimilitarism, the demobilization of the Continental Army was almost unobtrusive. Without an army any threat by dissident officers would have been meaningless, as Armstrong confessed to Gates,[67] and the evidence is lacking that the privates would in any event have followed their officers into the interior of the country.[68] The process of demobilization proceeded, with a small nucleus on hand to deal with the evacuation of New York City. Then, within months, the whole army was discharged except for a small force of Indian fighters. By proclamation Congress thanked the "armies" for their "long, eminent and faithful service," and ordered them discharged or permitted to retire from the service.[69] Just to keep this tiny force evoked tense debates in Congress. Alexander Hamilton and fellow committeemen of the distinction of James Madison, Oliver Ellsworth, and James Wilson had argued for a modest peacetime military establishment as well as a peacetime navy. Hamilton's eloquent warning that "the want of an army lost the liberty of Athens" fell on deaf ears, as Congress was in no mood to heed this modern Demosthenes. Nor was the country.[70] Contrariwise, James Monroe, a delegate from Virginia, argued that even a peacetime army needed for the protection of the Western settlers might pose a threat to American liberties. Congress cut down the original proposal for enlisting an army for three years from a total of 896 men to a mere 450,[71] and in June 1784 it discharged all its forces except for 83 privates at Fort Pitt and West Point and a few officers above the rank of captain.

The lesson of Newburgh had been quickly grasped by both the public and Congress. Despite Shays' Rebellion, frontier disorders, disunion threats, the maintenance of British troops on American soil, and Indian military activities on the Southern frontier, the delegates at the Federal Convention were not in the least dissuaded from the necessity of putting the army under civilian authority. The President was designated as commander-in-chief of the army, the navy, and the militia when called into national service, while even the chief executive's authority over military affairs was circumscribed by the Framers, who conferred upon Congress the power to declare war and limited military appropriations to a period of two years.

The last days of the Revolutionary Army were humiliating. When Secretary of War Benjamin Lincoln arrived at New Windsor before disbandment, he failed to bring along the Morris notes for three months' pay and even tried to borrow a few dollars to assist officers needing travel money.[72] Impoverished soldiers went home after begging their way and were soon forgotten. The pension claims filed at a much later time remain as mute testimony to the inability of so many of the Revolutionary War veterans to make their adjustments to a peacetime economy.[73] It was almost as though a people's war had been won without the presence of an army.

Postscript: By 1787, few of the troops still held the loan office certificates given them in final settlement. Most had been forced to sell them to speculators or creditors for a fraction of their ultimate worth. The Framers indubitably knew this when they included Article VI in the Constitution, which reads: "All Debts contracted and Engagements entered into, before the Adoption of this Constitution, shall be as valid against the United States under this Constitution, as under the Confederation."

CHAPTER 3

Congress and the People

THE question where sovereignty originally resided in Revolutionary America has been recently criticized as "a continuing if fruitless debate from the nineteenth century to the present over the priority of the union or the states."[1] Most of those who oppose the view that sovereignty originated in the nation not the states have relied for their authority on the Articles of Confederation and the relatively brief debates thereon. It should be borne in mind, however, that the Articles did not go into effect until March 1, 1781, almost seven years after the initial Congress had begun to take united action on behalf of the American people.

In point of fact the issue of precedence was central to the burgeoning Revolutionary and post-Revolutionary controversy over the locus of sovereignty between radicals (later called Antifederalists) who supported rather extravagant claims to state sovereignty and the conservatives (later mistermed Federalists) who adopted a more continental view, stressing sovereignty as residing in the *people* rather than the *states.*

A review of the evidence makes it clear that a national government was in operation before the formation of the states. It was the people who initiated the holding of the First Continental Congress, which met from September 5 to October 26, 1774. Even before passing the Declaration and Resolves denouncing British repressive measures, the First Congress adopted the Continental Association of nonimportation and nonconsumption of British goods. Noteworthy were those clauses establishing extralegal machinery for enforcement. A committee was to be elected in each county, town, and city to execute the Association, violators to be punished by publicity or boycott. On the higher level, Congress pledged to boycott any province which failed to keep the Association—a provision clearly indicating Congress's perception of itself as a superior authority to the colonies in these pre-Revolutionary measures and imparting the prestige and authority of Congress to local leaders whose own status was unclarified. Then by calling for the election of new committees to replace those appointed irregularly, Congress arranged not only to provide them with a new mandate but to hold a referendum on its own policies as well. As one recent commentator has concluded, "By extension, Congress too would be able to argue that its authority flowed from the express will of the people."[2] Delegates to that Revolutionary assemblage were selected in disregard of colonial assemblies and by other extralegal means.

Finally, the First Congress in turn issued the call for its successor, the Second Congress, which convened on May 10, 1775. Notwithstanding repeated adjournments and movements from site to site under the exigencies of war and even mutiny, the Second Congress continued to function throughout the war as "The Congress," assuming the title conferred upon it by the Articles of Confederation "The United States in Congress Assembled" on March 2, 1781, holding its last session on March 2, 1789.[3]

To determine which came first, chicken or egg, one has to examine the methods by which delegates were selected to the two Congresses. In general, the delegates to both Congresses were selected by the *people* of the colonies, not by the colonial governments, a significant distinction. Delegate selection was accomplished in a number of different ways—by Revolutionary committees, polling of freeholders, elections by illegal assemblies in defiance of royal governors, and Revolutionary conventions. These steps may have been fortuitous in part; but in the main they sprang from the exigencies of the Revolutionary situation. The chart at the end of this chapter is submitted to clarify the relation of the Continental Congress to the colonies and states and the methods of election employed.

The selection of delegates to the First Congress took place in the spring and summer of 1774, after adjournment of the regular winter meeting of most colonial assemblies. Thus, unless a governor had called a special session of the colonial legislature that year, the assemblies could not legally meet or act. Hence, a majority of the delegates to this Congress were chosen by popular or Revolutionary bodies. Only four out of the twelve colonies represented in that Congress elected delegates through their regular assemblies, and two of these were in fact extralegal. In Delaware, the assembly session was called by the speaker rather than the governor; in Massachusetts, the General Court held its session in defiance of the governor. Only in Pennsylvania and Rhode Island, the first a proprietary colony, the second a self-governing one, did the regular assemblies elect delegates to the Congress without interference from their respective governors. In neither did the royal government exercise control over the convening of the legislature.

On September 5, 1774, the delegates to the First Congress assembled—save Georgia, the only unrepresented colony. In their formal resolutions, they described themselves as the delegates appointed or elected "by the *good people* of the several colonies."[4] In sum, the evidence establishing the fact that the selection of delegates to the First Congress occurred largely outside the colonial legislative bodies supports Story's contention that the Continental Congress was organized "with the consent of the people acting directly in their primary, sovereign capacity," and that the Union was "spontaneously formed by the people of the United States."[5]

While disaffected groups of colonists initiated the First Congress, that body issued, as one of its concluding actions in October 1774, the call for the Second Congress to convene on May 10, 1775.[6] The instructions went out to all "the Colonies, in North America" to choose deputies. They were instructed to elect, at town and district meetings deputies to a provincial congress, which in turn would choose delegates to the Congress at Philadelphia.[8] The procedure embarked upon was extralegal, if not subversive. The delegates of the Thirteen Colonies were chosen during the winter and early spring when most provincial assemblies held their regular session. Fearful that the assemblies would be prorogued by Crown-appointed governors, the people in eight of the colonies chose to elect their delegates through extralegal assemblies or conventions, deliberately bypassing the legally constituted assemblies.[9]

As a result of the vacuum created by the disintegrating authority of the colonial assemblies and royally appointed governors, whom the upstart Revolutionary colonial congresses or conventions ignored,[10] the Second Congress assumed the initiative in establishing Revolutionary governments in the colonies and ultimately transforming them into states. Extralegal committees of public safety, patterned after the Revolutionary committees set up in England during the Puritan Revolution and in the American colonies during the upheavals of 1689, had sprung up in several colonies to fill this vacuum. On July 18, 1775, the Continental Congress recommended that those colonies lacking such committees set them up in recess.[11] By 1777, every single colony had complied with this directive. Congress was also instrumental in giving these extralegal bodies a uniformity of title throughout the Thirteen Colonies, and in at least five colonies, it played an initiating role in their formation.[12]

Even more significant and certainly more pertinent to the issue of the precedence of Congress was the role of that body in the formation of the states themselves. It was Congress which issued the call to the people of the colonies to organize state governments. At the start this was done on an ad hoc basis. In New Hampshire, the first province to make the transition to statehood, the Committee of Safety and the Exeter Convention sought the guidance of Congress in July 1775.[13] Acting on the prompting of John Adams and the New Hampshire delegates, the Continental Congress passed a resolution on November 3, 1775, authorizing New Hampshire to set up a civil government.[14] The following day, a similar authorization was extended to the inhabitants of South Carolina.[15] Both took steps to carry out Congress's mandate. On January 5, 1776, New Hampshire adopted a form of "Civil Government for this colony,"[16] while the South Carolina legislature adopted its constitution on March 26, 1776.[17]

The historic date which should settle this issue is May 10, 1776. On that day Congress, spurred by a groundswell from within a cluster of colonies, generalized its previous practice of calling upon individual colonies by issuing a broad resolution urging the provinces to organize state governments:

Resolved, That it be recommended to the respective assemblies and conventions of the United Colonies, where no government sufficient to the exigencies of their affairs have been hitherto established, to adopt such government as shall, in the opinion of the representatives of the people, best conduce to the happiness and safety of their constituents in particular, and America in general.[18]

Commenting on the passage of this resolution, John Adams observed: "It was indeed on all hands considered by Men of Understanding as equivalent to a declaration of independence: tho a formal declaration of it was still opposed by Mr. Dickinson and his Party."[19] If Adams considered this resolution a de facto declaration of independence, he would soon see that the real one ran not far behind.

The Declaration of Independence was by its own words "a declaration by the representatives of the United States of America in General Congress assembled." Since only four state governments, three of them provisional, had been formed prior to the Declaration,[20] it was Congress—not a confederation of "sovereign states" —that proclaimed American independence from Great Britain. In essence, it was Congress which declared the colonies to be "states." That is the way the first Chief Justice of the United States saw it, when in *Chisholm* v. *Georgia*,[21] he characterized the Declaration as the act of the whole people of the united colonies by the instrumentality of their representatives. Indubitably, John Jay, if pressed, would have conceded that the "whole people" excluded from its constituency the substantial segment opposed to independence, and he might even have admitted that it excluded the politically voiceless.

The Great Declaration, an act of paramount and sovereign authority, dissolved the political connection with and allegiance to Great Britain. In waging war against Great Britain, as in declaring independence, Congress acted for the people rather than as an agent of thirteen separate states. As early interpreted by the Supreme Court, the transfer of sovereignty "from the crown of Great Britain" to "the [American] people" constituted the legal significance of the Declaration.[22] The Court perceived the period of congressional government from September 1774 to March 1, 1781, as an exercise of power derived from the people, expressly conferred through the medium of state conventions or legislatures, and, once exercised, "impliedly ratified by the acquiescence and obedience of the people."[23]

How did the colonies perceive the assumption by Congress of the role of national sovereignty? They accepted the initiative of Congress, along with its authority, in their transformation into thirteen states exercising only internal sovereignty.[24] Thus, for example, the ten state constitutions which provided methods for electing delegates to the Congress implicitly acknowledged that the Union was as durable as the states, that the enacting state was a permanent member of the Union, and that the Union was endowed with extensive powers.[25] More significant, none of the state constitutions claimed powers necessary for the conduct of national defense and foreign affairs.[26]

In turn, one might properly inquire, what was Congress's self-perception of its sovereign authority? So far as the First Congress is concerned, that body exercised the substance, if not the title, of national sovereignty. It passed "resolves," essentially legally effective acts.[27] It adopted a Declaration of Rights and Grievances.[28] Significantly, the First Congress's most important exercise of authority, its nonconsumption and nonimportation resolves, constituted an agreement on the part of the delegates of Congress "and the inhabitants of the several colonies, whom we represent" in which all the delegates bound themselves and their "constituents" to adhere to these resolutions.[29] While some matters agreed upon in the Congress were submitted to the colonies for their approval, the Petition to the King, the Address to the People of Great-Britain, and the Memorial to the Inhabitants of the British Colonies were issued on the responsibility of Congress alone.[30]

Although the First Congress acted as a national assembly without actually denominating itself as such, the Second Congress consciously regarded itself as the embodiment of "the United Colonies." It first employed the term "United Colonies" on June 7, 1775, in a resolution for a Continental day of humiliation, fasting, and prayer.[31] Ten days later, in commissioning General Washington, it described him as commanding "the army of the United Colonies."[32] On June 22, it resolved that "the twelve confederated colonies" be pledged for the bills of credit it now resolved to emit.[33] Early in July, Congress adopted the Jefferson-Dickinson draft of the Declaration of the Causes and Necessity of Taking Up Arms, issued on behalf of "the United Colonies of America,"[34] along with an Address to the Inhabitants of Great Britain from "The Twelve United Colonies by their Delegates in Congress."[35] Similar phraseology was employed in the approved draft of a "Speech to the Six Confederate Nations,"[36] and in an Address "to the People of Ireland."[37] More conclusive than the assertion by Congress that it spoke on behalf of the "people" or "the inhabitants" was its assumption of the direction of the war operations and its determination of instructions for peace.

With the exception of a few intractable states' righters, such as Thomas Burke of North Carolina, the overwhelming number of Founding Fathers supported the view that the United States in Congress Assembled acted in the capacity of an independent sovereign state. Even the concession of equality of voting by the former colonies in Congress can scarcely be construed as indicating that Congress considered itself merely an agent of the colonies or states rather than of the people, for the decision in favor of equal voting was a gesture of conciliation to the smaller states rather than a recognition of state sovereignty.[38] In fact, the proposal for equality of voting was made by John Jay,[39] quickly to become an arch-continentalist, while others, like Benjamin Rush, who advocated proportionate voting in the Second Continental Congress, denied that the Union was composed of "totally independent States."[40]

In accord with Rush's perception of the locus of national sovereignty, a long list of leading statesmen of the era can be cited, including James Wilson, James Madison, Benjamin Franklin, John Adams, Robert Morris, and George Washington. There is, perhaps, no clearer enunciation of this position in the years prior to the adoption of the Articles of Confederation than the Circular Letter from Congress "to their Constituents." Prepared by its president, John Jay, and adopted on September 8, 1779, the document accompanied Congress's resolutions "for stopping the further emissions of bills of credit."[41] "For every purpose essential to the defense of these states in the progress of the present war, and necessary to the attainment of the objects of it," President Jay informed the states, "the States now are as fully, legally, and absolutely confederated as it is possible for them to be." This remark has peculiar relevance, because the Articles of Confederation had already lain on the calendar for a good two years and still lacked ratification by one state. Here was the president of Congress, acting on behalf of that body, declaring that such unanimous ratification was not necessary, a position supported in some part by the fact that the Articles were silent on the number of states needed for ratification (Article XIII might have been construed as a ratification by the delegates as agents for their states). To support his interpretation, Jay cited, first, the credentials of the delegates to the First and Second Congresses to show that they were instructed to establish a Union to oppose the oppression of Great Britain and redress grievances, and, second, the Declaration of Independence. With respect to the latter, he asked: "Was ever confederation more formal, more solemn or explicit?" Finally, he cautioned that it would be "a mistake to believe that the Union would end when its objects were attained."[42]

From distant Montpelier James Madison was moved to respond to Jay's "Address" in a paper critical of Congress's monetary policy, but not published for a dozen years. Its nationalistic tone could have come from Jay's own pen. Therein Madison treated the United States as an indivisible unit, speaks of "our currency" as American currency, of "public credit" as the credit of the United States, and "domestic loans" as those of the whole country. Quoting with approval Jay's assertion that "these states now" are "fully, legally, absolutely confederated," Madison concluded that until the war debts were paid, the Confederation could not be dissolved "consistent with the laws of God or man." Madison discerned "a sense of common permanent interest, mutual affection . . . the importance and splendor of the union," all "conspiring to form a strong chain of connection, which must forever bind us together."[43]

In sum, congressional government was a creation of the people of the colonies or states acting in a revolutionary capacity. Stepping into a vacuum of political power in the transitional period before formal war, Congress assumed the military initiative, imposed a boycott on trade, issued the call to the people of the colonies to organize state governments, voted for and declared independence, and was viewed by the former colonies, by most of the Revolutionary leaders, and by itself as exercising the substance of national sovereignty.

This distinction between external sovereignty exercised by Congress and internal sovereignty reserved by the states was widely recognized. Public figures such as John Jay, Benjamin Rush, James Duane, and Alexander Hamilton understood the test of a sovereign state to be its capacity to exercise external sovereignty. For example, Secretary for Foreign Affairs Jay asserted in 1786 that the thirteen state legislatures had "no more authority to exercise the powers [of war and peace] or pass Acts of Sovereignty on these points, than any thirteen individual Citizens."[44] Benjamin Rush observed that a sovereign state in Europe was held to be one possessing the power of making war and peace, forming treaties, and the like.[45] The majority of the first Supreme Court similarly understood external sovereignty to be the essence of statehood and denied that the states had ever exercised it.[46] It may be added that the view propounded by Rush, and seconded by the early Supreme Court, that the capacity to enter into relations with other states is an essential attribute of national, as opposed to state, sovereignty, remains an accepted tenet of international law.[47]

If any of the former colonies pretended to be sovereign states, as the terms were understood even then in international law, they failed to make apparent those intentions. A possible exception was the submission by Governor Thomas Jefferson to the Virginia state legislature of the Treaty of 1778 with France for ratification—a mistake that was not repeated on later occasions.[48] Indeed, Congress's right to conduct foreign relations—wartime defense and diplomacy, including the negotiation of treaties—stood unchallenged throughout the Revolutionary period, even before the formal promulgation of the Declaration.

The submission of the Articles of Confederation for ratification by the states entailed no diminution of the *external* sovereignty of Congress, although, as we shall see, it did materially diminish its powers in other respects and in ways pertinent to the long-range conduct of diplomacy. Article IX conferred on Congress "the sole and exclusive power" over war and peace and foreign affairs.[49] In fact, the Treaty of Peace with Great Britain was ratified solely by Congress acting for the United States and merely referred to the states for observance. Despite the provision of Article IX of the Articles of Confederation that "no State shall be deprived of territory for the benefit of the United States," the treaty nonetheless altered the boundaries of eight states.[50] The notion that a state might have its boundaries determined without its consent was hardly consistent with the concept of a fully sovereign state.[51]

Direction of National Defense

The start of the shooting war gave the early actions of the Second Continental Congress a special urgency, and in meeting the challenge of events, it clearly assumed war powers. It imposed an embargo on all provisions to the British fisheries in America,[52] determined to put the colonies "in a state of defence,"[53] and urged the Provincial Convention in Massachusetts to set up a provisional government.[54] The most noteworthy acts of sovereignty were undertaken during June of 1775. First, Congress created a Continental military establishment[55] (some units in the Continental Army had "CONGRESS" stitched on their headdress). Second, it took steps to make the militia an effective fighting force.[56] Third, it authorized the emission of bills to finance the defense of the colonies.[57] To supplement its regulations for the organization of a Continental Army, Congress adopted the Articles of War and established a hospital and medical service.[58] In October, Congress authorized a Continental Navy, and the next month, adopted a set of "Rules for the Regulation of the Navy of the United Colonies."[59]

Once independence was declared, Congress went so far as to arrange and support an interim state-operating regime where a power vacuum existed within a state. In the early spring of 1777, Congress appointed members to the supreme Executive Council and the Board of War of Pennsylvania and established a committee to confer with the President over the emergency situation in that state. Since the state council and assembly were in recess, the committee advised Congress, "the executive authority" of the state was "incapable of any exertion adequate to the present crisis." It urged the President and such other officials as were available on the state council and Boards of War and Navy to "exercise every authority to promote the safety of the State" until such time as the legislature and Council could be convened. It further recommended that the commanding officer of the Continental forces in Philadelphia afford "every possible assistance" in carrying out such measures as may be recommended to him by such interim authority, and that Congress pledge to cooperate in facilitating every measure deemed conducive to the safety of the state. Congress so resolved.[60]

Diplomacy and Treaties

Diplomatic endeavors commenced as early as November 29, 1775, when Congress appointed a five-man Committee of Correspondence to contact the European powers.[61] On September 26, 1776, it named a committee to prepare plans for treaties of commerce with foreign nations.[62] From 1776 onward, without exception, American diplomatic commissions negotiated treaties which contained such unequivocal terms as "the two parties," "the said two nations," "the two states," "the two republics," "of either nation," or "both nations."[63] The treaties of commerce and alliance with France, as Mr. Justice Chase later wrote, evidenced that Congress "possessed the great rights of external sovereignty."[64] It was Congress that appointed diplomatic representatives abroad and issued instructions and commissions in the name of the United States and letters of credence explicitly in its own name.[65] Acting under such a commission, John Jay was instructed to procure a treaty between Spain and "the citizens of the United States."[66] Adams referred to his commission from the United Provinces as having been "lately received from my sovereign the United States of America in Congress Assembled."[67]

An early test of Congress's treaty-making power involved state challenges to its Definitive Treaty of 1783 with Great Britain.[68] By Article V of that treaty, Congress agreed to recommend to the state legislatures the restitution of all estates belonging to British subjects which had been confiscated, and by the sixth article, it stipulated that no further confiscation nor prosecutions would be initiated because of a person's role in the war. The New York legislature passed a series of statutes in defiance of these treaty provisions. The first challenge to these measures was in the 1784 case of *Rutgers* v. *Waddington*.[69] In the course of his opinion, Mayor James Duane of New York, presiding over the Mayor's Court, the predecessor of the Court of Common Pleas, observed: "The foederal [*sic*] compact hath vested Congress with full and exclusive powers to make peace and war. This treaty they have made and ratified, and rendered its obligation perpetual.[70] Alexander Hamilton, chief counsel for the defendant, took to the press to defend the unpopular decision. In "A Letter from Phocion," he asserted:

Does not the act of confederation place the exclusive right of war and peace in the United States in Congress? Have they not the sole power of making treaties with foreign nations? Are not these among the first rights of sovereignty and does not the delegation of them to the general confederacy so far abridge the sovereignty of each particular state? Would not a different doctrine involve the contradiction of *imperium in imperio*?[71]

The issue of the supremacy of treaties made by the United States was settled by Congress in April 1787, when Congress resolved that treaties were part of the laws of the land, and that a state could in no way undertake to abridge these obligations.[72] Foreign Secretary Jay's activist role in maintaining the supremacy of national treaties carries special weight since he was intimately involved in the negotiation and formal ratification by Congress of most of the eight treaties signed with foreign nations during the Confederation years.[73] Jay, bearing in mind that the Treaties of 1778 with France were gratuitously ratified by Virginia (significantly, by no other state),[74] did not submit these treaties to the states for their ratification. Congress fully effected ratification of these later treaties on its own authority, sending them to the states for their information only and with a directive to observe their provisions.[75]

Perhaps the most formidable threat to congressional power to enter into treaties on behalf of the people of the United States were the proposals of Russia[76] and Austria,[77] the co-mediators of the American War for Independence, for separate negotiations between England and each of the thirteen states. These proposals were endorsed by the Comte de Vergennes,[78] France's foreign minister, as a means of extricating his country from the conflict without entirely abandoning the American cause, for he felt that England would be more willing to accede to a subdivided independent America than it would to a centralized sovereignty of all the former colonies.[79]

John Adams, appointed minister plenipotentiary by Congress in the fall of 1779 to negotiate a peace and commercial treaty with Great Britain, learned of the Russo-Austrian proposals. At a July 1781 conference with Vergennes, Adams sought to dissuade the French minister from supporting the plan for separate negotiations with the states. Adams pointed out that the states could not be represented in negotiations with European powers without recognition of their independence as separate sovereignties—a status foreclosed by the Articles of Confederation, ratified and communicated to the courts of Europe, and as "universally known as any Constitution of Government in Europe." The Articles, Adams briefed the French foreign minister, expressly delegated to the United States in Congress Assembled the power and authority to negotiate with foreign powers. It would be "a publick Disrespect" for any power to apply directly to the governors or legislatures of the separate states, and it would be an error and a misdemeanor for a state official to receive and transmit such a communication to his provincial legislature. In short, "[t]here is no method for the Courts of Europe to convey any Thing to the People of America, but through the Congress of the United States, nor any way of negotiating with them, but by means of that Body." With these constitutional obstructions in mind, Adams strongly urged Vergennes to discountenance the notion of "summoning Ministers from the thirteen states."[80]

This exchange ended France's interest in the proposal. Henceforth, it was clear to America's ally as well as to the mediating powers that negotiations were to be conducted with a single nation, the United States of America.

Admiralty Jurisdiction

Since most of the powers of Congress over matters of war and peace, the army and navy, and external affairs were exercised without challenge, it may be significant to focus on the narrower areas where congressional authority was contested by some of the states. While the creation, supply, and direction of naval operations were implicitly conceded by all thirteen states as falling within congressional authority, the issue of jurisdiction over admiralty was only resolved after an intense and prolonged struggle. Congress very early set up a committee "to hear and determine finally upon all appeals brought to Congress" from the courts of admiralty of the several states. Under a measure adopted in 1775,[81] appeals were referred to special committees. In January 1777, Congress created a Standing Committee on Appeals, which would serve as a judicial body.[82] Under Article IX of the Articles of Confederation, Congress was given the power of creating "courts for the trial of pirates and felonies committed on the high seas," and Congress exercised this prerogative on April 5, 1781, by designating certain state judges to sit in such cases.[83] One can identify 104 decided admiralty cases over an eleven-year period, including some 49 that resulted in outright reversals of the state courts.[84]

Although in most cases execution of the federal court's judgments proved routine, some of the states undertook in various ways to narrow congressional appellate jurisdiction in admiralty. Virginia, for example, sought in 1779 to deny Congress admiralty jurisdiction over cases in which both litigants were citizens of that state.[85] In the previous year a Pennsylvania statute declared that the findings of the jury "shall establish the facts without reexamination or appeal."[86] This provision ran counter to Article IX of the Articles of Confederation, which empowered Congress to establish courts of final appeals "in all cases of captures." No state had raised any objection to Congress's authority in this area prior to ratification.

An appeal in the case of the sloop *Active*,[87] condemned in the Pennsylvania Court of Admiralty in Philadelphia, brought Congress and Pennsylvania at loggerheads over the issue of congressional appellate jurisdiction in admiralty. The Standing Committee of Congress, in defiance of the Pennsylvania statute, reexamined the facts and reversed the Pennsylvania court decree.[88] The Pennsylvania admiralty court refused to execute this new decree on the ground that the jury's findings of fact were conclusive under the statute. A special committee of Congress proceeded to uphold its own Committee on Appeals and recommended an appropriate resolution,[89] which Congress adopted in March 1779.[90] The resolution affirmed the power of congressional appointees to examine decisions of fact as well as law in appeals from state courts of admiralty, whether the decisions be rendered by judge or upon a jury verdict, and to issue a final decree.

Exercising the power to declare a state law unconstitutional for the first time during the American Revolution, Congress, in words written by Thomas Burke, hitherto known as a leading states' rightist, resolved "that no act of any one State can or ought to destroy the right of appeals to Congress in the sense above declared." In words assertive of the fundamental tenets of national sovereignty, Congress went on to declare:

That Congress is by these United States invested with the supreme sovereign power of war and peace:

That the power of executing the law of nations is essential to the sovereign supreme power of war and peace:

That the legality of all captures on the high seas must be determined by the law of nations:

That the authority ultimately and finally to decide on all matters and questions touching the law of nations, does reside and is vested in the sovereign supreme power of war and peace:

That a controul by appeals is necessary, in order to compel a just and uniform execution of the law of nations.[91]

Furthermore, Congress asserted that investing a state jury with the unreviewable authority to determine the legality of captures at sea would mean that "juries would be possessed of the ultimate supreme power of executing the law of nations"; that to concede to juries a power so uncontrolled would be to accept

a construction which involves many inconveniences and absurdities, destroys an essential part of the power of war and peace entrusted to Congress, and would disable the Congress of the United States from giving satisfaction to foreign nations complaining of a violation of neutrality, of treaties, or other breaches of the law of nations, and would enable a jury in any one State to involve the United States in hostilities.

Such a construction, Congress contended, was "inadmissible for these and many other reasons."[92]

On a roll call ten states voted in the affirmative, and Pennsylvania along with delegate Witherspoon of New Jersey voted in the negative. Significantly, in terms of New Hampshire's own *Lusanna* litigation,[93] that state's only voting delegate on this occasion, George Frost, voted in the affirmative on both ballots.[94]

As a result of the controversy over the *Active,* Congress sought to strengthen its admiralty jurisdiction. On January 15, 1780, it established a Court of Appeals in Cases of Capture, elected and commissioned the judges,[95] and transferred the cases pending before the Committee of Congress to the new court.[96] On March 27, 1781, some three weeks after the final ratification of the Articles of Confederation, it reasserted its authority to seize prizes of the enemy in a sweeping resolution drafted by James Madison. The resolution authorized both "the fleets and ships of these United States and such vessels commissioned by letters of marque and reprisal by the authority of the United States in Congress assembled," to seize all vessels and goods belonging either to the king of Great Britain or to "his subjects or others inhabiting" any of the territories or possessions of the king. To ensure execution of this resolve, Congress authorized the state courts of admiralty to take judicial cognizance of such seizure and condemn such ships or goods "according to the course of admiralty and the law of nations."[97] Impliedly, Congress reserved to itself final appellate jurisdiction, which was explicitly recognized in Article IX of the Articles of Confederation.

If Pennsylvania accepted, albeit reluctantly, federal appellate jurisdiction over prizes, New Hampshire proved more intransigent. The seizure of the brigantine *Lusanna* in 1777 not only raised the same constitutional and jurisdictional issues as that of the sloop *Active*, but ultimately drew from the United States Supreme Court an opinion defining the limits of state sovereignty in admiralty. The protracted litigation over the seizure of the *Lusanna*[98] illustrates the role of the earliest permanent judicial bodies with a national jurisdiction—Congress's Court of Commissioners and its successor, the Court of Appeals in Cases of Capture.

Lusanna involved a prize taken by a certain New Hampshire privateersman in 1777. The brigantine was libeled in the Court Maritime of the State of New Hampshire and the ship and her cargo were decreed forfeit. Twice the court denied the appeal to Congress on the ground that the applicable New Hampshire statutes provided for appeal only to the state Superior Court.[99] The appellant petitioned Congress for review, and Congress, having already decided, in the dispute over the *Active*, that it possessed jurisdiction in prize appeals by virtue of the war power, agreed to consider the case. The case was heard on January 15, 1780, by the newly established Court of Appeals in Cases of Capture.[100] The court reversed the sentence of the New Hampshire court and ordered restoration of the property to the claimants.

Since the state courts would take no action to enforce the decree, the case lay dormant until the new federal court system was established by the Judiciary Act of 1789. Then in 1793, the United States Circuit Court for the District of New Hampshire directed commissioners to assess the damages, and a final decree was awarded in 1794.[101] The case came before the Supreme Court on a writ of error as *Penhallow* v. *Doane,*[102] and was argued and decided in the February term, 1795. In lengthy opinions Justices Paterson, Iredell, Blair, and Cushing agreed that the Court of Appeals, sitting after the ratification of the Articles of Confederation, which confirmed congressional appellate authority in admiralty, was validly constituted and had jurisdiction. Paterson[103] and Blair[104] held that the inherent war power of the Continental Congress was sufficient to validate jurisdiction in the period before the Confederation. Iredell agreed that Congress, prior to the Articles of Confederation, "did exercise, with the acquiescence of the states, high powers of . . . external sovereignty,"[105] but argued that these powers were originally conveyed by the people of each of the several provinces separately rather than jointly.[106]

If the resolves of Congress and the specific provision of the Articles of Confederation, indubitably prompted by the litigation over the seizures of the *Active* and *Lusanna,* were not by themselves dispositive, the ruling of the Supreme Court conclusively established Congress's appellate jurisdiction in admiralty, while affirming the supreme sovereign power of Congress in war and peace during the period prior to the adoption of the Constitution.

Settling Interstate Disputes

Article IX of the Articles of Confederation authorized the setting up by Congress of a court for the settlement of territorial jurisdictional land disputes between the states. Where the parties could not agree on the composition of the court, Congress would, by a complicated selection process, name the judges, whose judgment would be "final and decisive." In only one case, however, did an Article IX court sit, and that was at Trenton in 1782, where the court upheld Pennsylvania's jurisdiction over the Wyoming Valley, an area contested by Connecticut.[107] In other cases the disputes were settled by compromise agreements between the parties.

Congressional Power to Compel National Allegiance

The right of a state to command the allegiance of its inhabitants has long been an essential attribute of sovereignty.[108] This general right authorizes the requirement of the taking of loyalty oaths, the definition and punishment of treason, the requirement of nationalization or naturalization, and the admission or exclusion of aliens. During the Revolutionary years, notwithstanding an occasional challenge from the states, Congress successfully asserted national authority over these matters.

1. *Treason as a National Offense.* Congress—not the states—formulated the definition of treason against the United States. Not only did Congress dissolve the bonds of allegiance to the Crown, it substituted a new national allegiance and provided sanctions for its breach. The affair of Benjamin Church, the army's chief surgeon and a resident of Massachusetts, precipitated congressional action in the area of treason. Upon the interception of a ciphered letter conveying information for transmission to the British military and its positive identification as having been written by Church, Washington brought the suspect before the Council of War. The Council convened on October 4, 1775, and unanimously decided that Church's act was criminal, but felt that the sentences listed in the Articles of War, keyed to the sanctions imposed by general courts martial,[109] were inadequate in light of the enormity of his offense. Washington then proposed to Congress that the Articles be amended to provide a more appropriate disposition for military treason.[110] When the Massachusetts House of Representatives, in turn, appealed to Congress that it could not prosecute its domiciliary for treason because it was not an independent state,[111] Congress acted swiftly to punish Church. On November 7 it ordered Church's confinement in a Connecticut jail.[112] Earlier in October a congressional committee had conferred with Washington and urged Congress to authorize the death penalty for the military treasons of mutiny, sedition, and correspondence with the enemy.[113] Congress amended the Articles of War accordingly.[114]

The inducement for congressional action with respect to civilian treason was considerably more colorful than the misdeeds which precipitated the military treason response. It took the so-called Hickey Plot of June 1776, involving charges of counterfeiting and conspiring to instigate an armed uprising and to assassinate Washington, to impel Congress to extend its treason law to civilians. Thomas Hickey, a private in Washington's security guard, was found guilty of "sedition and mutiny, and also of holding a treacherous correspondence with the enemy."[115] Hanged the following day, he bears the unenviable distinction of being the first American to suffer death for treason. Then, at the request of a secret committee of the New York Provincial Congress, Washington apprehended Mayor David Mathews of New York City, also implicated in the Hickey Plot. Mathews's arrest rendered urgent the creation of a civilian treason offense. Congress's response was immediate: "[a]ll persons abiding within any of the United Colonies, and deriving protection from the laws of the same, owe allegiance to the said laws, and are members of such colony."[116] Such allegiance could also be expected of temporary visitors. All such persons levying war against any of the said colonies or giving aid and comfort to the king of Great Britain were deemed "guilty of treason" against such colony.[117] One specialist in the law of treason considers this action of Congress to have been a "de facto declaration of independence."[118]

Congress went on to recommend to the "several United Colonies" that appropriate laws be enacted to implement the resolve.[119] The states acted promptly, inserting treason provisions into their constitutions and promulgating treason statutes and oaths of allegiance.[120] Where the states were able to maintain authority within their borders and proscribe treasonous practices therein, Congress did not intervene; where they were unable to ensure the allegiance of their inhabitants, Congress interceded. Thus in Pennsylvania, where the Patriot government had been disrupted by the invasion of the British and their occupation of Philadelphia, Congress adopted a resolution making civilians liable to court-martial if they indulged in "traitorous practice."[121] Men serving in the Continental Army were tried by the military authorities, while civilians were tried by a reconstituted and augmented Pennsylvania Executive Council.[122]

In summary, Congress took the initiative in the area of treason legislation and its enforcement. The states normally enforced their own statutes, which owed their authorization to Congress[123] and were often adopted at its suggestion. Congress intervened, however, in those states where internal order had been wracked by the Revolution.

2. The Emergence of National Citizenship. Closely related to the sovereign's right to enforce the obligation of allegiance is its right to require national citizenship by means of the administration of oaths of national allegiance and naturalization procedures.

  (a) Oaths of National Allegiance. From his headquarters in Morristown on January 25, 1777, General Washington issued a proclamation, requiring all who had taken an oath of allegiance to Great Britain either to "take an oath of allegiance to the United States of America" or be treated as common enemies.[124] Washington's act was potentially vulnerable on two counts. First, Congress, wishing to guarantee the supremacy of the civil government over the military, had enacted a resolve forbidding any officer from imposing or requiring an oath of the inhabitants.[125] Second, Washington's edict may have contravened state authority. The latter point was discussed on the floor of Congress. One delegate, Abraham Clark of New Jersey, moved that the Washington resolve be nullified on the ground that it might "interrupt the due course of the Laws" enacted in certain states "for the trial and punishment of traitors and other offenders against the peace and liberties of the same," and on the additional ground that it was an unwarranted interference with "the free exercise of the Legislative or Executive powers of any State."[126] Congress referred the resolution to a committee of five, comprised of John Adams, Richard Henry Lee, Jonathan Dickinson Sergeant, who had seconded Clark's motion, Roger Sherman, and Thomas Heyward. The committee promptly reported a resolution, drawn up by John Adams, which declared that the proclamation did "not interfere with the Laws or Civil Government of any State; but considering the situation of the Army was prudent and necessary."[127] Congress, however, evidently regarding the issue as both sensitive and divisive, voted to table the committee resolution.[128]

  By avoiding a definitive stand on the issue, Congress impliedly upheld Washington, and the General proceeded to implement his proclamation. Clark, however, continued his opposition, regarding the oath not merely as a contravention of a congressional resolve, but a logical absurdity:

[I]t is Notorious [that] the General directly counter acted [sic] a Resolve of Congress of the 9th of March last, Strictly forbidding any officer to impose or require any Oath of the Inhabitants, and he requires an Oath of Allegiance to the United States when such an Oath is Absurd before our Confederation takes place, Each State requires an Oath to the Particular State. . . .[129]

Had Clark examined some of the oaths then being administered both by Congress and the states, he might have conceded the issue, for some sort of national as well as state allegiance was quite uniformly exacted. In the case of Congress, military officers and public officials were required to take an oath of allegiance to "the United States of America,"[130] and in the case of those states which exacted some sort of national as well as state allegiance, persons of dubious loyalty were forced to clear themselves.[131]

 (b) Passports and Naturalization in the Name of the United States. Although Congress sought to avoid a definitive resolution of the issue of national, as opposed to individual state, citizenship, it did not hesitate to issue passports in the name of the President of the Congress of the United States of America.[132]

Moreover, diplomats overseas without exception viewed themselves as agents of the United States of America, not representatives of the several states. Benjamin Franklin, American commissioner in France, for example, demonstrated his identification with the national government in the phraseology employed in the passports he issued,[133] and in his stand on the naturalization of aliens. In writing to John Jay, then unaccredited minister to Spain, Franklin indicated that, although he wished to receive explicit instructions from Congress on the policy of administering oaths of United States citizenship, he had issued oaths and passports in the name of the United States of America as a matter of course.[134] Henry Laurens, a peace commissioner in France from South Carolina who had earlier served as president of the Continental Congress, was unequivocal on the issue of United States citizenship. Confined to the Tower of London on a charge of high treason after his capture on the high seas in 1780, Laurens was released on bail on December 31, 1781. He conditioned his posting bond with the comment: "I hold myself to be a citizen of the United free and independent States of North America."[135] He did not explicitly claim to be a citizen of the state of South Carolina.

Whatever may have been the difference between Congress and Franklin or his consular agents—and it is not evident that Congress ever formally objected to the administration of oaths of national citizenship and national passports—the issue was settled by the Definitive Treaty of Peace of 1783, which recognized both "the Citizens of the United States" in Article VIII and the citizens of the separate states in Article VII. Neither British nor American peace commissioners appear to have contested this resolution of the issue, and there is no evidence of any challenge in Congress to the provisions of the treaty recognizing United States citizenship. In ratifying the treaty and directing the states to carry out its provisions, Congress asserted the authority of the Confederation to confer citizenship in the collectivity, as distinguished from the traditional rights of the separate colonies, assumed by the states, to grant state citizenship.[136]

Contributing to the growing acceptance of national citizenship in the Confederation years were the provisions in the Articles of Confederation for interstate comity and full-faith-and-credit. Under the latter, creditors from one state frequently brought suit in the courts of other states. The state courts had occasion to support the claims of nonresident citizens, as in *Bayard* v. *Singleton,* in which the plaintiffs contested a state law on the ground that it deprived them of the right to trial by jury. In upholding the plaintiff's argument, the court declared that "these plaintiffs being citizens of one of the United States, or citizens of this State by the Confederation of all the States; which is to be taken as a part of the law of the land unrepealable by an act of the General Assembly," could not be deprived by statute of the right to a jury trial.[137]

From a review of the historical evidence, it seems clear that the United States was created by the people in collectivity, not by the individual states. An analysis of the process of selection of delegates for the First and Second Congresses underscores the revolutionary role of the people of the colonies in the establishment of a central governing body. It was Congress that asserted the initiative in the formation of the States. It was Congress that assumed powers of war and peace. It was Congress that entered into treaties with foreign powers, and the issue of the supremacy of treaties made by the United States was settled even before the convening of the federal Convention in 1787. It was Congress which asserted its jurisdiction over admiralty on the basis of its "sovereign power of war and peace." And it was Congress that ventured to assert power to compel national allegiance.

The central government alone possessed those attributes of external sovereignty which entitled it to be called a state in the international sense, while the separate states, possessing a limited or internal sovereignty, may rightly be considered a creation of the Continental Congress, which preceded them and brought them into being.

The Relation of the Continental Congress to the Colonies and States

Colony/State	Elections for First Congress (1774) (1)	Elections for Second Congress (1775) (2)	Date of state constitution (3)	First election of delegates under new constitutions or as "states" (4)
Connecticut	Committee of Correspondence for the Colony chosen by the Assembly[a]	Assembly[a]	Provincial Charter retained until 1818[a]	October 2, 1776[a]
Delaware	Assembly session called by Speaker, Governor having declined to convene a session[b]	Assembly[b]	September 21, 1776[b]	November 8, 1776[b]
Georgia	Unrepresented	Provincial Congress, Parish of St. John (later Liberty County), Savannah having declined to send any delegates April 13, 1775; Provincial Convention, representing all except two parishes, elected delegates July 8, 1775[c]	February 5, 1777[c]	June 7, 1777[c]
Maryland	Delegates chosen by extralegal committees appointed by the counties[c]	Provincial Convention ("Meeting of the Deputies appointed by the several Counties")[d]	November 11, 1776[d]	February 15, 1777[d]
Massachusetts	General Court (in locked-door session held in defiance of Governor)[d]	Provincial Congress[e]	Provincial charter retained until ratification of state constitution, 1780[e]	December 10, 1776[e]
New Hampshire	Extralegal meeting of town deputies held at Exeter[e]	Convention of Deputies appointed by the towns[f]	January 5, 1776: adoption of "Civil Government for this Colony"[f]	January 23, 1776 (under new provincial constitution); September 12, 1776 (as "State" delegates)[f]

(continued)

The Relation of the Continental Congress to the Colonies and States *(continued)*

Colony/State	Elections for First Congress (1774) (1)	Elections for Second Congress (1775) (2)	Date of state constitution (3)	First election of delegates under new constitutions or as "states" (4)
New Jersey	Extralegal committees appointed by seven counties[f]	Assembly[g]	July 2, 1776[g]	November 30, 1776[g]
New York	Extralegal election in N.Y. City and County; slate endorsed by three other counties; Suffolk and Orange Counties sending their own delegates[g]	Provincial Convention[h]	April 20, 1778[h]	October 3, 1777[h]
North Carolina	Extralegal meeting of "deputies" (New Bern Convention of 32 out of 38 counties represented)[h]	Provincial Convention ("General meeting of Delegates of the Inhabitants of this Province, in Convention"), approved by the Assembly[i]	December 18, 1776[i]	May 4, 1777[i]
Pennsylvania	Assembly[j]	Assembly[j]	September 28, 1776[j]	March 10, 1777[i]
Rhode Island	Assembly[j]	Assembly[k]	Provincial charter retained until 1842[k]	May 7, 1777[k]
South Carolina	Extralegal "General Meeting of the inhabitants"; slate ratified later by Assembly[l]	Provincial Congress; slate ratified later by Assembly[l]	March 26, 1776 (temporary charter retained until 1778); replaced by 2nd Constitution, adopted March 19, 1778, effective November 1778[l]	January 10, 1777[l]
Virginia	Provincial Convention ("a general meeting of Delegates from the different Counties")[l]	Provincial Convention; ("convention of delegates for the counties and corporations in the colony of Virginia")[m]	June 29, 1776[m]	October 10, 1776[m]

Footnotes to this table appear on the following page.

Notes to Table on page 77-78

Column 1

a. *JCC*, I, 17–19.
b. *Ibid.*, 21–22.
c. *Ibid.*, 22–23; Arthur M. Schlesinger, *The Colonial Merchants and the American Revolution, 1763–1776* (New York, 1917), pp. 360–62.
d. *JCC*, I, 15; JA, *Diary*, II, 96–97; *FAA*, I, 421–23.
e. *JCC*, I, 15.
f. *Ibid.*, 19–20.
g. *Ibid.*, 19, 30; Roger Champagne, "The Sons of Liberty and the Aristocracy in New York Politics, 1765–1790" (Ann Arbor, Mich., University Microfilms, 1960).
h. *JCC*, I, 30; Schlesinger, *Merchants*, pp. 370–73.
i. *JCC*, I, 21–22; *FAA*, I, 607–08, 661.
j. *JCC*, I, 16–17.
k. *Ibid.*, 23–24; Schlesinger, *Merchants*, pp. 373–79; *FAA*, I, 671–72.
l. *JCC*, I, 23; *FAA*, I, 686–90.

Column 2

a. *JCC*, II, 15.
b. *Ibid.*, 18.
c. *Ibid.*, 44–48, 192–93, 240–41.
d. *Ibid.*, 18–19; reappointed at Annapolis, *ibid.*, 245.

e. *Ibid.*, 13–14.
f. *Ibid.*, 13.
g. *Ibid.*, 17.
h. *Ibid.*, 15–16 (April 22, 1775); the New York Assembly in February 1775 refused to appoint delegates to the Second Congress and adjourned April 2, 1775. *Ibid.*, I, 16, n. 1.
i. *JCC*, II, 19–20; the Convention's choice was ratified by the assembly, whose membership was virtually identical.
j. *JCC*, II, 17–18.
k. *Ibid.*, 50–51.
l. *Ibid.*, 20–21; *FAA*, I, 1116.
m. *JCC*, II, 19, 101–02.

Column 3

a. Charter not supplanted until 1818. F. N. Thorpe, ed., *Federal and State Constitutions, Charters, and Other Organic Laws, 1847–1851* (7 vols., Washington, D.C., 1909), I, 536.
b. *Ibid.*, 562.
c. *Ibid.*, II, 777.
d. *Ibid.*, III, 1686.
e. *Ibid.*, 1888, 1922 n.
f. *Ibid.*, IV, 2451.
g. *Ibid.*, V, 2594.
h. *Ibid.*, 2623.

i. *Ibid.*, 2787.
j. *Ibid.*, 3081.
k. *Ibid.*, VI, 3222.
l. *Ibid.*, 3241, 3248.
m. *Ibid.*, VII, 3812.

Column 4

a. *JCC*, VII, 11.
b. *Ibid.*, VI, 1000.
c. *Ibid.*, IX, 931.
d. *Ibid.*, VII, 131.
e. *Ibid.*, 25–26. On May 1, 1776, however, all commissions then current were terminated, the regnal phraseology dropped, and the "Government and People of the Massachusetts Bay in New England" were fixed as the source of authority for all writs and commissions thereafter issued. A. C. Goodell, et al., eds., *The Acts and Resolves, Public and Private, of the Province of Massachusetts Bay* (Boston, 1869–1922), VI, vi–xi.
f. *JCC*, IV, 177–78; VI, 920.
g. *Ibid.*, 1002.
h. *Ibid.*, IX, 906.
i. *Ibid.*, VIII, 411.
j. *Ibid.*, VII, 169.
k. *Ibid.*, VIII, 408.
l. *Ibid.*, VII, 129.
m. *Ibid.*, VI, 822–23.

CHAPTER 4

Congress and the States: Operating Under the Articles of Confederation

Framing the Articles of Confederation

A LTHOUGH Congress had called upon the states to set up their own governments and write their own constitutions, it operated without a formal written charter of its own for some seven years. When that charter, the Articles of Confederation, finally was ratified, Congress suffered a serious diminution of its authority and effectiveness as well as of its prestige both at home and abroad.

The start of a shooting war had called for centralized military and diplomatic operations, the latter to win friends abroad and secure foreign funds and arms. Even before Congress adopted the Declaration of Independence thoughtful men pondered the question of what sort of a union the people wanted, whether one created to meet the exigencies of the war situation and then disband, or a longer-range or even perpetual union; whether to choose one which would exploit the war effort to bring about national consolidation or one which would revise, or, if one prefers, preserve the powers traditionally exercised by the states when colonies.

Significantly, the early drafts were nationalistic in tone and would have conferred upon Congress crucial powers, some of which it would never in fact possess. Of the *six* drafts of a confederation now known to have been prepared in 1775 and 1776, Benjamin Franklin's seems to have been the first to have been submitted to Congress, and that was as early as July 21, 1775, when he appears to have done so on his own motion. A committed nationalist as well as a democrat, Franklin offered his plan as a tentative proposal or a "sketch" to serve as a basis for a more effective instrument. Timid delegates, fearful that the plan would foreclose reconciliation with England, made certain that no entry of the plan was included in the journals of Congress, but fortunately it was preserved in the archives by Congress's perpetual secretary, Charles Thomson.[1]

Entitled "Articles of Confederation and Perpetual Union," the Franklin proposal was revised by its author in January 1776. Vestiges of the plan managed to survive in the final Articles, but the meat of it died quickly. Franklin proposed a common treasury supplied by the colonies to defray the general expense of the Confederation, the taxes therefor to be laid in each colony by its own legislature. He suggested apportioning expenses according to the number of males between sixteen and sixty years of age. He would have had the delegates chosen annually, the respective numbers to be determined by the same number of male polls he used for determining allocation of expenses—one delegate for every five thousand polls. Pursuing this democratic notion of proportional representation, Franklin allotted to each delegate only one vote, a departure from the equal voting by states originally adopted by the First Congress and continued by the Second. Franklin was far-sighted enough not to limit the term of service of delegates.

Franklin's plan—proposed for a temporary union until reconciliation with Great Britain—would have conferred broad powers upon Congress: the determination of war and peace, the settling of disputes among the colonies "about Limits or any other cause if such should arise; and the Planting of new Colonies when proper." The latter idea Franklin borrowed from his own Albany Plan of 1754.[2] In addition, he would have conferred upon Congress jurisdiction over commerce, the currency, and the regulation of the armed forces, as well as the appointment of "all General Offices, both civil and military pertaining to the Confederacy." He would have empowered Congress to pass regulations relating to the "General Welfare." Franklin would have forbidden any colony from engaging in an offensive war with the Indians without the consent of Congress (Article X), while granting Congress the right to make alliances with the Six Nations and to ascertain the bounds of Indian lands for their protection against injustice and to provide relief at public expense for their wants (Article XI).

Franklin had other advanced ideas. He favored setting up an

Executive Council of twelve persons to be appointed by Congress to manage general Continental business during a recess of Congress, a mechanism to be incorporated in the Articles but exercised on only one occasion. He would have had amendments proposed by Congress adopted by a simple majority of the colonial assemblies (Article XII). While leaving the door ajar to reconciliation with England, Franklin insisted that, were such efforts to fail, "The Confederation is to be perpetual."[3]

Franklin had given some thought to the reserved powers of the states, but he spelled them out vaguely, proposing that "Each colony shall enjoy and retain as much as it may think fit of its own present Laws, Customs, Rights, Privileges, and peculiar Jurisdiction within its own Limits," including a right to amend its own constitution by assembly or convention (Article III). The wide powers granted Congress and the vagueness of the powers reserved to the states proved unpalatable to some delegates from colonies boasting sea-to-sea charters as well as to the particularists and states' righters who were not prepared to surrender as much of their authority as Franklin demanded.

Still, one recognizes the seeds that Franklin planted. They sprouted in Jefferson's territorial plan, in the Northwest Ordinance, as well as in the commerce clause of the federal Constitution. But they made no headway with the delegates in Congress when they were proposed. In many respects they provided for a centralized government far closer in powers and structure to the federal Constitution than any subsequent plan considered by Congress. The farsighted plan of Franklin found the delegates ill-prepared to abandon so many powers they assumed their respective colonies still possessed.

So far as we can determine, Silas Deane, a delegate from Connecticut fated to play a highly disputed role in the conduct of American affairs abroad, drafted a set of proposals for a confederation some months before Franklin.[4] This seemed to have served as a working paper for another draft prepared by the Connecticut delegates, possibly with Roger Sherman as its penman. Both drafts were terse and obviously tentative. The Deane proposals sought a compromise over the one-vote-one-state issue and strict reapportionment. He would have allowed colonies one delegate for every 25,000 "Souls" for the purpose of determining "Supplies of Men or Money," and for lesser measures as well. A simple majority would decide. However, on war and peace and broad general policy, a concurrence would be needed of both a majority of the colonies and a majority of the delegates. One might see here, if one is so inclined, the genesis of the Great Compromise of 1787, for which so much credit has traditionally been awarded to the delegates from Connecticut. The powers of Congress were broadly, even vaguely sketched, whereas to the states were reserved matters of internal police and legislation. In fact, the states were forbidden to levy duties without permission of Congress, the proceeds of such duties to go to the common treasury.

In one respect Deane moved even farther than Franklin in the direction of centralization. He would have had Congress appoint the governors and lieutenant-governors of the royal, but not the proprietary, governments, with lesser officers to be elected by the lower house of assembly to serve for good behavior, and with the right of appeal to Congress if they were "displaced and felt themselves injured." Thus neither the Deane nor the Franklin plans directed themselves to affirming Congress's authority during this transitional period before a formal constitution went into effect.[5]

Deane's plan suffered radical changes when the Connecticut Plan was published in early March of 1776. Therein Congress's powers were curtailed. It was not empowered to create more colonies or to act for the general welfare. The Connecticut Plan explicitly reserved to each colony "the sole government and direction of its internal police" and forbade Congress from imposing or levying taxes. Still, despite these reservations in favor of states' rights, the Connecticut Plan gave Congress exclusive power over foreign affairs, war and peace, and the regulation of the army. On all issues it required a majority of the colonies represented as well as a majority of the delegates present. Certainly on such vital issues as commerce and the settlement of Western Lands the Connecticut Plan marked a major retreat from Franklin's notions.

If the Connecticut Plan bore similarities to the Dickinson Plan as finally amended and seemed aimed at conciliating divergent state interests, it by no means spoke with the unanimous voice of Revolutionary leaders, of men like Joseph Hawley who as early as December 1775 had advocated "An American Parliament with legislative authority over all the colonies," or of still others who suggested that

Congress should play a large role in the reconstruction of provincial governments.[6]

It was only some days after June 7, 1776, when Richard Henry Lee proposed his resolution for independence, that Congress appointed a committee of thirteen to draft the Articles of Confederation. The bulk of the members were moderate to conservative delegates, who still left the door open to reconciliation with Great Britain. Only two delegates, the aged Stephen Hopkins and the activist Samuel Adams, could be labeled unreconstructed extremists.[7] A committee so composed quite logically turned to John Dickinson to draft the Articles. A man of learning and a gifted penman, Dickinson, ever the moderate, had difficulty in reconciling the conflicting viewpoints of his fellow committeemen. Edward Rutledge accused him of "the Vice of Refining too much" and feared that the resultant Confederation would be dominated by New England.[8] Dickinson took his criticisms seriously and recorded the disputes over every single article he proposed, incorporating reservations and changes suggested by his committee.[9]

In the draft Dickinson submitted to Congress, the "Confederacy," as he called it, was denominated "the United States of America." Therein the union between the states was to be "perpetual," a term also introduced in the Northwest Ordinance, which was to be described as a "perpetual compact," but the adjective was somehow overlooked in the federal Constitution. In distributing power between the central government and the states, Congress in effect was given the supreme authority. The significant Article III of the Dickinson proposal reads:

> Each colony shall retain and enjoy as much of its present Laws, Rights and Customs as it may think fit, and reserve to itself the sole and exclusive regulation and Government of its internal Police, in all Matters that shall not interfere with the Articles *(agreed upon by)* at this Confederation.

Dickinson would have limited state action even further by providing for religious toleration and prohibiting "any Law or Ordinance thereafter to be made in the Colony different from the usual Laws and Customs subsisting at the Commencement of this War" requiring dissenters to support established churches, nor would persons be disqualified by future laws from holding any office civil or military, nor should any further tests concerning religion be adopted, such liberties to be extended to the Confederation generally.[10] It was indubitably a profound disappointment to Dickinson, committed as he was to religious toleration and opposed to church establishment, to have to insert in the margin: "All this Article rejected." At this time it is evident that Congress shared the views of John Adams instead of Dickinson's. The Massachusetts Patriot favored religious toleration but believed that Congress should "never meddle with religion further than to say their own prayers, and to fast and give thanks once a year. Let every colony have its own religion without molestation."[11]

Dickinson's plan forbade the states to conduct foreign affairs or to enter into alliances "with each other" without the consent of the Union. It prohibited the states from discriminating against inhabitants of other colonies, especially in trade, where the inhabitants of each state were to enjoy the rights and privileges and immunities possessed by those of other states.

To make war or enter into treaties, Congress needed the votes of nine states. In fact, only one important restriction was imposed upon Congress. It could not levy taxes or duties except in managing the Post Office. Like the Franklin draft, the Dickinson version gave Congress the control of Indian affairs and of the settlement of "the boundaries of the states with charter claims to the South Seas." To these two provisions Dickinson appended a note and signed with his initials: "These claims to be submitted to Congress."

On the sticky question of representation, Dickinson cautiously observed the current practice by giving each state an equal vote in Congress, and on the equally sticky issues of taxation, he proposed that all charges of war and others incurred for "the general welfare" be defrayed out of a "Common Treasury," to be funded by taxes laid and levied by the respective state legislatures.

The draft seems to have been completed by July 4 because Dickinson did not attend Congress after that date. Thus, if he was willing to vote for independence, he demonstrated both irresolution and irresponsibility by not staying to explain and defend his draft Articles to Congress, which might have been readier to adopt them at a moment of high patriotism and sense of union than at a later time. Indubitably, some blame attaches to Dickinson for what happened when he left. Congress virtually stood the Dickinson draft on its head, suffering thereby both in power and prestige.

In Dickinson's absence his committee reported his draft, but with its own reasons, to Congress on July 12.[12] Thereafter it was intermittently debated for a whole year—not until October–November of 1777 did Congress agree upon a final version. And that is a story by itself.

The first target of attack on the Dickinson plan was the provision for *equal representation.* The opposition was led by the Pennsylvania delegation, with Franklin placing his magisterial authority behind the idea of proportionality, and John Adams and Benjamin Rush lending support. But the small states had their backs up, and made sure that the printed draft of August 20, 1776, included the *equal* voting provision of the Dickinson draft. The issue was to be raised from time to time. It was proposed, for example, that very small states receive one vote each and the other states one vote for each 50,000 inhabitants. This proposition failed, as did another to give each state one delegate for each 30,000 inhabitants. Once more the equality provision of the Dickinson draft stood the test of balloting. An unsuccessful attempt was made to specify that the nine states required for the passage of a declaration of war and provisions for the coinage of money and the apportionment of expenses should comprise an actual majority of the people of the United States, except Indians and blacks. Virginia, the largest state, was the sole supporter.

The second great issue arose over the basis of *taxation.* The Dickinson draft provided that the states were to supply funds in proportion to their total number of inhabitants of every age, sex, and "quality" except Indians not paying taxes. The states with large black populations were adamantly opposed, and Samuel Chase moved that each state's quota of taxes be in proportion to the number of white inhabitants only. Slaves were property, argued Chase. If Southern property were to be taxed, why not New England's mercantile property? After a sharp debate over the slavery issue, Chase's amendment was defeated along sectional lines, with the Northern states against it and the South (Georgia divided) for it.

Finally, as debate was resumed in October 1776, it was moved that taxes be based on the value of all property except household goods and wearing apparel. When that failed, it was moved that public expenses be apportioned according to the estimated value of all lands granted to or surveyed for individuals, including the improvements thereon. The amendment carried by five votes to four, with New Englanders resentful that they would be forced to pay an unjust share of the costs since they had a greater amount of settled land, while the South was managing to evade taxes on a third of their wealth—their slaves.

A third ingredient which some states swallowed very hard was the provision in the original Dickinson draft giving Congress control over the Western lands. The "landed" states managed to have this clause deleted from the final draft. As a result, the so-called landless states, led by Maryland, refused to ratify the Articles until control over the Western lands was restored to Congress.

This issue could hardly be settled on a disinterested basis. Many delegates from the landless states were land speculators, including Benjamin Franklin, James Wilson, Samuel Chase, Robert Morris, Samuel Wharton, and Charles Carroll of Carrollton. Similarly, speculation preoccupied delegates from Southern states boasting "sea-to-sea" charters, delegates whose concerns would later emerge during the debates over the Mississippi question. In the end, the West would prove the most divisive issue delaying the adoption of the Articles of Confederation.[13]

Fundamental to the final acceptance of the Articles of Confederation was the issue of *sovereignty*. When the draft Articles were first presented to Congress, none of the states'-rights particularists recognized the danger to state power inherent in the third article as it was then numbered, in which the reserved powers of the states were so vaguely defined. It was left for a maverick Irishman named Thomas Burke, a delegate from North Carolina, who arrived in Philadelphia early in 1777, to raise the issue. What precipitated the fight was the holding of a convention of New England states early in December to consider the progress of the war and to propose measures against inflation. Such a meeting in the view of James Wilson required the approval of Congress. Indeed, the Convention had sent their report to Congress with this end in mind. That was the way John Adams saw it, while Benjamin Rush denounced the meeting as usurping the powers of Congress.[14]

Burke had been gradually shaping his ideas of state versus federal sovereignty.[15] In a letter to Governor Richard Caswell of North Carolina, April 29, 1777, he indicated that two days of the week were devoted to discussing the Confederation and that a major innovation had been a new "declaration of the Sovereignty of the States, and an express provision that they be considered as retaining every power not expressly delegated." Then, Burke added, this provision occasioned a two-day debate in which he had argued that, unless the original Article III was changed, Congress "could explain away every right belonging to the States, and to make their own power as unlimited as they please." The profound significance of Burke's amendment seemed to catch everyone unawares, and, as the mover reported, "it was some time before it was seconded, and South Carolina first took it up."[16]

The opposition to Burke's amendment was led by James Wilson and Richard Henry Lee—clearly indicating that this was no conservative-radical confrontation. Yet when the question was put, eleven states voted yes, Virginia, no, and New Hampshire was divided.[17]

Burke's amendment significantly altered the locus of sovereignty in the Confederation. In its final form, it read (as Article II): "Each State retains its sovereignty, freedom and independence, and every power, jurisdiction, and right, which is not by this confederation expressly delegated to the United States, in Congress assembled."[18]

The nationalists would not soon forget the sweeping language of Article II. Madison's phrasing of what became Article X of the Bill of Rights in the federal Constitution reads: "The powers not delegated to the United States by the Constitution, nor prohibited by it to the States, are reserved to the States respectively, or to the people." The significant omission of "expressly" before "delegated" opened the gates to a broad avenue of implied powers for the federal government. In a notable decision John Marshall pointed out that the Tenth Amendment "omits the word 'expressly,'" an omission which he attributed to the desire "to avoid more embarrassments" caused by its inclusion in the Articles of Confederation.[19]

Burke, who had been pondering the draft Articles throughout the fall of '77, found fault with other sections of Dickinson's handiwork as well. He disliked the privileges and immunities clause, which in his mind would result in the absurdities of residents in other states having "the right of voting for Members of our Legislature," and suggested that the section be amended by adding the words "Not inconsistent with their respective Constitutions." He opposed having the state legislatures elect the delegates, which was contrary to the practice in North Carolina, where the delegates were annually chosen by ballot. He opposed prohibiting the states from entering into commercial treaties with foreign powers, as well as objecting to the prohibition of compacts between two or more states. He favored encouraging the states to build up their navies. As regards the ninth article, he would have left the United States sovereign in foreign affairs and war, but felt that "in all commercial or other peaceful Intercourse" the states ought to be "as separate Sovereigns." He disapproved of having "the United States" act as "the last resort on appeal in all disputes between the States." This would impose a judicial authority upon Congress which he felt could be better served by using Congress as an arbiter. He opposed allowing Congress to regulate the alloy of coin struck by authority of any of the states. "The power to increase the alloy," he argued, "is a power to pay off any Debt with less than the sum contracted for, and involves an extensive power over property," hardly the language of a radical. The power to borrow money and emit bills ought never to be in Congress, he argued, "but when given by the States upon special occasions." The state legislatures disagreed and further enlarged Congress's power over money. Congress voted down his proposal of a two-house legislature and rejected his idea of having delegates elected by popular ballot instead of by their respective legislatures. In fact, except for the crucial reservation of state sovereignty, Burke, who entered Congress long after the initial debates, found that his views were not shared by his fellow delegates. He was outvoted on the retention of the privileges and immunities clause of Article IV, on prohibiting states from entering into foreign relations without the consent of Congress or making interstate treaties without such consent, both of which provisions he had opposed. He even opposed continuing Congress after the conclusion of the war. Notwithstanding, the Articles as finally adopted still speak of "confederation and perpetual union" (Article I).[20] Before the debate on the final article had ended, Burke had succeeded in making himself a general nuisance. Delegates criticized his "obstinate Vanity," his "impudence," and one delegate even lamented his reappearance in Congress in March of '78 "to the universal sorrow etc. of every member."[21]

In fact, Burke was hardly a model of consistency even in his radicalism. He was the first to enunciate the principle that state laws conflicting with the resolves of Congress were null and void, and he did so more than three years before the Articles went into effect.[22] In the case of Gideon Olmstead, resuscitated in the federal courts a quarter century later, his arguments served as the basis for Chief Justice Marshall's determination that the colonies were confederated from the beginning and that federal power, within its assigned sphere, was supreme from the start of the Second Congress in 1775.[23]

Before its final adoption on November 15, 1777, the Articles as first proposed had been watered down by emendations, amendments, and changes in phraseology. First of all and much earlier, Dickinson's proposal for religious toleration and church disestablishment within the states was, as we have seen, rejected out of hand over the mover's own protest.[24] Then, in addition to adopting Burke's formula enlarging the sovereignty of the states at the expense of Congress, certain enumerated powers of Congress over commerce and the settlement of disputes between the states were eliminated or modified. The Dickinson draft had prohibited states from levying duties which conflicted with treaties entered into by Congress. Instead, as amended, a state was permitted to levy on foreign goods the same duties its own citizens were required to pay on imports, and each state was allowed to prohibit exportation and importation altogether, even to deny privileges in its ports to citizens of any foreign country which denied the same privileges to the citizens of that state as they permitted their own people or vessels.[25] The power of making treaties of commerce on the part of Congress was now confined to cases where such treaties would not restrain a state from levying such imposts and duties on foreigners as its own people were subject to, or from prohibiting the states from exporting or importing any "goods or commodities whatsoever" (Article IX). With the result that, under the Articles, Congress could regulate trade by treaty, but could provide no effective check upon conflicting state regulations—a deficiency which would cause Congress, its committees, and later secretaries of foreign affairs considerable embarrassment in the Confederation years ahead.

Under the final Articles major actions by Congress required the approval of nine states; amendments to that instrument, confirmation by every state legislature. Instead of placing disputes between the states in the hands of Congress, the final Articles made Congress the last resort on appeal—a move seemingly calculated to delay congressional intervention, with the result that Congress's role in dispute resolution between the states was invoked on only one occasion.

In short, a Congress lacking the power to levy taxes and to regulate commerce, and limited to powers directly conferred upon it (except where such powers were deemed inherent) proved a frail instrument of governance, a pale shadow of Franklin's bolder plan, and a sadly weakened version of Dickinson's scheme.

The Functioning of Congress as a Legislature and Administrative Body

The functioning of Congress both before and during the years of the Confederation was adversely affected by forced flights from Philadelphia under military necessity, by bad weather and wretched transportation which delayed delegates traveling to and from the sessions, and by the indifference and irresponsibility of the delegates themselves. The quality of its membership was shaped by delegate defections, which the principle of rotation introduced by the Articles served to encourage,[26] and by the rival attractions of more glamorous posts. In midwinter of 1776–77, when Congress was impelled to flee Philadelphia and take refuge in Baltimore to escape capture by the British forces, John Adams, who arrived on the scene quite late, made what was to prove a prophetic comment:

I have the melancholly Prospect before me of a Congress continually changing, until very few faces remain that I saw in the first Congress . . . Mr. S. Adams, Mr. Sherman, Coll. Richard Henry Lee, Mr. Chase and Mr Paca are all that remain. The rest are dead, resigned, deserted or cutt up into Governors, etc. at home.[27]

Adams himself would soon leave on a mission as peace commissioner. Diplomacy also claimed the services of Silas Deane, Arthur Lee, Benjamin Franklin, John Jay, and Henry Laurens. Other ex-delegates chose military careers, and still a third group found state posts more alluring.

Down to the last days of Congress, getting a quorum often proved extremely difficult, no matter how serious the issues remained to be debated or the treaty to be ratified. During vital debates over hand-ing the West over to Congress, some took flight. "Our House," wrote Laurens on October 16, 1778, "will be reduced in a few days to barely twenty or twenty-one Members." One might have thought that Samuel Chase and Charles Carroll of Carrollton would have remained to press the claims of their own land-bound state against those with spacious charters to the "South Seas." But they could not get away fast enough.[28] As late as January 1779, Laurens complained that there were "barely nine States on the floor representing about as many persons."[29]

Attendance did not improve once the Articles took effect. Quite the contrary. When Congress was forced to beat a hasty retreat to Princeton from Philadelphia because of the mutinous behavior of the Philadelphia militia, it took months to get a quorum together, and most of the time not more than six states were represented. Perhaps the most signal failure was the difficulty of getting a representation of nine states necessary to ratify the Definitive Treaty of 1783. At that time Congress was sitting in Annapolis, with President Mifflin impatiently awaiting a quorum on November 22, 1783. As late as December 16 Thomas Jefferson, then a delegate, wrote Edmund Randolph: "We have no certain prospect of nine states in Congress and cannot ratify the treaty with fewer. Yet the ratifications are to be exchanged by the 3d of March."[30]

As has been previously noted, the task of getting delegates from nine states to attend even this epochal event was an enormous chore. New Hampshire had one delegate in attendance; and it would require six weeks to bring another. South Carolina had only one in attendance, although another, Richard Beresford, lay sick in Philadelphia; no delegates had been elected yet from New York, and one of the Delaware delegates abruptly quit Congress to attend his "private affairs" at home. Finally, on January 13, 1784, two delegates from Connecticut appeared, and a solitary one from New Jersey. Then Beresford rose from his sickbed, providing the nine states necessary for ratification, which was accomplished the following day.[31]

To Thomas Jefferson's consternation, attendance began to fall away immediately after the ratification of the treaty, although matters of urgency were before the Congress for decision,[32] and it was increasingly difficult to maintain a quorum. Between the adjournment from Princeton and March 1, a period of four months, on only sixteen days were there as many as seven or eight states in attendance; at times, the attendance dropped to three.[33] Fast losing patience, Jefferson wrote Madison: "We cannot make up a Congress at all. We have not sat above 3 days I believe in as many weeks. Admonition after admonition has been sent to the states, to no effect. We have sent one to-day. If it fails, it seems as well we should all retire."[34]

It was not only the nonattendance of delegates but the poor quality of those who did make an appearance that especially concerned Secretary Thomson. Writing Jefferson in the spring of 1784, he observed: "I wish the states would send forward men of enlarged minds and conciliating tempers, that matters might not be precipitated and that time might be given for consolidating and strengthening the Confederacy," and ended with the ardent wish that it might be "lasting."[35]

Indeed, the difficulties of persuading delegates to attend seemed to increase as 1784 advanced. Some deeply concerned delegates like President Richard Henry Lee wrote Madison on November 26 that it might be a "necessary step" to call upon the states "to form a Convention for the sole purpose of revising the Confederation so far as to enable Congress to execute with more energy, effect, and vigor the power assigned to it, than it appears by experience that they can do under the present state of things."[36] As of that date Madison had not made up his mind, while four years later Lee would adopt a very different stance when he was confronted with the design for a more effective government crafted in Philadelphia.

The year 1786 proved no exception. Delegates in attendance requested David Ramsay of South Carolina, who was chosen to serve as chairman until President John Hancock should arrive—an event that never took place—to remind the state executives of their serious delinquency in the matter of representation in Congress. "The remissness of the States in keeping up a representation in Congress naturally tends to annihilate our Confederation. That once dissolved, our State establishments would be of short duration. Anarchy, or internecine wars would follow till some future Caesar seized our Liberties, or we would be the sport of European policies, and perhaps parcelled out as appendages to their several Governments."[37] The inattention of the states prompted the chairman to write privately to Dr. Benjamin Rush. "There is a languor in the States," he complained, "that forebodes ruin. The present Congress for want of more States has not the power to coin a copper. In 1775 there was more patriotism in a village than there is now in the 13 states."[38]

Issues were coming to a head. Vetoes by individual states had still blocked the impost. By this time New York was the only noncomplying state, and in what one delegate called "a moody fit," the lower house of the New Jersey legislature, in retaliation against New York's own thriving impost business, passed a resolution against granting the impost. This surprise move, although lacking legality, prompted Congress to dispatch a delegation to the New Jersey legislature to persuade its members to rescind their action. Charles Pinckney of South Carolina, one of the members of the congressional delegation, warned them of the consequences if the present Confederation were dissolved, "and an assembly of the states convened for the purpose of adopting a system calculated to render the general government firm and energetic." Would it not be reasonable, he asked, for the large states to insist upon a greater influence than they at present possess? His concluding council: New Jersey should instruct its delegates in Congress "to urge the calling of a general convention of the states, for the purpose of revising and amending the federal system." A fellow commissioner, William Grayson of Virginia, warned the Jerseyites that "in a new confederation you will be put in your proper place." The effect was dramatic. The New Jersey Assembly repealed its resolution, while, alas, New York refused to comply.[39]

If Congress had trouble with securing quorums during its years of power and authority, one can imagine what transpired once the Constitution was transmitted to the states for their action. By November 5, 1787, only five members answered the roll call; either because some states felt that the new Constitution would supersede the old Congress or because they were "indifferent about a larger Confederation upon any plan," they neglected to dispatch their delegates. If they prefer the Confederation upon the old plan, "they certainly ought to keep up their representation," Samuel Alleyne Otis argued. "And if they are zealous for the *new plan,* they ought to send delegates to prepare the way." He himself had no expectation "of a speedy adoption of the *New System.*"[40] All efforts to keep the old Congress alive were now unavailing, even though issues posed by the Western territory created by the Northwest Ordinance, Congress's supreme achievement, were pressing. And the battles against the *"New System"* were to be waged in the state ratifying conventions, not in the old and dying Congress.

The Executive and Administrative
Functions of Congress

Jealous as it was of centering executive and administrative power in a single person, actions that would set off antimonarchical alarm bells, Congress from the start delegated special functions to committees that exercised authority within guidelines set by Congress, to which body they were expected to report. During the first few months of its existence the Second Congress managed its business either through the whole body or through special committees. Due to the persistence and increasing complexity of administrative problems, a Standing Committee system was set up by Congress, among them the Secret Committee, the Committee of Secret Correspondence, the Naval Committee, and others. Delegates often served on multiple committees and were excessively overworked. For example, William Livingston served on eleven committees in one year; Thomas McKean served on no less than thirty-three committees and was chairman of five during one period in Congress; and during another, he was a member of nineteen committees and chairman of six.[41] To operate efficiently a compromise plan was worked out, a mixture of boards, some of whose members were delegates and some came from the outside.

Since this hybrid system proved an equally clumsy way of administering great affairs of state, a movement gathered headway for establishing departments under single heads who were not members of Congress. This was done in 1781, when Robert Morris of Pennsylvania was named Superintendent of Finance and Agent of Marine; Benjamin Lincoln, Secretary at War (in turn, succeeded by Henry Knox, also from Massachusetts); and Robert R. Livingston, Secretary for Foreign Affairs, and his postwar successor after an interim, John Jay, both of New York. With the end of the war the only single-headed departments that survived were those of War and Foreign Affairs, along with the Post Office. When on November

1, 1784, Robert Morris finally resigned, after a stormy period in the administration of the Treasury, the affairs of that department were, after an interval of a half a year, placed in the hands of a Board of Treasury. All three commissioners whom Congress elected resigned on one pretext or another, and finally on January 25, 1785, Congress chose John Lewis Gervais of South Carolina, Samuel Osgood of Massachusetts, and Walter Livingston of New Jersey to comprise the three-man board. In place of Gervais, who declined the honor, Congress settled on Arthur Lee, much to Thomas Jefferson's displeasure.[42] These commissioners gradually absorbed the various duties of boards and commissioners then operative to settle a variety of accounts stemming from war expenditures, including the Loan Officers, while the offices of comptroller and auditor were ultimately merged with the activities of the Board of Treasury.

The claims confronting the board were conflicting, perplexing, and almost impossible to systematize, and, although the terms of office of the three-man board were continued until March 10, 1789, the board was constantly harassed by investigating bodies and allowed little freedom of action. By the time the board's term came to a close, the finances of the Confederation were in a rocky state. It was a mystery to one observer how the Board of Treasury had managed to maintain the civil list, pay interest on the Dutch loan, and support the handful of troops in the Continental Army. Nathan Dane credited these achievements to the payments received from New York on requisitions, "the gleanings of new Emission money and a little tobacco from North Carolina," while another Treasury-watcher was convinced that "we must be in a very paralytic state at present."[43] This variety of experiences with committees, boards, and the single-headed executive of the Robert Morris era convinced the first Congress under the Constitution, after some debate, that a one-man head of the Treasury was the best alternative.[44]

The two single-headed departments of Foreign Affairs and War served as prototypes for operations in the same area under the federal government, functioning for a time under the same individuals, with Knox heading President Washington's war office and Jay, acting as Secretary of State ad interim until Jefferson took up his post, Jay's simultaneous service as Chief Justice notwithstanding, Jay's dual role was briefly duplicated by John Marshall at the onset of his Chief Justiceship. The Post Office department, established by Congress in 1775 with Benjamin Franklin as postmaster general, also continued as a single-headed operation under the federal government. Benjamin Hazard had managed to run the postal system on a paying basis between 1782 and 1789, by which date the country had seventy-five post offices and 2,400 miles of post roads. The Antifederalist Samuel Osgood of Massachusetts succeeded as postmaster general under President Washington, a position then not considered of Cabinet rank.[45]

The Committee of the States

It was obvious to all, even from the start, that the conduct of the war required a commitment to constant administrative oversight. Yet Congress was reluctant to allocate such authority to any one person. Franklin had proposed an "Executive Council" of twelve persons, with rotating terms which should have power to act "in the Recess of Congress to execute what shall have been enjoined thereby; to manage the general continental Business," to prepare an agenda for Congress, and to draw upon the general treasurer for monies necessary and appropriated by Congress, among its other duties.[46]

The Dickinson draft had provided for a Council of State (originally Dickinson wrote "Council of Safety") to operate during a recess of Congress. In its final form it was called "The Committee of the States," authorized to perform whatever functions would be deemed expedient by nine states.[47] It was not designed as an administrative body, nor, as one historian describes it, "a permanent bureaucratic staff of the central government." As Dickinson conceived it, the Council was to meet only during a recess of Congress.[48] Since Congress—and the point has been pressed before—so often failed to meet or lacked a quorum, one would have thought that essential administrative duties might have been performed by this body. In point of fact the Committee of the States was never called into being until the summer of 1784. Its ineffective efforts constitute one of the most dismal chapters in the history of the Congress.

What precipitated the incident was the question of whether Congress would continue in being after the consummation of peace. One might have thought that a "perpetual union" such as had been created by the Articles would have rendered such an issue superfluous, but the fact is that some states and some delegates now felt that Congress was irrelevant. Thomas Jefferson was not among them. His comprehensive mind grasped the many unsettled issues created by the peace and the need for dealing with the many new problems of nationhood. Before departing for Europe he was preparing reports on the Land Office, the coinage, and the Western Lands.[49] As a result of some sense of reality, Congress ordered a Committee of the States to hold an interim session and defined the committee's powers.[50] After the briefest of sessions the committee was forced to halt its proceedings, as its various members, starting with the New Englanders, mounted their horses and headed for home. In effect, the Committee of the States was dissolved, but six remaining members stayed on for another ten days before the committee was suspended. When the committee sought to reassemble, no one knew precisely where it would sit. John Francis Mercer, whose ambitions to become foreign secretary perturbed Jefferson,[51] traveled from Annapolis to Philadelphia in search of a nonexistent body, expressing his frustration in a letter to the irascible Jacob Read, then the South Carolina member of the Committee. "A desire that the State of Virginia might show her respect for the Confoederal Government (if it is not a prostitution of the name of Government to apply it to such a vagabond, strolling, contemptible Crew as Congress) will induce me to sit out a Couple of weeks here."[52]

The Committee of the States finally met and organized on June 4, choosing Samuel Hardy of Virginia as chairman. Then, after adjournment, it found that it could not reassemble a quorum until July 8. All that was accomplished was routine business, and in effect the New England members put finis to the meetings by departing, leaving the remainder without a quorum. To chairman Hardy the irresponsible indignity to which the deserting members had exposed the Committee of the States was unbearable and would "lessen the dignity of the foederal Government in the Eyes of our own Citizens as well as those of foreigners,"[53] and Secretary Thomson remarked pithily: "A government without a visible head must appear a strange phenomenon to European politicians and will I fear lead them to form no very favourable opinion of our stability, wisdom or Union."[54]

At long last Congress managed the incredible feat of assembling a quorum of delegates at Trenton on November 29, 1784, and quickly forgot the one occasion when the Committee of the States failed to serve the very function for which it was created. After adjourning on Christmas Eve, Congress removed to New York, which would be its permanent home for the remainder of its life.

The Presidents of Congress

The United States, known until 1781 as "The Congress," under the Articles of Confederation officially called "The United States in Congress Assembled," and under the federal Constitution, "The United States of America," has always had a "president." That functionary possessed, of course, far less authority and prestige before 1789 than he did subsequently, but he was a prestigious figure nonetheless. In all, from the First Continental Congress, which convened in 1774, to the last session of the Second Congress in 1789, fourteen different presidents were elected from nine of the thirteen states,[55] serving an average of a year apiece. One of the fourteen, John Hancock, held two widely spaced terms but never appeared in Congress on the later occasion.

Since these presidents exercised the first glimmerings of executive power under the central government, and since six presidents preceded the actual formation of executive departments, their role foreshadowed, however dimly, the presidency as we now know it under a federal Constitution which assumes a separation of powers unknown to the Congress of the pre-Confederation or Confederation years. Whatever authority the presidents exercised developed out of the necessities of the case and rested on slight legal foundation, but what they did and how they did it depended in no small measure on their personalities, their own conception of their roles in office, and the political situations which confronted the respective incumbents.

From the start, Congress had assumed the executive power. Soon that power was shared with the commander-in-chief, and then portions were parceled out to ad hoc committees. However, without express delegation, but from the necessities of the case, a degree of executive authority had always been exercised by the president of the Congress from that very first session on September 5, 1774, when Peyton Randolph, the Virginia aristocrat, was unanimously elected to the post.

The president was not only a presiding officer. As a delegate, he had the power to vote and to serve on committees like every other delegate. He received and answered letters addressed to the Congress and carried on correspondence with the state governors, the military commanders in the field, and American diplomats abroad. On occasion he was authorized to draft resolutions or addresses on behalf of the Congress, and even when they were drafted by others, they were invariably issued under his signature. He was in effect the administrative head of state, although no executive powers were ever formally conferred upon him either by the Congress or under the Articles of Confederation.

As Congress's social functionary, the president was its undisputed first member. Protocol demanded that the dais on which he was seated be elevated above that of all other government officers. It was the president who was expected to receive official guests, such as foreign notables, and extend hospitality. Their frequent dinners, levees, and balls established the congressional president as the ceremonial head of state,[56] and, indeed, foreshadowed the high tone set by President Washington under the federal Constitution.

Buried in Article IX of the Articles of Confederation is an authorization to Congress "to appoint one of their number to preside," with the provision that "no person be allowed to serve in the office of president more than one year in any term of three years," a restriction designed to limit the perpetuation of any power or influence the president might be able to wield by virtue of his tenure. However, even before the Articles of Confederation went into effect, the average length of presidential tenure was under a year, with Henry Middleton serving in that office for a mere five days, and John Hancock, the most durable incumbent, presiding for two years and five months. One advantage of rapid rotation in office was that it made it possible to have the majority of the states in turn represented in the presidency. In fact, nine of the thirteen states had delegates who were elected to and served in the presidency. Only New Hampshire, Rhode Island, North Carolina, and Georgia failed to fill that office with one of their own delegates.

Lacking specific authorization or clear guidelines, the presidents of Congress could with some discretion influence events, formulate the agenda of Congress, and prod Congress to move in directions they considered proper. Much depended on the incumbents themselves and their readiness to exploit the peculiar opportunities their office provided. All of them were sturdy individualists, with strikingly diverse traits, and some of them held strong convictions about the need to enhance executive power. Despite differences, however, they do lend themselves to a composite portrait. Except for the Scotsman Arthur St. Clair, all the presidents were native-born Americans. All were mature, experienced politicians who had, in addition, been actively involved in the creation and functioning of the Revolutionary infrastructure which underpinned the movement of independence and the call for the first Congress.

Hardly youthful revolutionaries, their average age at the time of election to the presidency was forty-seven. The youngest incumbent, John Jay, and also one of the most conservative, entered upon his duties in his thirty-fourth year; the eldest, Henry Middleton, served briefly in his fifty-eighth year. Seven of the fourteen were in their fifties at the time of their respective presidencies.

The majority of the presidents were well educated by the standards of the time. Peyton Randolph, the first president, and Cyrus Griffin, the last, were Middle Templars, whose attendance at the Inns of Court in London had given them their basic legal training. Griffin, in addition, had attended the University of Edinburgh, as had Arthur St. Clair, who also had been exposed to a brief term as an apprentice to a London anatomist. Of the remainder, most had the benefit of private tutors or had studied at the newly emerging academies. Least exposed to any sort of formal education appears to have been Nathaniel Gorham of Massachusetts, who early in life was apprenticed to a merchant. By contrast, there were at least three American college graduates—John Hancock, a Harvard man; John Jay, a graduate of King's College (now Columbia); and Thomas Mifflin, of the College of Philadelphia (later the University of Pennsylvania). Mostly the presidents were men of inherited wealth, which they enhanced by their own industry as planters, merchants, or lawyers. Perhaps the wealthiest among them were Henry Middleton, the great plantation owner of South Carolina, his fellow Carolinian, the merchant-planter Henry Laurens, and Boston's leading merchant shipper, John Hancock. Nearest to being a self-made man was Samuel Huntington of Connecticut, who found the expenses involved in maintaining his social position as president especially burdensome.

Prior to the adoption of the Articles of Confederation, three presidents decisively shaped events either because of the special situations that confronted them or by virtue of their activist personalities. The first was John Hancock; the other two, Henry Laurens and John Jay. Although the initiatives in the moves toward independence were taken by Richard Henry Lee, author of the resolution for independence (and a later president), and the two Adamses, Samuel and John, chief actors behind the arras (but not presidents of Congress), it was John Hancock as the president of the Congress who alone affixed his bold signature to that document upon its adoption on July 4, 1776, to which Charles Thomson, Congress's permanent nondelegate secretary, attested. "There!" Hancock is reported to have commented on his bold signature. "John Bull can read my name without spectacles, and may now double his reward of £500 for my head! *That* is my defiance."[57] Others were either too timid or too involved to sign for another month, and in some cases for a good many months. That document was a renunciation of allegiance to the king of Great Britain, an affirmation of the right of revolution, and a declaration of war. Since it sought to place the stamp of legality upon an act of secession from Empire, it had to carry a signature, and it was Hancock's that provided it with the necessary authentication, thereby singling out the president of Congress for the special animus of King and Parliament.

Although the Declaration of Independence stands out as the climactic achievement of Hancock's term of office (indeed, of his entire career), it must be recognized that under his presidency Congress had, more than a year before, initiated and asserted powers of external sovereignty. It had commissioned General Washington and set up a military establishment. It had emitted bills of credit. It had set up a secret committee to secure aid abroad. It had issued a call for the colonies to organize state governments. Granted that Hancock was not the active instrument in any of these initiatives, and that he would have much preferred the role of commanding general to that of president, yet they were all taken in his name, and his presidency marked perhaps the most creative span of congressional initiatives.

Finally, Hancock was the first American president to issue a farewell address. Although that practice can hardly be said to have been institutionalized that early, the circumstances surrounding it shed light on the incumbent's conception of his term of office. After dwelling in Philadelphia in a state that became his opulence, Hancock, upon the British occupation of the American capital, removed with his lovely young bride, Dorothy Quincy, to a variety of makeshift homes to which Congress was forced by military exigencies to resort—to Baltimore, back to Philadelphia, and thence to Lancaster and York. In taking his leave of Congress on October 27, 1777, Hancock declared that his impaired health mandated a leave of several months, but Congress jumped at the chance to replace him. A vote of thanks for his services in office was grudgingly accorded him.

Three days later Hancock was replaced by Henry Laurens, the affluent merchant-planter from South Carolina. The activist Laurens was also the first of the presidents to form a firm opinion of the need for strengthening executive power in the central government. Vain, combative, and indiscreet (he actually fought a duel with a fellow delegate, John Penn, while in Congress),[58] Laurens presided with little pretense of impartiality. At times his temper outran his prudence, and he almost came to blows with the fiery secretary Charles Thomson, who made no secret of his disapproval of the president's "outrageous language and insolent behavior." Possessed of a poor opinion of his fellow delegates, whom he found ruled by "venality, peculation and fraud," Laurens took little pains to conceal his opinion. Laurens' charges in "the present corrupt times" created something of a sensation when they were published in a Loyalist newspaper as a result of the interception by the British of a letter he wrote to Georgia's governor.[59] He was shocked at the widespread evidence of graft in the administration of the war by congressional committees and bureaus, and was highly critical of the way Robert Morris appeared to juggle tobacco shipments, whether on his own or the public account.[60]

Shocked by the generous terms that General Horatio Gates had granted to British General "Gentleman Johnny" Burgoyne on the latter's surrender at Saratoga in October 1777, Laurens was determined to block the implementation of the so-called Saratoga Convention, the surrender agreement. Bedridden with gout, Laurens was carried into the House to participate in the debate on this issue and played a major role in having the Convention abrogated. As a result, Burgoyne's captured army was not permitted to sail for England but was kept in captivity in America until war's end.[61] It was also during Laurens's presidency that the so-called Conway Cabal against Washington was uncovered, partly as a result of Laurens's own revelations to the General.

Laurens participated in debate more frequently than had any previous president, exercising his prerogatives as a delegate, at times the sole delegate from his state, and even speaking from the chair. There was, indeed, a special cast to his role. As president he joined forces with Samuel Adams of Massachusetts and Richard Henry Lee of Virginia to become the leader of the faction in Congress that was critical of the French alliance and, more particularly, highly suspect of the integrity of Silas Deane, one of the three commissioners dispatched by Congress to France. Deane's long-smoldering feud with Arthur Lee, a fellow commissioner, split Congress virtually in half.[62]

When Congress recalled Silas Deane from France, Laurens treated him on his arrival in Philadelphia as though his guilt had been incontrovertibly established. Deane took his case to the public through the medium of the press. Thereupon, Laurens moved to suspend hearings of the accused commissioner pending a committee investigation. When his motion failed of passage, he regarded it as a vote of no confidence and tendered his resignation in a dramatic and prolix farewell address.[63] If Laurens had hoped for vindication, he was to be quickly disabused. Congress accepted his resignation as they had Hancock's, and at once chose in his place a stalwart supporter of Silas Deane, the eloquent lawyer from New York, John Jay. Continuing as a delegate in Congress, Laurens quickly found a new target, Benedict Arnold, against whom charges of corruption had been levied by the Pennsylvania authorities.[64]

Jay's presidency of Congress marked the zenith of presidential activism during the years of the Continental Congress. He entered office when the factional dispute over the conduct of Silas Deane in Paris was raging, and it was soon brought to an all-time high when Thomas Paine, the brilliant penman who was serving as secretary to the Committee for Foreign Affairs, committed a gross indiscretion. In an effort to bring down Deane, Paine publicly disclosed secret information about French aid to the United States prior to the formal alliance of 1778. Even though France had been at war for almost a year, Paine's revelation was considered an embarrassment to France and a reflection on the king's honor. The French minister to Philadelphia, Conrad Alexandre Gérard, officially protested to Congress, insisting that Paine be disciplined and Congress repudiate his statement.

The result was a hearing in Congress resembling a trial for impeachment over which John Jay presided. Paine was called to the bar of the House and sharply questioned by President Jay. As a result of the hearing Congress dismissed Paine from office, although the latter had anticipated the move by resigning the post. In addition, Congress disavowed Paine's published disclosures and formally denied that prior to the alliance France had given America any supplies whatsoever. This, of course, is what we know as a "cover story," but Jay was instructed to pass the disavowal on to Minister Gérard, which he did with seeming relish.[65]

On more than one occasion, Jay as president asserted the fundamental tenets of national sovereignty. When Pennsylvania refused to accept Congress's jurisdiction over cases in admiralty, it was Jay who asserted that "Congress is by these United States invested with the supreme sovereign power of war and peace."[66] Throughout Jay's presidency, currency deterioration and price inflation proved major concerns shared by Congress and the states. In January 1779, he issued an "Address to the People on the Currency" in which the issuance of bills of credit was vigorously defended and blame for depreciation attributed to the enemy for widespread counterfeiting operations.[67] As resentment against speculation reached a fever pitch, Congress felt impelled to try more Spartan methods. In early September it placed a ceiling of $200 million on the emission of bills of credit and instructed President Jay to send out his "Circular Letter from Congress to their Constituents." In that impressive state paper, bearing Jay's inimitable style, the president called on the states to pay their taxes, advocated reducing the amount of currency in circulation and relying henceforth on loans and taxes. Reminding his readers that in the longer run the credit of the United States rested on the success of the war, Jay reassured them that "the independence of America is now fixed as fate, and the petulant efforts of Britain to break it down are as vain and fruitless as the raging of the waves which beat against her cliffs."[68]

Finally, much of Jay's presidency was taken up with debates over peace objectives. His experience as presiding officer over these stormy arguments prompted Jay to observe to Washington that "there is as much intrigue in this State House as in the Vatican, but as little secrecy as in a boarding school."[69] Jay left the presidency in October 1779 to take up his post as special envoy to Spain.

In the interim between Jay's presidency and the adoption of the Articles of Confederation, Congress was deeply concerned with defining its war aims, devaluing its currency, and resolving the thorny issue of half pay for officers. In the settlement of none of these issues did the subsequent presidents of Congress play decisive roles.

Instead, with the creation of new executive departments in early 1781, more and more executive and administrative duties, some of which had been exercised by the president, were now assumed by the new department heads or secretaries as well as the Superintendent of Finance and his collective successors, the Treasury Board, while the responsibility for corresponding with the new departments was delegated to the perennial secretary of Congress, Charles Thomson. Since the Articles of Confederation made no change either in the powers of Congress or in the character of the presidency, although it did explicitly limit the president's tenure, the presidency was if anything diminished in effectiveness after the Articles went into operation. An exception, perhaps, was the tenure of Elias Boudinot of New Jersey, who for a time in 1783 doubled as president and ad interim Secretary for Foreign Affairs and, in addition, chaired innumerable committees. It was his unhappy responsibility to lead the congressional delegates into humiliating exile in Princeton after a mutiny of the Pennsylvania line forced the Confederation government to quit Philadelphia.[70]

Although Richard Henry Lee of Virginia, both a renowned libertarian and a jealous advocate of states' rights, stands out as the most distinguished incumbent of the congressional presidency during the years of the Confederation, he exercised few independent initiatives in that office. Originally attached to the Eastern faction, he gradually shifted to the Southern bloc.[71] In fact, the prestige of the presidency declined along with that of the Congress itself. Indeed, John Hancock, although elected to the presidency again in 1785, never came to New York to perform the duties of office. His pretext was ill health, but as James Sullivan, a fellow delegate, remarked, "the President's chair" was "the Easiest in the Union for an invalid."

During Hancock's nonappearance Congress had imposed the duties of chairman upon David Ramsay, the noted historian of South Carolina, and Nathaniel Gorham of Massachusetts, in turn. On receipt of Hancock's letter of resignation, Congress chose Gorham to fill out the remainder of Hancock's term. Gorham, a prosperous Boston businessman and advocate of a strong central government, did something quite startling for a president. If we are to believe the later charges of James Monroe, he sent an invitation to Prince Henry, brother of Frederick II of Prussia, to become king of the United States, provided that the kind of constitutional change then being considered should be along British lines. If Gorham did so, he appears to have acted entirely on his own, or at the instigation of General von Steuben, without authorization of Congress or any committee thereof, nor did he take Congress into his confidence.[72]

The most important piece of legislation ever enacted by the Congress of the Confederation was the Northwest Ordinance, which Congress, sitting in New York, adopted in July of 1787 while the Constitutional Convention in Philadelphia was drafting the new charter of federal government. It so happened that the Ordinance was passed during a fortnight's absence of the president of Congress, General Arthur St. Clair. Since St. Clair was named governor of the new territory in October of 1787, there is still a cloud of speculation over whether he was instrumental, first, in seeing that a tutelary system rather than outright self-government would be an initial stage of territorial government, thereby enhancing the powers of the governor, and second, whether his appointment was a quid pro quo for his support. One of the very few cases of conflict of interest on the part of a president of Congress, the curtain had dropped without the issue being settled.[73]

There has been a good deal of brouhaha about who was the *first* president of the United States. Most vocal have been the supporters of the claim of John Hanson, of Mulberry Grove, Maryland, who held tenure during the year beginning in November 1781. The fact that Hanson was of Swedish origin made him stand out from most of the other incumbents of the congressional presidency. Except for John Jay, who boasted that he did not have a drop of English blood in his veins, the remaining twelve claimed British ancestry. But ethnicity, with due obeisance to the enthusiasm of Scandinavian-Americans, has little pertinence to the issue. It has been claimed that Hanson was the first president of the United States in Congress Assembled. But the claim is tenuous. Hanson was the first of the presidents of Congress to begin his presidential service at the start of the federal year provided by the Articles of Confederation, but he was not even the first president to serve under the newly adopted Articles of Confederation, since both Samuel Huntington of Connecticut and Thomas McKean of Delaware preceded him as presidents under the new government. Were the functioning of Congress under the new Articles to be the criterion, then a strong case could be made out for Huntington. But even stronger cases could be made out for Peyton Randolph of Virginia, the first president of both the First and Second Continental Congresses, or for John Hancock, the president of Congress when that body declared its independence.

Considering the character of the office, its limitations in explicit powers and tenure, and the fact that most executive functions were assumed by the departmental secretaries created under the Confederation, it is clear that one is describing an incumbent who was but first among equals in the Congress, a far different position from the chief executive whose powers were enumerated by the Framers of the federal Constitution. If you ask any schoolchild who was the first President of the United States, he or she will answer, hopefully, George Washington. And it would be correct.

Secretary of Congress

Of more practical importance than the presidency to the functioning of Congress and to its continuity as a governing body was its permanent secretary. That post was filled from the start of the First Continental Congress and held without interruption through each succeeding Congress until its last session, a span of fifteen years, by a remarkable scholar-politician, Irish-born Charles Thomson. Teacher, champion of Indian rights, agronomist, and critic of the proprietary government of his home state of Pennsylvania, Thomson was one of the earliest to espouse the radical cause in pre-Revolutionary years.

As secretary, Thomson recorded all the measures voted on by Congress, including roll calls, but not debates, published all orders, resolves, and declarations approved by Congress, and attested to the authenticity of proclamations and treaties. He corresponded with the states, issued passports, letters of marque and reprisal, even news releases, and published the journals. He kept what amounted to a congressional reference library. He was charged with safeguarding the Great Seal of the United States (in the design of which he had a hand) and affixing it to documents as directed by Congress. For these duties he was paid a salary which climbed to $3,000 per annum.[74]

A committed nationalist, Thomson exercised considerable weight on men and measures in after-hour councils. A combative personality, he not only had a contretemps with President Henry Laurens, but on one occasion he was cained by James Searle, a Pennsylvania delegate, and "returned the salute." For brief periods he assumed a larger role, taking on the duties of Secretary for Foreign Affairs in the interim between Robert R. Livingston's resignation and Jay's assumption of the duties of that office. During the temporary absence of Arthur St. Clair, he was the only executive in the Congress at the time the Northwest Ordinance was adopted, and its antislavery provision doubtless gladdened his heart. It was Thomson who drew up and signed the rather tepid resolve of Congress to submit the new federal Constitution to ratifying conventions of the states, a document which he strongly supported. It was he who received the electoral votes cast for President and Vice President under the new Constitution and delivered them to Congress on April 6, 1789, and it was he whom Congress selected to travel to Mount Vernon and notify Washington of his election.

Never included as an officer in the new government, Thomson devoted his remaining years to translating the *Septuagint* from the original Greek, a very considerable feat of scholarship. Before the war had ended, John Jay appealed to Thomson to "devote one Hour in the four and twenty to giving posterity a true account" of the "Rise, Conduct, and Conclusion of the American Revolution," a story not to be cluttered with battles and sieges, advances and retreats, but concentrating on "the political story," the one aspect that in Jay's judgment would be the most subject to "misrepresentation." Regrettably, Thomson did not take the "Hint," for no one had a fuller command of the central role of Congress in the Revolution.[75] Evidently deciding that discretion was the more prudent course, Thomson not only did not take the "Hint," but burnt many of his papers, possibly even an unfinished account of the war. About "our great men," Thomson confessed, "I shall not undeceive future generations."[76]

CHAPTER 5

The People and the States:
Constitution-Making and Constituent Power

LORD SHELBURNE, who proved a better friend of America than any of his immediate successors, held some curious conversations with Henry Laurens when that American peace commissioner was paroled after a long confinement in the Tower of London. Early in 1782 the then Colonial Secretary had cautioned the South Carolinian that the Americans might not be prepared for the sacrifices that a severing of the bonds of Empire entailed. In one of his interchanges Shelburne let it be known that he feared lest by separating from Great Britain, the United States lose the benefit of the Habeas Corpus Act. He pursued this point by dispatching his legal adviser, Sir William Meredith, to present Laurens with a volume that the latter had just written on the Habeas Corpus Act.[1]

Laurens pointedly replied: "You cannot liberate a prisoner with so much facility as we can do in America." Having just spent an extended stay in a British prison, Laurens might well have been considered something of an authority on that phase of English law, and certainly an unlikely choice to heed Shelburne's warning. Apparently it had never occurred to Shelburne or to his legal adviser that the thirteen United States were perfectly free to incorporate into their revised legal codes and newly created constitutional systems as much of English law, rights, and liberties as they might wish to adopt or retain, and that to a large extent this had been done long before independence.

In singling out the writ of habeas corpus—providing for the right of the individual confined by the authorities to a court of enquiry into the cause of his detention—Shelburne had clumsily chosen a weak example. Since the British Habeas Corpus Act of 1679 failed to mention the colonies, its applicability to America was considered moot.[2] On occasions, such as in South Carolina in 1692 and in Massachusetts three years later, the colonial legislatures enacted the writ of habeas corpus as provided by the English Habeas Corpus Act. In each case the act was disallowed, in the former by the Proprietors, in the latter case by the Privy Council.[3] Despite such inhibitions, and the evidence in New York that summary trial was permitted of persons charged with offenses less than the degree of grand larceny who were unable to provide bail within forty-eight hours,[4] the right of the colonies to the writ of habeas corpus rested on the common law and seems to have been widely utilized despite the lack of statutory protection.[5]

Had Shelburne been as well informed about the constitutional and legal changes that were taking place during the American Revolution as he had once been about colonial affairs, he should have known that prior to his conversations with Henry Laurens most American states had in their written constitutions or by legislation included protections for virtually all of the rights later protected by the federal Bill of Rights.[6]

The traditions of imposing limits on the powers of government and providing protections for the individual were long familiar to the English settlers of Britain's North American colonies. From Runnymede down through the English Bill of Rights of 1689, a heritage of protected liberties and rights had become part and parcel of the thinking of colonials about fundamental constitutional guarantees. To be doubly sure, they early asserted fundamental rights of their own, notably in such instruments as the Massachusetts Body of Liberties of 1641, which embodied rights and liberties far in advance of contemporary England; and other examples may come to mind, such as the Charter of Liberties adopted by the New York Assembly in 1683. Aside from instances where the colonists themselves affirmed such guarantees, there were those contained in charters granted by the Crown or the Proprietors, notable among them being the "Concessions and Agreements of West Jersey" of 1676, the Pennsylvania "Frame of Government" of 1682, and that province's Charter of Privileges of 1701, not to mention the unworkable and highly speculative Fundamental Constitutions of Carolina of 1669.

In sum, by the time of the American Revolution, the inhabitants of the Thirteen Colonies were thoroughly imbued with the notion of government operating under limitations and protections laid down by the King in Parliament, the respective proprietors, or, in the case of the self-governing colonies, by their ancestors. They had early put to the test in a limited way the notion that government rests upon the consent of the governed. The Mayflower Compact of 1620 asserts the intention of setting up "a civil Body Politicks," and the patentees of the Massachusetts Bay Charter of 1629 had by the Cambridge Agreement, concluded soon after the grant of the charter, constituted an understanding to transfer control of the government to those who were actually to emigrate to the new colony.

None of these instruments, however, were fundamental law in the sense that the word was employed in Revolutionary years. Charters could be altered by monarchs, and were; territories could be sliced off, the rights restricted. Even the unwritten English constitution could be changed by act of Parliament, although colonial lawyers had ambivalent feelings on that issue, especially in the light of Coke's assertion in Dr. Bonham's Case that in a case where "an Act of Parliament is against common rights and reason, or repugnant or impossible to be performed, the common law will controul it, and adjudge such Act to be void."[7] As modern scholars adjudge this case, Coke did not confer upon the courts the power of judicial review. He was stating a canon of construction rather than a constitutional theory, reminding the courts of their duty to construe statutes strictly in order to bring them into conformity with accepted legal principles. Americans came increasingly to construe these words literally as a statement that there was a fundamental law limiting Parliament's powers.[8] This elastic interpretation of Coke would find its way into the American doctrine of constitutionalism, and, more specifically, into the supremacy clause of the federal Constitution. The evolving doctrine of judicial review was an innovation which distinguished American from English concepts of constitutionalism.

To the American Patriots, fundamental law signified more than the preservation of individual rights and liberties. The concept embraced binding frames of government which provided the bases for their notion of constitutionalism. When, in 1779, Barbé-Marbois, the debonair young secretary of the French legation, made a trip to New England, he was shown the old oak near Hartford where the Charter of Connecticut had been hidden at the time of the creation of the Dominion of New England in 1686. On a legal technicality the Crown lawyers decided that, having never been given up, it had never been invalidated.[9] The Charter Oak, which outlived the marquis by a score of years, was to the people of Connecticut a symbol of an inviolable constitutional grant. Indeed, the charter was cherished so dearly that its inhabitants kept it for their state constitution, merely purging all references to royal activity, a procedure Rhode Island had previously adopted; the latter's charter, an archaic instrument which restricted suffrage to freeholders and their eldest sons, was not to be supplanted until Dorr's Rebellion of 1743. Rhode Island finally responded to pressure and adopted a written constitutional incorporating a liberalized suffrage. The people of the other eleven colonies found it both prudent and even necessitous to adopt written constitutions, and did so over a four-year span.

As a matter of fact, Connecticut notwithstanding, charters could be revoked and changed at will, settlement rights could be curbed by the king, as was done by the Royal Proclamation of 1763, and territory once granted could be transferred to other governments by parliamentary act, as happened with the Quebec Act of 1774, which transferred to Canada territory north of the Ohio claimed by a number of American colonies. Long-cherished rights ("a man's house is his castle") could be placed in jeopardy, as with the Writs of Assistance;[10] seventeenth-century principles of no taxation without representation were obviously deemed by the framers of the Stamp Act as not applicable to the colonies; and traditional fishing rights, to maintain which the blood of many a New Englander had been shed in four intercolonial wars, were wiped out by a punitive act of Parliament. Judges could be appointed, contrary to colonial custom, at the pleasure of the Crown rather than for good behavior. In short, as the Patriots saw it by 1775, the rights of Englishmen and the principle of government by consent of the governed were being rapidly eroded.

That the great innovative feature of the American Revolution was the doctrine of constitutionalism is a tribute to the role of Patriot

THE WOUNDS OF WAR

1. Trinity Church. Gutted by fire in 1776, this, the tallest structure in New York City, was not rebuilt until after the British evacuation in 1783. From a sketch by a British officer during the Revolution (Emmett Collection, New York Public Library)

2. State House at Annapolis, Maryland. Site of General Washington's address resigning his commission, December 23, 1783, and of the ratification of the Definitive Peace with Great Britain, January 14, 1784 (Maryland State Archives)

3. Federal Hall, New York City. Site of the Confederation Congress, 1785–89, and remodeled for President Washington's inauguration, April 30, 1789, with a restored Trinity Church in the background (From a contemporary print)

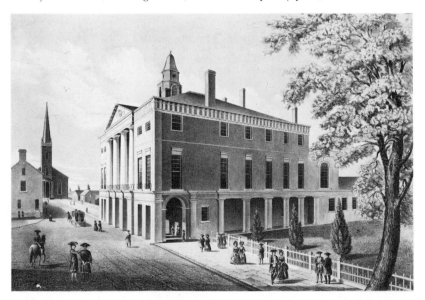

5. Phillis Wheatley. Black slave and female poet, whose verses were acclaimed in both Boston and London (Engraving, unidentified artist after Scipio Moorhead, National Portrait Gallery, Smithsonian Institution, Washington, D.C.)

4. Frontispiece to *The Contrast*, a major postwar satirical comedy by Royall Tyler, first produced by the American Company at New York's John Street Theatre, April 16, 1787

6. Lewis Hallam the Younger. British actor and copartner with John Henry of the American Company, a principal troupe in the restoration of the drama in postwar America (Courtesy of The Players, New York)

7. Foederal March. Composed by the immigrant musician Alexander Reinagle for the parade in Philadelphia marking the ratification of the Constitution (Courtesy of the Music Division, Library of Congress)

9. Nathaniel Gorham. Portrait by Charles Willson Peale (Independence National Historical Park Collection)

8. Henry Laurens. Painted by John Singleton Copley while the former President of Congress was a prisoner in the Tower of London (The Capitol, Washington, D.C.)

10. Arthur St. Clair. Portrait by Charles Willson Peale (Independence National Historical Park Collection)

11. Charles Thomson. Congress's permanent secretary. Portrait by Charles Willson Peale (Independence National Historical Park Collection)

12. Henry Knox. Secretary at War. Portrait by Charles Willson Peale (Independence National Historical Park Collection)

13. Robert Morris and Gouverneur Morris. The superintendent of finance and his deputy —Robert Morris (right) and Gouverneur Morris. Portrait by Charles Willson Peale (Courtesy of the Pennsylvania Academy of Fine Arts)

14. John Jay. Secretary for Foreign Affairs. Portrait by Gilbert Stuart (Courtesy of the State Department, Washington, D.C.)

15. Thomas Jefferson. Minister to France. Portrait by Charles Willson Peale (Independence National Historical Park Collection)

16. John Adams. Minister to the Court of St. James's. Portrait by Charles Willson Peale (Independence National Historical Park Collection)

17. Benjamin Franklin. Portrait by Joseph Duplessis (National Archives)

18. James Monroe. (Independence National Historical Park Collection)

19. Joel Barlow. Poet, entrepreneur, and diplomat, and author of *The Vision of Columbus*. Portrait by Robert Fulton (Courtesy of the National Portrait Gallery, Smithsonian Institution, Washington, D.C.)

20. Noah Webster. Educator and lexicographer. Engraving by unknown artist in Webster's *American Spelling Book* (Boston, 1789) (Courtesy of the National Portrait Gallery, Smithsonian Institution, Washington, D.C.)

lawyers. On the eve of the Revolution they were evolving a rationale for establishing a constitutional republic, or republics, as one may prefer. Stressing the Whig notion of compact and its violations, lawyers shared with theologians like Jonathan Mayhew a leading role in demonstrating both the necessity and the virtue of resistance to oppression. They skillfully wove together various intellectual strands. They drew upon the covenant theology of New England, borrowed from Enlightenment writers ranging from Locke to Rousseau. They misconstrued English legal history, idealized pre-Norman law, resting their case on the common law and the rights of Englishmen. When these examples provided insufficient support, they turned to natural rights and notions of higher law. The fact that American pamphleteers, some of whom would be Constitution-shapers, hewed to the Whig party line and found reinforcement from English radical thinkers of the early eighteenth century to dissidents like John Trenchard and Thomas Gordon, co-authors of *Cato's Letters,* suggests that they were looking backward for their models. They were discovering them in the great English reforms of the seventeenth century—even in the republican experiment under Cromwell. Their opponents, Loyalist lawyers as well as British jurists, were defending a very different English constitution, the one that had evolved in the course of the eighteenth century.[11]

At the completion of the task of adopting the Massachusetts Constitution of 1780, Samuel Cooper, the well-known preacher, in a sermon delivered before Governor Hancock, declared: "Is not a country a constitution—an established frame of laws; by which a man may say, 'we are here united in society for our common security and happiness. These fields and these fruits are my own: the regulations under which I live are my own; I am not only a proprietor in the soil, but I am part of the sovreignty of my country.'"[12]

In nonlegal language the Puritan preacher was reiterating the timeless phrases of Thomas Jefferson, to the effect that government of necessity derives its authority from the consent of the governed, or, as Robert R. Palmer has phrased it, "the people is a constituent power."[13] Now the idea of government resting upon the consent of the governed as asserted in formal compacts was hardly novel or an invention of the Americans. Nevertheless, the mechanism for giving reality to popular sovereignty, a collective bundle of constitutional principles, evolved over a relatively few years and emphasized written constitutions. Basic to constitutionalism was the principle that a constitution drawn up at the people's behest and ratified by the people must be distinguished from an ordinary statute subject to change or repeal by the legislature. Such an instrument became fundamental law transcending ordinary legislation. These principles evolved in stages and did not become formalized until the ratification of the federal Constitution. It was the people of the states, rather than Congress, who demonstrated the road to constitutionalism and reiterated on every appropriate occasion the doctrine of popular sovereignty.

That deeply rooted conviction in America that the foundations of government rest upon the consent of the governed served to explain the attachment of a substantial body of the inhabitants to the cause of independence, while providing the underpinning for the concept of constituent power. One can locate the roots of a people's government in the early Revolutionary mechanisms, the elaborate infrastructure, linking artisans and merchants. In New England one can find the hand of the church, the town meeting, the county convention, the militia, and the provincial council and assembly joining forces to recruit a broad-based support for revolution.

From these dual steps—the setting up of revolutionary machinery on both the Continental and the state levels—emerged, as we have seen, a system of dual sovereignty. A logical extension of the notion that government rested upon the consent of the governed was the acceptance and incorporation by this dual constitutional structure of the doctrine of resort to "first principles," embracing the right to amend or change a constitution, a task that proved impossible to achieve on the federal level until 1787 while meeting less resistance on the part of the people of the respective states. Significantly, James Madison in the 40th and 49th *Federalist* asserted the people's transcendent right to alter and abolish their political institutions, an assertion that he later included as a prefix to his proposed draft of the Bill of Rights which disappeared from the final version.

Congress followed up its directive to the colonies to organize their own state governments by setting forth the reasons for such a step. Its phrasing was coopted in the preamble to the New York Constitution of 1777. Therein the New York draftsmen informed their constituents:

The present Government of this Colony, by Congress and Committees, was instituted while the former Government, under the Crown of *Great Britain,* existed in full force, and was established for the sole purpose of opposing the usurpation of the *British* Parliament, and was intended to expire on a reconciliation with *Great Britain,* which it was then apprehended would soon take place, but is now considered as remote and uncertain.[14]

The themes of popular sovereignty and of formation of government by compact are central to all state constitution-making. They were sounded even before the congressional directive of May 15, 1776, when Richard Henderson, founder of the Transylvania Company in what is now Kentucky, called a convention of representatives of four small settlements, which adopted a constitution Henderson had written. Addressing the delegates, Henderson reminded them that "if any doubt remain amongst you with respect to the force or efficacy of whatever laws you now or hereafter make, be pleased to consider that *all power is originally in the people"* and "the laws derive force and efficacy from our mutual consent."[15] True, this was not state-making in any formal sense but an operation guided and directed by a proprietary group, yet these borderers managed to set up a quasi-government which functioned some four years. Indubitably this irregular example of popular sovereignty and compact confirmed Lord Dunmore's appraisal of it as "a dangerous example to the people of America."[16]

One could cite innumerable examples of declarations on the grass-roots level of popular sovereignty as the basis of government during these innovative years. In Massachusetts the people of Pittsfield petitioned the General Court on May 29, 1776, urging the adoption of a state constitution and proclaiming "that we have always been persuaded that the people are the fountain of power."[17] A fortnight later the mechanics of New York City instructed their delegates in the New York Congress that they were now "vested with the power of framing a new Constitution for this Colony" as "every man . . . is, or ought to be, by inalienable right, a co-legislator with all the other members of that community."[18]

Echoing the sentiments of the Great Declaration, the new state constitutions asserted that the people were the sole source of legitimate power, and while implicitly recognizing the delegation of power to the people's representatives, insisted on the accountability of the latter to their constituents. Thus, the Virginia Bill of Rights of June 1776: "All power is vested in, and consequently derived from the people. . . . Magistrates are their trustees and servants, and at all times amenable to them."[19] Or take Delaware's, the first to be adopted after independence had been declared: "All Government of Right originates from the people, is founded in Compact only, and instituted solely for the Good of the Whole."[20]

Even before the colonies received the congressional directive of May 10–15, 1776, to form their own governments, a few found it necessary to set up provisional constitutions. What many of the states sought was guidance. Would it be possible, some asked, for Congress to provide a uniform model constitution for the states? And if not, should they accept as a basis the models of their colonial governments, the system of "mixed government," and the checks and balances they were accustomed to and had long cherished as a part of Parliament's victories in the seventeenth century over the royal prerogative? Congress was disinclined, and for two reasons: In the first place, a substantial segment in Congress felt that such action would be tantamount to a declaration of independence; secondly, Congress was doubtful whether a uniform frame of government could take into consideration the differences among the states, differences that might well warrant distinctive rather than uniform frames of government. Thirdly, Congress was itself a unicameral body which exercised executive as well as legislative functions, and would soon take on a limited judicial role.

The matters were privately discussed in Philadelphia in the fall of '75 in talks by Richard Henry Lee with John Adams. Lee found Adams's ideas both fresh and original, and suggested that he commit them to paper. Adams obliged in a short letter dated November 15, 1775. What he proposed was a lower house chosen by the people; an upper legislative chamber picked by the lower house (his model, obviously, the Massachusetts Charter of 1691); and the governor and other executive officers to be annually elected by joint ballot. The governor was to possess the veto, command the armed forces, and have the power of appointment of lesser officials and magistrates, subject to the approval of the upper chamber. This plan, as Adams advised, might be put into operation at once; but for the longer term, and as soon as affairs took on a more peaceful aspect, the legislature might enact a law providing for the annual election of the governor and the upper house.[21] John Adams, for one, felt that "the Barons of the South and the Proprietary Interests in the Middle Colonies" were reluctant to adopt a republican system, a reluctance compounded by what Adams viewed as "that avarice of Land, which has made upon this Continent so many Votaries to Mammon, that I Sometimes dread the Consequences."[22]

Hardly had Adams's letter to Lee gained currency when Thomas Paine electrified America with the publication on January 10, 1776, of *Common Sense*. Therein Paine, with the Pennsylvania provincial model somewhat in mind, threw out some "hints," not plans. He advocated an annually elected unicameral house, founded on much more equitable principles of representation than currently prevailed in Pennsylvania and some other colonies. He would have given the legislature the power to elect its own president, confined its business to wholly domestic matters, and made it subject to the authority of the Continental Congress. Nor did he feel that an independent executive branch was necessary at either the state or the federal level.[23] Combining legislative and executive business in one body clearly contravened Adams's notions of separation of powers and checks and balances. Paine's hastily thought-out scheme prompted Adams to issue a pamphlet in the form of a letter to George Wythe, bearing the title *Thoughts on Government*, and enlarging on the substance of his earlier letter to Lee.

Adams and Paine, so opposite in personalities as in ideologies, shared one principle in common. They both opted for a republican constitution, but while the latter reached this goal by way of social contract, the former, pursuing Montesquieu, argued that virtue was the peculiar attribute of the citizens of a republic.[24]

How republicanism shaped the state constitutions and how each state in its own way paid tribute to the principle of popular sovereignty can perhaps best be illustrated by examining the variety of models which the people adopted for their respective states. The two that were adopted prior to the formal call of Congress on the states to organize governments, those of New Hampshire and South Carolina, were adopted provisionally. Both states in the post-Declaration era supplanted their provisional frames of government with more detailed constitutions. Two others by a small margin of time anticipated Congress's vote for independence. These were Virginia and New Jersey, and both constitutions endured for more than half a century. Three others set up written constitutions right after July 4, 1776—Pennsylvania, Maryland, and Delaware. New York's Constitution of 1777 avowed its own acknowledgment of popular sovereignty in the following words: "No authority shall, on any pretence whatever, be exercised over the people or members of this State but such as shall be derived from and granted by them."[25]

Only in a restricted sense could the very early constitutions be considered instruments of the people. Wartime necessity, the occupation of parts of the colonies, if not all, by enemy troops, meant that rump bodies assumed the responsibility for making constitutions. Nor was opportunity usually available for formal ratification by the people. Significantly, it was Massachusetts, once freed from the dangers of invasion, that came closest to embodying the notions of constitutionalism that were brought to perfection by the Constitutional Convention of 1787 and the ratifying conventions in the months following.

What was unique about the American system of constitutionalism was that it not only proclaimed the supremacy of constitutions over ordinary legislative acts and—unlike the British constitution—was written down, but that, in addition, it evolved over time a distinctive mechanism of production or creation, if you will. That production involved a series of steps—the drafting of constitutions by bodies chosen by the people specifically for that purpose, rather than by ordinary legislatures, and ratified by special ratification conventions again chosen by the people.

Objections to having constitutions written by the regular state legislatures were voiced as early as 1776 in resolutions adopted by the Massachusetts town of Concord, which asserted:

The Supreme Legislative . . . [is] by no means a Body proper to form and Establish a Constitution or form of government; for reasons following. First, because we conceive that a Constitution in its Proper Idea intends a system of Principles established to secure the subject in the possession and enjoyment of their rights and privileges, against any encroachments of the Governing Part. Second, Because the same Body that forms a Constitution have [sic] of consequence a power to alter it. Third, because a Constitution alterable by the Supreme Legislative is no Security at all to the Subject against any encroachment of the governing part on any, or on all of their Rights and privileges.[26]

Only Massachusetts, in its mechanism and constitution-drafting, was permitted the wartime luxury of a specially elected constitutional convention. American constitutionalism would also develop other unique features, some of which appeared immediately, others evolved with time—a republican system, bills of rights, checks and balances, separation of powers, judicial review, and federalism.

In South Carolina, Virginia, and New Jersey, Revolutionary legislative bodies assumed the task of framing constitutions although they lacked the authority. Seven states held elections in contemplation of the writing of constitutions, and in New York a special election was held for that purpose. In Pennsylvania the assembly was thrust aside, and a province-wide conference laid down regulations governing the election of a convention. That body, while chosen primarily to write a constitution, was also authorized to enact legislation. While Delaware and Maryland issued calls for special conventions, North Carolina attempted to frame a constitution by a Revolutionary Congress, but the action was deferred to a new, specially elected Congress of October 15, 1776.

If the notion of formal conventions chosen by the voters was not yet universally recognized or in a number of instances not feasible owing to military events, so likewise did the state assemblies or conventions that drafted constitutions lack uniformity of representation. New York's Congress, the fourth since 1775, was elected from among a large enfranchised group comprising every Patriot freeman in New York City and Albany and every freeholder elsewhere.[27] Pennsylvania seemed on paper to have the most democratic franchise for its convention. It permitted any taxpayer or small property holder to cast a ballot for members of the convention, but in apportioning delegates allotted twice as many to the western counties as to the eastern and barred substantial numbers of conservatives who did not at that time approve the movement for a new constitution. Virginia and South Carolina operated in reverse, allotting proportionately far more delegates to the Tidewater than to the rest of their respective states, and like disproportions were evident in the Maryland allotment.[28]

The constitutional mechanism for framing and ratification upon which the federal drafting and ratifying process was most closely modeled was that of Massachusetts. The draft constitution which a convention submitted to the towns for ratification in 1778 was considered by the inhabitants as defective, as it lacked a bill of rights and other features deemed essential. It was defeated by a resounding vote of 9,972 to 2,083. Once again the legislature, now in a chastened mood, asked the people to authorize a convention, which was done. On this issue all freemen over twenty-one were entitled to vote. Happily John Adams, who had just come home from France, was able to guide the deliberations of the convention and, eventually, to draft the constitution. This second effort was submitted to the towns and accepted. The process of drafting and ratification was denominated by Adams as having been carried out "in the most legal manner of which I find any example since the days of Lycurgus."[29]

Following Montesquieu, most American lawmakers shared the conviction that the enjoyment of political liberty required a separation of powers. So the First Continental Congress affirmed in its "Letter to the Inhabitants of the Province of Quebec," directly quoting "the immortal Montesquieu."[30] Although the Continental Congress itself did not embody this principle in its own unicameral structure, it was affirmed in various state constitutions, notably in those of Virginia, New York, and Massachusetts. Thus, the Virginia Bill of Rights of June 12, 1776, following the lead of John Adams's "Thoughts," provided the classic statement:

That the legislative and executive powers of the State should be separate and distinct from the judiciary; and that the members of the two first may be restrained from oppression, by feeling and participating the burdens of the people, they should, at fixed periods, be reduced to a private station.[31]

As one scholar has pointed out, "this was the first constitutional document since the Instructions of Government, under which Britain had been governed from 1653 to 1657, to include the principle of separation of powers in express terms."[32] Along with the concept of balanced government, separation of powers, utterly ignored under the Articles of Confederation, would become a cornerstone on which the federal constitutional structure was to be erected. While the federal Constitution embodied the doctrine of separation of powers in its tripartite structure, its failure to enunciate the principle provided a ground for criticism by the Antifederalists and impelled James Madison to devote essays on the subject in *The*

Federalist. To satisfy those who wished to have a more explicit statement incorporated in the Constitution, Madison framed one based on the statement in the Virginia Constitution, intending it to be included in the Bill of Rights. Congress, however, failed to adopt it among the twelve amendments it transmitted to the states for ratification.

Since Congress both before and under the Articles of Confederation functioned without a separate executive, the state constitutions in this respect provided a model for the federal Constitution, although the degree of authority these instruments were prepared to entrust to the governor or president (as he was sometimes designated) varied widely. This is understandable. The war was being waged ostensibly against the abuse of magisterial power by kings or governors, as well as by Parliament. Sentiment was pervasive toward shackling executive power. In this respect no state went farther than Pennsylvania, whose constitution totally eliminated a governor. Instead, his role was assumed by an executive council of thirteen, elected directly by the people every three years. The council was headed by a president—elected by a joint vote of the council and the legislature. The title of president was also used in Delaware, New Hampshire, and South Carolina.[33]

In contrast to the weak or plural executive provided by the Pennsylvania example stood the New York model of a relatively strong executive, with powers limited in certain areas. When the state's framers heard how Pennsylvania's executive council was functioning in crisis, the New Yorkers were appalled. James Duane reported from Philadelphia that he was astounded to learn that the executive council had adjourned for a month. "Executive adjourned, say you, how is this possible?" Duane predicted that, since "the Civil Governeurs have in effect abdicated" their authority, Congress would have to take over the operation of the state.[34] This prediction proved accurate. Congress was obliged to step in and authorize the president of Pennsylvania, "with as many members of the Executive Council as could be convened," to assume "every authority over the state boards of war and navy until such time as the legislative and executive authorities could be convened."[35] Contrariwise, New York's framers believed that the state executive should have responsibility for continuously enforcing the laws while the legislature need only meet periodically. New York's Constitution of 1777 empowered a popularly elected governor to call the legislature into special session and prorogue it for a maximum of sixty days. The governor commanded the state militia and navy. All government officials were commissioned by him and reported to him. He was to correspond with the Continental Congress and the other states, and, most important, he was "to take care that laws are faithfully executed."

On the other hand, the New York framers made a point of curbing two powers which had been exercised by royal governors but had been a special target of criticism by the populace—the executive veto and the power of appointment. The result was two striking innovations. As a compromise the framers instituted a council of revision, consisting of the governor, the justices of the Supreme Court, and the chancellor. The governor, or any two of the others, would have the authority to "revise" or veto all legislative bills subject to re-passage by a two-thirds vote of the legislature. In another compromise the framers set up a council of appointment, comprising one senator from each district, with the governor having a casting vote, "but no other vote."[36]

A still stronger executive was set up under the third model, the Massachusetts Constitution of 1780. Annually elected, he was given authority to summon a council to direct the affairs of the state and with their consent to adjourn or prorogue the legislative body. As in New York, he was in command of the states' armed forces, but unlike the latter state, he was given the power of appointment, "with the advice and consent of the Council." He had a limited veto which could be overriden by a two-thirds vote of the legislature. To make sure that he would act for the public good and uphold "the dignity and character" of his office, he was given "an honorable stated salary" amply sufficient for those purposes.

It was in its conception of the role of the legislative branch that Pennsylvania deviated sharply from most of its sister states. Discarding widespread notions of checks and balances and mixed government, the Pennsylvania Constitution of 1776 set up a unicameral legislature, elected annually, with no property qualifications being required either of the legislators or of the voters. While a variety of radicals in the state—George Bryan was not a delegate but his views were reflected by James Cannon, Timothy Matlack, and Dr. Thomas Young, among others[37]—supported the unicameral plan, it is clear that the influence of Benjamin Franklin and Thomas Paine was especially evident in the design for the legislature. Franklin's little story to illustrate the defects of the bicameral system is legendary. Drawing an analogy to the snake with two heads, each of which pointed a different course toward the brook, he tells us that, as a result, "the poor snake died of thirst."[38] To nail down the notion of rotation in office, the constitution provided that assemblymen might not serve than four terms and the councilmen not more than one between seven years. Only Georgia and Vermont followed Pennsylvania's unicameral experiment.

The unbalanced constitution with its all-powerful legislature threw the moderates and conservatives, or "Anti-constitutionalists," as they were called, into a paroxysm of fury. Only the threatening military situation deterred them from attempting to kill the constitution without by any means putting an end to a degree of violent partisanship perhaps unparalleled in any other state in the era of the Confederation, Rhode Island excepted.[39]

As with the federal Constitution, which, with its tripartite branches of government, took the preferred state constitutions for its model, so in both state and federal instruments the judiciary received minor attention. What the states' draftsmen did was virtually to carry over the colonial court and legal systems with a few innovations. Most of the changes occurred at the highest level, the inferior and local courts continuing largely untouched. The details of judicial organization and procedure were left to the legislature, just as the federal Constitution would leave such details to Congress.

The courts that emerged under the state constitutions bore many likenesses to past models—superior courts by various names, which had jurisdiction over inferior civil and criminal courts. Chancery courts administered equity in most states except in New England, where equitable relief had from the beginning been administered by courts of common law. Accordingly, chancellors or chancery courts continued well on into the national period when court reforms merged law and equity. In New York this was not accomplished until the constitutional revision of 1846, and in New Jersey not for another hundred years.

Weak as the judiciary seemed on paper in contrast to the all-powerful legislative branch, which usurped both executive and judicial powers, there were within the states judges who were prepared to declare to the legislature, as did George Wythe, the Virginia chancellor, "Here is the limit of your authority; and hither shall you go, but no further."[40] By dicta and by hair-splitting *ratio decidendi* the state courts cautiously crafted the doctrine of judicial review, according to which the courts could assume the authority to determine the unconstitutionality of acts of the state legislatures, a power that the federal courts were specifically given in the Judiciary Act of 1789.[41]

Conscious of the novel and even undemocratic notion that unelected judges would or could declare state laws unconstitutional, few judges of the Confederation era were prepared to risk the threat of impeachment by legislatures or the ire of large segments of the public by explicitly asserting the power of judicial review. James Iredell of North Carolina, a jurist soon to sit on the bench of the United States Supreme Court, proved less inhibited. A constitution, as he viewed it, was not only "a fundamental law" but also a special popularly created "law in writing," one that "limited the powers of the Legislature, and with which every exercise of those powers must necessarily be compared." When judges were confronted with the choice of deciding between "the *fundamental unrepealable* law" laid down by the people and an ordinary legislative enactment contrary to the constitution, Iredell saw no reason for hesitancy. "They must simply determine which law was superior," he declared, asserting that the judges could not "wilfully blind themselves" to the superior authority of the written constitution.[42]

Significantly, one of the most ardent and influential proponents of judicial review was Alexander Hamilton. His doctrines were enunciated both as counsel in a highly controversial case that arose shortly after the occupation of New York City, and in the polemical writings it inspired. The case was *Rutgers* v. *Waddington*. The defendant was a wealthy Tory whom the female plaintiff sued for trespass for occupying her brewery during British military rule. The suit was brought under a recent act of the state legislature, the Trespass Act, giving an action in law against Loyalists who occupied or purchased the real or personal property of Patriots during the war years.[43] That statute was enacted before the New York legislature learned the terms of the Preliminary Peace of November 30, 1782, barring such legislation. Brought at the height of anti-Tory feeling, the suit by Rutgers for back rent for the occupancy of the premises made the Mayor's Court, and James Duane, mayor and presiding judge, the focus of national attention, with leading members of the bar enlisted on both sides of the case. As chief counsel for the defense, Alexander Hamilton, who had already defended in the press the supremacy of the Treaty of Peace over state legislation,[44] urged upon the court that the judiciary had a responsibility to interpret the law, and that such interpretation should include a comparison of state or national law. The plaintiff's case, he argued, was barred by the law of nations, the Treaty of Peace, the court's right of judicial review, and, finally, by the common-law rules of statutory interpretation. Hamilton insisted that Congress had been given the exclusive power to conclude treaties of peace and that observance on the part of the states was obligatory. Any state law in violation of the treaty was ipso facto void, and it was the duty of a state court to refuse to give effect to such a law.

Mayor Duane made a politic judgment, distinguishing between occupation by the Loyalist defendant by permission of a British civilian commissary, during which period he paid no rent, and occupation under authority of the British military commander, when all those occupying Patriot premises were ordered to pay rent to the British agent for the Vestry for the Poor. The treaty, Duane held, would protect the defendant for the time he occupied the property under authority of the latter, whereas occupation under orders of British civilians was contrary to the treaty. Accordingly, damages were awarded for the period of occupation under British civilian authority. While the court deftly straddled the issue and seemed purposefully ambiguous,[45] the decision was violently attacked, and Hamilton, never one to back down, strenuously defended it in his continuing *Phocion* letters.[46]

In the 78th *Federalist* Hamilton, on the one hand, sought to reassure his readers that under the new Constitution, "the judiciary, from the nature of its functions, will always be the least dangerous to the political rights of the constitution, because it will be least in a capacity to annoy or injure them." The executive holds the sword, the legislative branch the purse, but the judiciary, lacking either sword or purse, possesses "neither Force nor Will but merely judgment, and must ultimately depend upon the aid of the executive arm for the efficacy of its judgments." If, then, the judiciary was the weakest of the three branches, as Montesquieu described it, it is the least likely to endanger the liberties of the people. Nonetheless, since "no legislative act" contrary to the Constitution "can be valid," it is the proper function of the judges, Hamilton argued, to choose the Constitution in preference to the statute, "the intention of the people to the intention of their agents." The line of argument from *Rutgers* v. *Waddington* to the 78th *Federalist* is straight as an arrow.

Hamilton's remarks on judicial review first appeared in print on May 28, 1788.[47] His views hardly reflected the opinions of the average state legislator, if we can draw inferences from the bitter experience suffered by the Rhode Island judiciary when it attempted to exercise the power of judicial review. In this state the contest between court and legislature reflected the wide economic gulf between a relatively impoverished rural population, the backbone of the "country party" opposed to a Continental impost and a firmer national union, and an affluent mercantile group in the towns. The "country party," resentful of the weight borne by its constituency of taxes and mortgages, unseated the commercial interests in the April election of 1786. They then lost no time in emitting £100,000 in bills to be loaned at interest on landed security. To enforce the law, the legislature provided for summary trials of creditors who declined to accept the bills in payment of debt. Upon such declination the debtors could discharge their debts by depositing the required sum in bills with the county judge. Depreciation was instant and swift. To the newly elected legislature the solution was to impose a fine ranging from £6 to £40 upon any person refusing to accept the bills.

Business responded negatively. In every town, shops shut down. Unemployment was widespread.[48] The inhabitants of neighboring Massachusetts and Connecticut refused to ship their produce and manufactured goods to Rhode Islanders. While the legislature stood fast and the populace was sharply divided, the courts revolted. A test case in September 1786, *Trevett* v. *Weeden*, was carried to the Superior Court by a stubborn Newport butcher who was defended by General James M. Varnum. A member of Congress, Varnum had voted for the impost and then been defeated for reelection. The court defied the legislature by refusing to administer the penalty for noncompliance provided in the statute on the ground that it lacked jurisdiction. The lower house then summoned the justices before it and administered a stern reprimand, but failed to impeach them. The precedent stood, but at the next election all of the judges save one were defeated for reelection. Varnum's brief in published version had maintained that the act enforcing the recent paper money bills under which the defendant was indicted did not provide for a jury trial or right of appeal and was therefore "unconstitutional and void." The legislature had, Varnum argued, overstepped the bounds set by the people in their charter or constitution, and such fundamental laws could only be changed by the people and not by their legislatures.[49]

Followed shortly thereafter by the North Carolina case of *Bayard* v. *Singleton,*[50] in which the state's Supreme Court declared an act of the legislature void, it is clear that Varnum, Hamilton, and Iredell had laid the ground for curbing willful legislatures and preparing the public to accept judicial review of state legislative acts by federal courts and, ultimately judicial review of acts of Congress. By 1787 the judiciary might still have seemed the "least dangerous branch," but its potentialities in the system of checks and balances were gradually gaining recognition.

In sum, the experiment in state constitution-making provided a depth of experience upon which the Framers of the federal Constitution drew, in addition to their awareness of European examples and of venerated political theory. Speaking of the Massachusetts Constitution, John Adams quite rightly referred to it as "Locke, Sidney, and Rousseau and De Mably reduced to practice."[51] Separation of powers, checks and balances, a strong executive, an independent judiciary could be found in some, if by no means all, of the state constitutions, while the need to add a Bill of Rights to the federal Constitution attested to the popularity of the provisions almost universally incorporated by the states either in their constitutions or their evolving legal systems.

These state constitutions molded the character of America's emerging political system. As one minister who engaged in the process of constitution-making in Massachusetts predicted, "If America preserves her freedom, she will be an asylum for the oppressed and persecuted of every country; her example and success will encourage the friends and rouse a spirit of liberty through other nations, and will probably be the means of freedom and happiness to Ireland and perhaps in time to Great Britain, and many other countries."[52]

CHAPTER 6

The New Nation's First Depression

I N the year 1784 there were no gurus on Wall Street to predict economic calamity. In fact, stock speculators did not begin to assemble under Wall Street's buttonwood tree until 1792.[2] Economics hardly a science then, if that claim can be made for it now, stood forth in complete disarray. Some Americans held grimly to mercantilist notions which they had imbibed as part of the old British Empire; others were enticed by the new laissez-faire theories of the philosophes and Adam Smith.[3] There were protectionists and free traders; hard money men and paper money champions; pro- and anti-bank advocates; and the opposing parties were at each other's throats for most of these depression years. If there was one thing the nation lacked, it was a business consensus.

The reasons for what, in depth and duration, proved to be the most serious economic setback suffered by Americans since the earliest days of colonial settlement, are not difficult to unearth. War's privations had fostered a pent-up demand for goods. For a brief time there seemed to be a surplus of specie accumulated as a result of French funds, the expenditure of the French armed forces in America, Dutch loans, wartime privateering, trade with the foreign West Indies, illicit trade in wartime, and relatively high prices for farm products, to the farmers' advantage. A false sense of prosperity had been created, a prosperity unevenly distributed both geographically and by class. Some fattened on profits—war contractors, privateers, farmers, speculators, and engrossers. Others found that the prosperity had been maldistributed. Planters and small farmers whose farm buildings had been destroyed, whose livestock had been purloined, whose slaves had been "liberated" by British invaders, and whose tobacco warehouses had been burnt down hardly shared in wartime prosperity. Least of all was it a prosperity that touched the men in the armed services.

War's end brought a rush to buy goods at the market where the best terms were available, at the lowest interest rate, for comparatively long terms, and for goods that Americans found familiar, desirable, and purchasable in small lots. The market for such wares was afforded by the British. French goods were much dearer than English, and luxury exports like champagne were, to most American palates, no more appealing than cider.[4] The Dutch likewise found it initially impossible to compete with Britain in the American trade.[5] Anxious to recover what had been to them an extremely lucrative source of revenue—their American customers—and to discourage American investment in competing manufactures, English businessmen were not hesitant about extending credit once again and dumping goods in excess of any realistic demand. Indeed, the British government encouraged exports to America by according such exports the same sort of drawbacks, exemptions, and bounties that had been granted formerly on exports to the Thirteen Colonies.

First came a brief price rise as a result of temporary shortages, followed by a sharp slide in prices and wages in America. Urban wage rates dropped from an index figure of 23 in 1785 to 17 in 1789 and did not show any substantial upturn until 1791, while the wages of farm laborers in Massachusetts had shriveled to a low of 40 cents a day by 1787.[6] In the wake of price and wage declines came mounting indebtedness as the network of credit covered the country. Inland traders and shopkeepers had been extended credit by coastal merchants and shopkeepers, and in the interior the former had in turn extended credit to small farmers and artisans. When the credit bubble burst, a combination of indebtedness and unemployment resulted, and to a degree of severity Americans had never previously experienced. As a mournful procession of protested bills of exchange were returned to America, credit from abroad finally stopped, with resultant bankruptcies taking place in both Europe and America.[7]

The situation can, as a start, be documented by adverse balance of trade figures. United States imports of British goods for the years 1784–86 were valued at £7,591,935, while U.S. exports to Britain amounted to about a third, or a reported sum of £2,486,058.[8] A slightly variant year-to-year breakdown of trade between England and America for the entire period of the Confederation only serves to accentuate the hugely unfavorable balance of trade (figures in sterling):[9]

	Imports	Exports
1783	1,435,220	314,058
1784	3,413,417	701,199
1785	2,078,744	725,892
1786	1,493,255	743,644
1787	1,794,217	780,449
1788	1,709,928	883,618
1789	2,306,529	892,296

This unfavorable balance of trade did not include such items as interest charges, profits of British merchants who sold directly to planters in the South, and the cost of slaves purchased from British firms. Thus, as gold and silver stocks were quickly depleted,[10] exports proved grossly inadequate to bridge the gap, and a credit crisis proved inevitable.

Writing with the advantage of hindsight, that irrepressible speculator James Wilson attributed "the disagreeable state of our commerce" to "extravagant and injudicious importation. We seem to have forgot," he added, "that to pay was as necessary in trade as to purchase." Those who paid in specie diminished the circulation of money; those who made no remittance at all impaired American credit. "The phenomenon," observed Wilson, "spread over the different parts of the United States, and thus every operation, foreign and domestic, had an injurious effect on credit, our circulation, and our commerce."[11] If the depression in part can be attributed to a credit binge by Americans in buying goods abroad, it also can be put down to overspeculation in land, notably in the purchasing of confiscated Loyalist estates in such states as Maryland, where inveterate speculators like Samuel Chase had rushed to buy enormous tracts of land and sought relief from the financial burdens they were now shouldering by state emissions of paper money.[12]

Despite an overwhelming body of evidence to the contrary, sympathizers with the Antifederalist position have charged that the bad times of the postwar years were the figment of the imagination of nationalist propagandists. Inklings of this view can be found among contemporary Antifederalist writings.[13] It was easier, however, to deny the evidence of severe economic conditions when one was several generations removed from the Confederation years. One of the earliest of the nineteenth-century writers to expound the conspiracy thesis without supporting evidence was Henry B. Dawson, a learned military historian of the American Revolution, who also devoted himself to studying the role of the masses in that war and had a penchant for picking controversial issues which he fought with relish and passion.[14] As Dawson would have it, the Federalists or nationalists conspired to falsify the true conditions of the period in a deliberate effort to create panic and undermine the government of the Confederation.[15]

It was to be Charles A. Beard who would provide the most significant amplification of the thesis of Dawson and his followers in his *An Economic Interpretation of the Constitution of the United States* (New York, 1913). Therein Beard contended that the country was not depressed but prosperous, and that what John Fiske had called "The Critical Period" was really not so critical after all, but, drawing heavily upon Dawson's article, "a phantom of the imagination produced by some undoubted evils which could have been remedied without a political revolution."[16] Without pointing to the inconsistencies between Beard's *Supreme Court and the Constitution* published the previous year, and the repudiation of his economic determministic thesis in his later *The Republic* (1943) and his *Basic History of the United States* (1944), we find him in *The Enduring Federalist* (1948) describing conditions in the Confederation period in language that would have gratified Fiske and perhaps shocked Bancroft.

Beard's inconsistencies and his latter-day virtual repudiation of his own allegations about the state of the economy during the Confederation years failed to deter Merrill Jensen, who in his magisterial study *The New Nation*[17] finds the period of the Confederation "one of extraordinary economic growth." As evidence, he contends that more merchants owned more ships at the end of the 1780s than they had at the beginning of the Revolution, and that by 1790 the export of agricultural products was double what it had been before the war. He speaks of labor shortages in this period (true for a time among ironworkers), when workmen walked the streets seeking jobs, when fishermen by the thousands were idle, and foreclosures and bankruptcies occurred on a scale unparalleled in the history of the country up to that date.

The evidence of those who would find prosperity during and immediately after 1784 is hardly supportive of the conspiratorial thesis. Channing, for example, speaks of the period as one of "economic readjustment," and argues that the country "commercially and industrially" had regained its prosperity by 1789 and was on the high road to it in 1786.[18] The movement of prices provides him with no support. Even the sober Andrew C. McLaughlin, who accepted the thesis of a critical period, conceded that there was "some tribulation," which he largely qualified as regards the extent of the trade downturn. He finds the latter largely confined to New England, while insisting that the charge that the country was "forlorn, destitute, and poverty-stricken" is exaggerated.[19] McLaughlin's evidence: Chastellux's *Travels*, which were undertaken in America in 1781 and 1782, two to three years before the onset of the depression, and a letter of John Jay to Thomas Jefferson in Paris, wherein the former is describing the nation's potentialities for prosperity while deploring the existence of "much public and private distress."[20] Later on McLaughlin refers to the Confederation years as "the dismal period."[21]

Recent economic historians take a down-to-earth position, preferring the traditional view of America's first depression. They are reinforced by Tench Coxe, the knowledgeable financial expert from Philadelphia who would reflect on how the affairs of the country "had fallen into a very disagreeable condition in the year 1786."[22] What the facts reveal is a prolonged business slowdown whose impact was uneven. New England and the lower South suffered much more than the Middle States, which benefited by prevailing high prices for farm crops, and the Chesapeake, which seems to have benefited by the ability to sell tobacco to England and to France and other parts of the European continent as well.

It has been pointed out that our trade with Great Britain, our leading customer, was less in 1790 than it was at the start of the Revolution, although the population of the country had expanded from 2,500,000 to some four million. America was now subject to Britain's restrictive trade measures, excluded from the lucrative

British West Indian trade (except for smugglers), and liable to all the discriminatory duties levied against foreign bottoms in its direct trade with other countries. Furthermore, the demand for staple exports was no longer expanding. Tobacco exports remained stationary, while rice exports actually declined between 1777 and 1791, and the fisheries industry was operating at approximately 80 percent of the prewar level.[23] Even when allowance is made for the shift of America's West Indian trade to the French and Dutch West Indies in this period and for illicit trade, the per capita value of all U.S. exports was considerably less in 1790 than prior to the war.[24]

Those who view the Confederation years through Antifederalist spectacles are encouraged by the tone heard in correspondence of American statesmen with foreigners. It is perhaps significant that when Franklin, Jefferson, and Robert R. Livingston expressed in their letters to foreign correspondents a more roseate view of conditions than other Founding Fathers, they were making these observations to Frenchmen or to Englishmen. They were understandably seeking to reassure friends and well-wishers of Americans abroad that the country was not headed for collapse. Such assertions must be discounted as shrewd propaganda. Jefferson, as he was passing through Boston on his way to France, confessed to his closest political ally, James Madison, that the conviction was "growing that nothing could preserve the confederacy unless the bond of union, their common council, could be strengthened."[25] Yet, when in France, he reassured Jean-Nicolas Démeunier that the United States was in no danger of bankruptcy and that, with certain minor exceptions, "the Confederation is a wonderfully perfect instrument."[26] Similarly, when Franklin wrote to M. Le Veillard on March 6, 1786, that "America was in higher prosperity,"[27] he ignored the statistics to the contrary that are unfolded in this chapter. Again, when Livingston wrote Lafayette in April 1787 that commodity prices were higher than before the war, he was evading the real issue of how far they had dropped since the coming of the peace.[28] If Lafayette had had the opportunity of reading the French consular correspondence from America with the Marquis de Castries, the Minister of Marine, he would have found a far more somber picture painted by experts on the scene, who repeatedly warned of a flood of bankruptcies in America and advised caution on the part of French businessmen.[29]

The concept of a prolonged depression is bolstered by the general downturn of commodity prices which took place in the aftermath of peace, with lows established in the years 1788–89. The fall of prices has been attributed to the outflow of specie and to the behavior of European prices of major export staples. The result, however, was to make the burden of governmental debt heavier, to increase the discontent of the debtor class, and even to contribute in some degree to civil unrest, notably to Shays' Rebellion, which receives separate treatment in this study. Businessmen, mechanics, and artisans witnessed a Confederation government incapable of controlling the money supply, of paying interest on the public debt, or of regulating and encouraging foreign and domestic commerce. Little wonder that these groups recognized the grim necessity for setting up a stronger central government.

Examples from the Philadelphia wholesale market: farm crops dropped from 101.72 in January 1784 to 82.06 in 1790, rising smartly to 105.74 the following year. In the same year, January 1784, sugar dropped from 122.70 to 76.69 by the following January and was even lower, 75.16, in 1789. Staves and barrels which commanded an index figure of 74.05 in 1784 slumped to 42.72 in 1790, while breadstuffs were one of the few items that showed little range, from 79.43 in 1784 to 70.16 in 1788, while beef slumped from 130 to 98, tumbling again after a brief recovery in 1786.[30]

It was much the same story in Charleston, where the average price of rice declined from £15 4s. (current) per hundred pounds in 1784 to 10s. in 1789; combined wholesale prices in rice, deerskins, corn, pitch, tar, turpentine, and indigo dropped from an index figure of 240 in 1780 to 160 in 1785. The weighted index of imported products fell from 110 in 1784 to as low as 50 the following year, and at 90 in 1790 had not fully recovered from the start of the depression.[31] This downward movement was more serious for South Carolina producers than the figures indicate, for prices as measured in specie fell even more rapidly. After the state of South Carolina authorized the first printing of paper money, it remained at par for about two years, but from May 1787 to 1791 circulated at a discount which was ordinarily about 10 percent.[32]

The prolongation of this first depression after independence is attested to by other than quantitative data. Commenting on conditions in Charleston in the spring of 1788, one merchant wrote: "The scarcity of money in this country is inconceivable; indeed the difficulties in this state increase. It is not easy to say how and when they will alter." Another declared that "since ever I knew this place, people never were so backward on their payments, nor trade at such a stand."[33]

The ratification of the federal Constitution seems to have laid a basis for economic recovery, but no change in the downward direction of commodity prices was under way even at the time of the inauguration of the federal government.

Aside from over-purchasing on credit by Americans and the dumping by the British of manufactured goods, the depression in America was sharply exacerbated by a series of British political decisions made in the midst of the negotiations in Paris for a trade treaty and prior to the Definitive Peace. The Preliminary Articles of Peace contained this clause: "It is agreed to form the articles of the Proposed Treaty, on such Principles of liberal Equity, and Reciprocity, as that partial advantages (those seeds of Discord!) being excluded, such a beneficial and satisfactory Intercourse between the two Countries, may be established, as to promise and secure to both perpetual Peace and Harmony."[34] Significantly, this proposed agreement on trade disappeared from the Definitive Treaty of Peace.

Once Shelburne was out of office, to be succeeded by the improbable North–Fox ministry, chance of liberal trade concessions to the Americans faded rapidly, much to the discomfiture of David Hartley, who had replaced Richard Oswald as commissioner to the Americans in Paris. Fox, who now dominated the negotiations, proved sticky, negative, and obstructive, and in no aspect of the peacemaking was Fox's meddling more inept and its consequences more mischievous than in his negotiations with the Americans over trade issues. His predecessor, Lord Shelburne, was wedded to the principle of free trade, indubitably encouraged by his friend and confidant the Abbé Morellet. Shelburne recognized a peace as "good in the exact proportion that it recognizes" the "great principle of free trade."[35] True, his own Cabinet had rejected the article drafted by John Jay providing for reciprocity between England and America[36] on the ground that the executive had no authority to alter the operation of the Navigation Laws. It was understood, however, that such matters would be covered by a treaty of commerce.[37] Backed by an American merchant lobby in London, a bill was accordingly drafted permitting American produce for the time being to enter British ports on the same footing as though British-owned, while treating American ships carrying such produce as those of other foreign states. During this interim period the bill would have permitted American ships to carry American goods to British colonies and islands in America and to export any goods whatsoever from such British possessions. Duties and charges would be in both cases the same for British-owned merchandise, transported by British ships and crews.[38]

By the time the trade bill was introduced, Shelburne was out of office, and Pitt, still holding on as Chancellor of the Exchequer, sounded lukewarm. Fox advocated caution, and even Burke, another long-reputed friend of America, compared the proposed legislation to a one-sided courtship. "Great Britain was extremely fond in her wooing, and in her love fit was ready to give largely; whereas to my knowledge, America had nothing to give in return."[39]

It was William Eden, Privy Councillor to the North–Fox coalition, who proceeded to demolish the proposal. His argument reflected a careful reading of a tract just published, entitled *Observations on the Commerce of the American States.* Its author, Lord Sheffield, marshaling an imposing array of statistics, argued that Americans must be treated as foreigners and not permitted to enjoy those branches of the carrying trade with the Empire in which they had previously participated, notably the trade in foodstuffs and timber with the British West Indies. Now Britain could regain the British West India carrying trade, nor need the British be concerned about losing the American market for British manufacturers. The Americans, he argued, could not get along without them, and British shipowners could carry the manufactured goods there. His major theme: for years to come Americans would be economically helpless.

The shipping and exporting lobby preferred Sheffield's arguments to those found in Adam Smith's *Wealth of Nations,* a work published in 1776, which mustered impressive arguments for free trade. The government in power ignored Adam Smith, nor were European continental businessmen persuaded. As one European observer remarked, "Dr. Smith, who had never been in trade, could not be expected to write well on that subject any more than a lawyer upon physick."[40] In America, though, Smith was gaining some currency, for free trade arguments had long been popular.[41]

The final rebuff to America's reciprocal trade initiatives came on July 2, 1783, when an Order in Council was issued barring American ships from the West India trade.[42] Its author, William Knox, a longtime public official and diehard Tory, claimed that the order, which he had first drafted as a bill, entitled him to have engraved upon his tombstone a tribute for "having *saved the navigation of England.*"[43] The Order in Council opened up a grievous and festering wound in Anglo-American relations, and disclosed that the shooting war was to be succeeded by one of intense commercial rivalry between the erstwhile belligerents. Although British shipping and manufacturing interests would reap a short-term harvest, the British West Indian planters found that they were now forced to pay exorbitant prices for salt, fish, and timber from Canada, especially Nova Scotia, and Honduras, since the cheaper supplies from New England had been cut off (smuggling aside). The island planters would suffer a mortal injury by this impairment of their competitive position.[44]

If Britain's prohibition against American trade with the British West Indies ultimately boomeranged, the more immediate effects were devastating to New England and severely damaging to the Middle States. The impact of the depression on America's diverse regions merits careful analysis. The Royal Navy found it impossible to interdict violations by American shippers of the Orders in Council, as Horatio Nelson, then an obscure naval officer stationed in Antigua, found out to his chagrin. Despite British warships, illicit trade brought substantial quantities of foodstuffs to West Indian islands like Jamaica, and American shippers soon found how frequently the island ports were thrown open to prevent starvation. In addition, by false registries and in collusion with English relatives engaged in similar ventures, the illicit trade never dried up completely, while such complicity of British island officials with American shippers could be matched in the French islands.[45]

New England was especially hard hit by the British trade prohibitions. The heaviest blows were sustained by fishing, shipping, and whaling, and their recovery was slow. As compared with the prewar year of 1766, for example, ship entries at American ports in 1788 showed a decline of 23 percent for ships arriving from all the West Indies; of 46 percent for ships coming from the British West Indian islands. The shrinkage of West Indian trade affected both fishing and shipbuilding in New England. Comparing the years 1765–75 with those of 1786–90, the proceeds from New England fish shipped to all the West Indian islands dropped from $448,000 to $284,000 a year[46] between 1786 and 1790 as compared to 1765–75, as shown by the following table:

Statistics of the Cod-Fishery of Massachusetts from the year 1765 to 1775, and from 1786 to 1790.[47]

Towns	From 1765 to 1775			From 1786 to 1790		
	Vessels annually employed	Tonnage	No. of men	Vessels annually employed	Tonnage	No. of men
Marblehead	150	7,500	1,200	90	5,400	720
Gloucester	146	5,530	888	160	3,600	680
Manchester	25	1,500	200	15	900	120
Beverly	15	750	120	19	1,235	157
Salem	30	1,500	240	20	1,300	160
Newburyport	10	400	60	10	460	80
Ipswich	50	900	190	56	860	248
Plymouth	60	2,400	420	36	1,440	252
Cohasset	6	240	42	5	200	35
Hingham	6	240	42	4	180	32
Scituate	10	400	70	2	90	16
Duxbury	4	160	28	9	360	72
Kingston	6	240	42	4	160	28
Yarmouth	30	900	180	30	900	180
Wellfleet	3	90	21	—	—	—
Truro	10	400	80	—	—	—
Provincetown	4	160	32	11	550	88
Chatham	30	900	240	30	900	240
Nantucket	8	320	64	5	200	40
Weymouth	2	100	16	3	150	24
In Maine	60	1,000	230	30	300	120
Total	665	25,630	4,405	539	19,185	3,292

These statistics are buttressed by the comment of the British agent George Beckwith that New England seafarers had "suffered more by the Act of Independence than any part of the Country, from the decay of their shipbuilding and the effect which the dismemberment of the Empire has produced on their oil and fish in foreign markets."[48] The most telling evidence was provided in Jefferson's masterly "Report on the American Fisheries," submitted as Secretary of State, in which he shows that the fish catch during the Confederation years was "too small to afford a living to the fishermen," and resulted in the withdrawal of vessels from the fishing and whaling industries and a wholesale exodus of fishermen to Nova

Scotia. Jefferson attributed these conditions to the loss of the Mediterranean markets, to the exclusion of markets "of some of our neighbors," to high duties in other countries, and to bounties "to the individuals in competition with us."[49]

Before the war, one fourth of the value of fish exports had come from trade with Mediterranean countries, fish and other articles carried in American ships sheltered by the British flag, and protection money paid by the British government to Tripoli, Tunis, and Algeria to buy off the Barbary pirates. In the postwar years, Barbary pirates in effect drastically curtailed the sail of fish products to the Mediterranean as they quickly embarked upon a program of seizing American vessels, enslaving sailors, and demanding tribute.[50]

Whaling suffered an even heavier blow. Between 1772 and 1775, some 150 vessels were engaged in whaling, largely out of Nantucket. That number had shrunk to fifteen in 1785, rising to a mere thirty-six two years later. Similarly, the barrels of whale oil brought into Nantucket steadily declined from an estimated 30,000 barrels in the years 1772–75 to 12,000 barrels for the years 1787–88.[51] In December 1783, Britain slapped a prohibitive import duty of £ 18 3s. a ton on American whale oil, a duty which was estimated to have ruined the whale industry and deprived Massachusetts of half its total of exports to Britain. In that state the whaling fleet declined by two thirds between 1775 and 1789, with particular hardship felt at Nantucket.[52] Jefferson, when minister to France, strove valiantly to have the duty on whale oil imposed by that country reduced, but the results seem to have been minimal.[53] Meantime, France sought to lure the Nantucket whalers to Dunkirk.

Shipbuilding proved one of New England's heaviest casualties. With the coming of peace, ships newly built in the states were no longer considered British vessels as they had been under the Navigation Laws, which had entitled them to engage fully and freely in all British commerce. As foreign vessels, New England ships were barred from nearly all trade with British ports. That vigorous industry, which had hitherto flourished from a constant stream of British orders based on cheaper costs, ready access to ship timber and masts, and an available supply of artisans, now felt the drying up of British orders. Massachusetts yards laid only fifteen or twenty ships in 1785; only eleven keels in all New England in 1789. The loss of shipbuilding orders had been estimated as running as high as

£100,000 a year.[54] Brissot reported that only three vessels were built in Newburyport in 1788 as against ninety in 1772.[55] Accompanying the decline of shipbuilding was a corresponding downturn of the timber industry, a decline which devastated the economy of northern New England. Brissot reported in 1787 finding many residences in Portsmouth "in ruins, women and children in rags . . . everything announces decline."[56] Verily, the New England shipbuilding and lumber industries had come to a standstill by the close of the Confederation years.

The Middle States were by no means exempt from the effects of the depression. In New York prices dropped sharply, a trend not reversed until 1788 or mid-1789, cash was scarce, shipyards idle. Throughout 1785 the Chamber of Commerce complained of trade "daily in the Decline and languishing under fatal obstruction," while the tune, "stagnation in trade," re-echoed constantly in the New York press the following year.[57] Labor unrest and attempts of mechanics, who were mostly entrepreneurs, to protect themselves against dumping and low wages marked these years in New York City, which also witnessed working-class efforts to change the political complexion of the legislature.[58] In foreign trade, however, New York customs receipts show a favorable turn beginning in 1787, for which year receipts amounted to some £48,000, rising to £70,000 in 1788.[59]

New York's neighbor, New Jersey, sank more and more into debt, doubly burdened by heavy charges exacted by middlemen in New York and Philadelphia, by differences in exchange rates of currency, freight charges, duties levied by both New York and Pennsylvania on imposts, and prevailing low prices for farm products.[60]

The prohibition by the British government in July 1783 of the carrying of grains and livestock, among other products and articles, to the British West Indies, severely injured the economy of the provision states, including Pennsylvania. In Philadelphia, flour dropped from an index figure of 120 to 95 during the depression years (despite the technological breakthrough of Oliver Evans's automatic flour mills, first put into operation after 1783 and first introduced by the Ellicott brothers on the Patapsco River, their use spreading quickly to the Baltimore area); beef from 120 to 98; pork from 130 to 90; iron from 155 to 100; and naval stores from 120 to 65.[61] The Middle States, particularly New Jersey and Pennsylvania, long heavy exporters of bar iron, which the British permitted to enter free of duty, failed to recover their export markets, amounting as late as 1790–92 to a mere 16 percent of the substantial exports of that product to Britain before the war.[62]

The decline in the export trade in furs particularly hit the Northern states, notably Pennsylvania and New York. The war cut the Northern states out of this traffic, for since the British continued in violation of the Treaty of 1783 to hold such key posts as Dutchman's Point and Pointe-du-Fer at the head of Lake Champlain, at Oswegatchee on the St. Lawrence, at Oswego on Lake Ontario, at Niagara on the U.S. side of the Niagara River and below the Falls, and at Detroit and Michilimackinac, the Canadian fur traders out of Montreal now enjoyed a monopoly of the trade routes to the interior by way of the St. Lawrence River and via Indian tribes west of Lake Superior. It is estimated that at least half of the £200,000 annually received by Britain from the fur trade in the postwar years came out of the pockets of Americans excluded from the fur traffic in the Old Northwest.[63] In the lower South, Pensacola and New Orleans dominated the fur trade, while St. Louis was the entrepôt from which the French traders ruled the fur trade of the lower Mississippi Valley prior to the Louisiana Purchase. Even undisputed areas proved barren because of the alliances formed in 1784 between the Creeks, Chickasaws, and Choctaws to accept Spain's protection, to ban the American fur traders from their territory, and to trade on a preferential basis with a British firm operating out of East Florida. Border wars waged by frontiersmen of Georgia and Tennessee, breaking out in the summer of 1785, and rising in intensity in 1787–88, brought the Southern Indians into even tighter alliance with the Spaniards.[64]

Thus, the recovery of the fur trade both in the Northwest and the South proved a major issue of American diplomatic negotiations with both Britain and Spain, and merits further mention in the diplomatic section.

Before the war, the pinelands of North Carolina had been beneficiaries of bounties paid to produce naval stores—tar, pitch, and turpentine—but by 1788, naval stores exported to Britain were not even a third as valuable as before the war, while the New England states now constituted the chief market for such Carolina products.[65]

The lower South was as badly savaged by the depression as any other region. Rice, its major export product, had, in the Confederation years, to surmount the handicap of slave losses to the British, with a resultant labor shortage and low production. From 277,124,000 pounds of rice exported from South Carolina and Georgia in the four years 1770–73, the exports for a similar span, 1783–86, declined to 46 percent of the earlier total.[66] In addition to the production handicaps, the new trade policy of the British government proved severely restrictive. Before the war, the British had encouraged the export of rice to the foreign West Indies and to points in Europe south of Cape Finisterre. Now Britain imposed high duties on such imports, forcing the planters to trade directly with continental Europe. As a result, the price of rice collapsed in 1783, only to recover for a few months briefly the following year, and then drastically drop for another two years.

In colonial times, indigo, a product of South Carolina, enjoyed a British bounty; with independence, the bounty was dropped, and indigo shipments in 1785 were half what they were before the war. Even in the year of the ratification of the Constitution indigo exports stood at 30 percent below the 1775 level.[67] By this date, competition of the British East Indies was having its impact on South Carolina and would ultimately lead to the abandonment of the cultivation of this product. The result of the hard-hit naval stores and rice and indigo production was to reverse the favorable balance of trade position that the Carolinas had enjoyed with Great Britain before the war.[68]

In sum, as a result of extensive war damage, slave losses, British trade policies, and the general postwar depression that spread to all the states, South Carolina was in a severely crippled economic state for some years after the war. Henry Laurens, for example, wrote in 1786 that he was frequently reduced to a dollar in cash. Edward Rutledge's black slaves were on the verge of starvation, suffering in the wake of the British devastations and the economic paralysis that followed. Hard up though Laurens was, he managed that same year to respond to a plea of Rutledge's overseer that "the negroes won't have a bite after next Sunday," scraping together a hundred bushels of "corn, peas, and rough rice from Mt. Tacitus plantation to supply your negroes for the rest of the season."[69]

Judging from the piercing cries emitted by Chesapeake tobacco growers and Virginia debtors generally, one might assume that this area was the very worst victim of the depression. In fact, the evidence hardly supports that inference. Hence, this region has been left to the last because it alone was favored by special trade arrangements with France.

While a number of planters had switched from tobacco to wheat in the prewar years, that course was now largely reversed on expectations of a resumption of a flourishing tobacco trade. The British raids had swept the fields of many black hands and tobacco warehouses had been special targets for the incursions of Mathew, Arnold, and Cornwallis. As a result, the quick restoration of tobacco production to prewar levels was out of the question. It took almost a decade to come near that figure. The production problem is revealed by the following records of Virginia's tobacco exports:[70]

Annual Average	Hogsheads
1770–72	67,247
1783–84	49,497
1784–85	55,624
1785–86	60,380
1786–87	60,041
1787–88	58,544
1788–89	58,673
1790–91	56,288
1791–92	61,203

Some of the shortfall was made up by the shift of tobacco production from Maryland and northern Virginia southward, including North Carolina and the lower South. The combined total of tobacco exports, including these relatively new producing areas, revealed that tobacco exports in total recovered their prewar levels by the year 1785, with the deficiencies of the Chesapeake states made up by the Carolinas and Georgia.[71]

While tobacco shipments to Great Britain from Williamsburg declined by one third during the years 1784–91,[72] the substantive change lay not so much in the total as in the direction of exports, since before the war all North American shipments had gone to Great Britain.

The significant change in the direction of imports in the Confederation years is explained by the fact that, despite incomplete data, France and the rest of the European continent seem to have siphoned off perhaps 35 percent of such shipments. However, what is especially remarkable is that, despite the elimination of the United States from such benefits as had ensued from the English Navigation Laws, Britain initiated desperate efforts to continue to serve as entrepôt for the tobacco traffic from the United States. While barring shipments in American vessels to the British West Indies, that nation by an Order in Council of June 6, 1783, opened British ports to American tobacco in British *or* American vessels, and in the same year Parliament, by waiving the first penny per pound of the duty to be paid in cash at entry and by permitting the duty to be bonded, facilitated a resurrection of the tobacco trade in order to compete with French ports like L'Orient and Dunkirk. In addition, American tobacco, now that the United States was independent, could be carried directly to Ireland and the Channel Islands, traffic forbidden during the war. Thus, the British and Scottish factors, with easy credit and familiar goods, won back their old Virginia customers.

For the British there was only one cloud on the horizon, and that was France. French officials both in America and at home hoped to supersede the British in the tobacco trade with America. Vergennes, in particular, now serving as the principal minister on Maurepas's death, had counted heavily on France's gaining tangible economic benefits from the postwar trade with America to make up for its great sacrifices in the late war. France proceeded to liberalize the tobacco trade with the French West Indies, by the *arrêt* of 1784 established seven free ports for tobacco in France, and was behind efforts to unite the export trade in the hands of a single American firm.[73]

First, Franklin managed to procure a commission for his grand-nephew Jonathan Williams and the latter's father-in-law, Franklin's old friend William Alexander, to supply the French. Indeed, the old doctor's alertness to business opportunities for himself, his kinsfolk, and his friends belied his years. But theirs was a speculation based on the assumption that, with war's end, tobacco prices would decline. Instead, British purchases in America buoyed tobacco prices by 1785 and, unable to fulfill the contract, Alexander was succeeded by his secret partner, Robert Morris. But while tobacco prices remained relatively high, the price of imported goods bought in

America dropped sharply as a result of the acute depression. The only way to sell imported items in Virginia was at auction. French consular correspondence is replete with complaints about the poor prospects for French business as a result of this monopolistic arrangement and warned that Virginia's businessmen would be thrown into the arms of the English.[74]

When Jefferson supplanted Franklin as minister to France, the former revealed in his correspondence a doctrinaire hostility to monopoly. In justice to that immensely talented diplomat, it should be said that Jefferson not only reacted as a Virginia debtor and tobacco planter, but as a well-informed diplomat who consistently argued with Vergennes to persuade the French minister that tobacco sales would rise in France if the Farmers-General tobacco monopoly could be terminated, an eventuality which, he insisted, would prove beneficial to Franco-American trade.[75] His argument ignored the fact that the monopoly for fiscal reasons chose to buy at least 80 percent of its tobacco in the United States and insisted on having its production prohibited in France.

Both the monopoly and the Robert Morris contract were at issue, and Lafayette served as Jefferson's willing intermediary in advocating open trade in France subject only to an import duty. A commission set up in February 1786 ruled that the Morris contract should run its course to the end of 1787, but be neither renewed nor extended thereafter. Jefferson's contention that Morris had driven down tobacco prices by almost 50 percent, causing the inhabitants of Maryland and Virginia a loss of £300,000 sterling, has failed to persuade one careful scholar of the subject.[76] In any event, the financial crisis of the French government had by 1789 caught up with the tobacco trade and forced the hard-pressed Farmers-General to make drastic reductions in their tobacco purchases. Hence, despite Jefferson's strenuous five-year effort to enlarge Franco-American trade as the basis for a close Franco-American connection, tobacco was more heavily directed toward Britain than ever before, and the British had even taken over a considerable share of the carrying trade between France and America. By 1791, and after a long fight, France abolished the tobacco monopoly.[77]

So far as America was concerned, the French arrangement had little or no impact on tobacco prices, which, after rising swiftly following the war, dropped 50 percent by 1785, costing Virginia and Maryland £400,000 in one year.[78] Chesapeake planters returned once more to their chronic condition of depression, characterized by lack of specie and an increasing indebtedness to British merchants above and beyond prewar debts which in many cases remained to be settled.

Attempts to Turn the Tide

State Tariffs. To secure revenue, prevent dumping of foreign goods, and protect emerging native industries, a majority of the thirteen states levied tariffs on imports, a source of income they denied to Congress. On the positive side, it should be said that portions of these tariffs did provide protection to local industries, which were not slow in pressing their respective cases,[79] and promoted innovation and invention thereby, thus confirming a warning of minister John Adams to the Court of St. James's.[80] Industries that enjoyed such protection included hardware, woolen and cotton cloth, hats, and sailcloths.[81] On imported products competing with such industries, duties as high as 15 percent were imposed. Foreign consuls, notably the French, were alarmed by the sweeping character of the tariffs enacted in such states as Massachusetts and New Hampshire, rates which drew protests and threats of retaliation.[82]

So far as France was concerned, the trade balance with America continued to be unfavorable. For example, exports to the United States declined from 7.2 million livres in 1786 to 5.6 million in 1788, while imports from the United States dropped less dramatically, from 13 million livres in the former year to 12 million livres in 1788.[83]

A second type of import was taxed to discourage the export of specie. The targets fell into the luxury category, including items like jewelry, silverware, carpets, and silks. A third target consisted of articles not then produced in America in quantities sufficient to meet the people's needs, items such as books, china, glassware, and coaches. Finally, to raise revenue, duties were imposed on foreign liquor. With time, the number of articles subject to tariffs was increased and rates upped to as much as 25 percent ad valorem.

In addition, eight states enacted retaliatory laws against British shipping in order to benefit American shipowners and seamen, including discriminatory tonnage duties on British vessels entering their ports.[84] Six states went even further, imposing special taxes on goods imported in British ships. In New Hampshire, Massachusetts, and New York, the rates were twice as high as those on goods imported in American ships; in Rhode Island, treble duties were exacted; in North Carolina, a special duty of 20 percent ad valorem was assessed.[85]

Indubitably such tariffs encouraged the production and sale of American manufactured products and lured European workmen, who were once again being recruited.[86] A rapidly developing shoe industry in Lynn was selling its wares far beyond the confines of its own state.[87] The products of nailmakers in Providence, Stamford, and Norwalk reached the entire Atlantic seaboard, as did hats from New England and paper from the Middle States. Buttons were being turned out so successfully that some were even being shipped to Europe, and a Boston sail manufacturer was filling orders from various parts of the Union. The expansion of water mill technology facilitated production at gristmills, sawmills, tanneries, carding machines, and fulling and paper mills.[88] The machinery perfected by Oliver Evans of Philadelphia for cleaning, grinding, cooling, bolting, and barreling grain without manual operation represents an early instance of complete mechanization of manufacturing, from raw materials to finished commodity. Under such a system, six men, mostly employed in closing barrels, could annually convert 100,000 bushels of grain into flour.[89]

After 1789, textile production expanded rapidly, particularly as a result of the use of Cartwright's machinery by Samuel Slater, with cotton first being spun in the United States in a plant opened by Moses Brown at Pawtucket, Rhode Island. In short, while the technological revolution missed the Confederation by a hair's-breadth, the rapid expansion of preindustrial technology had registered a considerable impact in the Revolutionary and Confederation eras.[90]

On the negative side, the state tariffs failed to provide a truly common market within the thirteen states, a major objective of the later federal Constitution. In addition to being discriminatory,[91] they lacked uniformity in the degree of protection offered home industry and production, and their objectives diverged as regards the trade patterns they sought to shape. The Southern states, along with Delaware, either failed to impose any protective duties or taxed them lightly out of an evident desire to encourage British shipping and gain an advantage thereby against the Northern states as an exporter of American products.[92] Moreover, state legislative policy contributed to unnecessary risks on the part of shippers, since there was no guarantee that the state might not change the rules of the game after contracts had been entered into on the basis of a tariff schedule then in operation. A multitude of varying details on rates and schedules imposed by the separate states vexed businessmen and curtailed initiative.

Only a federal tariff with uniform rates could resolve such conflicts and uncertainties and provide shippers and manufacturers with the protection they needed. The Articles of Confederation did not confer that power on Congress. Hence, the shipping and manufacturing interests, including the mechanics, artisans, and seamen in their employ, increasingly pushed proposals to remove the power over commerce from the states and deposit it securely in Congress.[93]

One eminent scholar of the Confederation era regards the state tariffs as "strikingly effective," and as contributing to the growth of American commerce after the war. His main evidence is the complaint of British shipowners as late as March 1787 that state tariffs were giving American ships "an advantage in trade between the two nations."[94] On the other hand, he points out, virtually every British merchant questioned by the Privy Council felt that the tariff to be imposed by the new national government would prove more favorable to them than had the legislation of the states.[95] As Merrill Jensen sees it, the artisans and manufacturers were, in the Confederation years, the chief beneficiaries of the state tariffs; after 1789, it was the merchants. However, the record of U.S. manufacturing strides after 1789 is hardly confirmatory of this conclusion.

A contrary argument would be found in the writings of *The Federalist.* In No. 12, Hamilton describes the advantages of having one government guarding the coastline to bar foreign contraband, insists that the national government would raise duties to a higher level than the states (a long-term eventuality, however), and in *Federalist* No. 7 argues that interstate trade regulation made some states tributary to others. New York, for example, "from the necessities of revenue," might levy duties on its imports, a great part of which "must be paid by the inhabitants of Connecticut and New Jersey." States like New Jersey and North Carolina, lacking suitable ports, were sufferers from the tariff discrimination. James Madison observed that "New Jersey, placed between Philadelphia and New York, was likened to a cask tapped at both ends; And North Carolina, between Virginia and South Carolina, to a patient bleeding at both Arms."[96] Such discrimination, Hamilton insisted, could not long remain uncontested.

It is hard to uncover any other issue in American history upon which there was so much general agreement as there was on conferring upon Congress the supreme power over commerce. Yet, time after time, proposals to achieve just such an end were blocked. In the spring of 1784 Congress, prodded by a special committee and a request of the merchants of Pennsylvania, widely endorsed by businessmen throughout the other states, asked the states for a grant of power to pass navigation laws, to prohibit the import and export of goods of countries not having treaties with the United States, and to forbid the subjects of foreign nations to import goods from other than their own countries, save where exempted by treaty. Unless such action were taken, especially in view of British restrictions on the West India trade, Congress warned that "our foreign commerce must decline, and eventually be annihilated."[97]

The states procrastinated, and even the merchants felt that the proposal did not go far enough. What they sought was a permanent grant to Congress of a general power to regulate trade.[98] This was precisely what James Monroe proposed late in 1784 by way of amending the Articles, but the defects in the proposals were that they deferred too much to the sensibilities of the states. The proposition would have had all duties collected by authority of the states and expended to the use of the state in which they were paid. In fact, it was in sharp contrast to the impost of 1783 which was before the states for approval.[99] With pros (the Northern shipping interests) and antis (the agrarian opposition) divided, the proposed amendment never got out of Congress, blocked by even those who saw "the necessity but fear the consequences," Monroe reported to Jefferson.[100] Again, in March of 1786, Congress, after a survey of state actions on the previous proposal, once more futilely called upon the states for the grant of such power.[101]

In sum, the Americans had won the war and stood perilously close to losing the peace. Only a unified government capable of establishing the nation's credit on a firm foundation, of controlling foreign and interstate commerce, empowered to levy tariffs not only for revenue but also for protection of native industries, and establishing a consistent foreign policy bolstered by military and naval sanctions could point the economy in a steady upward course and lead to rapid economic development. As the months of depression dragged into years, a consensus was growing among Continental-minded politicians, merchants, manufacturers, and mechanics that a new constitutional structure held the solution to the nation's economic concerns.

The first step in that direction was taken in September 1786 when, in response to Virginia's invitation, an interstate commercial convention gathered at Annapolis. Lacking a quorum of states, that body took no formal action; but, as we shall see, it did issue a call for a convention at Philadelphia to discuss not only commercial problems but *all* matters necessary "to render the constitution of the Federal government adequate to the exigencies of the Union."

The Philadelphia Convention responded affirmatively to the irregular call. The Framers, in Article I, section 8, of the Constitution, conferred upon Congress the power "to lay and collect Taxes, Duties, Imposts, and Excises" (all duties, imposts, and excises to be uniform throughout the United States), and "to regulate Commerce with foreign Nations and among the several States, and with the Indian tribes." Section 9 prohibits the levy of taxes or duties on exports "from any State" or the granting of preferential regulations of commerce or revenue "on one state over those of another," nor should vessels bound to, or from, one state "be obliged to enter, clear, or pay duties to another."

The result was the Tariff of 1789,[102] transferring the drama of tariffs from the state to the national stage and guaranteeing that levies would prove a major source of congressional debate and sectional dissension for a century and a half to come.

Banks and Credit. Thomas Paine, both man of the people and speculative entrepreneur, put his finger on the emerging crisis when, in 1780, he observed that the American states were "in want of two of the most essential matters which governments could be destitute of—money and credit."[103] Men like Paine, Hamilton, Gouverneur Morris, and Robert R. Livingston all argued that the credit pinch of the Confederation years was tightened by the absence of a nationwide banking structure. European banks operated in England, France, Sweden, and the Netherlands, whose Bank of Amsterdam was widely publicized in Adam Smith's *Wealth of Nations*. Experiments in both land and silver banks had been initiated briefly in colonial Massachusetts, but the nation had operated for the greater part of the war without such fiscal and credit facilities.

To meet the limited needs of the war effort there was set up in July of 1780 the Bank of Pennsylvania, which, under operations continuing for about a year and a half, provided a subscription list to a loan fund for the army with repayment guaranteed by Congress.[104] The Bank of Pennsylvania lacked the functions of a modern commercial bank and its scope was too limited for a young man of Alexander Hamilton's probing financial imagination. As early as September 1780, he proposed that Congress erect a national bank on the joint credit of "the public and of individuals," which for a limited period would even be permitted to coin money.[105] A half year later he presented a full-blown banking plan in a lengthy letter to Robert Morris. Drawing upon economic ideas of British writers like Richard Price, David Hume, and Malachy Postlethwayt, he proposed a national bank, to enjoy a banking monopoly for some thirty years, and to have shares in the amount of £3,000,000, including security in land, and to be tax free. The United States, the particular states, and foreigners would be permitted to subscribe. The bank would be authorized to lend money at 8 percent, to lend money to Congress, and to be responsible for the redemption of all paper then emitted. Its banknotes were to be received in payment of all customs duties and taxes. Recognizing that the United States at war's end and for some time thereafter would have "a national debt," Hamilton had no qualms, but insisted that "a national debt shall be a national blessing."[106]

Hamilton's plan was perhaps too grandiose for its time, but the more modest Bank of Pennsylvania did prepare the way for setting up a true commercial bank, the Bank of North America, which managed to have its charter squeak through Congress in May 1781. As Superintendent of Finance, Robert Morris subscribed on behalf of the government slightly more than 50 percent of the Bank's capital. Beginning operations in January 1782, the Bank was required to report to Morris at the close of every business day the state of the cash account and the notes issued and received. There was no limit set on the note issues, no requirement as to reserves, but the notes were made receivable for all taxes and debts to the United States, as Hamilton had proposed. While some constitutional questions were raised about the power of the United States in Congress Assembled to charter a bank,[107] that institution obtained charters or recognition of its national character from many of the states; some of them even granted it a monopoly of banking within the state. Not only did the Bank succeed in attracting private investors, who soon bought out the government shares, but it proved enormously useful in the handling of government finances. The Bank loaned the government money to tide it over temporary deficits, discounted its bills, and brought a degree of order into the collection and expenditures of the federal treasury. It handled funds of state and municipal agencies as well, along with a large commercial business, lending money on short-term credit. In short, from the point of view of both the businessman and the Congress it was a great success.[108]

The success of the Bank of North America spawned two other banks in the Confederation era. Alexander Hamilton, bypassing the state legislature, set up a "money" bank, the Bank of New York, and succeeded in obtaining an initial capital of $500,000. The bank set a discount rate at 6 percent, a thirty-day limit on loans, and permitted no renewals. It opened for business on June 9, 1784.[109] "Bankomania," as some critics called the movement, led to the establishment of a third bank during this period, the Bank of Massachusetts in Boston, chartered by the state legislature in February 1784, with a capital of £500,000, with accounts kept in Mexican dollars as was the case with the Bank of North America. Discounting rules were similar to those of the New York bank, with interest subtracted at the time of the issuance of the loan.[110]

The Paper Money and Debtor Relief Movements. The three banks operating in the Confederation years proved far short of providing the emergent nation with the credit facilities it needed to develop its economy in what was still a preindustrial stage, or to provide urgently needed relief to hard-pressed debtors. A shortage of currency cramped the economy of the Confederation years and spread debt across the nation. Specie quickly became extremely scarce, largely hoarded in seaboard towns, and lacking in uniform value. Rates of exchange varied from state to state. Although the medium of exchange for business transactions was the Spanish milled dollar, with other foreign coins in circulation as well, and although the

Continental Congress adopted the dollar in 1785,[111] this action did not effect a change in the money in circulation in the states. Rates varied from region to region. In Boston, the dollar was valued at 6 shillings; in New York, at 8; and in Philadelphia at 7s. 6d. In the Southern States, rates varied from a high of 32¼ s. to a dollar in South Carolina, to as low as 5 to the dollar in Georgia.[112]

The three banks extended short-term credit to merchants and shipowners, while refusing long-term loans to farmers, artisans, manufacturers, and land speculators. For long-term loans one had to seek out private moneylenders and usurers, the only source for private loans in the interior areas. Even in Massachusetts, however, where the sectional division seems especially evident and where the credit crunch was perhaps the most severe, the private lenders of the backcountry—shopkeepers, local officials, and traders—lent out, it is estimated, more than 85 percent of the region's money, often at exorbitant rates of interest, to farmers for home and farm mortgage payments, barn repairs, breeding cattle, or paying taxes. Understandably, Western moneylenders, as well as Easterners, were equally opposed to such radical nostrums as moratory legislation and reform of the judiciary, all favored by a majority of the region's voters.[113] Each one of the thirteen states found creditors arrayed against debtors without taking into account the massive claims of English and Scottish creditors for prewar debts, a subject that will be treated in the diplomatic section. Contrary to tradition as the Populist-Progressive historians would depict it, the division was neither geographical nor a clear-cut alignment of the rich against the poor. While this writer cannot accept the contention of a foremost authority on the history of banking that the "poor debtor" was a "myth,"[114] especially in light of the situation in New England in the late 1780s, there is no question that many rice and tobacco plantation debtors would scarcely be classified as "poor," and certainly not the big Maryland land speculators—Samuel Chase, Charles Ridgeley, and William Paca.[115] Thus, as Bray Hammond shows, men of substance, but in debt, in states like Maryland, Pennsylvania, and the Carolinas—and, one must add, Virginia, with its heavy prewar debt of planters to British and Scottish businessmen—had considerable in common with agrarian debtors.[116] In some states like Pennsylvania and Maryland, it was the speculative rich debtors who took the initiative in seeking relief through paper emissions. Thomas Paine described "a set of men who go about making purchases upon credit, and buying estates they have not wherewithal to pay for; and having done this, their next step is to fill the newspapers with paragraphs of the scarcity of money and the necessity of a paper emission, then to have a legal tender under the pretence of supporting its credit, and when out, to depreciate it as fast as they can, get a deal of it for a little price, and cheat their creditors; and this is the precise history of paper money schemes."[117]

In Maryland, the pressure to provide cheap money was spearheaded by Samuel Chase, financially embarrassed by the enormous tracts of confiscated Loyalist lands that he had bought. His proposal in 1785 for a paper money emission was opposed by his arch enemy Charles Carroll of Carrollton. By rejecting the bill, the state Senate split the conservative faction that had ruled the state since the Revolution and reversed emergency relief measures enacted during the war.[118] In South Carolina, bills of credit on the security of land were issued (acceptable in tax payments, but not legal tender) largely for the relief of debts incurred by planters for slave purchases. These bills passed at par and then at a modest discount, whereas the North Carolina emission of 1786 shrank to more than half of its face value. New Jersey issued legal tender bills of credit to be loaned to citizens on the security of unmortgaged real estate, but the bills were not accepted in New York and Pennsylvania, where, as James Madison pointed out, "all trade in New Jersey is carried."[119]

In New York the paper money partisans, so far as can be ascertained, comprised artisans, laborers, war veterans, small shopkeepers, along with land speculators. Their opponents rallied round the Chamber of Commerce of New York City, an organization of prominent businessmen, which adopted resolutions opposing legislative action and secured six hundred signatures to an anti-paper money petition. That was not enough to halt the passage of legislation in 1786 and again in 1787 authorizing bills of credit to be lent on real estate or plate at 5 percent, with two enactments passed in this period to relieve bankrupts. New York paper suffered only a moderate depreciation after initially passing at par.[120]

Although what Madison disdainfully called "a rage for paper

money" swept the states, he was able to keep it from inundating Virginia. Under his leadership the lower house refused to acknowledge the emission of paper money while still forgiving part of several levies and making it possible to meet others from hemp, flour, and tobacco warehouse receipts.[121] Virginia proved to be in the minority, for by 1786 seven states had resorted to paper money emissions in one form or another.

Most fiercely was the battle waged in Rhode Island, where the pro-paper country party was bitterly contested by the merchants. Outside the state, conservatives viewed Rhode Island as a center of riot and anarchy. In the *Anarchiad,* that satire in verse recounting the follies of the Confederation years, Rhode Island's apostasy from civilization was thus denounced:

> Hail! realm of rogues, renown'd for fraud and guile.
> All hail, ye knav'ries of yon little isle.
> There prowls the rascal, cloth'd with legal pow'r.
> To snare the orphan, and the poor devour;
> The crafty knave his creditor besets,
> And advertising paper pays his debts;
> Bankrupts their creditors with rage pursue
> No stop, no mercy from the debtor crew.
> Arm'd with new test, the licens'd villain bold,
> Presents his bills, and robs them of their gold.

In fact, the legal tender issue authorized by the legislature in May 1786 was more sweeping in character than in any other state and precipitated an historic clash between the legislature and the judiciary, in which the latter clearly affirmed the power of judicial review. What distinguished Rhode Island from the other paper money states was that the emission per capita was the largest and the legal steps taken to make it acceptable as legal tender unparalleled. All a debtor had to do was to deposit the bills with any county court judge in payment of his creditor. Anyone refusing to accept the bills at face value was liable to a fine of £100, triable in special three-judge courts without a jury. The enforcement provisions divided town against country and caused a "convulsion," as Madison described it. The "convulsion" prompted John Jay to raise a query as to how long the people of Rhode Island would remain obedient to "the very extraordinary and exceptionable laws passed, for compelling them to embrace the doctrine of the political transubstantiation of paper into gold and silver."[122]

Inevitably the contest over paper money brought on that classic confrontation between legislature and judiciary previously treated. In the end, both sides won. The legislature repealed the penalties for noncompliance and within six months all but one of the judges had returned to private life.[123] Five years later, after the federal Constitution was in effect, the legislature of Rhode Island appears to have acquiesced in a decision of the state court holding the legal tender statute invalid "on the principle that by the adoption of the Constitution that act was virtually repealed."[124] Finally, the crisis in Massachusetts and New Hampshire created by the impasse between creditors and debtors and the obdurate position of the states themselves brought on the violent collision to be treated hereinafter.

By way of postscript, it is interesting to note that almost at the last minute a provision was inserted into the federal Constitution by the Committee of Style forbidding states to emit bills of credit or to "make anything but gold or silver coin a tender in payment of debts; pass any bill of attainder, ex post facto law, or law impairing the obligation of contracts" (Article I, section 10). This last clause was added to make sure that the term "ex post facto," which normally refers to criminal cases, would be framed to fit civil cases as well. It was prompted directly by a response to the paper money, insolvency, and stay laws which had been passed in mounting numbers just prior to the adoption of the Constitution. Rufus King had failed to persuade his colleagues on the floor in late August of 1787 of the usefulness of imposing some restraint on the power of the states to "interfere in private contracts." When the Convention considered this prohibition on September 14, it accepted the addition by the Committee of Style without a murmur, pausing only to tighten it slightly. No such prohibition was imposed upon the Congress, however, despite the efforts of Elbridge Gerry.[125]

No statesman was more eloquently explosive on the subject of paper money and moratory legislation than Madison, with perhaps Rufus King a close second. In *Federalist* No. 10, Madison prophesied that "a rage for paper money, for an abolition of debts, or for any other wicked or improper project, will be less apt to pervade the whole union than a particular member of it." Appropriately, Madison is entitled to the last word on this subject. In *Federalist* No. 54, he stoutly advocated the constitutional prohibition against the issuance by the states of bills of credit and the impairment of contracts. "The extension of the prohibition of bills of credit," argued Madison,

must give pleasure to every citizen, in proportion to his love of justice, and his knowledge of the true springs of public prosperity. The loss which America has sustained since the peace from the pestilent effects of paper money on the necessary confidence between man and man, on the necessary confidence in the public councils, on the industry and morals of the people, and on the character of republican government, constitutes an enormous debt against the states chargeable with this unadvised measure, which must long remain unsatisfied; or rather an accumulation of guilt, which can be expiated no otherwise than by a voluntary sacrifice on the altar of justice, of the power which has been the instrument of it.

In a closing argument, by way of summation, Hamilton in *Federalist* No. 85 joins Madison in condemnation, with a moral note that touches the heights of hyperbole:

. . . the precautions against the repetition of those practices on the part of the state governments, which have undermined the foundations of property and credit, have planted mutual distrust in the breasts of all classes of citizens, and have occasioned an almost universal prostration of morals.

Changing Trade Patterns

For those who believed that commerce was the lifeblood of America's recovery from its economic slump, much attention was given to new initiatives in opening up nontraditional patterns of trade. The restrictions that the British imposed, both on trade with their West Indies and their home ports, were so severe that one is inclined to overlook the fact that restrictive trade measures were also being imposed by America's ally, France, and in turn by Louis XVI's ally, Spain, and that the Mediterranean was initially closed to American ships by the depredations of the Barbary pirates. Efforts to negotiate treaties with the European and North African states will be considered in chapter VIII.

The one significant trade breakthrough that occurred in the Confederation years was the opening to China and India. Having successfully seceded from the British Empire, the United States had sacrificed certain trade advantages it had hitherto enjoyed, but it was by the same event liberated from restrictions forbidding Americans from trading eastward of the Cape of Good Hope and from importing the products of Asia and the East Indies except from Britain. Furthermore, a French ruling in 1784 permitted American ships to use islands in the Indian Ocean as ports of call.

The Americans seized quickly upon the loopholes and liberties. First, the sealanes to China were opened, and with them a market in the United States for teas, silks, spices, and chinaware, as well as an export market for ginseng, a wild forest medicinal plant, and in later years for furs from the Pacific Northwest. The initiative came from a consortium of Morris, Duer, Parker, and John Holker that would finance the first extensive trading voyage to China via the Cape of Good Hope. The *Empress of China,* of 360 tons, sailed from New York in February 1784, laden with 40 tons of ginseng and other goods. The vessel stayed four months in Canton, returning to New York on May 11, 1785, with a cargo of teas, silks, nankeens, chinaware, and cassia, and netting a profit of $37,000 on an outlay of $120,000. This venture was duplicated by the *Grand Turk,* financed by Elias Hasket Derby of Salem, and later voyages by John Brown of Providence.[126]

Trade with India, encouraged by Richard Tilghnam of Baltimore, was inaugurated in 1786 by the voyage of the *Chesapeake* of Baltimore, commanded by Captain John J. O'Donnell. As a mark of special favor, the ship was exempted by the Supreme Council of Bengal from all customs duties, and the government of India followed with an order that American ships at the East India Company's settlements should be treated in all respects as the most favored foreigners, a policy confirmed by Article XIII of the Jay Treaty with Britain of 1794. In fact, it was estimated that before 1790 the total American tonnage in the Indian ports exceeded that at Canton.[127]

These new trade patterns, as well as prospective ones, prompted John Jay, the Secretary for Foreign Affairs, to establish a consular system to handle duties previously performed by commercial agents.[128] Consuls, at Jay's prodding, were designated in some nineteen foreign ports.[129] Appropriately on Jay's recommendation the consular post at Canton was filled by Samuel Shaw, supercargo on the initial voyage of the *Empress of China*.

One regrettable result of the trade obstacles confronting postwar America was the temptation to resume the slave trade with Africa. Between 1783 and 1785 seven thousand blacks were reputed to have been imported into South Carolina. The *Maryland Journal* reported in June 1785 that American vessels, "mostly from Boston," abounded on the Guinea coast, carrying New England rum to be exchanged for slave cargoes.[130]

A most troublesome trade issue, however, revolved around negotiations for a consular convention with France that would be acceptable to both the Secretary for Foreign Affairs and the minister to France, Thomas Jefferson. The lengthy negotiations and the relatively satisfactory results for the United States will be treated in the section on diplomacy.

In sum, a key aim of American diplomacy was to open trade with countries with whom the Americans as colonists had lacked direct trade relations or to secure commercial treaties which would augment such trade as existed. Commercial treaties with the Dutch, the Swedes, and the Prussians were made, as well as one with Morocco toward the end of the Confederation era as a step toward freeing American shipping and seamen from depredations of the Barbary pirates, whose attacks had effectively closed the Mediterranean to American trade.

CHAPTER 7

A Cautiously Transforming Egalitarianism

THE Constitution proclaims itself to be a creation of "We the People." As the nationalists who drafted it were to interpret the Preamble, that document was adopted by ratifying conventions of the *people of the states* rather than by the states themselves, and its sanctions went directly to the people.[1] Under this new charter of governance, many Americans would enjoy rights and privileges unparalleled in the contemporary world. One could argue that the Constitution reflected that cautiously transforming egalitarianism which marked the Revolutionary era.

The fact is that, unlike the Great Declaration, which, as one perceptive scholar has observed, "introduced an egalitarian rhetoric to an unequal society,"[2] the Constitution has no place for the word "equality." The Framers were more concerned about creating an effective national government than in underpinning notions of equality, which they deemed unrealistic if not unattainable. Some of the Founding Fathers were rather emphatic on the subject. "All men are men, and not angels," John Adams observed, "nor are they lions or whales or eagles." In fact, "the most that equality of nature amounts to," Adams concluded, is that they were "all of the same species."[3] James Madison frequently remarked on the inequality of talents, wealth, and conditions of men, perhaps most notably in the 10th *Federalist,* while James Wilson told his law students that the declaration that all men are created equal was not meant to apply "to their virtues, their talents, their dispositions, or their acquirements. In all three respects," he concluded, "there is, and it is fit for the great purposes of society that there should be, great inequality among men."[4]

What the Founding Fathers were committed to was equality of opportunity, an equality made possible by the availability of freehold land under a national land system devised for an expanding frontier. Equality of opportunity would not be curbed by special privileges, monopolies, titles of nobility, or hereditary honors, and would be promoted in the states by the abolition of primogeniture and entailed estates and a variety of other reforms in education and in criminal and civil law. The reformers did not aim at social leveling, which the Founding Fathers would have looked on with abhorrence. Still, James Madison did keep the door ajar. The due process clause in his Bill of Rights would provide a plastic conception, one day to be expanded to include rights which even Madison did not envision. The incorporation principle adopted by the Supreme Court of our century fixed upon the states as well as the federal government the restraints of a number of the first Ten Amendments, the intention of Madison's proposed draft in which Congress had not concurred.

The equality that foreign travelers found in America at the time of the adoption of the Constitution was evident in a decline of deference, a trend that fell short of overthrowing the divisions of society by orders or classes. What the American Revolution produced was a sweeping change in the elites: the Patriot Whig elite now supplanting royal officials and affluent Tories. A half century later Tocqueville might fix upon the equality of social condition as "the salient feature of American society," but the destruction of gentry leadership that he was witnessing did not occur in the years of the Confederation.

In short, what observers noted was a cautiously transforming egalitarianism. Political upward mobility was indubitably advanced. In most states Catholics and Jews were enfranchised and church establishment terminated. Despite the existence of property qualifications for voting—qualifications that are sidestepped in the Constitution, which leaves such matters to the states—in practice 50 to 80 percent of the adult white males were enfranchised, although voter turnouts in these years seldom exceeded 36 percent of adult males. The franchise was not really a serious issue among the working class, which had already substantially won the franchise. What working people were concerned about was their suitability for elective office and their power to control their representatives once they were elected.[5] So far as holding federal office was concerned, neither the Articles of Confederation nor the federal Constitution prescribed any property qualifications. Only the Northwest Ordinance set a minimum requirement for its representatives to the territorial assemblies of 210 acres of land in fee simple within the district they represented.

Impressive strides were made in the Confederation years in correcting the inequitable representation of the interior and the upcountry, often highlighted by moving state capitals from tidewater to upland. By issuing copious amounts of paper currency, anathema to a James Madison, or by shifting taxes from polls to property, or from equal acreage to ad valorem taxes, the states were in effect shifting the burdens from the poor to the rich—from the debtor to the creditor—but *not* universally, or we would not have had Shays' Rebellion concluded only months before the convening of the Federal Convention.

In no area is the egalitarian impact of the American Revolutionary era more visible than in the opportunities for new men to enter government as well as business and the professions. The Philadelphia grandee who complained that the Revolution brought all the "dregs" to the top may have had in mind New Jersey's "poor man's lawyer" Abraham Clark, or New York's Abraham Yates, Jr., shoemaker-lawyer and unreconstructed Antifederalist, or the Pennsylvania frontier trio of John Smilie, William Findley, and Robert Whitehill. In the same category one could cite such delegates at the Philadelphia Convention as Irish-born William Paterson, son of a tinplate worker, and the Connecticut Yankee Abraham Baldwin, self-educated son of a blacksmith, who represented Georgia to which state he had removed. All bypassed the social hierarchy despite their lack of polish and their meager educational backgrounds. Indeed, socioeconomic mobility of the pre-Revolutionary and Revolutionary years has been a recent focus of significant investigation, and the emergent picture is conflicting, both urban and rural. Clearly the rich were getting richer while the less affluent were also improving their economic prospects, albeit at a decidedly slower pace.[6] However, even the most critical of foreign observers would grudgingly concede that ranks were not fixed as in Europe, while wealth and reputation were fluid and variable.[7]

Certainly the omission of the word "equality" from the Constitution did not deter the working people in the cities and larger towns from giving overwhelming support to the Constitution. Indeed, one of the remarkable stories of the period is the transformation of a radical anti-Tory working class into a fervent supporter of an effective national government which would impose uniform tariffs, prevent foreign dumping, and encourage domestic manufactures. That alliance toward the close of the Confederation period of free labor with business and professional people was evidenced in every leading town where the respective states' ratification of the Constitution was celebrated by grand parades, in which participants were arrayed by trades, occupations, and professions. Far from regarding the Constitution as a reaction and betrayal of the American Revolution, as unreconstructed Antifederalists viewed it then and Populist-Progressive historians have depicted it in more recent times, the urban working men hailed it as a fulfillment of the purposes for which the war had been fought—national independence.

The Movement for Law Reform

The property-conscious common-lawyers who played so conspicuous a role in the movement for independence from Great Britain and in the drafting of state constitutions and bills of rights, as well as in their sponsorship of the federal Constitution, were neither millenarians nor utopians. True, the reforms they sought in the field of private law had both an egalitarian and a humanitarian end, but one could hardly deem them revolutionary. Such reforms as were achieved were effected through the legislatures, not the courts. The role of the judge had not yet been regarded as one of making new law but rather in the "exposition of the existing" law.[8] The proposals for reform, while in part a response to the felt needs of a new republican order, clearly reflected the reformist impulses of the European philosophes. As one scholar has felicitously described the process, "it was Americans who not only embraced the body of Enlightenment principles but wrote them into law, crystallized them into institutions, and put them to work."[9]

The fact that the most comprehensive movements for reform

occurred in Virginia and Pennsylvania is in no small part a tribute to Thomas Jefferson and Benjamin Rush. Of all Americans of that era, Jefferson's commitment to reform proved the most encompassing and, in terms of his personal commitment, the most enduring. Serving in the Virginia House of Delegates from October 1776 until June 1779, Jefferson, with the support of a few prestigious colleagues, sought to republicanize the legal system "with a single eye to reason, and the good of those for whose government it was formed." In the comprehensive sweep of his program, Jefferson's law revisions stood unrivaled. By June of 1778 he and his colleagues on the Committee of Revisors had proposed 127 bills ranging from land reform to liberty of conscience and public education.[10]

A movement of long duration, covering proposals never embodied in a single enactment, including education and reforms of the institution of slavery, both bypassed, the program first successfully targeted the land law, by which Jefferson hoped to supplant "an aristocracy of wealth" with "an aristocracy of virtue and talent." Jefferson achieved a notable success in 1776 with the enactment of a statute declaring tenants in tail of land or slaves to be holders in fee simple, and subsequently in 1785 by the enactment ending primogeniture (descent to the first-born son). Emulating Virginia's example, the other states abolished primogeniture except in New England and Pennsylvania, where partible descent (including other children) had always been the rule (with Rhode Island as the notable exception). Some of the state laws ended or transformed the character of entails (restricting ownership to inheritable life estates), thereby paying tribute to the pervasive notion that legal devices for the descent and distribution of land must, so far as possible, provide an egalitarian base for unfettered landholdings.[11]

What was important here to Jefferson was the principle rather than the result. Entails acted as a clot, stopping the free circulation of land, whose liquidity was desperately needed by a heavily indebted planter class, and the practice set a poor example for the egalitarian society that Jefferson envisioned. True, an entail, prior to this legislation, could be docked by a private legislative act, but the process was costly, the enactment had to be approved by the Privy Council in England, and the proper people abroad had to be taken care of to ensure that the act of entailment would not be disallowed. Now with one bold stroke Jefferson had converted entails to fee simple holdings.[12]

The egalitarian effects of the abolition of entails and primogeniture have, we now believe, been given undue weight. Diggers in county courthouses have shown that, although there were some large estates held in fee tail, like the bulk of the estate of Thomas, sixth Lord Fairfax of Cameron, ending entail did not bring about substantial redistribution of landholdings. Most Southern planters made ample provisions in their wills for the younger children in their families and a number of legal decrees for breaking entails were already in wide use.[13] Indeed, if one stops to compare large landholdings in the South during the age when entail and primogeniture were in operation with the national period, when partible descent prevailed, one soon discovers that the later period witnessed a far more extensive consolidation of landholdings than had characterized pre-Revolutionary times, attesting to the far greater leverage exerted by economics and technology than by the laws on the statute books.

Jefferson properly considered a reform of the real property laws as central to transforming a land-structured society in an egalitarian direction. As he interpreted legal history, the introduction of feudalism into England by the Normans brought about a system of inequality that was not appropriate for emigrants to America, persons who, as he put it, "were laborers, not lawyers." To make sure that the undistributed land was considered as belonging to all the people, he advocated legislation striking at feudalism by making land allodial. Other states quickly followed suit. In Virginia and elsewhere, notably in Maryland, quit rents were abolished, and manorial privileges, as in New York, were relegated to oblivion without however affecting the leases governing the rented lands.[14] Thus the marginal vestiges of feudal control had largely disappeared by the time of the adoption of the Constitution, and Americans could look forward to acquiring fee simple land in freehold tenure and hopefully to a country where wealth did "not form a permanent distinction."[15]

The confiscation of the immense Tory estates and the opening up of the West provided a magnificent opportunity to create a society of small freeholders. However, unless quick action were taken, the land jobbers and monopolizers were certain to assume the initiative. So prescient a statesman as Jefferson anticipated the problem. He sought unsuccessfully to incorporate curbs on the ownership of the unappropriated lands in the various drafts he formulated for the Virginia Constitution of 1776. His Land Office Ordinance of 1779, which speculators managed to evade, had similar purport; his Ordinance of 1784 was one of the most notable pieces of legislation of the old Congress under the Confederation[16] and deserves separate attention. Jefferson was not alone in his concern. So voracious a land speculator and engrosser as Robert Morris warned Congress in 1782 that "a large proportion of America is the property of great landholders," who "monopolize without cultivation."[17]

If more democratic landholdings resulted from the confiscation of Tory estates, that was not the initial purpose of the attaints of their owners and the sale of their properties. The forfeitures were imposed for punitive and fiscal reasons, not out of egalitarian concerns, and the pattern of distribution of Tory lands varied from colony to colony and from county to county. In New York City and Annapolis, expensive urban properties were acquired by speculators and wealthy investors. To the contrary, in rural Dutchess County, New York, and on Philipsburgh Manor, as well as in Frederick County, Maryland, manor tenants exercised preemption rights and became freeholders as a result of confiscations. Small landowners in New Jersey's Somerset County found extreme difficulty in picking up forfeited estates, as confiscations proved a windfall to wealthy insiders. Not only that, but when estates were broken up they often went to enlarge the holdings of adjacent farmers, thereby leading to a concentration rather than to a break-up of holdings. A complex subject, indeed, and one that merits a precise area-by-area investigation before any valid generalization can be drawn about what seemed on paper to have the broadest social implications of any of the Revolutionary measures adopted by the American Patriots. The evidence, still tentative, does suggest that rural holdings were, if not at once, then in time subdivided. Urban properties went from the affluent of one camp to those of the other.[18] In some states such as Massachusetts actual confiscation was carried out on a limited scale and the Loyalists were remarkably successful in protecting their property.

A major target of law reformers in the years under review was the system of penal laws, varying from state to state. Whether the punishment of delinquency commanded attention because of concern over an apparently rising incidence of crime during and after the war, it is clear that American reformers sought to adapt to their respective states the notions of Italy's great penological reformer, Cesare Beccaria, and of England's John Howard.[19]

To Jefferson, the criminal law had become a moribund relic of judicial legerdemain.[20] In the preamble to his bill for a complete reform of the penal code, he defined the legislature's duty as the arranging "in a proper scale the crimes which it may be necessary to repress, and to adjust thereto a corresponding gradation of punishment." Not only did Jefferson feel that punishment should be proportionate to the injury, but, committed as he was to the "reformation of offenders," he was persuaded that capital punishments "exterminate" instead of reform. However, his Bill No. 64 "for proportioning crimes and punishments" and limiting capital crimes to murder and treason was finally defeated, but emerged in 1796 in legislation, by which time the example of Pennsylvania and the ripening of public opinion, Jefferson explained, provided a more receptive climate for penological reform in Virginia.[21]

Jefferson, who had spent considerable time in Philadelphia in attendance at the Continental Congress, was impressed by the advice to the legislature of that state contained in the Pennsylvania Constitution of 1776, wherein the legislators were directed to make punishments "less sanguinary, and in general, more proportionate to the crimes,"[22] and Pennsylvania's amended penal laws of 1785 carried a preamble emphasizing the importance of correction and reform as a deterrence to crime.[23] Accordingly, the death penalty was reduced to four crimes. Other felons were subject to sentence to hard labor instead of being executed or corporally punished as formerly.

If Pennsylvania moved further ahead in its program of penological reform than any other state in these years, it was in no small measure a tribute to the ceaseless activities of that extraordinary humanitarian Dr. Benjamin Rush. Edinburgh- and London-educated, Rush combined politics and medicine with moral and practical reforms. A firebrand revolutionary, renowned as a teacher of chemistry and medicine, an American pioneer in what we would now call psychiatry, ceaselessly active in organizations whether scholarly or reform-minded, he opposed slavery and the slave trade, and proposed far-reaching educational reforms. Preferring more emphasis on practical rather than classical studies, favoring education for women and girls as well as for men and boys, he saw the need for each generation to instruct the next in the necessity of republican virtue.[24]

Rush managed to devote considerable attention to penal reform, influenced by the English prison reformer John Howard, as well as by Beccaria. He opposed capital punishment, and his paper, *An Enquiry into the Effects of Public Punishments upon Criminals and upon Society*, read at the home of Benjamin Franklin on March 9, 1787, forecast the future development of penology in America for the next hundred years. Arguing that public punishments were inconsistent with the goals of reforming, deterring, or isolating dangerous criminals, he proposed instead their solitary confinement in a large building to be constructed in a remote part of the state, where prisoners

The Walnut Street Prison in Philadelphia. Facing the State House Yard, now Independence Square (From an engraving by W. Birch)

would be put to work in complete silence. His Philadelphia Society for Alleviating the Miseries of Public Prisons advocated separating hardened criminals from first offenders, as well as separating the sexes and the debtors. Rush's reforms were enacted in part in 1789–90. While the proposed model penitentiary was not then provided for, the latter act called for the erection in the jail yard of tiny cells for hardened offenders to perform their tasks, isolated from the common yard by a wall. Rush's campaign against capital punishment led to legislation limiting the death penalty to murder in the first degree, while the Walnut Street Prison, with its solemn atmosphere and work ethic, bore testimony both to Rush's reformist zeal and to Howard's blueprint.[25]

Pathbreaking though Pennsylvania and Virginia may have been in the area of penal reform, they were not matched in these years by the remaining states. Despite minor limits on capital crimes, elsewhere no meaningful changes in the criminal law were instituted during the remainder of the eighteenth century.[26] This was true of law reform in general during the years of the Confederation. Save for liberalizing the divorce law in some states, continuing the practice of arbitration in legal disputes, and minor reforms in procedure and practice, the major reforms in the law were left to be dealt with in the century that followed.[27] The instrumental role that the courts would play in the undergirding of an entrepreneurial society was but faintly visible in the years before the Constitution went into operation.

The Movement for Liberty of Conscience

Indubitably the most important reforms of the Revolutionary and postwar years were achieved in the area of freedom of conscience and in efforts to end religious discrimination at law. So pervasive was the movement's impact on American society that central aspects of it have already been addressed in the initial chapter of this book. The movement really had three targets. It aimed at establishing freedom of conscience; the removal of civil or political disabilities on dissenters, Deists, and non-Christians; and the disestablishment of the churches.

The first of these was most easily addressed. Beginning with Virginia, the bills of rights and constitutions of all states guaranteed religious freedom with the exception of South Carolina, which made no mention of religion. These provisions fell far short of ending discrimination against various sects. Religious tests for officeholding in a number of states such as Massachusetts and Pennsylvania effectively barred Catholics, Jews, and atheists. Such restrictions were rather quickly removed in some states—by Virginia in 1785, by Georgia in 1789, by Pennsylvania and South Carolina in 1790, and by Delaware and Vermont in 1792 and 1793, respectively. Still other states were slower to respond.[28]

What one must bear in mind in connection with the movement for disestablishment, initiated by Jefferson and carried through in Virginia by Madison, is not only that the laws affected the Church of England, which had been established in the Southern colonies and the four lower counties of New York, but that in some six states multiple establishments existed, testimony to the pluralistic character of religion in America by the time of the Revolution, with the rapid rise of dissenting denominations. In such states, establishment included the church of every Christian denomination and sect with sufficient number of adherents to form a church. In some cases Protestantism was established; in others, Christianity. In such states where multiple establishment existed, one church was not preferred to others, even in New England where the Congregational Church was dominant.[29] Disestablishment, initiated in Pennsylvania in this period by its Constitution of 1776 and successfully accomplished in Virginia as a result of Madison's heroic efforts, both literary and political, was also effected between 1777 and 1790 in New York, Delaware, New Jersey, North Carolina, and Georgia, but was not completed in such multiple establishment states as those of New England until the nineteenth century, with Rhode Island the pioneer exception, for it never did have an established church.

Even the Continental Congress found itself involved in the controversy. In 1785, a committee of the Congress dominated by New Englanders proposed a plan for the settlement of the Western states that set aside lot number 29 of each township for the "support of religion" or for charitable purposes, the determination to be made by the majority of inhabitants of each township. Congress defeated the proposal. James Madison's adverse reaction was prompt: "How a regulation so unjust in itself, so foreign to the authority of Congress, so hurtful to the sale of public land and smelling so strongly of antiquated Bigotry, could have received the countenance of a committee is truly a matter of astonishment."[30] But that was not quite the end of the matter. Following the adoption of the Northwest Ordinance, and while Madison was attending the Constitutional Convention, Congress on July 23 authorized the sale by the Board of the Treasury of large tracts of land to the Ohio Company's agent, the Reverend Manasseh Cutler, a wheeler-dealer from New England, with the provision that lot number 29 of each township be given for the support of religion. This arrangement may be seen as an attempt to reconcile Article I of the Northwest Ordinance providing for liberty of conscience with the third article declaring that "religion, morality, and knowledge being necessary for good government and the happiness of mankind," schools "and the means of education shall forever be encouraged."[31]

Hence the extraordinary action of the old Congress, taken while the Constitutional Convention was in session, undergirds the importance of the restriction upon Congress imposed by the First Amendment (and now by incorporation imposed upon the states as well). It is significant, too, on the basis of their own disestablishment laws, that of the eleven states that ratified the First Amendment, only Vermont and New Hampshire failed to subscribe to the proposition that the support of religion and churches should be a personal and voluntary matter, and that any financial assistance by government to religion constituted an establishment of religion and violated its free exercise.[32]

Persons Forgotten

The movement for reform, with its egalitarian overtones, constitutes only a part of the story, however. The original Constitution we now recognize to have been basically a document of governance for free white propertied adult males, free from dependence upon others. Left out of its text, or dealt with ambiguously, were the forgotten people—those bound to servitude, white or black (slavery was implicitly rather than overtly recognized), debtors, paupers, Indians, and women, most of whom were not considered a part of the political constituency. True, the Founding Fathers held diverse views on the score of blacks, Indians, and women, but managed to sidestep a direct confrontation on each of these issues.

Poor Whites. Let us now focus on these forgotten people—in numbers, a majority of the nation's inhabitants in 1787. It may, perhaps, come as a surprise to learn that so many white males fell into this category. In one form or another these people were victims of the harsh laws relating to indebtedness. Perhaps our comprehension of and sympathy for the plight of the debtor in the early national era may be quickened when we realize that mortgage foreclosures in the 1980s have exceeded any total since the Great Depression years, and that this cyclical problem is still not resolved. In the 1780s, as Shays' Rebellion highlights, the burden of debt in the wake of the first depression in our national history (one beginning in 1784 and continuing down through the establishment of the national government) spared neither poor nor rich. Victims of the speculative orgies of the 1790s like Robert Morris, William Duer, and even Supreme Court Associate Justice James Wilson, attest to the unrelenting pressures against delinquent debtors.

The men who drafted the Constitution, men of the stamp of Madison, Hamilton, Gouverneur Morris, and Rufus King, were determined that debtor relief in the form of paper money issued by the states and various forms of moratory legislation should not be tolerated. In *Federalist* No. 10, Madison expressed his satisfaction that under the Constitution, "a rage for paper money, for an abolition of debts, for an equal distribution of property, or for any other improper or wicked project, will be less apt to pervade the whole body of the Union than a particular member of it." And the Constitution reflected Madisonian thinking. It forbade states to issue bills of credit, "make anything but gold or silver coin tender in payment of debts," or enact laws "impairing the obligation of contracts."

Voltaire pointed out that in England, "if a poor fellow cannot readily pay a little money when his hands are at liberty, the better to enable him to do it, they load him with handcuffs." Voltaire's satirical observation would have been as applicable to the United States at the time of the adoption of the Constitution. Despite the passage of a considerable body of remedial legislation providing partial release from imprisonment for debt, reform of the debt laws in the early national era had a low priority; but there had always been an alternative. Because of the continuing labor shortage, laws enacted in colonial days releasing the debtor from prison to serve his creditor or his assigns for a period of time sufficient to discharge the debt remained on the books during the Confederation years, with Massachusetts having the dubious honor of lodging in jail the most highly publicized number of insolvent debtors or selling them off as servants.

While a variety of organizations for the relief of insolvent debtors lobbied for a reform of this system, at best only partial relief was provided by the states on the eve of the Federal Convention. In fact, if there was a reform movement against incarceration of defaulting debtors, it clearly was directed toward the merchant and the speculator, not the workingman and the small farmer. Such discrimination was frankly avowed by Zephaniah Swift, the Connecticut jurist writing toward the close of the century. Swift differentiated between the honest and the fraudulent debtor as regards treatment at law, while making a further distinction between laboring men and persons of substantial property, a distinction that few would be willing to accept as valid in our own time.[33] In sum, at the time of the adoption of the federal Constitution the elimination of servitude for white debtors was still several decades away, as was the abolition of imprisonment for debt. Save for seamen, who were not relieved from their compulsory labor obligations until federal legislation in the twentieth century, liberal insolvency laws had by the 1830s virtually ended specific performance of labor contracts by white workers.

Aside from the usual category of debtors, whether from trade or as farm mortgagors, there was a substantial body of indentured servants, largely redemptioners, who were bound to labor for periods of years as determined by written agreements or by the custom of the respective colony or state in return for passage from Europe. In effect, they were contract laborers. Outcroppings of protest arose against a system which was riddled with fraud. It separated families. It imported women on occasion for immoral purposes. It exploited labor, largely unskilled farm labor, without any wage payments except freedom dues at the end of the servant's term—usually a suit of clothes, a gun, and a hoe. With the heavy wave of immigration that followed the coming of peace a substantial number of the new arrivals came as redemptioners, although the numbers declined as a multitude of free workers deluged the labor market and hired hands became an integral part of the economy. However, vestiges of the redemptioner traffic could still be found in Pennsylvania,

Delaware, and Maryland well into the third decade of the nineteenth century.

At least apprentices to trades, who now faced serious competition from "green hands," including women and children used in the factory system, might take comfort from the prospect of expanded business activity anticipated as a result of the establishment of the new federal government. Contrariwise, bound servants discovered no tangible benefits from the two great national charters of 1787—the Northwest Ordinance and the federal Constitution. Each made a special point of protecting the property of masters in their servants. While barring slavery and involuntary servitude in the new territory (a prohibition honored in the breach so far as white servants were concerned), the Northwest Ordinance provided that "any person escaping into the same from whom labor service is lawfully claimed in any one of the original States" might be lawfully reclaimed (Article VI).

Article IV of the federal Constitution contains a similar provision for the return of persons escaping from labor service, while the so-called Fugitive Slave Law of 1793 nailed down the details of enforcement. Clearly, the protections that the new national government provided were protections for property owners, not for bound workers, white or black. Even when in later years imprisonment for debt was technically abolished, except for fraud, forms of debt servitude and contract labor continued to survive or surface well into the nineteenth century and in some instances much later.

The pool of white labor was swollen by two types of convict labor. The first, which attempted to resurface after the Revolution, comprised persons convicted of crimes or felonies in England, Scotland, and Ireland, and transported to the colonies for long terms; the second, of persons who were sentenced in the colonies to labor service in lieu of satisfying penalties exacted for a variety of crimes, mostly against property. In the six decades before the American Revolution some thirty thousand convicts were transported to America, more than two thirds of whom went to the Chesapeake colonies.[34] Despite hostile community feeling, convict shipments continued so long as employers felt it profitable to exploit their labor. During the Confederation years the British, despite America's newly won independence, attempted to dump convicts in this country, and in some cases succeeded. The intermittent operation of this surreptitious practice brought protests in the form of a resolution from the Continental Congress as late as September 1787, and a recommendation to the states to forbid the practice. The First Federal Congress was obliged to levy a tax on "the importation of certain persons," a tax aimed at convicts as well as slaves. Blocked in America, the British were forced to turn to Botany Bay to solve their convict problem.[35]

Another category of convict servants ranked among the forgotten people. This group comprised persons convicted of a variety of crimes under state laws, including larceny, arson, and bastardy. Traditionally, such malefactors had been sentenced by colonial courts to corporal punishment and to make multiple restitution of the value of the property stolen or damaged. Since invariably the prisoner was unable to make such restitution, he or she would become a judgment debtor and as such bound out to service by the court, a system well entrenched in Massachusetts and Pennsylvania in this period, with Indians, free blacks, and white servants customarily receiving heavier sentences to servitude than the rank and file of free whites.

Another, and a very substantial, addition to the labor market came from penalizing absentee or runaway servants by requiring them to serve an additional term amounting to as many as ten days for every day's unauthorized leave—a practice notably found in the tobacco states.[36]

Bastardy posed a special problem to early American communities, and the use of servitude for this offense continued down to relatively recent times in some states. The states continued their colonial practices of imposing additional terms of service on women servants for extramarital pregnancy, while selling into servitude the putative father for a four-year term when he defaulted in his obligation to enter into recognizance to provide a stated maintenance for the illegitimate child until the latter reached the age of twelve. The proceeds of such a sale of labor services were applied to the child's upkeep. In South Carolina the practice was not ended by law until 1847, and in North Carolina not until 1939.[37]

As the penitentiary system initiated in Pennsylvania with the start of the Revolution spread to other states, experiments began with programs of prison labor, but the practice of hiring out convicted persons to outside employers still continued.[38]

The word "welfare" appears twice in the Constitution. The Preamble declares the promotion of "the general Welfare" to be one of the purposes of the new government the Constitution is establishing, and Article I, section 8, empowers Congress to provide for "the general welfare." Does that suggest that it was the intent of the Framers to provide a welfare state, or a welfare program for the indigent poor and the unemployed? If they did so intend, they would have radically departed from the limited range of activities conducted by the Confederation government under the Articles of Confederation. Article IV of that earlier charter declared as its collective purpose "the better to secure and perpetuate mutual friendship and intercourse among the people of the different states of this Union, the free inhabitants of these states—paupers, vagabonds, and fugitives from justice excepted—shall be entitled to all privileges and immunities of free citizens in the several states." The corresponding section of the Constitution, Article IV, section 2 (the comity clause), drops the reference to paupers and vagabonds and simply reads: "The Citizens of each State shall be entitled to all the Privileges and Immunities of Citizens in the several States." Since the states retained the power to determine their own rules of citizenship, though not of naturalization, and since the comity clause has always been narrowly interpreted by the Supreme Court, no conclusive evidence can be discovered of an intent either to develop a nationally enforceable standard of equality or to extend privileges and immunities to the poor and the homeless.[39] "The day may come," one scholar suggests, "when the general doctrine under the fifth and fourteenth amendments recognizes for each individual a constitutional right to a decent level of affirmative governmental protection in meeting the basic human needs of physical survival and security, health and housing, work and schooling."[40] That time has not yet arrived, although recent generations have seen the federal and state governments making halting moves in such a direction. It certainly had not arrived when the Constitution was framed and ratified. Then poverty, pockets of which could be found in every state, was dealt with by binding out the poor to private persons or housing them in almshouses or workhouses. In rural New England, public auctions of paupers to the lowest bidder resulted in separating families and the constant shifting of indigent persons from location to location, as they were often sold off on a monthly or quarterly basis.[41] This system, both impersonal and inhumane, was found in the other states as well, and was perpetuated in the Northwest Territory.

Along with paupers, the authorities lumped into one unsavory category vagrants, transients, and "strollers," any or all of whom could be jailed, dumped in the workhouse, or hired out as laborers for wages. If defaulting, they could be sold at public vendue for terms ranging from six months to a year and a day, a sentence legislated in South Carolina the same year the Constitution was adopted.[42] In Georgia, they could be shipped out of the state.[43] However, by the Confederation era the trend in the larger cities was to place the indigent poor and the temporarily unemployed in workhouses or almshouses, which, as the New York law stated it, served also as a house of correction for "Beggars, Servants running away or otherwise misbehaving themselves, trespassers, Rogues, and *poor people* refusing to work."[44] As a consequence, the indigent, the homeless, the unemployed, and the transient poor remained subject to state and local controls or assistance long after the Constitution was ratified.

Black People. The word "slavery," Abraham Lincoln would one day note, was "hid away in the Constitution just as an afflicted man hides away a wen or cancer which he dares not cut out at once, lest he bleed to death." Lincoln's metaphor was peculiarly apt to the framing of the Constitution. Implicitly rather than overtly did the Constitution recognize slavery through its three-fifths formula for enumeration, its slave trade compromise, and its provision for the return of fugitives "to service or labor." Slavery may have been the subject of heated remarks during the Philadelphia Convention, but nowhere in the final draft of the Constitution does the word "slave," "Negro," or "black" appear. The drafters were guilty of more than negligent omission, since at the time they were debating the issues concerning black people, one seventh of the population of the thirteen states was held in slavery, with a sprinkling of free blacks enjoying at best a quasi-freedom.

Indeed, there is no doubt about the readiness of the Northern states to cut a deal on the slavery issue in order to preserve the Union. Still, the slavery compromises at the Philadelphia Convention do not accurately reflect the extent of the conflict then being waged between those moved by humanitarian, religious, and Revolutionary impulses on the one hand, and others accepting the necessity of compromise to preserve a Union threatened with division if not dissolution. Even Southerners were found to reflect such humanitarian impulses. That colorful and contentious planter and ex-slave trader, Henry Laurens, was perhaps the first Southerner to avow privately his readiness to apply the ideals of the Great Declaration to the bondsmen and women on his estates.[45] Yet so vaunted a liberal and humanitarian as Thomas Jefferson would soon find that efforts to ameliorate slavery in his own state would get nowhere and, if persisted in, could be politically damaging. We know that he tried unsuccessfully to write into the Virginia Constitution of 1776 a provision that "no person hereafter coming into the state would be held in slavery."[46] Not long after, in his original draft of the Declaration of Independence, he had ascribed to George III, among other wrongful acts, his insistence on continuing the external slave trade, only to see it stricken out by his fellow delegates. The record does not show that Jefferson put up any kind of fight to save this rhetorical, if substantively illogical, section.[47] Jefferson's notes of July 2 state that the clause was stricken "in complaisance to South Carolina and Georgia," adding, "Our Northern brethren felt a little tender for they had been pretty considerable carriers of [slaves]."[48]

Jefferson's antislavery efforts were not yet exhausted, however. In his 1783 draft of a new constitution for Virginia, he provided for the freedom of all children born of slaves after the year 1800, but the proposition was defeated. Again, and shortly thereafter, he attempted to bar slavery in the territories in the first territorial law of 1784, a remarkably democratic and anticolonial document, but his proposal was defeated by one vote, the delegates voting by states.[49] "The fate of millions unborn," Jefferson would later comment, "was hanging on the tongue of one man, and heaven was silent in that awful moment." Thereafter Jefferson proved much more ambivalent on the slavery issue. In his *Notes on Virginia* in 1785, he continued to favor gradual emancipation, while failing to include any such program in his revision of his state's laws. Whether Jefferson was conscious of his deep-seated anti-Negro feelings, which found expression in his view about the mental inferiority of the blacks, or whether as a political realist and later national party leader he yielded to conventional opinion, are arguable propositions to which numerous historians have addressed themselves.[50]

One must concede that the Revolution acted as a spur to the manumission of slaves in the South as well as the North, in most cases the beneficiaries of such freedom being the elderly, the infirm, and persons of mixed blood. Those making such bequests by will frequently avowed that they were prompted by reasons of humanity and conscience, and sometimes made respectable provisions for the well-being of their manumitted slaves. In general, however, laws enacted in the South permitting manumission were usually designed to prevent the master from shifting support of unwanted free blacks to the public. Since self-hiring was considered a device to circumvent curbs on manumission or an initial step to freedom, the practice was usually frowned upon by city ordinances and state laws, but the prohibitions were still evaded.

In short, aside from a few timid steps taken and the actions of individual slaveowners motivated by humanitarian impulses, the South during the years of the Confederation did little to ameliorate the condition of slavery. Instead of loosening the shackles, the South in most cases tightened such loopholes as existed. Instead of slavery declining in the upper South, a myth to which some historians have continued to cling, there is a considerable body of evidence to the contrary.[51]

Indubitably the sentiments voiced in the manumission instruments of these years could be matched by the pro-slavery petitions addressed in 1784 and 1785 to the Virginia General Assembly. The 1,244 signatures attached to these petitions evidence considerable opposition to manumission and overt hostility to the efforts of Quakers, Methodists, and others to ameliorate the condition of the blacks. To these petitioners, there was nothing hypocritical about their Revolutionary rhetoric in stressing property rights and liberty while denying such rights to the black population.[52] As such petitions and much other documentation underscore, most Southerners consistently regarded black men and women as outside the constituency and not included in the phrase "all men are created equal."

When one turns to the North, one finds a different and more complex set of attitudes. Largely as the result of pro-manumission organizations, whose leadership was primarily Quaker and Federalist, five Northern states, in addition to Vermont, which acted prior to its admission to the Union, initiated programs of manumissions before the Federal Convention assembled in May of 1787. Two other states followed soon thereafter. The antislavery activities were favored not only by their elitist leadership, including a Franklin, a Jay, and a Hamilton, but by factors of demography and the labor market. Of the Northern states, only New York had a substantial black population. Free labor was increasingly available and resentful of slave competition. The public authorities encouraged the white population to settle and guard the frontiers, while racial undercurrents, such as fear of miscegenation, should by no means be discounted. Slavery disappeared at a faster rate where blacks made up proportionately a smaller segment of the population. On the other hand, where the slave population was relatively substantial, notably in New York, manumission was tenaciously resisted. Of the states that adopted gradual emancipation statutes, New Jersey delayed the effects of abolition the longest, while its neighbor to the south, the state of Delaware, maintained slavery even after the Civil War. As late as February 8, 1868, both houses of the Delaware legislature by joint resolution rejected a proposed amendment to the state constitution prohibiting slavery or involuntary servitude, and despite the fact that the Thirteenth Amendment had become a part of the organic law of the land on December 18, 1865, the sale of free Negroes persisted beyond that date in Delaware.[53] Obviously, even though Delaware had adopted a limited manumission law back in 1787, the egalitarian impulse of the Revolutionary generation stirred not a ripple in that state.

It was one matter for Northern states to adopt measures ending slavery. It was another to carry them out. For example, Pennsylvania, the first state to pass a law for the gradual abolition of slavery, listed the ownership of some slaves as late as the census of 1840. Nor did the bill of rights affixed to New Hampshire's constitution of 1783 immediately bring slavery to an end in that state. Some one hundred and fifty slaves were reported in the New Hampshire census of 1790, after which the numbers shrank rapidly. There were still some thousand slaves in Rhode Island in 1790, underscoring the "gradual" nature of that state's emancipation act of 1784. Despite the Quock Walker Case in Massachusetts wherein Chief Justice William Cushing held that slavery was "as effectively abolished as it can be" by the assertion in the state's bill of rights "that all men are free and equal; and that every subject is entitled to liberty,"[54] slaves continued to be bought and sold in Massachusetts. Gradually the institution disappeared, either because the blacks now considered themselves free and quit their masters or because nervous owners disposed of their human property to Southern purchasers. By 1790 it had totally disappeared.

In New York, despite the valiant efforts of the New York Manumission Society organized in 1785, every step toward emancipation was contested. The proposition to free the slaves put forward by Gouverneur Morris and John Jay at the time of the drafting of the Constitution of 1777 disappeared from the final draft, and the proslavery forces, largely Antifederalist, held off gradual emancipation until July 4, 1799, when a Federalist governor, the committed antislavery leader John Jay, signed the legislative measure.[55]

Pregnant with historical potentialities were the antislavery lobbying efforts of the Pennsylvania and New York Manumission Societies in the summer of 1787. On June 2 of that year the Pennsylvania Society, probably at the initiation of its secretary, Tench Coxe, memorialized the Federal Convention to suppress the African slave trade, and a similar petition was drafted by the New York Society's president, John Jay. Knowing at first hand the sentiment of the Southern delegation on the slavery issue, Franklin, the Pennsylvania Society's president, suggested that the petition be let to "lie over for the present."[56] In turn, Alexander Hamilton, who had taken leave of the Convention some weeks before but had attended enough sessions to have gauged the temper of the delegates on this supersensitive issue, seems to have persuaded the New York Society to withhold its petition.[57] This was really a lull before the storm. Hardly had the First Congress, under the new federal government, begun its sessions when that body was confronted with petitions from antislavery groups, the first of these bearing the signature of Benjamin Franklin.[58] One day a rivulet would flood its banks and could not be harnessed.

On the national level the antislavery movement did score one notable victory, however: the inclusion by the Continental Congress of a provision in the Northwest Ordinance, lifted from Jefferson's earlier effort and moved on the floor by Nathan Dane, prohibiting slavery in the territories north and west of the Ohio. Almost at the very moment this vote was recorded, the delegates in Philadelphia were fashioning a series of compromises on slavery to avoid offending the sensibilities and to secure the votes of their Southern collaborators.[59]

What is especially revealing about popular opinion on this issue is the fact that, save for Rhode Island, which was late in coming into the Union and did in 1790 propose a constitutional amendment condemning the slave trade, not one ratifying convention submitted, among the several hundred amendments proposed, a single one dealing with slavery. Rather, one finds that the humanitarian impulse, however spiritedly advanced by abolitionist groups in the North, had limited impact in the free states in the years following the Constitutional Convention. Instead, we see decades marked by the passage of discriminatory legislation that kept free Negroes in the North in a status of quasi-bondage, excluded them in most states from the polls and the militia, managed to keep them off juries, while even barring their entry in some states. Segregation was widespread.[60]

When, in the March 25, 1820, issue of his antislavery journal *The Philanthropist,* Elisha Bates asserted that a "system of oppression is in full force against the man of color in the free states," he stood on solid ground. In the South, it goes without saying, the humanitarian impulse did not survive the Revolutionary era. Only a few years following the adoption of the Constitution the cotton gin and the use of long staple or sea island cotton fastened slavery on the South and Southwest, with a steady stream of slave manpower moving thence from the upper South.[61]

The Revolutionary impulse had shriveled, and that "dark gloominess hanging over the land," which John Woolman had perceived before the American Revolution began, still permeated American society both in the so-called free states and in the rest more firmly attached than ever to their "peculiar institution."

Native Americans. The brief reference to the Indians in the federal Constitution scarcely suggests the magnitude of the problem the Native Americans posed to the nation's security and expansion or the difficulties confronting the Indians in obtaining equitable treatment at the hands of competing sovereignties—Congress and the states. The Constitution grants Congress the power "to regulate commerce with foreign nations and among the several States and with the Indian tribes" (Article I, section 8). Save for the clause dealing with apportionment and direct taxes, excluding Indians "not taxed," the Constitution mentions them nowhere else.

At the Philadelphia Convention, Madison, who had long been irked by the ambivalent powers over the Indians granted under the Articles, proposed a more explicit provision, one that would confer upon Congress the power "to regulate affairs with the Indians as well within as without the limits of the United States." But by the time his proposal emerged from committee, it was reduced to the simple phrase, "and with the Indian tribes."[62] To this phrasing there was no recorded dissent. Terse and even cryptic as the phrase reads, Congress assumed thereunder the power to legislate trade and intercourse with the Indians. This supremacy over the states in Indian affairs was buttressed by the role the Constitution gives the Senate in treaty-making and by Congress's war powers.[63]

After their experience in war and postwar years at the hands of Western settlers and the states, the Indians might have been expected to welcome the apparent assertion of paramount authority over their affairs by the new federal government. By bad luck or miscalculation the Indians, with few exceptions, had allied themselves with the British against the Patriots. Hence, most white inhabitants, especially the frontier settlers who had experienced at first hand the ferocity of Indian warfare and had retaliated in kind, shared the view that the Indians deserved no more consideration than did the Loyalists whose lands had been forfeited and many of whom had been forced into exile. In most states they were denied civil rights and the right to vote.[64]

Both Congress and the states considered Indian lands a prize of war and a portion thereof as reparations for Indian hostility.[65] Their control would guarantee the security of Western settlement. Accordingly, Indian lands would be offered in lieu of back pay to officers and soldiers, sold to meet the debts incurred in fighting the war and to help defray the current expenses of government. To add to the complications, Indian lands lay athwart boundaries in dispute between such states as Massachusetts and New York, Pennsylvania and New York, and Virginia and Pennsylvania, among other contested areas.

Persistent tension in Indian-white relations was exacerbated by a growing disparagement of Indian life and culture and a deeply negative view of the potentialities for the assimilation or amalgamation of the Indians. With a few notable exceptions, among them Anthony Benezet, Thomas Jefferson, and John Jay, the Founding Fathers reflected the racist notions of the general public.[66]

In *The Federalist* No. 3, John Jay noted that "not a single Indian war has yet been occasioned by the aggressions of the present Federal government, feeble as it is, but there are several instances of Indian hostilities having been provoked by the improper conduct of the individual States, who either, unable or unwilling to restrain or punish offences, have given occasion to the slaughter of many innocent inhabitants." Jay obviously had in mind the massacre of the Christian Indians at Gnadenhutten in Ohio in 1782; and, in response, the torture and murder of Colonel William Crawford by the Delaware some months later.[67] Frontier tension reached its apex in 1786-87, with Secretary at War Knox informing Congress in the fall of '86 of Indian warfare in the Northwest and then, during the Federal Convention, reporting on July 18, 1787, that a war with the Creek and Cherokee tribes was imminent due to violations of the tribes' hunting grounds reserved to them in federal treaties.[68]

From the Indians' point of view, the full extent of the tragedy of the late war had become evident with the signing of the Preliminary Articles of Peace in Paris on November 30, 1782. Although Britain, France, and Spain had each in turn sought to curb American expansion, ostensibly out of concern for the Indians, no mention of the Indians can be found in the Preliminary Articles or in the Definitive Treaty of the next year. Instead, the British ceded to the United States lands occupied in substantial part by the Indians as far west as the Mississippi, as far north as the Great Lakes, and as far south as the northern border of the Floridas, which Spain regained.[69] Neither during the peace negotiations nor in the ratification of the treaty by Congress were the Indians ever consulted. Once the Preliminaries were signed, the British officials in America who dealt with the Indians tried to keep the terms of the treaty from them, but the news spread and aroused both indignation and apprehension among Britain's loyal allies.

The perceived need of white Americans for a national Indian policy had deep roots. One may trace it at least as far back as Franklin's Albany Plan of Union of 1754, which would have conferred upon the "President-General" exclusive regulation of Indian affairs. The problem sparked the Royal Proclamation of 1763 and the setting up of Superintendents of Indian Affairs for the Northern and Southern Departments. Between the Indians and the ever-expanding white settlers stood the royal government, presumably as the formers' protector. With a fighting rather than a declared war between England and its colonies under way, the Continental Congress had, on July 12, 1775, set up three departments to manage Indian affairs, "to preserve peace and friendship" with the said Indians, and to "prevent their taking any part in the present commotions."[70]

When drafts for the Articles of Confederation were initially proposed in the Continental Congress, first Franklin and then Dickinson would have conferred complete jurisdiction over Indian affairs upon Congress; but in its final form the Articles of Confederation contained a germ of ambiguity, which bedeviled relations between Congress and the states over Indian affairs for the entire span of the Confederation. Thus, Article IX, clause 1, granted Congress the "sole and exclusive right and power of determining peace and war . . . [and] entering into treaties and alliances. . . ." However, clause 4 of the same article, while presuming to reinforce the previous provision giving the United States in Congress assembled "the sole and exclusive right and power" of "regulating the trade and managing all affairs with the Indians," added the descriptive phrase "not members of any of the States," and tacked on the proviso that "the legislative right of any State within its own limits be not infringed or violated."[71]

Although some of the states assumed that the descriptive limitations over Indian affairs contained in the final Articles seriously curbed the authority of Congress, that body exercised some bold initiatives during the years of the Confederation. First, to clarify the authority of the federal government vis-à-vis the states, Congress issued a Proclamation on September 22, 1783, forbidding "all persons from making settlements on lands inhabited or claimed by the Indians, without the limits or jurisdiction of any particular State, and from purchasing or receiving any gift or cession of such lands or claims without the express authority and direction" of Congress. The Proclamation declared any such purchase or settlement lacking such authority null and void.[72]

Secondly, in pursuance of its asserted authority over Indian affairs, Congress, through federal commissioners, concluded a series of treaties with the Indians, starting in October 1784 with the Treaty at Fort Stanwix, New York. That treaty, made with the Iroquois Confederacy, included two members, the Oneida and Tuscarora tribes, who had been allies of the United States, while the remaining four had openly sided with the British. The latter were forced to make substantial concessions, including the abandonment of all Iroquois claims to land in the Old Northwest. In turn, the government guaranteed the territorial integrity of their allies, the Oneida and the Tuscaroras—a pledge that was never honored. Governor George Clinton of New York disputed the authority of Congress over tribal lands within the borders of the state, tried to obstruct the federal agents from concluding with the Indians, despite the fact that James Madison, along with Lafayette, attended the sessions, and in defiance of the opinion voiced by Madison at that time upholding Congress's authority to make such treaties.[73] Subsequently, in 1785 and 1788 Clinton coerced the Oneidas into turning over Indian title to over five and a half million acres of their aboriginal land, threatening to withhold state protection against trespassers on their lands if they persisted in refusing outright sale. Both New York "treaties" were concluded without the consent of the Confederation government or even its participation.[74] In addition, the Confederation government made treaties with the Wyandots and the Cherokee, both in 1785, and the following year with the Shawnee, the Choctaw, and the Chickasaw.[75]

As it moved toward replacing coercion by diplomacy in dealings with the Indians, the federal government in 1786 set up a Northern and a Southern Department for Indian Affairs to execute "such regulations as Congress shall, from time to time, establish respecting Indian affairs," and asserting exclusive power over trade with the Indian tribes.[76] A further step was taken in the spring of 1787, when at John Jay's prodding, Congress adopted a supremacy resolution, holding treaties of Congress binding on the entire nation.[77] The term "treaties," a later Supreme Court held, applied to Indians as well as "other Nations," basing its authority for negativing state actions contrary to Indian treaties on the supremacy clause of the Constitution (Article IV, clause 2), which took as its model the earlier congressional resolution.[78]

A fourth step taken by the old Congress was the adoption in July of 1787 of the Northwest Ordinance, whose Article III provided that "the utmost good faith shall always be observed towards the Indians; their lands and property shall never be taken from them without their consent; and, in their property, rights, and liberty, they never shall be invaded and disturbed, unless in just and lawful wars authorized by Congress; but laws founded in justice and humanity shall, from time to time, be made, for preventing the wrongs being done to them, and for preserving peace and friendship with them."[79]

Throughout the years of the Confederation the issue of the Indians and their lands proved of continuing concern to the old Congress, whose protective measures toward the Native Americans were systematically flouted by states, speculators, and impatient settlers. The discussions at the Philadelphia Convention reflected the concern of the leadership over this gnawing problem. True, the reference to Indians in that document may have been tantalizingly terse, but henceforth the new federal government conducted its business with the Indians on the assumption that its authority in that area would now be undisputed. If ambiguities remained after the adoption of the federal Constitution, they should have been extinguished by the clear prohibition of state purchases of Indian land contained in the Indian Trade and Intercourse Act of July 22, 1790, and its subsequent reenactments.[80]

The Constitution inaugurated a change in Indian policy, both legal and political. Purchase now replaced conquest, but without extinguishing the government's determination to acquire all Indian lands as far as the Mississippi. A new breed of Americans and a new breed of leaders, in contempt of the Constitution, would in the longer run achieve the wholesale annexation of Indian lands, a ruthless program, one incompatible with notions of amicable Indian-white relations and even with the amalgamation of the Indians into the mainstream of American life.[81]

Women. No woman sat at the Constitutional Convention nor at any state ratifying conventions. No woman cast a vote for a delegate to the latter. Still, so deep-dyed an Antifederalist as Pennsylvania's George Bryan conceded that the female sex, at least in his state, was pro-Constitution. His explanation: "They admire General W."[82] That admiration was widely shared by the opposite sex as well, and indubitably persuaded many Antifederalists to support the new charter of government which it was commonly believed the General would head. If the cult of personality played a role in public opinion about the Constitution, in the case of women it clearly prevailed over interest.

From "We the People" of the Preamble to the frequent references to "persons," "People," or "inhabitants" in the document itself, a case could be made that the Constitution was gender-blind. In determining the intent of the Framers, however, it would have been helpful if they had given us a hint as to whether their use of the masculine pronoun to describe the President and Vice-President and, with one exception, the qualifications of representatives and senators, was employed in a generic sense or was meant to exclude women.[83]

Giving to the Framers the most liberal intention in their use of pronouns, one can argue that the Constitution did not explicitly bar women from federal office, while conceding that the election or even appointment of women to fill national posts were ideas whose time had not yet come. Jefferson, who loathed political conversations with the women of Parisian salons, expressed the hope that "our good ladies . . . are contented to soothe and calm the minds of their husbands returning ruffled from political debate."[84] When President, a hint from Albert Gallatin, his Secretary of the Treasury, that the President might consider appointing women to the public service, evoked this sharp rejoinder from Jefferson: "The appointment of a woman to office is an innovation for which the public is not prepared, nor am I."[85] Had Hamilton been alive, he might well have shared his political opponent's sentiments. *The Federalist* contains only one reference to women and that is in Hamilton's No. 6, in which he warns his readers of the perils posed to the safety of the state by the intrigues of courtesans and mistresses. Jefferson, who did not usually endorse Hamilton's political views, betrayed a like concern over the wiles women might exercise. At an advanced age he made a point of remarking that even the purest democracies would find it necessary to exclude women from the suffrage "to prevent deprivation of morals and ambiguity of issue."[86]

Such antifeminist prejudices did not evaporate quickly but lasted well into the early national era. So preeminent a bluestocking as Mercy Otis Warren, who corresponded on political issues with Jefferson, John Dickinson, and Mrs. Macaulay Graham, the English historian, aroused the wrath of the irascible John Adams, whose literary jousting with his wife Abigail over this subject is now legendary. Adams did not take kindly to Mercy Warren's treatment of him in her *History of the Progress and Termination of the American Revolution*, published in 1805. "History is not the Province of the ladies," he observed caustically, a view in which Mercy's nephew, Harrison Gray Otis, heartily concurred.[87] John Adams's insensitivity toward his wife's arguments for political justice were revealed privately to James Sullivan. "Depend upon it, Sir," he declared, "it is dangerous to open so fruitful a source of controversy and altercation as would be opened by attempting to alter the qualifications of voters; there will be no end of it. New claims will arise; women will demand a vote, lads from twelve to twenty-one will think their rights are not enough attended to, and every man who has not a farthing will demand an equal voice with any other in all acts of state. It tends to confound and destroy all distinctions, and prostrate all ranks to the common level."[88] In the republic of John Adams, "distinctions" must not be destroyed and women must know their place.

Since the Constitution laid down no voting requirements but left suffrage qualifications to the states, the latter failed to seize the opportunity at the time of ratification and widen the franchise.[89] On the local level, however, there was a certain degree of ambiguity about franchise qualifications. The New England towns continued to make distinctions upon issues on which "freeholders" and "male inhabitants" might vote. In Adams's own town of Braintree, voting on most issues seems to have been open to "the freeholders and other inhabitants," impliedly permitting women property holders to vote. However, the voter and tax lists of Massachusetts reveal that few women holding taxable estates of significant value continued to exercise the local franchise, for, as Abigail Adams pointed out, restrictions involving the ownership of property by married women except in the case of marriage settlements or special arrangements sharply curtailed the number qualifying. Nevertheless, in New England and in some of the Middle States unmarried women with property, as well as widows of proprietors, did participate in making proprietary decisions.[90] In addition, one finds increasing evidence in the 1780s of tax-paying widows joining men in exercising the right of petition to the state legislatures.[91]

More weighty legislation involving provincial or state issues and elections was restricted to male voters. Women were deliberately excluded from the Massachusetts state franchise, along with slaves and minors, as Theophilus Parsons explained in the *Essex Result* (1778), not only because they were "so situated as to have no wills of their own," but out of the conviction of the delegates to the state constitutional convention that women should be confined to their housewifely role and not encouraged to engage in "promiscuous intercourse with the world, which is necessary to qualify them for electors."[92]

What was true of Massachusetts was true everywhere, with one exception—New Jersey. The provision of its constitution that "all the inhabitants . . . of full age . . . worth fifty pounds" could vote was interpreted to include unmarried women otherwise qualified. Some women pounced upon this loophole and exercised the franchise in local elections held in the 1780s and 1790s. Women's votes in 1797 in favor of the Federalist candidate for the state legislature from Elizabethtown are believed to have affected the outcome of the election. In 1807, however, following several allegations of fraud, an amendment was passed which took away the privilege.[93] Framers of state constitutions in other states, like New York and Georgia, were meticulous about avoiding such loopholes and carefully chose the word "male" to describe a voter's necessary qualifications.[94]

Our concern with the treatment of women in the Constitution and their political rights, or lack thereof, in the states should not lead us to conclude that the status of women was unchanged in this period. Appreciable gains were scored by women in conducting business of their own and in securing access to better education.[95] With the coming of the Revolution, the role of Republican motherhood was especially esteemed. Women were recognized as models and teachers of civic virtue. A woman could now more easily obtain a divorce and enjoyed other rights at law which would have been denied her in England at common law.[96] True, these gains were modest and no decisive breakthrough occurred until the married woman's property reform legislation of the nineteenth century. In fact, the era of the Constitution by no means revolutionized the status of women or conferred upon them equal rights. One must accept the judgment of St. George Tucker, who remarked in the first edition of his *Commentaries* on Blackstone, which he published in 1803: "I fear there is little reason for a compliment to our laws for their respect and favour to our female sex."

* * * *

So much for the forgotten people of the original Constitution. The history of the Constitution is the story of the ways in which constitutional rights and protections came to be extended to all the excluded groups we have examined, and of how that great charter of governance has been broadened by amendment, judicial interpretation, and practice to underwrite a system of participatory democracy which is still a model for other nations.

CHAPTER 8

In Diplomacy: Friction and Frustration

I N the course of the secret sessions of the Philadelphia Convention, a New York newspaper reported the reply of an Englishman when told that the United States would eventually retaliate against British trade restrictions. "Pish!" he scoffed. "What can the Americans do? They have neither government nor power. Great Britain could shut up all their ports. Americans take measures against Great Britain, indeed!" Reams of correspondence between John Adams, America's minister to the Court of St. James's, and John Jay, America's Secretary for Foreign Affairs, were encapsulated in that snide remark.

Relations with Great Britain and other major powers during the Confederation years would make it abundantly clear to the Framers of the new Constitution that the federal government must be given power to regulate commerce as well as exclusive power over tariffs and that its treaty powers be buttressed with sanctions. Unless foreign states were convinced that the new government possessed ample powers in all these respects, along with an independent treasury, they would regard the United States as impotent to retaliate against discriminatory measures and they would hold the trump card in all negotiations.

The man to whom Congress now delegated the management of foreign affairs was John Jay, returned to New York in July of 1784 after his triumph in Paris. Assuming his duties in late December of '84,[1] he took office with the assurance that he could pick his own staff, that he would be the sole vehicle for communications on foreign affairs and with state governors on such matters. He also had the privilege—unique among nondelegates—of appearing before Congress even though he was not a member of that body, a privilege of which he availed himself with great regularity. He submitted recommendations, drafted resolutions, and exercised outside that chamber in conversations with European ministers, consuls, chargés, and agents an influence that the journals and papers of Congress can do no more than suggest. A secret act authorized Jay to inspect at his discretion any letters in the Post Office that might involve the "safety or interest of the United States."[2] It is understandable that Jay, who had suffered indignities abroad, where his letters were systematically examined before reaching him, would have hesitated to exercise this singular power, and there is no evidence that he ever did so.

Operating in New York City out of Fraunces Tavern,[3] some blocks south of where Congress was then sitting at the old City Hall, Jay worked with a minuscule staff comprising one secretary, part-time translators, two clerks, and a doorkeeper-messenger.[4] Jay was charged with securing the enforcement of the Treaty of Peace with Great Britain, including the removal of British troops from American territory. It was his responsibility to have foreign trade restrictions against American goods and shipping lifted or replaced, to oversee the making of a commercial treaty with Great Britain, a consular convention with France, as well as a treaty with Spain settling boundaries, trade, and the navigation of the Mississippi. It was his additional responsibility to see that the provisions of commercial treaties made with the Dutch, the Swedes, and the Prussians (the last ratified early in his term of office) were carried out, to engage in talks or oversee negotiations with states lacking treaties of amity with the United States, to free American hostages from Algerine captivity, and to end piratical depredations against American shipping off the Atlantic coast and in the Mediterranean by making a treaty with Morocco.

British-American Issues

Of all the postwar problems confronting the Confederation, the most exigent stemmed from differing interpretations of the Definitive Treaty on the part of the United States and Great Britain. These differences imperiled frontier security, held up Western settlement, and had profoundly adverse repercussions on America's foreign trade. The treaty recognized the independence of the United States, ceded to America a vast territory stretching from the Great Lakes in the north to Spanish Florida in the south and from the Atlantic to the Mississippi. From this entire area the British had bound themselves by the treaty to evacuate "with all convenient speed." On parchment, the treaty underwrote the future expansion of the United States and protected the fishing rights or "liberties" of New Englanders off the Canadian coast.

While enthusiastic about these provisions, a good many Americans had second thoughts about the concessions to the British that their own peace commissioners had found it necessary to make. Many tobacco planters were unhappy about the fourth article providing that "creditors on either side shall meet with no lawful impediment to the recovery of the full value in sterling money of all bona fide debts heretofore contracted." Although the balance was heavily weighted in favor of British creditors, state statutes and state courts effectually blocked the recovery of their claims. Jay quickly found that this pledge to creditors (mostly on the other side of the ocean) was difficult to carry out.

The response was especially hostile to the fifth article, by which Congress pledged to recommend to the state legislatures the restitution of all properties "of persons resident in districts in the possession of his Majesty's Arms, who had not borne arms against the United States." There was less than cordiality manifest toward persons "of any other description," as the treaty described them, who were to be free to enter the United States and remain twelve months to obtain a restitution of their confiscated estates. The American commissioners, while warning their British counterparts that the United States under the Articles lacked the power to bind the states, had included a provision pledging Congress to recommend to the states "a reconsideration and revision" of laws on the subject of confiscation in order to render them "consistent, not only with justice and equity, but with the spirit of conciliation." Congress had also agreed to recommend that confiscated Loyalist properties be restored to their original owners on their refunding to persons now in possession the bona fide prices they had paid in purchasing such properties. The sixth article went even further, pledging that no person "shall on that Account suffer any Loss or Damage in his Person, Liberty, or Property," and that those confined be set at liberty, while prosecutions initiated be discontinued.[5] Considering the lack of sanctions possessed by Congress, these treaty pledges amounted to a set of prayers dependent upon the good will of the separate states for their execution.

Let us first examine the protracted dispute over the articles on the debts. Resistance to debt collection was most adamant in Virginia, slightly less unyielding in Maryland. In the two great tobacco plantation states where the bulk of the debtors resided, political passions over this issue reached fever pitch. During the war the legislatures of both states had passed acts enabling their citizens to pay all or part of their debts owed British subjects into their respective state loan offices with state or Continental currency. Upon making payment, the debtor received a certificate to certify that the debts had been paid. Most debtors waited, however, until the depreciation of paper money made it possible to pay off their debts at a fraction of their real value. In all, the Virginia state treasury received £275,554 of paper money, with a sterling value of £15,044, to discharge the British debt; in Maryland, £144,474 had a sterling value of £86,744. In effect, this device amounted to a settlement in Virginia on an eighteen-to-one basis on average—virtual repudiation; in Maryland, to a settlement of 60 percent, a more respectable figure.[6]

A second obstacle to resuming effective diplomatic relations with Great Britain was the continued violation in the American states of the treaty pledges regarding the Loyalists. The issue rated a lower priority in England than that of the English and Scottish debtors, who systematically bombarded the home government with petitions for relief because the British government had set up a commission to deal with Loyalist claims and provided substantial relief to this category of petitioners, paying out some $22 million in claims.[7]

Jay could observe, he could investigate, he could record, and he could recommend, but he could not act. Every single state had legislated against the Tories, either confiscating Loyalist estates or imposing heavy taxes on such properties.[8] The bitter animosity toward the Loyalists which prevailed at the peace slowly ebbed with passing years. Within limitations the New England states gradually relaxed their prohibitions against the return of Loyalists to America.[9]

A much tenser situation prevailed in New York, where both downstate merchants and upcountry tenants had supported the British cause. In that state shrill cries were raised at war's end, notably after the evacuation of the British Army from New York City, that Tories who had not quit the state be expelled or disfranchised. Responding to the clamor, the state legislature in 1784 enacted a sweeping law disfranchising all who had been British officials, who had helped the British in any way during the war, who had left the state, or who had actually joined the British armed forces. Countering the demand for reprisals were more moderate-minded public figures like John Jay and Alexander Hamilton, who urged, in Jay's words, a policy of "clemency, moderation, and benevolence."[10]

The issue was brought to a boil by the passage of the New York legislature's Trespass Act, which provided a remedy in law, permitting Patriots whose property had been occupied by Loyalists or British subjects during the war to recover damages, and prohibited the pleading of military orders by way of justification. Enacted in March of 1783 and reenacted over a veto by the state's Council of Revision, the statute opened the floodgates to Patriot claimants. Most celebrated among the numerous cases arising under the Trespass Act was the case of *Rutgers* v. *Waddington*, previously treated.

Bitterly assailed by the radical anti-Tory party, Hamilton defended his course in two pamphlets under the pseudonym of "Phocion," in which he urged moderation for ex-Tories and strict observance of the terms of the Treaty of Peace.[11] A few years later Hamilton maneuvered through the legislature a bill repealing the Trespass Act, and in 1788 the legislature repealed all laws contravening the peace treaty.[12]

South of New York anti-Tory legislation was universal, if varying in degree of execution. Pennsylvania, in addition to the substantial Loyalist population in Philadelphia, claimed a substantial body of those objecting to war on religious grounds, chiefly Quakers and Mennonites. In that state, a sweeping "Test Act" of 1777 required white male inhabitants to take an oath renouncing fidelity to George III under penalty of forfeiting both civil and political rights.[13] Due to the efforts of the conservative Republican faction the test laws were repealed in part in 1786, enabling the bulk of the adult males to vote, and the following year the last of such discriminatory laws was taken off the books. Instead, one had to declare allegiance to the state before voting or holding office. The issue was not easily resolved since nearly five hundred Tories in Pennsylvania had been attainted for high treason in absentia.[14]

The Loyalist problem in the South was compounded by the fact that the Tories of the Tidewater were relatively recent immigrants from England or Scotland, while in the Carolinas backcountrymen —Highland Scots, Scotch-Irish, and some Germans—had conducted a fierce civil war against the Patriots. All in all the Southern Tories were by culture, religion, and sectional unrest the weakest. As a group, the Southern planters were Patriots. In Virginia, the issue was crystallized with the peace treaty, and, aside from the debts, a far more inflammatory issue in the tobacco states, the Loyalist problem seemed largely centered around Norfolk, where, despite a proclamation issued by Governor Benjamin Harrison in July of 1783 forbidding the return of all those who had left the state in 1777, many Loyalists had already returned and were facing popular justice. Within two years the legislature removed the bars except against those who had borne arms against the United States, while still denying the returnees the right to vote or hold office. On the score of the Loyalists, who had suffered little in the way of confiscation in Virginia, the state finally repealed its discriminatory legislation.[15]

While late in pressing anti-Loyalist legislation, South Carolina, of all the Southern states, provided the theater of bitterest conflict over the issue. What precipitated the intense anti-Tory feeling was the fall of Charleston to the British in 1780. Patriot leaders were dispatched on prison ships to St. Augustine, their lands confiscated, and their slaves taken. In response, the South Carolina legislature in January 1782 passed a series of acts, singling out some 286 "known" Loyalists, confiscating the estates of others, and fining still others 10 or 12 percent of their total estates in return for pardons. The evacuation by the British brought about a more lenient policy courageously advocated by Christopher Gadsden, who had fought the anti-Tory legislation "inch by inch," as an unjust, impolitic creed."[16] A number of estates were exempted from confiscation and many Loyalists readmitted to citizenship.[17] News of the Treaty of Peace aroused tensions anew. In Charleston the marine Anti-Britannic Society, led by Alexander Gillon, stirred up fierce anti-Tory feelings, but in the end the counsels of moderation prevailed. By the close of 1786 most of the confiscated estates had been returned or some form of compensation provided even though the confiscation laws had not been repealed.[18]

Although acts of banishment remained on the books, in some cases for more than a generation,[19] and despite the large number of refugees who had chosen exile in Nova Scotia, the West Indies, or the mother country, others stayed behind and rather quickly reestablished themselves; still others—the most notorious Loyalist leadership excepted—were permitted to return. With the backing of his old friend John Jay, the lawyer Peter Van Schaack came back to New York to teach law students at Kinderhook. Joshua Waddington stayed on in New York City to become a director of Hamilton's Bank of New York. Other returnees to New York included Josiah Ogden Hoffman, who later became the state's attorney general, and his law partner, Cadwalader David Colden (Tory governor Colden's grandson), and even that unreconstructed Tory the Reverend Samuel Seabury made it back to New York as a missionary of the Church of England, now as an Episcopalian. Neutralists like William Samuel Johnson were accepted in political society. Johnson was to become president of Columbia College, an architect of the Connecticut Compromise, and chairman of the Committee of Style at the Constitutional Convention. In Pennsylvania, Tench Coxe stayed on to play a significant role at the Annapolis Convention, later serving as Assistant Secretary of the Treasury and commissioner of the revenues under Hamilton. Pennsylvania proved hospitable to returning Benjamin Chew, who, once chief justice, would become president of the High Court of Errors and Appeals in 1790, while Benedict Arnold's father-in-law, Edward Shippen, became the state's chief justice in 1799. A few returned to America to serve the Crown, notably Bostonian Sir John Temple, as consul general, and Phineas Bond, as vice consul in Philadelphia. Those who stayed or returned to the States made their peace with their former neighbors, would be mostly numbered among the supporters of the Constitution, and would become stout Federalists.[20]

Creditors and Loyalists kept up a bombardment of the British Foreign Office, as John Adams, America's minister at London, constantly reminded Jay.[21] Both Adams and Jay realized that debts and continued confiscations were inextricably tied to Britain's removal of its troops from frontier posts, as pledged in the Definitive Treaty. The continued occupation of the garrisons by the British Army jeopardized the security of the northern frontier and blocked vital trade routes.[22] Continued treaty violations on the part of the Americans served to dampen such sentiment as existed in England for a reciprocal trade treaty to which the Preamble of the Preliminary Articles looks forward.[23] Above all, to men of probity like Jay and Adams such violations reflected on America's public faith.

To rebut British charges that treaty violations by the United States had in fact preceded Britain's, Jay needed to ascertain the facts. In compliance with a request of Congress, he conducted an extensive correspondence with all the state governors to determine the degree to which the states had complied with the Proclamation of January 14, 1784, recommending the restitution of estates confiscated from the Loyalists during the war, as well as the rescinding of laws or judicial decisions blocking the recovery of debts with interest due British creditors.[24] Even before all the data had been digested, Jay had enough evidence at hand to conclude that this was not the propitious moment to press the claims of Americans for property (chiefly slaves) removed by the British Army during wartime so long as some of the states still retained on their books laws impeding British creditors from collecting their debts, laws which state courts, he found, continued to uphold. Having formed a preliminary judgment, Jay reached the conclusion by the fall of '86 that the United States was the initial violator of the treaty's provisions, a view which he expounded in a searching, comprehensive, and judicious report to Congress.[25]

In that report, Jay made no effort to conceal his hostility to slavery. Rather did he rebuke delegates by labeling their insistence on the return of the blacks carried away by the British as inconsistent with humanitarian principles. He advocated, instead, compensation by the British government to their claimant owners. The issue transcended so narrow a point, Jay insisted. What was at stake was the enforcement upon the states of the obligations of national treaties. In April 1787, the Secretary pressed Congress to resolve that treaties constitutionally made become "part of the law of the land," and be considered as "not only independent of the will and power of [state] legislatures," but also binding and obligatory upon them, and that state laws repugnant to the treaty be forthwith repealed.[26] Considering the sharp division in the country over such issues as the debts and confiscation, Congress's response was extraordinary. It unanimously adopted a letter to the states drafted by Jay, calling upon them to comply with the treaty.[27] This resolution laid the foundation for the inclusion in the federal Constitution of the supremacy clause (Article VI, section 2).

An assertion of seemingly uncontested sovereign power, the congressional resolution was honored in the breach, notably by the state of Virginia, whose creditors had been able to put off the day of reckoning, protected as they were by state laws and state judges. The ratification of the Constitution, however, brought dismay to the entire congregation of debtors and revived the hopes of Tories whose property had been confiscated, particularly after 1783.[28] British and Scottish creditors soon deluged the United States circuit courts, as well as Virginia's own courts, with suits to recover their claims. Despite pro-creditor decisions in both federal and state courts, the issue of British debts remained unresolved until the Jay Treaty of 1794, and the dispute was at length settled by a compromise formula adopted by the Convention of 1802. The claims recognized and paid from the U.S. Treasury constituted less than a third of what the Committee of Merchants had demanded, but finis was at length written to a protracted and divisive issue.[29]

Since Jay made a fetish of secret diplomacy, particularly with regard to his ongoing Spanish negotiations, and his report to Congress on the treaty violations by the states had been made in secret, it does seem unpardonable for him to have divulged to Sir John Temple, the British consul general, the substance of his findings. Jay asked his confidant not to disclose the information "in this country." Acting on what seemed an obvious hint, Temple relayed the news at once to Carmarthen, the British Foreign Secretary.[30] Jay's remarks, only serving to bolster Carmarthen's contention that the Americans were the prior violators of the treaty's terms, earned him a reputation abroad as a well-wisher of Britain.

On the issue of prior violations, Jay might well have been both more cautious and more discreet. Had he been privy to the correspondence between the home government and Canada's officials, he would have been astonished to learn that on April 9, 1784, Lord Sydney, Secretary of State for Home Affairs in the Pitt Cabinet, addressed a dispatch to Sir Frederick Haldimand, Governor-General of British North America, instructing him that, in view of the vagueness of the treaty's stipulation for evacuation "with all convenient speed," such a move might be delayed "at least until we are enabled to secure the fur traders in the Interior Country and withdraw their property."[31] The very next day George III proclaimed the ratification of the treaty and promised "sincerely and faithfully" to observe its provisions![32]

While alert to frontier dangers, Jay was not ready for war unless assured that France would support America, an assurance Thomas Jefferson, our minister to France, could not obtain for him.[33] The facts were, as Jay soon ascertained, that Canadian officials, dissatisfied with the boundary settlement and responsive to their fur traders, were conducting a systematic program aimed at maintaining ties with potential Western secessionists, a connection to be exploited at the propitious moment. "They hold the posts," he remarked to Adams, "but they will hold them as pledges of enmity."[34] By the summer of '86 Jay could inform Jefferson that the British government at New Brunswick was not only extending its jurisdiction farther than the treaty permitted but was apparently stirring up trouble between the Indians and American settlers. "How far" the Indians might "be instigated by our Neighbours is not decided," he commented with his customary caution, "but the Asperity observable in the british Nation toward us, creates Surprises that they wish to see our Difficulties of every kind encrease and accumulate."[35]

Almost to the end of his tenure as Secretary, Jay sought a resolution of the problems of the posts. He asked Congress for authorization to conclude a convention with Great Britain creating a commission to determine the value of American property carried away during the war and to arrange for the evacuation of the Western posts after the states had complied with Jay's circular letter calling for the repeal of laws repugnant to the treaty.[36] The commission proposal, later incorporated in the Jay Treaty, was not implemented at this time. Instead, even as late as January 1789 Jay was responding to reports of secessionist efforts pressed by the British and former Loyalists in collusion with residents in the Kentucky country.[37] In sum, the price of peace had been fixed by Canadian officials, and it amounted to American renunciation of the Old Northwest. Never repudiated by the home government, the Canadian officials had incited the Indians to warfare while taking pains to preserve the Indians' attachment to Great Britain, nor were they above encouraging secession by American settlers. And so matters remained unsettled during the Confederation years.[38] After the new federal government was inaugurated, the fortuitous combination of a military defeat of the Indians and the Jay Treaty of 1794 obliged the British to evacuate from the northern and western territories of the United States.

Shrouded in a thick mist of divergent maps, claims, and counterclaims, the northeastern boundary was most stubbornly contested at the peace table. The river denominated in the treaty was called the St. Croix, which in fact turned out to be two more or less parallel streams emptying into Passamaquoddy Bay: the Magaguadavic—the first river west of the St. John's and evidently the river intended by the treaty—and the Schoodic, nine miles to the west of the former at its mouth. While not far apart at their outlets, the two streams diverge at their alleged respective sources by some fifty miles. Exacerbating the issue was the speed with which the British government granted lands in the disputed area to the Loyalists once the Definitive Peace was signed.[39]

Since the boundary of Maine (then a part of Massachusetts) was involved, Congress as early as January 1784 had asked Governor John Hancock to ascertain whether Nova Scotia was encroaching on his state's territory and to demand the recall of British subjects so trespassing. In October 1785 Congress had the documents collected by Hancock dispatched to Adams, with instructions to settle the boundary dispute by a commission (along the lines Jay had proposed) if it could not be done "in the ordinary mode of negotiation."[40] Lacking assurances from France that it would support America's territorial claims against Britain and

Spain, Jay urged Congress to avoid demanding "a categorical An-swer," while at the same time advising that the nation be placed on a war footing.[41] The Northeastern boundary dispute, like the other differences with Great Britain over the Treaty of 1783, re-mained unsettled as the Confederation drew to a close. Later Jay, in the treaty bearing his name, would arrange to have his long-favored mixed commission established to settle the controversy. When at length it was resolved, the decision in favor of the Schoodic River rested on dubious grounds and was less than fa-vorable to the United States.

On assuming office, Jay had quickly recognized that the gravest threats to the new nation were external in origin. They were not to be found in the possible secession of western territories, or disputed boundaries, or unsettled differences with Spain, or even domestic insurrection that lay ahead. The threat was to the prosperity of America jeopardized by British dumping and trade exclusion, ac-tions which contributed almost immediately, as we have already seen, to the onset of an acute depression in the United States. "I may reason till I die to no purpose," declared John Adams as early as June of 1785. "It is unanimity in America in measures, which shall confute the British sophisms and make them feel, which will ever produce a fair treaty of commerce."[42] That unanimity was never achieved under the Confederation and, consequently, no trade treaty would be forthcoming.

In London, Adams had pressed promptly for a reciprocal trade treaty and the removal of the severe trade and shipping restrictions quickly imposed on the United States even before the Definitive Treaty was signed. He soon discovered his efforts to be fruitless. Within six months from the start of his mission he confessed that he was a complete "cypher," and that British retaliatory trade mea-sures and prohibitions on the export to America of tools and other products used in American manufacturing revealed the true "spirit of this country toward the United States." In short, in trade matters, "the Friends of America are reduced to Doctor Price and Doctor Jebb."[43] Adams came up with the only sensible answer: impose discriminatory duties on British products.[44] Of course, Adams un-derstood that such a policy could not be initiated under the strait-jacket imposed on Congress by the Articles of Confederation. The only hope lay in enlarging the powers of Congress, and in that view he was fortified by the prospects held forth by Lord Carmarthen in a closing conference.[45]

In sum—and Adams and Jay surely would have agreed—the refashioning by the British government of its mercantilist policy in the postwar years to discourage American competition in shipping, trade, and manufactures may well have contributed more to the convocation of the Constitutional Convention of 1787 and to its success than, as one distinguished scholar has remarked, "many who sat in that august body."[46]

Promoting Trade Relations with Continental Europe

Reestablishing trade relations with Great Britain constituted but one facet of America's postwar trade policy. Trade in general, it was widely believed, should be established with all nations and on a liberal basis. Such efforts had been initiated from the start of the Revolution. John Adams's "Plan of Treaties," drafted in 1776, reflecting the example of the Franco-British commercial treaty of 1713 as well as contemporary notions of the French philosophes, included provisions for commercial reciprocity and establishing free trade not only between Europe and America but also with other nations.[47]

Treaties subsequently concluded and derived from the "model treaty" laid down what became an article of faith in America's longer-term treaty negotiations: free ships make free goods. A policy espoused by little-navy nations, it would give nations the right to trade with belligerents while drastically restricting the list of contraband goods, even excluding naval stores and foodstuffs.[48] These principles were embodied in the Treaty of Amity and Commerce made with France in 1778.[49] The French treaty served as the prototype for future commercial treaties. Before the war had ended, treaties had been concluded with the Netherlands and Sweden. The latter treaty, signed by Franklin on April 3, 1783, contained a new article permitting each party, both being neutral, to convoy the other's ships in time of war.[50]

Following the signing of the Definitive Peace, Congress prepared instructions, in part drafted by Jefferson, to guide the American commissioners in Paris in negotiating treaties of amity and commerce with virtually all the powers of Europe.[51] The treaty with

Prussia, the first to follow the Swedish treaty of 1783, like its predecessor which Adams had negotiated with the Dutch, contained a most-favored-nation clause but without the conditional provision found in the French and Swedish treaties.[52] It also embraced certain humanitarian features, for which Franklin had been pushing for some years, notably the immunity of noncombatants in wartime and decent treatment of prisoners of war. The article providing that contraband goods on neutral ships could not be confiscated in wartime, but merely detained, with reasonable compensation for resulting loss to the proprietors, was to raise pertinent issues as late as World War I.[53] The treaty had in fact little effect on the pattern of trade in these years. The expectations of the Prussians that American tobacco, rice, and indigo would be exchanged in substantial amounts for Silesian linens and Saxon procelain[54] failed to materialize in any significant way.

Negotiating With Non-Treaty States

While still in Paris, Franklin had initiated conversations with a number of European states looking toward commercial treaties with the United States. Despite the valiant efforts of our ministers abroad, no treaties were concluded during the Confederation years with Denmark, the Austrian Netherlands and the Empire, or with Sardinia, the Papal States, Tuscany, Saxony, Portugal, and Russia.[55] Still, some of these states appointed agents in America who kept watch on both commerce and political developments in the Confederation and on discriminatory duties levied by the states against the ships and imports of their respective nations. The Austrian agent lobbied to have discriminatory duties against his nationals removed from states like Pennsylvania, Maryland, and South Carolina, while still informing his home government of the pressing need for a commercial treaty with America.[56]

Jay, who saw no haste in concluding treaties with European nations that lacked territorial possessions in the Americas, felt that it was now too late to draw back from negotiating with those prepared to enter into such treaties, while advocating the prudent steps of incorporating in such treaties provisions limiting their duration "to a short Term so that any inconveniences arising thereof should not be of long duration. Circumstances," he advised Congress, "will by that Time probably place the United States on more advantageous Ground, and enable them to make Treaties far more beneficial than any that can now be expected."[57] He anticipated the likelihood that a strengthened central government would put the United States on a more even footing in further negotiations.

Portugal, with its vast holdings in South America, was a notable exception to Jay's deliberate course. Considering the great importance of American trade with the Iberian peninsula,[58] Jay and Congress placed a high priority on this treaty. Negotiations were undertaken abroad jointly by John Adams and Thomas Jefferson, with a project drawn up along the lines of the Prussian treaty, but one snag after another developed. Influential mill operators in the environs of Lisbon opposed including a stipulation for the admission into Portugal of American flour. Nor were the Portuguese ready to accept the broad definition of contraband the Americans had inserted in their draft.[59] In point of fact, Jefferson and Adams affixed their signatures to a draft treaty, but the Portuguese court held up the treaty and ministers from the two nations were not exchanged until 1791.[60]

The trade treaties that had been negotiated during and after the Revolution were treated with a certain indifference by the individual thirteen states; resentful foreign nations, through their consuls or agents, found it necessary to protest discriminatory state actions. Sweden, for example, had occasion to complain of restraints and duties imposed by several states in violation of the principle of reciprocity which was the basis for the Swedish-American treaty. In a prudent response, Jay drew up a resolution putting Swedish ships on the same footing as American vessels trading in Sweden.[61]

The Enigma of Franco-American Relations

The issue of how "perpetual" the Franco-American alliance was lurked below the surface throughout the Confederation years, only to flare up with the start of the French Revolution and further destabilize the one-party (or no-party) system that seems to have characterized American politics with the inauguration of President Washington.

In America, the Peace of 1783 raised a series of questions about Franco-American relations. Would France consider itself bound by the '78 alliance to assist the United States in evicting the British from the occupied posts? What, if any, action would France take if the United States continued to defer payments of principal and interest due that nation and its military officers? Would France back the United States against the depredations of the Barbary pirates? Would France support America in its controversy with Spain over the opening of the Mississippi to navigation? Would France pursue a liberal policy toward American trade both in the West Indies and the metropolis?

The answers were mostly negative. The French foreign archives, then not open, confirm the impression of America's Foreign Secretary that France was unenthusiastic about seeing a strong and viable new nation emerge across the Atlantic. Against the Barbary pirates, despite promises written into the Treaty of 1778, France offered only empty expressions of good will.[62] Privately, the French backed Spanish actions against the United States on the Mississippi. France's foreign office frowned on the use of force by the United States against Spain and insisted on negotiations as the only viable approach.[63] The French minister to the United States in 1787, the Marquis Éléanor-François Moustier, who regarded the American government as a "phantom of democracy," even ventured to raise with his superiors the hope that France would reestablish its North American empire in the region between the Alleghenies and the Mississippi, with headquarters in New Orleans in order to block American efforts to gain control of the lower Mississippi.[64] His abrupt recall, however, suggests that his judgment was not widely respected at home. Hardly the most reliable reporter, Edmund Genêt, when he took up his post in 1793 as minister to the United States from the new French republic, submitted to the State Department official documents not only underscoring the pro-Spanish role of the statesmen under Louis XVI but even revealing that France had been anxious to see that the new federal Constitution would never be ratified. As Montmorin, Vergennes's successor, wrote Otto, the French chargé in August 1787, "it suits France to have the United States remain in its present state" and not "acquire a force and power" which it "would probably be very eager to abuse."[65]

A crucial question was whether France would respond to the mutual guarantee of each other's possessions under Article XI of the Treaty of Alliance by putting pressure on Great Britain to evacuate the posts. On this topic, Vergennes proved evasive. When Jefferson, on prodding from Jay,[66] put the question to him, Vergennes indicated doubts about the actual boundaries of the United States. "I told him there was no question what our boundaries were," Jefferson reported to Jay, adding, "I feared however to press this any further *lest a reciprocal question should be put to me;* and therefore diverted the conversation to another object."[67]

As might be expected of Jay, he was entirely supportive of the claims for back pay with interest of France and French officers who had fought in the American Revolution. Satisfaction of debts, an issue raised by the French early in Jay's secretaryship, was a matter of honor to Jay, who was not prepared to justify any moratorium or default. Rather did he seize on this issue as another example of the weakness of the central government and of Congress's lack of coercive powers to provide the needed funds.[68] On the issue of the debts, both public and private, the French evidenced understanding and restraint.[69]

It was in the commercial rather than the political area, however, that the French seemed more inclined to make some concessions, albeit they did not come up to the expectations of the Americans. Following the Treaty of Amity and Commerce with France, that nation had opened its West Indian ports to American products as a "temporary indulgence."[70] That indulgence did not survive the war. By a decree of August 30, 1784, seven free ports in the French West Indies were opened to the chief American articles of trade except salt pork, and four ports in France were declared free.[71] Free ports were not the equivalent of a free market, however, and several royal decrees of 1784 and 1785 cut severely into American trade with Martinique, Guadeloupe, and Haiti, barring wheat and flour exports to those islands as well as imports from them of sugar, coffee, cotton, and cocoa, a restriction that especially hit the Middle States. Certain bounties favored French fishermen and French bottoms.[72] In addition, preferential tariffs imposed in France on whale oil and tobacco carried in foreign bottoms provided the subject of a considerable correspondence between Jay and Jefferson. Through the latter's efforts, with strong help from Lafayette, some reductions of tariffs were secured on American whale oil.[73]

As has already been noted, tobacco, a major commodity in the French trade, was handled in these years between the French Farmers-General which enjoyed a domestic monopoly on the sale of the product, and a few select businessmen in America, notably Robert Morris. Although Jefferson, with Lafayette's support, failed to bring the tobacco monopoly to an end, some of its harsher features were softened in favor of American shippers and planters by an *arrêt* of 1787 which had the effect of diluting the monopoly.[74] That measure, which lowered duties on many American products, provoked "a violent opposition" from the mercantile community in France, so Jefferson reported.[75] Jay was gratified with the results of Jefferson's diligent and even aggressive intercession with the French government in trade matters. Hopeful of a much freer trade connection between the two nations than even then existed, Jay could not afford to be optimistic about the prospect. "Toleration in Commerce," he wrote Jefferson, "like Toleration in Religion gains Ground, it is true; but I am not sanguine in my Expectation that either will soon take place in their due Extent."[76]

A desire to facilitate commercial relation between the two nations was the ostensible reason for the controversial Consular Convention, the centerpiece of Franco-American diplomacy in the Confederation years. The protracted negotiations which this treaty entailed revealed Jay to be both a zealous defender of American sovereignty and a captious critic of any formal agreement in which the draftsmen of Versailles had a hand.

The Franco-American Treaty of Amity and Commerce of 1778 incorporated an article providing reciprocal rights of appointing consuls, whose functions were to be regulated by a separate agreement to be worked out later.[77] The French government quickly commissioned a consul general with the power to appoint consuls in America. Contrariwise, Congress appointed consuls in France but refrained from delegating such a power to its commissioners abroad.[78] However, despite insistent prodding from French officials, some eleven years were to elapse before a Consular Convention was ratified by both parties.

Early in 1782 Congress adopted a "Scheme for Convention,"[79] along lines proposed by France, and forwarded it to Franklin for implementation. Objections were raised by Thomas Barclay, consul general in France, as well as by Franklin, to a particular provision which forbade consuls from engaging in trade. Franklin objected on practical grounds. He felt that such a prohibition would require

Congress to provide a scale of salaries for consuls that it could ill afford.[80] Madison, however, kept Congress in line, and Franklin, bowing to Congress, pressed ahead and signed with Vergennes a Consular Convention,[81] which did not come to the attention of Congress until the early summer of 1785.[82]

Meantime, Jay had assumed the post of Secretary for Foreign Affairs. Even before taking office, however, Jay had, in his brief tenure in Congress on his return to America, scrutinized the Congress's "Scheme" and found it faulty. Accordingly, he introduced a resolution expressing the sense of Congress to delay or suspend the negotiations. Gerry seconded the motion which Congress, lacking information that the Convention had already been signed in France, adopted on December 14, 1784, appointing Jay to be chairman of a committee to revise the "Scheme" of 1782.[83] A week later Jay became Secretary for Foreign Affairs, but the resolution of suspension reached Franklin after the signing was a fait accompli. On January 17, 1785, Congress now replaced Jay with Gerry as chairman of the revision committee.[84]

In his July 6, 1785, report, Jay submitted the 1784 Convention to rigorous reexamination. Its provisions, he argued, exceeded the authorization of Congress's "Scheme." One initial point made by Jay concerned the departure in the Convention from the title by which the new nation was designated, which was changed from "the United States of North America" in the "Scheme" to "the Thirteen United States of North America." The latter, as Jay reminded Congress, excluded from its scope "all such other states as might be before the ratification of it or in the future created by, or become parties to the Confederacy." Since this was written two years before the adoption of the Northwest Ordinance, it is evident that Jay anticipated the rather rapid addition of new states to the Union to be formed out of the territories, a point of view that accorded with his anticolonial principles. Instead of enhancing the role of Congress in foreign affairs, Jay observed, by adhering to the "Scheme" according to which consuls were directed to present their commissions to "the United States in Congress assembled," the Convention stipulated that they should do so in "their respective states according to the form which shall be there established." Did "states" refer to the two nations, parties to the Convention, or to the thirteen separate states of the Confederation? Reminded long before by John Adams of Vergennes's readiness during the war to bypass Congress and deal with the states in the mediation process,[85] Jay was determined to clear up this ambiguity. He also agreed with Barclay and Franklin on the need for excising the provision forbidding consuls from engaging in trade. Sensitive as all Huguenot descendants understandably were to the issue of religious toleration in Catholic France, Jay complained of the omission of the sixth article of the "Scheme" giving consuls the right to have chapels in their residences. Pointing to the absence of religious reciprocity in France, Jay reminded Congress that in America, Catholicism was "freely professed." The eighth article offended the lawyer in Jay in opening the door to ex parte affidavits made before consuls, affidavits not subject to cross-examination.

Jay discovered a more substantial difference when he compared the twelfth article of the "Scheme" with the tenth article of the Convention. The latter authorized consuls to arrest captains and masters of vessels, along with seamen, passengers, or deserters, to sequester them and "even send them back respectively from the United States to France or from France to the United States." At the time he could find no such authorization in the "Scheme," but he would later acknowledge that the copy on which his charge of discrepancy was founded had erroneously omitted this provision of the "Scheme," which had in fact conferred such authorization.[86] Jay was still not content with the provision and found the Convention even "more ineligible" than he had previously adjudged.[87] One of Jay's most telling points related to the Convention's authorization of the consul's power to issue affidavits as a bar to the right of expatriation, an affidavit which could be upheld to the exclusion of all counterproof.

Jay was understandably perturbed about the variance of the fourteenth article of the Convention from the sixteenth article of the "Scheme." The weight the former seemed to give to registration of Frenchmen in the United States with their respective consuls or vice consuls (reciprocally for American citizens) seemed to preclude the naturalization of Frenchmen in America and evidenced, along with the previously mentioned authorization of consular affidavits, an obvious intention of the French government to curb emigration and naturalization by its nationals.

Above and beyond these specific objections, Jay in his concluding observations revealed his deep suspicions about stationing foreign consuls in America. This would serve, he felt, as a French political intelligence apparatus in the United States, an apparatus that the United States had no intention of duplicating in France. Considering that it was Thomas Jefferson who suggested to Jay the appointment of agents at four French ports "for the purpose of intelligence," Jay's concern seems both naive and ironic.[88] Contrariwise, Moustier was concerned about setting up in the United States an efficient consular establishment for commercial purposes.[89]

Significantly, an examination of the correspondence of French consular officials in America with their home Ministry of Marine shows a strong predilection to facilitating and promoting trade with America, along with a generally optimistic and friendly view of America's prospects. Quite in contrast are the reports in these years of the French chargé d'affaires, whose views were shaped to reflect the Foreign Office's suspicions of America's ambitions and its preference for a continued weak and disunited America that would lend itself to domination by its ally. The reports regularly sent by French consuls in America to the Ministry of Marine consisted chiefly of comments on commercial and financial affairs in America, with considerable emphasis on French residents and their misbehavior.[90] Some attention was also paid to examining the state of American maritime law.[91] In fact, it was the role of the consuls in dealing with disputes between French residents in America that led one of their number, Martin Oster, to urge upon the home authorities the necessity of a consular convention "to give complete jurisdiction over all ship captains, merchants, and other subjects of the King."[92] There was some perceptive reporting on such subjects as steamboat navigation[93] and the progress of the ratification of the Constitution. However, the reports are bare of anything that could smack of military intelligence in any meaningful sense.

Finally, to Jay the lawyer and zealous advocate of American sovereignty, the system of extraterritoriality which the Convention would have established, with its grant to consuls of certain judicial powers in litigation between their own nationals, was abhorrent and unlikely to be tolerated in the long run.

Jay's concern must have been based on the reports he himself was reading from American commercial agents located outside the United States. Around the time Jay was preparing his report to

Congress, he would be the recipient of significant intelligence from Oliver Pollock, the U.S. commercial agent at Havana, combining military and political information with commercial data and observations.[94] There is no evidence that he discouraged Pollock's diligence. In short, the kind of intelligence gathering Jay objected to on the part of French consuls was widely practiced by consuls and commercial agents of all the powers, including the United States.

In view of its objectionable features, Jay recommended that Congress reject the Convention. Most likely because he recognized the well-known effectiveness with Congress of France's diplomatic representatives in America, Jay declined to disclose the details of his report to the French chargé, Louis Guillaume Otto. Instead, he notified him that the American minister in France would officially inform the French court.[95] Congress had forty copies of Jay's report printed under an injunction of secrecy, but, as usual, someone in Congress leaked the information to Otto, who managed to obtain a copy and forward it to Vergennes. Jay's tight-lipped attitude toward the French chargé stands in sharp contrast to his indiscreet conversation with Sir John Temple, the British consul general, wherein the Secretary disclosed the essence of his report to Congress on infractions of the British Treaty of 1783.[96]

Jay's analysis of the Consular Convention's defects made a profound impression on Congress. The Convention "is universally disapproved," Monroe wrote Jefferson in August 1785.[97] Still, it was not until October 3, 1786, that Congress formally approved Jay's report presented some fifteen months earlier, and an impatient Jay forwarded the revised instructions to Jefferson the very same day.[98] If Jefferson was taken aback, he never revealed the fact. Instead, he agreed to do "the best" he could "for the reformation of the Consular Convention, being persuaded that our states would be very unwilling to conform their laws either to the Convention, or to the Scheme."[99] On this "difficult" and "delicate" business, Jefferson now embarked. With patience and scrupulous attention to detail he managed to secure agreement on a final draft of the Consular Convention, incorporating most of the important recommendations contained in Jay's instructions.

Jefferson's own analysis of the variances between the first Consular Convention and the revised one discloses the extent to which Jay's preferences were incorporated in the latter. Writing to Jay on

November 14, 1788, the day the new Convention was signed, the American minister reported the principal changes to be the following:[100]

The clauses of the Convention of 1784, cloathing Consuls with the privileges of the law of Nations, are struck out, and they are expressly subjected, in their persons and property, to the laws of the land.

That giving the right of Sanctuary to their houses is reduced to a protection of their Chancery room and its papers.

Their coercive powers over passengers are taken away; and over those whom they might have termed deserters of their nation, are restrained to deserted seamen only.

The clause allowing them to arrest and send back vessels is struck out, and instead of it they are allowed to exercise a police over the ships of their nation generally.

So is that which declared the indelibility of the character of subject, and the explanation and extension of the 11th article of the treaty of Amity.

The innovations in the Laws of evidence are done away.

And the Convention is limited to 12 years duration.

In addition, the new Convention used the term "United States of America" and provided for the delivery of commissions to and their reception by officials from the federal government. While exempting consuls from personal and military service, it subjected them in all other instances to the law of the land. It reduced the right of sanctuary in their houses to protection alone of the Chancery room and its papers. The revised Convention omitted the obnoxious features controlling emigration and nationality; it took away the previously granted coercive power of consuls over passengers, save for "deserted seamen only." Finally, the limitation of the treaty's duration to twelve years amounted to a mere two years longer than Jay had recommended.

In short, the Convention that Jefferson had finally signed might have been deemed a triumph for a less exacting man than Jay; but the Secretary was not fully content. It failed to meet Jay's insistence that *all* extraterritorial features of the consulate be omitted, as consular jurisdiction was retained in civil cases arising between nationals of the consul residing in his jurisdiction. On this point, Jefferson conceded that he was unable to budge the French. Nor was there any reference to the toleration of religious worship on the part of the consuls.

Without much enthusiasm, Jay reluctantly decided to recommend the ratification of the Consular Convention. His report was made, not to Congress, but to the Senate under the new Constitution, and that body ratified the agreement in July 1789.[101] In the long run, regardless of the efforts put forth by the representatives of both nations to obtain an appropriate Consular Convention and to sustain and improve trade between France and the United States, the new republic failed to return to France the solid dividends that Vergennes had anticipated would ensue at war's end. Throughout the years under review the balance of trade ran in favor of America,[102] while the British Isles rather than France continued increasingly to provide the bulk of the products America was importing,[103] a preeminence based upon credit and local preference for British goods and British prices.

Confrontation with the Barbary States

One of the earliest foreign crises to confront the Confederation was the interdiction of American shipping approaching and entering the Mediterranean. Stepped-up hostilities against American ships and seamen by the Barbary states, numbering Morocco, Algiers, Tunis, and Tripoli, constituted a serious economic blow to New England and, to a lesser extent, to the Middle States. The sale of fish, lumber, and flour to Mediterranean ports like Malaga, Barcelona, and Leghorn had contributed in colonial times substantially to rectifying the unfavorable colonial balance of trade.[104] Now, with American shipping unprotected, the postwar era found trade to that area severely crippled by the piratical operations of the northern African states.[105]

Congress and its diplomats abroad had anticipated the problem once the protection afforded by the British Navy was withdrawn from American ships, and made a variety of efforts to secure aid from friendly European powers, including in the Franco-American Treaty of Amity and Commerce an undertaking by Louis XVI to employ his "good offices" in protecting American commerce from the Barbary pirates, and a similar provision contained in the Dutch treaty of 1782.[106] Yet despite the efforts of John Jay, the British could not be persuaded to include such a pledge in the Definitive Treaty.[107] Indeed, Britain saw every advantage in declining to assist its former colonies and new trade rivals in this and other ways.[108]

The series of crises was inaugurated on October 1, 1783, when Moroccan pirates seized the American ship *Betsey* and her crew, who were held hostage at Tangier. Although ship and crew were released in mid-July 1785, largely through the good offices of Spain and the energetic efforts of William Carmichael, the U.S. chargé d'affaires at Madrid,[109] two other ships, the *Maria* and the *Dauphin*, along with their crews, were seized and taken to Algiers. Soon Congress was to learn the lurid details of the captivity of American ship captains and their crews.[110]

Congress first turned its efforts to ransoming the captives and buying peace, authorizing a sum not exceeding $80,000 to secure treaties from all four Barbary powers.[111] That sum, however, fell far below the expectations of the various avaricious intermediaries employed by the Barbary states.[112] Either to build a navy, which had been largely demolished or dismantled by the war, or to pay the ransoms demanded was beyond the resources of Congress. Since America's credit hardly justified floating another loan abroad, Jay advised putting the issue squarely up to the states. Their response, as anticipated, was discouraging, and Jay was impelled to warn Congress that "until such time as they furnish Congress with their respective portions of that sum the depredations of those barbarians will, in all probability, continue to increase."[113] "These requisitions produce little," Jay wrote to Jefferson of Congress's efforts to get the states to assume the burden of building a navy, "and Government (if it may be called a Government) is so inadequate to its object that essential alterations or essential Evils will take place."[114] Lacking a navy and lacking funds, Secretary Jay evidenced little enthusiasm for the various proposals that were hatched for a collective security pact with such maritime powers as Portugal, the Kingdom of the Two Sicilies, Denmark, Sweden, and Malta, or for joining in organizing a naval force of allied powers to guard the Mediterranean.[115]

Only in the case of Morocco were the Barbary negotiations brought to a satisfactory conclusion in these years. Thomas Barclay, the consul general in Paris, managed to purchase a treaty with that state which Congress ratified in 1787.[116]

Neither Congress nor the states confronted the continuing humiliations suffered by American trading vessels in waters in which the Barbary pirates operated. For years American seamen continued to rot in North African jails or to be sold into servitude. Two decades would elapse before the first of the successful expeditions was launched by a rebuilt American navy toward securing unmolested transit of American merchantmen through the Mediterranean, and it was not until 1815, with Stephen Decatur's smashing victory against Algiers, that the Barbary states ceased their ransom demands.

CHAPTER 9

The West and the Mississippi

Settling and Governing the West

THE vast territorial gains achieved at the Definitive Peace held out the promise of seemingly limitless continental expansion while posing a variety of perils to the young nation. Could the West, cut off from the thirteen states by a mountain range, be effectively governed and permanently united with the original states? Would not so expansive an empire pose a threat to republican liberties and, as one Antifederalist writer put it, "degenerate to a despotism"?[1] Nathaniel Gorham, president of the Continental Congress in 1786, wondered whether one could seriously suppose that this vast country will over a longer span "remain one nation."[2] Rather, was it not likely that the new territory would ally itself with one or the other of the rival sections, thereby diminishing the power of the section less fortunate? Or would the more distant territories secede and set up a confederacy of their own?

Before such troubling issues could properly be resolved, the rival land claims of the states had to be determined and the opposing interests of settlers—often squatters—Indians, and speculators reconciled, if possible. States with old and vaguely worded "sea-to-sea" charters, notably Virginia, found themselves pitted against others with defined and limited boundaries, such as Pennsylvania and Maryland. Pennsylvania and Virginia, for example, quarreled over their rival claims to the Pittsburgh region until they agreed in

1779 upon an extension of the Mason-Dixon line—formerly the southern boundary between Pennsylvania and Maryland—as the dividing line between the two states. Virginia, despite its military dominance in the disputed area, ratified the agreement on condition that its titleholders be secured in their lands.[3]

New York had long-standing territorial disputes with both Vermont and Massachusetts. Vermont, on the basis of New Hampshire Grants which antedated the American Revolution, had virtually from the outbreak of the war demanded recognition by Congress as "a free and independent State," an example of self-creation which others sought to duplicate.[4] The secessionist movement in Vermont was strenuously resisted by New York, many of whose prominent figures had speculated heavily in Vermont lands, confident that New York's jurisdiction over the New Hampshire Grants, resting as it did on a grant made by Charles II to the Duke of York, would prevail. Compounding the secessionist threats were the backstairs negotiations conducted with General Haldimand, commander of the British forces in Canada, for a separate treaty favorable to Vermont, a blackmail tactic pressed by the colorful Ethan Allen, his brothers Ira and Levi, and Thomas Chittenden, who, save for a single year, governed Vermont from 1778 to 1797.

Governor George Clinton and the New York delegates in Congress managed to keep the issue from being resolved until 1791, when the conflicting claims of all parties were more or less satisfactorily settled and Vermont was admitted into the Union as the fourteenth state. From John Jay, who was dispatched to Congress in 1779 to support New York's case, we have perhaps the pithiest comment on New York's ineptitude in this controversy. "The Vermont Business," he remarked in uncharacteristic language, has been "bitched in its last as well as first Stages."[5] With time, the New York Federalist came to realize that the admission of Vermont to the Union would serve as a counterpoise to Kentucky's accession, thus maintaining the political balance of the sections.[6]

New York appeared similarly inept in handling its western boundary dispute with Massachusetts. New York claimed the lands west of the Hudson on the basis of occupation and possession, defending the validity of Dutch title to much of the boundaries in dispute, a title resting on treaties with the Six Nations and their tributary Indian tribes. Massachusetts rested its counterclaim on the "sea-to-sea" clause in its old charter of 1629, a charter vacated in 1684 and replaced by one in 1691 which managed to obscure while redefining its boundaries.[7]

Here was an opportunity for the parties to resolve a pre-Revolutionary controversy by resort to the new interstate machinery created by the Articles of Confederation. The Articles made Congress the "last resort on appeal" in such interstate disputes. Under Article IX, the agents of the parties to the issue were to appoint judges by joint consent. Failing agreement, the judges would be named by Congress, with the federal court ruling to be final.[8] Congress authorized both parties to select judges, and after considerable delay both sides agreed upon a panel. However, the federal court was never convened, as both parties feared a definitive judicial ruling. Preferring instead a negotiated settlement, the two states conferred full authority on their respective agents. By a compromise agreement reached in December 1786, New York's sovereignty and jurisdiction were recognized over all lands within its claimed limits between the Hudson River and Lake Ontario, while the "right to the soil" claimed by Massachusetts over some six million acres west of the Fort Stanwix Line was confirmed, with the exception of a strip a mile wide along the Niagara River, retained by New York.[9] The settlement touched off an era of land company speculation while clearing the way for a heavy influx of settlers into the formerly disputed area.[10]

Although territorial disputes had evoked brief armed clashes of Virginians over Pittsburgh settlers and a shortlived confrontation between Yorkers and Green Mountain Boys, no dispute over property and jurisdiction was as prolonged and ferocious as the conflict between Pennsylvania and settlers from Connecticut in the Wyoming Valley lands (later Luzerne County), claimed by the former. From the very start of the Revolution speculators, supported by sizable numbers of armed settlers from Connecticut, sought to defend their title under the Susquehannah Company against Pennsylvania and its claimants. Here was a classic conflict between a small state whose pretensions rested on an ancient "sea-to-sea" charter and possession by settlers encouraged by land speculators vis-à-vis a much larger state with fixed boundaries. Having confiscated the territorial claims of its own proprietors in 1779,[11] Pennsylvania felt less inhibited about disputing the claims of proprietors claiming title from other states.

Once the Articles of Confederation had been ratified, Pennsylvania initiated Article IX proceedings to resolve its differences with Connecticut. This proved to be the only instance when Congress's special court decided an interstate territorial issue. Meeting at Trenton in December 1782, the court upheld Pennsylvania's jurisdiction over the Wyoming Valley but not its title to the disputed land. Rather, it expressed the hope that the Connecticut settlers dwelling within its borders would have their settlements confirmed. The Pennsylvania Council chose to evade the issue. It eulogized the United States for having displayed "a very singular and truly dignified example of a people who have wisdom and virtue enough not to waste in civil commotion the happiness and glory acquired by a successful opposition to their foreign enemies."[12] Rhetoric was no substitute for conciliation, however. Instead of pursuing the prudent advice of the congressional court, the Pennsylvania legislature, pressed by its own claimants to the disputed lands, dispatched the militia to drive off the sullen Connecticut settlers. In response, the Susquehannah Company organized a corps of fighting settlers under the leadership of a tough frontiersman named John Franklin. The Connecticut men even sought to carve out a separate state, to include the Susquehannah Valley, which embraced parts of both Pennsylvania and New York, had Oliver Wolcott draft a constitution for them, and welcomed a visit of Ethan Allen and his Green Mountain Boys to give a fillip to their secessionist movement. Following regrettable bloodshed, Pennsylvania acceded to the settlers' demands and confirmed the title of bona fide claimants.[13]

All through the years of the Confederation, years dominated by "the passion for emigration,"[14] rumors of secession were in the air and conspiratorial plots abounded. Land settlers and speculators threatened to bring about the secession of Kentucky from Virginia and Tennessee from North Carolina. The unsavory James Wilkinson bestrode the Western scene devoting himself to the task of separating Kentucky from Virginia in order to turn it over to Spain, for whom he served as a secret agent, while leaders like the legendary scout and pioneer Daniel Boone denied that the demand for separate statehood was "intirely against the voice of the people at

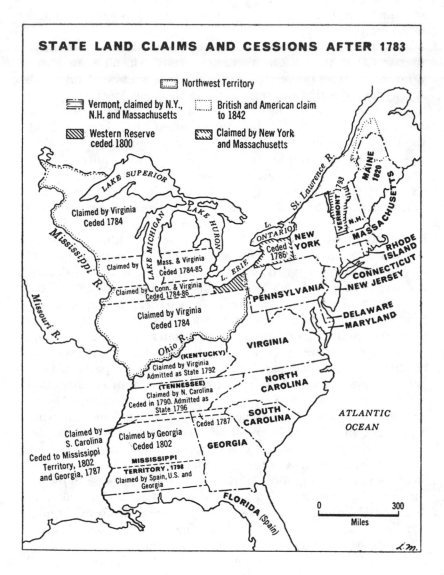

State Land Claims and Cessions After 1783 (From Francis S. Philbrick, *The Rise of the West,* in *The New American Nation series*)

Large." Nonetheless two conventions were held in Kentucky in 1785, the second asking for peaceful separation for Virginia, and successive conventions pressed the same demands. As we shall see, the Jay–Gardoqui negotiations, holding out the prospect of closing the Mississippi to Western trade for some twenty-five years, helped fire the flames of secession. A conciliatory Virginia legislature resolved the issue by the passage of an enabling act providing statehood for Kentucky under Virginia's direction while guaranteeing Virginian land grants in the region. Despite persistent calls for separation, Kentucky's admission to the Union had to wait, however, until the establishment of the new federal government, when the state's powerful speculators felt that they could confidently establish their claims against a majority of the settlers, many of whom were squatters.[15]

In both Kentucky under the early leadership of Richard Henderson and his Transylvania Colony and the western area of North Carolina, separatism took on Revolutionary overtones, with early attempts to provide role models for the principle that "all power is originally of the people."[16] In western North Carolina, settlers led by a local official, Arthur Campbell, a man who was both resident settler and land speculator, sought to create a new state south of the Ohio to include both Kentucky and Tennessee. Countering his move, the North Carolina legislature snatched away millions of acres of the state's western portion by an act of 1783. With strange inconsistency, that legislature first ceded the western part of the state to Congress in 1784 and then revoked the cession. While these dubious operations were being carried on in the eastern part of the state, a majority of its western settlers were pressing for the creation of a new state of "Franklin," temporarily adopting the North Carolina Constitution as an interim charter. Summoning their own legislature in 1785, they found that body controlled by speculators who arranged to validate all land grants in North Carolina.

The issue had become clearcut: democratically minded settlers, with Arthur Campbell's followers as the core group, opposed by a more conservative Eastern-oriented faction headed by Franklin's governor, John Sevier. What the Campbell group sought was a one-house legislature, manhood suffrage, voting by ballot, and even a popular referendum of all laws before final passage. What the opposition pushed for was a much less democratic constitution modeled on North Carolina's. When, in 1787, North Carolina sought to control the election, the opposing factions came to blows. After a precarious four-year existence the "Franklin" movement collapsed, North Carolina momentarily reestablished jurisdiction, then ceded its western claims. The region was organized in 1790 as the "Territory South of the River Ohio," with William Blount as governor, and was admitted into the Union as a state in 1796.[17]

Ineffectual as the Congress under the Confederation proved to be in most areas, it scored its greatest success in its arrangements for the public domain and its statesmanlike provisions for the settlement and the admission of new states. However, before it could exercise uncontested authority in the West, it had to have its jurisdiction over the areas confirmed. The need of centralized control of Western Lands had long been evident. The spectacle of hordes of squatters contesting every inch of the ground with speculators, and of both groups subject to fierce Indian retaliation, furnished compelling reason for centralized control. The subject had been tackled at the Albany Congress of 1754, but sea-to-sea charters of some of the states and the issues pressed by land companies in still others postponed the obvious decision. Shelburne was quite right in referring to "the nonsense" of the charters. The four southernmost colonies, claiming to the "South Sea" (Pacific Ocean), had been implicitly limited by the Franco-British negotiations of 1763 to extend only to the Mississippi. New York never claimed even as far west as the Mississippi but only into the Ohio-Michigan area, under a highly dubious deed from the Iroquois. The claims of Massachusetts (John Adams notwithstanding) and Connecticut to distant lands separated by neighboring colonies were visionary. Yet, as we have seen, Massachusetts would secure title, if not jurisdiction, to a goodly part of western New York, and Connecticut ultimately received western territory equal to its own area in satisfaction of its pretensions.[18]

The point has been made that the entire Northwest had been Crown land, "ungranted and unoccupied, although some claims for military bounty grants had attached to it" under the Proclamation of 1763.[19] Virginia's interest in the area was a mere expectancy, as were the expectancies for sale or settlement held by Virginia's rival claimants. With the Definitive Peace, the question whether title to these vast areas passed to the states or to the United States caused bitter controversies.[20] Fortunately, the issue was resolved by the cession of Western Lands by all the claimant states, a precondition to Maryland's adoption of the Articles of Confederation set by that state back in 1778. Virginia, by its cession in 1780, fulfilled Maryland's terms of admission, while prudently conditioning its cession with the provision that all ceded lands (save military bounties) be laid out in new states and be "a common fund for . . . members of the Confederation."[21]

What has been hailed as "the greatest date and act in the history of American federalism"[22] occurred on October 10, 1780, when Virginia stipulated that the lands so acquired should be "formed into distinct republican states, which shall become members of the federal union, and have the same rights of sovereignty, freedom, and independence, as the other states."[23] Virginia's cession was voted on January 2, 1781; Maryland ratified the Articles on February 2. On March 1, 1781, the Confederation was legally established with the delivery of the deeds of New York and Virginia and Maryland's long-delayed signature to the Articles.[24]

The land cessions provided Congress with an incomparable opportunity for creative statesmanship, and its delegates responded to the challenge. So did the land speculators. Fortuitously, Thomas Jefferson happened to be serving in Congress in 1784 as a delegate from Virginia, and his far-sighted republican and anticolonial goals were reflected in Congress's initial proposal. As chairman of the committee to draft an ordinance for the new public domain, Jefferson presented a plan which embraced a temporary government in the West. He would have divided the domain into ten districts, ultimately to become states. Whenever a particular territory numbered twenty thousand people, it was to call a convention, adopt a constitution, and send delegates to Congress. Then when the population of the territory equaled that of the free inhabitants of the smallest of the thirteen states, the new state was to be admitted to the Union on an equal footing. Its attachment was understood to be permanent; it was expected to pay its share of the federal debt, maintain a republican government, and exclude slavery after 1800. With only a few changes—but fatefully the dropping of the no-slavery clause—Congress adopted the program yet never put it into effect.[25]

Perhaps Jefferson's departure to take over Franklin's ministry in

Paris made the difference, but it is unlikely that even Jefferson, had he remained in Congress, could have overcome the opposition of land speculative interests, pro-slavery advocates, and Eastern conservatives in the final shaping of a compromise land and territorial policy that was less egalitarian and consensual than he had envisioned.

Jefferson would have given the public domain to the settlers on the ground that they would still have to pay their share of the national debt. Furthermore, as a realist he recognized that many settlers would occupy the land whether or not they had paid for it, while the settlers' presence both as security and income production would far outweigh the payment exacted by the government. The Virginian's view did not prevail, however. The Land Ordinance of 1785 divided the West into townships, each containing thirty-six square miles. Four sections in each township were to be reserved for the United States, along with one third of the gold, silver, and copper discovered. In each township, lot 16 was set aside for a public school (a proposal to reserve a lot for the support of the religion of a majority of the residents narrowly missed passage). After survey the land was to be put up for sale at public auction in minimum lots of 640 acres—an amount largely out of the reach of the poorer prospective settlers—at a price of not less than a dollar an acre, payment to be made in specie, loan office certificates reduced to specie value, or certificates of the liquidated debt of the United States. In addition, the act set aside bounty lands promised the army during the war.[26] The surveys proved a tediously slow process, and by 1787 just four ranges of townships starting at the western boundary of Pennsylvania had been completed.

Even these provisions for land sales at public auction did not satisfy the speculators. In July 1787 the Ohio Company Associates, a New England group of Revolutionary War veterans, spearheaded by Benjamin Tupper, General Rufus Putnam, Samuel Holden Parsons, and that skillful lobbyist the Reverend Manasseh Cutler, an ex-army chaplain, offered to buy a million and a half acres (actually 1,781,760 acres) lying beyond the survey for a dollar an acre payable in loan office certificates issued to officers and soldiers of the Continental Army. This was a great deal for the associates since national debt certificates were selling on the open market at 10 cents on the dollar.[27] To win a key ally, the associates proposed making General Arthur St. Clair territorial governor. At that time St. Clair was serving as president of Congress.

The deal had smooth sailing. Not only did Cutler's group get the million and a half acres but also an option on another five million. As part of the understanding, St. Clair was elected the first territorial governor and Winthrop Sargent, one of the Ohio Company principals, territorial secretary. A few months later Congress sold a million acres (a twenty-mile strip east of the Great Miami) to John Cleves Symmes, a delegate to Congress from New Jersey. The speculators moved fast in contrast to the prospective settlers who refused to be rushed to the first public auction of Ohio lands that fall, a sale which brought in a meagre $176,000. The fact is that the small homesteaders descended on the public lands as squatters, defying Congress, the Indians, and the speculators, clashing with both state and federal troops on the frontier, and in effect forcing the hand of Congress to set up a territorial government. Out of the two main speculative operations two chief settlements emerged—Marietta, founded by the Ohio Company group, and Cincinnati, out of the Symmes patent, the latter town to become a major military and commercial outpost of the new territory.

On July 13, 1787, at the very moment when the delegates in Philadelphia were on the verge of adopting the Great Compromise of the Constitution, Congress, sitting in New York, enacted the Northwest Ordinance. Of all the legislation adopted by the Congress of the Confederation, the Great Ordinance proved to be that body's most seminal achievement. Perfectionists have criticized it because it did not grant instant democracy to the new territories.[28] Had the territorial ordinance been Jefferson's instead of the handiwork of Nathan Dane, the Massachusetts jurist, and his collaborators, George Bancroft felt that it would have marked "an era in the history of universal freedom," and some recent historians have also faulted Congress for drastically changing Jefferson's plan of 1784 in a quasi-colonial direction.[29]

In reality, Jefferson's plan incorrectly gauged public opinion. The South was not ready to abolish slavery in future territories south of the Ohio. Eastern conservatives were not ready to turn the territories over to what they regarded as lawless elements suffering from

An ORDINANCE for the GOVERNMENT of the TERRITORY of the UNITED STATES, North-West of the River Ohio.

BE IT ORDAINED by the United States in Congrefs affembled, That the faid territory, for the purpofes of temporary government, be one diftrict; fubject, however, to be divided into two diftricts, as future circumftances may, in the opinion of Congrefs, make it expedient.

Be it ordained by the authority aforefaid, That the eftates both of refident and non-refident proprietors in the faid territory, dying inteftate, fhall defcend to, and be diftributed among their children, and the defcendants of a deceafed child in equal parts; the defcendants of a deceafed child or grand-child, to take the fhare of their deceafed parent in equal parts among them: And where there fhall be no children or defcendants, then in equal parts to the next of kin, in equal degree; and among collaterals, the children of a deceafed brother or fifter of the inteftate, fhall have in equal parts among them their deceafed parents fhare; and there fhall in no cafe be a diftinction between kindred of the whole and half blood; faving in all cafes to the widow of the inteftate, her third part of the real eftate for life, and one third part of the perfonal eftate; and this law relative to defcents and dower, fhall remain in full force until altered by the legiflature of the diftrict. ——— And until the governor and judges fhall adopt laws as herein after mentioned, eftates in the faid territory may be devifed or bequeathed by wills in writing, figned and fealed by him or her, in whom the eftate may be, (being of full age) and attefted by three witneffes; ——— and real eftates may be conveyed by leafe and releafe, or bargain and fale, figned, fealed, and delivered by the perfon being of full age, in whom the eftate may be, and attefted by two witneffes, provided fuch wills be duly proved, and fuch conveyances be acknowledged, or the execution thereof duly proved, and be recorded within one year after proper magiftrates, courts, and regifters fhall be appointed for that purpofe; and perfonal property may be transferred by delivery, faving, however, to the French and Canadian inhabitants, and other fettlers of the Kaskaskies, Saint Vincent's, and the neighbouring villages, who have heretofore profeffed themfelves citizens of Virginia, their laws and cuftoms now in force among them, relative to the defcent and conveyance of property.

Be it ordained by the authority aforefaid, That there fhall be appointed from time to time, by Congrefs, a governor, whofe commiffion fhall continue in force for the term of three years, unlefs fooner revoked by Congrefs; he fhall refide in the diftrict, and have a freehold eftate therein, in one thoufand acres of land, while in the exercife of his office.

There fhall be appointed from time to time, by Congrefs, a fecretary, whofe commiffion fhall continue in force for four years, unlefs fooner revoked, he fhall refide in the diftrict, and have a freehold eftate therein, in five hundred acres of land, while in the exercife of his office; it fhall be his duty to keep and preferve the acts and laws paffed by the legiflature, and the public records of the diftrict, and the proceedings of the governor in his executive department; and tranfmit authentic copies of fuch acts and proceedings, every fix months, to the fecretary of Congrefs: There fhall alfo be appointed a court to confift of three judges, any two of whom to form a court, who fhall have a common law jurifdiction, and refide in the diftrict, and have each therein a freehold eftate in five hundred acres of land, while in the exercife of their offices; and their commiffions fhall continue in force during good behaviour.

The governor and judges, or a majority of them, fhall adopt and publifh in the diftrict, fuch laws of the original ftates, criminal and civil, as may be neceffary, and beft fuited to the circumftances of the diftrict, and report them to Congrefs, from time to time, which laws fhall be in force in the diftrict until the organization of the general affembly therein, unlefs difapproved of by Congrefs; but afterwards the legiflature fhall have authority to alter them as they fhall think fit.

The governor for the time being, fhall be commander in chief of the militia, appoint and commiffion all officers in the fame, below the rank of general officers; all general officers fhall be appointed and commiffioned by Congrefs.

Previous to the organization of the general affembly, the governor fhall appoint fuch magiftrates and other civil officers, in each county or townfhip, as he fhall find neceffary for the prefervation of the peace and good order in the fame: After the general affembly fhall be organized, the powers and duties of magiftrates and other civil officers fhall be regulated and defined by the faid affembly; but all magiftrates and other civil officers, not herein otherwife directed, fhall, during the continuance of this temporary government, be appointed by the governor.

For the prevention of crimes and injuries, the laws to be adopted or made fhall have force in all parts of the diftrict, and for the execution of procefs, criminal and civil, the governor fhall make proper divifions thereof—and he fhall proceed from time to time, as circumftances may require, to lay out the parts of the diftrict in which the Indian titles fhall have been extinguifhed, into counties and townfhips, fubject, however, to fuch alterations as may thereafter be made by the legiflature.

So foon as there fhall be five thoufand free male inhabitants, of full age, in the diftrict, upon giving proof thereof to the governor, they fhall receive authority, with time and place, to elect reprefentatives from their counties or townfhips, to reprefent them in the general affembly; provided that for every five hundred free male inhabitants there fhall be one reprefentative, and fo on progreffively with the number of free male inhabitants, fhall the right of reprefentation increafe, until the number of reprefentatives fhall amount to twenty-five, after which the number and proportion of reprefentatives fhall be regulated by the legiflature; provided that no perfon be eligible or qualified to act as a reprefentative, unlefs he fhall have been a citizen of one of the United States three years and be a refident in the diftrict, or unlefs he fhall have refided in the diftrict three years, and in either cafe fhall likewife hold in his own right, in fee fimple, two hundred acres of land within the fame:—Provided alfo, that a freehold in fifty acres of land in the diftrict, having been a citizen of one of the ftates, and being refident in the diftrict; or the like freehold and two years refidence in the diftrict fhall be neceffary to qualify a man as an elector of a reprefentative.

The reprefentatives thus elected, fhall ferve for the term of two years, and in cafe of the death of a reprefentative, or removal from office, the governor fhall iffue a writ to the county or townfhip for which he was a member, to elect another in his ftead, to ferve for the refidue of the term.

The general affembly, or legiflature, fhall confift of the governor, legiflative council, and a houfe of reprefentatives. The legiflative council fhall confift of five members, to continue in office five years, unlefs fooner removed by Congrefs, any three of whom to be a quorum, and the members of the council fhall be nominated and appointed in the following manner, to wit: As foon as reprefentatives fhall be elected, the governor fhall appoint a time and place for them to meet together, and, when met, they fhall nominate ten perfons, refidents in the diftrict, and each poffeffed of a freehold in five hundred acres of land, and return their names to Congrefs; five of whom Congrefs fhall appoint and commiffion to ferve as aforefaid; and whenever a vacancy fhall happen in the council, by death or removal from office, the houfe of reprefentatives fhall nominate two perfons, qualified as aforefaid, for each vacancy, and return their names to Congrefs; one of whom Congrefs fhall appoint and commiffion for the refidue of the term; and every five years, four months at leaft before the expiration of the time of fervice of the members of council, the faid houfe fhall nominate ten perfons, qualified as aforefaid, and return their names to Congrefs, five of whom Congrefs fhall appoint and commiffion to ferve as members of the council five years, unlefs fooner removed. And the governor, legiflative council, and houfe of re-

Northwest Ordinance

a "depravity of manners" and "but little less savage than the Indians."[30] The speculators in Western Lands, both North and South, were sure to have a say in the final arrangements. Lastly, to secure the frontier, Congress had to come up with a stronger government than Jefferson's plan provided. As Nathan Dane, the principal author of the Ordinance, later wrote: "We wanted to abolish the old [Jefferson's] system and get a better one . . . and we finally found it necessary to adopt the best system we could get."[31]

If the Northwest Ordinance signaled the reestablishment of the colonial system from which the original states had only just escaped, it must be conceded that the stage of tutelary government was meant to be temporary and in principle devoid of any notion of permanent dependency. True, for some people that meant a goodly wait for statehood—twenty-three years for Illinois, thirty-seven for Michigan, and fifty-one for Wisconsin. Still, as a model for the whole world of admitting territories to statehood on an equal footing, the Northwest Ordinance was an unprecedented anticolonial measure and a centerpiece of American federalism.

The Ordinance combined a structure of territorial government and a schedule of admission to statehood with a set of provisions regarding property, contracts, and basic civil rights. In its initial stage the territory was to be governed by a governor, secretary, and judges appointed by Congress. The second stage would be reached when the territory comprised five thousand free adult male inhabitants. At that point the settlers were entitled to have their own bicameral legislature. When the territory attained a population of sixty thousand free inhabitants ("male" significantly omitted), it was eligible to admission as a new state to be "on an equal footing with the original states in all respects whatsoever." Ultimately, it was planned, from three to five states were to be created out of the Northwest Territory.

Some of the most significant substantive provisions were contributed by Dane, including the clause prohibiting slavery (with prompting from Rufus King), another prohibiting the enactment of any law impairing the obligation of contracts, and a law establishing inheritance of land on the basis of an unqualified fee simple and equal division in intestate succession. One authority considers the latter provision the first of two great steps toward democracy in the disposal of public lands; the second was taken by Congress in gradually adjusting the law governing those lands to favor a first squatter.[32]

The structural sections of the Ordinance were followed by a set of provisions "considered as articles of compact between the original States and the people and States in the said territory and forever [to] remain unalterable, unless by common consent." These included freedom of "peaceable" worship, habeas corpus, trial by jury; proportionate representation in the legislature; judicial proceedings to be conducted according to common law; availability of bail; moderate fines and avoidance of cruel and unusual punishments; protection of property by due process; prohibiting the enactment of laws impairing the obligation of contracts; forbidding slavery but permitting the recovery of persons escaping from one of the original states "from whom labor or service is lawfully claimed"; calling for dealings with the Indians with "the utmost good faith"; providing that the constitution and government "so to be formed, shall be republican"; and that the territories and states so formed "shall forever remain a part of the Confederacy of the United States of America, subject to the Articles of Confederation, and to such alterations there as shall be constitutionally made, as well as to the laws of Congress."[33]

While the fame of the Ordinance deservedly rested on these compacts, the governmental structure it innovated proved hospitable to the opening of the West. The Ordinance served as a model for the admission of states in other parts of the Union, and did so at a crucial moment, since the federal Constitution then being drafted managed to avoid any mention of territories. The votes and acts of Congress conclusively demonstrate that it was the sense of the nation that the United States should become an extended republic with safeguards for civil liberties, and ultimately stripped of the vestiges of colonialism. The legality of the Ordinance was confirmed by act of the federal Congress in 1792.[34]

The Mississippi Question

Of all the diplomatic negotiations conducted during the years of the Confederation, those with Spain, though inconclusive, had the most profound impact on American politics, most clearly disclosed sectional tensions barely lurking below the surface, and were of paramount concern to the West. Significantly, none of the major issues between the two nations which Jay had sought to settle in Madrid during the years 1780–82 had been resolved in early 1785 when Jay took up his post as Secretary for Foreign Affairs. Barriers to American commerce with the Spanish dominions had again been raised with the ending of the war. The claim of the United States to the free navigation of the Mississippi to the sea was still denied by Spain. Boundaries were still in dispute. Spain did not recognize the Mississippi as the western boundary of the United States, while the northern boundary of West Florida was still in contention. Related to the boundary controversies was the contest in progress between the two nations for the preponderant influence over the Indians in the Southwest.

As regards the thorniest of these issues, the opening of the Mississippi to American trade, Congress, while Jay was in Spain, had altered his instructions to permit him in return for a Spanish alliance to withdraw his insistence upon the free navigation of the Mississippi below 31° NL. Jay prudently made the revised offer to Florida-blanca of limited duration and contingent upon Spain's acceptance of it. Should Spain decline, Jay made clear, the United States would reserve all its rights to the Mississippi.[35] Jay's conversations in Paris with the Conde de Aranda, Spain's ambassador, were similarly inconclusive, while disclosing that France sided with Spain in the latter's effort to restrain the territorial pretensions of the Americans.[36]

By war's end Congress was no longer prepared to surrender its claim to the free navigation of the Mississippi. On June 3, 1784, it instructed the American negotiators that they were not to relinquish or cede "in any event whatever" the free navigation of that river "from its source to the ocean."[37] Although the port of New Orleans lay along the east bank of the Mississippi and although Spain held both banks of that river upwards of two hundred miles from the sea, a navigational servitude had been placed on the lower reaches of the river by the Treaty of Paris of 1763, providing for the free navigation of that river "in its whole breadth and length, from its source to the sea, and expressly that part, which is between the said island of New Orleans, and the right bank of that River, as well as the passage both in and out of its mouth."[38] Once Spain had reconquered the Floridas, it regarded that servitude as canceled.[39] Contrariwise, in their preliminary peace negotiations both Jay and Richard Oswald assumed the continuation of the 1763 servitude, and relied on it in their inclusion in the Preliminary Treaty of the provision for the free navigation of the Mississippi from its source to its mouth to be available to both the subjects of Great Britain and the citizens of the United States.[40] To a westward-expanding America the free navigation of the Mississippi was deemed crucial. Not only would the river's unobstructed navigation sustain and buoy Western land values, but to Western settlers the river's free passage for shipping products to market provided enormous cost advantages compared with the alternative trans-mountain routes.

Despite the American argument that the surrender by the Definitive Treaty of 1783 of Britain's western territory to the United States transferred not only the property but the servitude of the river as well, Spain abruptly terminated the special privileges granted during the war to American traders in Havana and New Orleans,[41] and on June 26, 1784, instructed the governor ad interim of Louisiana to proclaim that, until the boundaries of Louisiana and the Floridas should be settled, Americans would not be allowed to navigate the Mississippi within Spanish territory.[42]

The evidence is now clear that Spain hoped to resolve these issues by negotiation; but as prospects for a long-term settlement dimmed after 1786, Spanish officials carried on a series of intrigues with Western settlers to promote Western disaffection, albeit the frontiersmen took the initiative in such dealings.[43] Meantime, neither the state of Georgia nor the United States lost any time in making treaties with the Southwest Indians to bring them under American protection and to recognize the line of 31° NL as "the southern boundary of the United States of America,"[44] including areas in dispute between Spain and the United States. Not to be outdone, the Spanish government made treaties with three of the four tribes of the region, in which the Indians put themselves under Spanish protection and entered into alliance for the defense of Louisiana and West Florida, for which latter purpose the Creek Indians were given Spanish arms.

In addition to the prohibition of Americans from navigating the Mississippi, other Spanish trade restrictions kept the two powers in a state of tension. Although the special privileges Spain had granted Americans during the war to trade in Havana and New Orleans were now terminated, trade between peninsular Spain and the United States was permitted to continue at the sufferance of Spanish municipal decrees. Spanish vessels continued to enter American ports on what amounted in practice to be a most-favored-nation basis, but lacked formal treaty protection.[45] Since neither trade matters nor the other outstanding issues could be settled between Aranda and the American commissioners in Paris, these, too, were deferred to the end of the war.

To negotiate with the United States on these outstanding issues, Spain dispatched to America a special plenipotentiary with the title of *encargado de negociós,* literally, chargé d'affaires, but without the precise significance of the latter title. The plenipotentiary was Don Diego de Gardoqui, whose father had headed the firm of Gardoqui and Sons, which had been the go-between for the funneling of secret military stores to the American revolutionaries. During the period of the war, Don Diego had held a subordinate post in the Ministry of Finance at Madrid and served as an unofficial contact between the Spanish government and Jay, America's unaccredited minister.[46] Gardoqui's departure from Spain for the United States had long been anticipated by Jay, but with the *festina lente* tempo prevailing at the Spanish court, the Spaniard's arrival in the United States, which had seemed imminent in the summer of 1781,[47] did not materialize for a full four years.

Gardoqui was bound by specific instructions. He could accept the boundary line of East Florida laid down in the British-American Treaty of 1783, but he was instructed to reject the 31° NL line therein stated for the northern boundary of West Florida. Nor was he permitted to relinquish Spain's right to the exclusive navigation of the Mississippi River where it ran between Spanish banks. As regards claims of the United States west of the Appalachians, he was urged to press for a Spanish eastern line to be bounded by the Apalachicola River above its junction with the Flint and Chattahoochee, then down that river to the Ohio and along the Ohio to the Mississippi. But this line was negotiable. For any counterproposal regarding this boundary, Gardoqui was ordered to await instructions from Bernardo de Gálvez, Captain General of Louisiana and Cuba. Spain, so Gardoqui was instructed, was prepared to agree to reciprocal most-favored-nation privileges, including liberal treatment of American ships at Spain's peninsular ports. If, in order to secure recognition of Spain's right to the exclusive navigation of the Mississippi and the boundary of West Florida, Gardoqui deemed it necessary to proffer a treaty of alliance with a mutual guarantee of possessions in North America, in accordance with Jay's proposed draft treaty of September 22, 1781, the *encargado de negociós* was so authorized.[48]

Jay's instructions, in turn, provided little room for compromise, the commercial aspects of the negotiations excepted. On August 25, 1785, Congress, acting on the recommendations of a committee comprising Elbridge Gerry, James Monroe, and William Samuel Johnson, specifically instructed Jay that any treaty he made should stipulate the right of the United States "to their territorial bounds and the free navigation of the Mississippi, from the source to the Ocean, as established in their treaties with Great Britain," and enjoined him not to conclude "any treaty, compact, or convention" until he had previously communicated it to Congress and received the approval of that body.[49] Congress soon left the door slightly ajar to boundary concessions. What touched off the conciliatory gestures were the complaints of Gardoqui to Jay about the activities of agents of Georgia in signing treaties with a few irresponsible representatives of the Creek Indians ceding land in the southwestern part of the present state limits, as well as incursions into the area of settlers from other portions of Georgia.[50] Jay was instructed by Congress on October 1 to express concern about "the unwarrantable attempts of any Individual of these States to disturb the good understanding which so happily subsists" between Spain and the United States "and which they hope will be perpetual." Without waiving any territorial claims, Jay was told to notify the *encargado de negociós* that "every subject of controversy will be ultimately adjusted to the mutual satisfaction of both parties."[51] Jay could well have considered this to be a broad hint that America's boundary pretensions were not inflexible, a view that the Secretary adopted in his negotiations.[52]

In sum, the real sticking points in the negotiations were the navigation of the Mississippi, which Gardoqui was forbidden to yield, and the boundaries of West Florida and the east bank of the Mississippi, on which last subject the instructions of the opposing sides diverged sharply.

Even before Jay received his formal instructions, he had, by July of 1785, begun preliminary talks. Gardoqui had a plan of action which he described to his superiors in Madrid. In essence: pay assiduous court to both John and Sarah Livingston Jay. Right on target though Gardoqui might have been about Jay's bump of self-esteem and abiding affection for his wife, he was far off the mark in his belief that they were fortune-hunters like most Americans.[53] Throughout his career, and certainly in his relation with the *encargado de negociós,* Jay was the soul of propriety. Even the royal gift to Jay of a Spanish horse would not be accepted until he received the consent of Congress, while the American Secretary for Foreign Affairs politely declined Gardoqui's presents intended for Jay's wife.[54]

Both Jay and Gardoqui kept records of their talks. The latter carefully summarized his conversations with Jay and reported them either to Bernardo de Gálvez or to Floridablanca. In turn, Jay kept a letterbook, copying therein his correspondence with the Spanish envoy, relevant instructions and proceedings of Congress, and his reports to that body for the entire period of his negotiations with Gardoqui covering the years 1785–89.[55]

What does not appear either in Jay's letterbook or in his reports to Congress are the "Brief Summary Notes" of a conference, penned early in February 1786 by Gardoqui and transmitted to his home government. The "Notes" suggest a wide divergence between what Gardoqui led his superiors to believe about the terms of a tentative agreement and what Jay acknowledged in his reports to Congress. If Gardoqui was accurately reporting the terms of agreement—and Samuel Flagg Bemis does not venture to challenge the Spaniard's account[56]—Jay had agreed not only to the commercial articles but also to a military alliance to defend the territories of both Spain and the United States in North America.

Jay's failure to inform Congress that he was negotiating a military alliance to defend territories in dispute between Spain and the United States, the boundary concession of Gardoqui notwithstanding, might be ascribed to plain prudence or even deception. Surely Jay must have realized that it would be difficult enough to obtain the votes of the minimum nine states necessary to forgo the navigation of the Mississippi without having them agree to additional terms which would have offered palpable advantages to Eastern commerce and Northern frontier security without perceptible gains for the South and West.

Can Gardoqui's account be taken at face value? One must keep in mind the optimistic tenor of Gardoqui's early dispatches to Spain. One also must realize that the territorial concession which he added as marginalia to his report on the tentative agreement on trade seems contrary to his written instructions. Does it not seem extraordinary that Jay failed to include, either among his own papers and notes or among those he submitted to Congress, any confirmatory memorandum suggesting that he had come to an agreement at this time on boundaries? Is it not a more plausible inference that the Secretary was prepared to sound out Congress about forgoing the navigation of the Mississippi in order to win a highly attractive commercial agreement, again assuming that the boundaries defined in the Treaty of 1783 would prove acceptable to Spain?

That the Jay–Gardoqui talks were still at a tentative stage and that no meeting of the minds along the lines of the Gardoqui memorandum to Floridablanca had been attained even months later is evident from Gardoqui's letter to Jay of May 25.[57] Therein, the Spaniard, while rejecting America's claims to the navigation of the lower Mississippi on the basis of the British servitude, proposed to recommend to the king that America's possessions be guaranteed. No mention now of the mutual defense treaty he had articulated almost four months earlier.

Recognizing that the Mississippi question was the stumbling block, Jay decided to ascertain congressional sentiment among Southern delegates by sounding out James Monroe. In retrospect Jay's approach to Monroe, who was to prove Jay's *bête noire* in this negotiation, may have seemed imprudent. In fact, the Secretary for Foreign Affairs had some ground for feeling that the upper South, notably Maryland, which had no Western Land claims or urgent need to utilize the Mississippi, and, more particularly, Virginia, might go along with his proposal. Soundings had disclosed that a number of prominent Virginians were sympathetic. Washington, who with the support of the legislature of his state had, as we have seen, formed the Potomac Company to open a route to the western country from tidewater Virginia by connecting the Potomac and Ohio rivers, had been circulating the opinion that the immediate settlement of the West would people a territory lacking the cement of "interest," which would bind it to the Union, its inhabitants having "no predilection for it."[58] Richard Henry Lee, with whom

Jay had had frequent contacts during the Virginian's recent service as president of Congress, shared Washington's views and was an ardent advocate of Jay's proposal,[59] and so did Henry Lee, who came to Congress in the winter of '86 as a delegate from Virginia.[60] Even in the lower South support could be found among at least one eminent figure for deferring the Mississippi question. Writing to Jay in November of 1786 on his return to Charleston, Edward Rutledge reported:

The subject of the western waters I found was in the possession of many of our people on my arrival. Various are their opinions; the majority of those, with whom I have conversed, believe we should be benefited by a limited cession of it to Spain, or rather a cession for a limited time. But then we must take care and be explicit on one head: we must not be called upon by Spain at a future day to guarantee the cession. That will be absolutely impracticable; she should understand clearly the extent of our engagement. If from our relinquishment at present, she can obtain for a number of years the exclusive navigation of the river, it is well—it will stop migration, it will concenter force, because the settlers can have no vent for the productions of that country but down the Mississippi, and, therefore, think they will not be fond of immediately inhabiting her banks.

But when the time should arrive that would find the inhabitants "very numerous," it then would be worth while for Spain to yield the navigation of the Mississippi and "divert their minds from conquest."[61] Not even Northerners like William Samuel Johnson or Rufus King could have expressed this Southerner's views more aptly.

Hence, without perhaps anticipating the violent reaction his disclosures would prompt, Jay approached James Monroe in December of 1785. He reported to the Virginia delegate Spain's intransigence on the subject of the Mississippi and broached the idea of having the United States forbear the use of the river within exclusively Spanish limits for some twenty-five or thirty years, throwing out a feeler about the prospects of Congress's appointing a committee to control him in the negotiation. Since it was Monroe who had drawn up the binding instructions for Congress back in August of '85, the Virginian felt a sense of personal outrage, reminding Jay that Virginia's delegation was barred by its own state's instructions from complying. Jay appears to have sounded out sympathetic

Northern delegates as well. In June 1786 we find Rufus King, a confidant of Jay's, and one who incorrectly foresaw little connection between the Atlantic states and the trans-Appalachian settlements, strongly backing a trade treaty with Spain and prepared to have such a treaty stipulate "that the U.S. should forbear to use the navigation of the Mississippi for 20 or 25 years"—Jay's precise language. Such a treaty, King argued, would be of "vast importance to the Atlantic States."[62]

Monroe, who suspected King and certain New England leaders of toying with the idea of a separate confederation, felt quite differently. For reasons which are by no means clear, Monroe held his fire until August 12, 1786, when he sat down and reported the conversation of more than a half year earlier to Virginia's governor, Patrick Henry.[63]

If Jay was forewarned by Monroe's initial reactions, he was not deterred from presenting the very same proposal to Congress on May 29, following the receipt of a memorandum six days earlier from Gardoqui summarizing Spain's position.[64] Jay's recommendations precipitated the stormiest debate in the brief annals of the Confederation Congress and one that saw that body sharply divided along sectional lines. On May 31 Congress named Rufus King of Massachusetts, Charles Pettit of Pennsylvania, and James Monroe, to a committee to consider Jay's report and make recommendations.[65] After a delay of two months the committee recommended its own discharge, a recommitment of the Spanish matter to a committee of the whole, and a request to Jay to appear before Congress and give that body full information on the subject under review. These recommendations were made on August 1 by King and Pettit, Monroe apparently refusing to join. Congress approved them without delay.[66]

Pursuant to Congress's request, Jay appeared before Congress on August 3. His remarks were designed to persuade his hearers of the advantages of the trade treaty, the terms of which, as Jay reported, he and Gardoqui had tentatively agreed upon. The terms provided for (1) reciprocity; (2) the establishment of consulates; (3) admission into Spain and its European islands and into the United States of the manufactures and products of either country (American tobacco excepted), with duties based on exact reciprocity; (4) Spain's commitment to order masts and timber to be paid for in specie; and

(5) while Spain's European islands as well as peninsular Spain were to be open to reciprocal trade but not Spanish America. Jay sought to assure Congress that flour and other commodities from America would surely find their way into Spanish America via the Canaries.

In short, a good deal for America, as Jay described it. However, for the successful negotiation of the Spanish treaty, America had to forgo its claim to the navigation of the Mississippi through Spanish territories. Why not do so for, say, twenty-five or thirty years, Jay proposed, since this was, in his words, "not *at present* important," nor likely to be so for that proposed time span. We lose nothing, argued lawyer Jay, since "they who take a lease admit the right of the Lessor," and after twenty-five or thirty years the West would be so heavily populated that Spain would recognize the impracticality of denying the right. As to the Florida boundary, he believed it better "to yield a few acres than to part in ill-humour."

Jay proceeded to paint a gloomy picture of the alternative—the rejection of the trade treaty. "Unblessed with an efficient government, destitute of funds, and without public Credit either at home or abroad, we should be obliged to wait in patience for better days, or plunge into an unpopular and dangerous War with very little prospect of terminating it by a peace, either advantageous or glorious."[67]

The subject of the Spanish negotiations occupied the attention of Congress in committee of the whole, first on August 10 and then over several days between the 16th and 23rd of that month.[68] The debates brought into dangerous focus the sharp differences on the subject between Northerners and Southerners. Charles Pinckney took up the cudgels for his section in perhaps the lengthiest speech, delivered on August 16. Denying that the commercial treaty offered real reciprocity, he particularly denounced the forbearance of the navigation of the Mississippi on the ground that the sale and disposition of the lands ceded in the Western territory had always been considered by Congress as providing a sufficient fund for the discharge of the domestic debt. Predicting that the Western settlements would inevitably turn to the Mississippi, Pinckney warned that this would lead to a severance of the ties between East and West.[69] James Monroe stressed the lack of reciprocity in the commercial treaty and downplayed the value of the sale of masts to Spain. It was William Grayson who let the cat out of the bag by declaring that the Spanish treaty "would destroy the hopes of the principal men" in the Southern states of establishing the future fortunes of their families. In refutation, Rufus King queried whether one "must sacrifice the interest and happiness of a Million" people to promote the interests of a few "speculating landjobbers." He warned that failure to buy time might lead to a war for which America was ill-prepared. "The fact is," King reminded his fellow delegates by way of summation, that "you cannot use the River for twenty years."[70]

Without seeking to ascertain the real motives behind Southern opposition, which two constitutional scholars, echoing James Monroe's charges, impute to the dimming of the bright prospects of Southern political power to be augmented by the addition of new states to the Union,[71] it might be illuminating to learn how an astute foreign observer of the contemporary scene reacted to the debates. Louis Guillaume Otto, reporting to the Comte de Vergennes on September 10, 1786, found the ground for the "vigorous opposition" of the Southern states in "the great preponderance of the northern states." "To incline the balance to their side," Otto saw the Southern states as neglecting "no opportunity of increasing the population and importance of the Western territory, and of drawing thither by degrees the inhabitants of New England, whose ungrateful soil only too much favors emigration." As separate states, the new territories would be entitled to representatives in Congress and thereby "augment greatly," as Otto put it, "the mass of the Southern states."[72]

The issue was joined on a motion from the Massachusetts delegation to strike out limitations in Jay's instructions.[73] With Congress divided along sectional lines, that body voted seven states to five in favor of repealing Jay's original instructions.[74] By the identical vote Congress instructed Jay to insist on the 31st parallel as the Florida boundary.[75] The first vote outraged the Southerners, and the second failed to placate them. They now gave warning that they would refuse to ratify any treaty signed under the amended instructions which lacked the concurring vote of nine states, in effect writing finis to the Jay–Gardoqui negotiations. North Carolina delegate Timothy Bloodworth, reporting to Governor Richard Caswell, placed the issue in a larger constitutional context. "If seven States can carry a treaty, or in other words will persist in the measure," he observed,

21. Alexander Hamilton. Portrait by Charles Willson Peale, circa 1791 (Independence National Historical Park Collection)

22. *Phocion.* A pamphlet containing two newspaper essays published by Alexander Hamilton in 1784 urging strict observance of the Treaty of Peace with Great Britain (The New York Public Library)

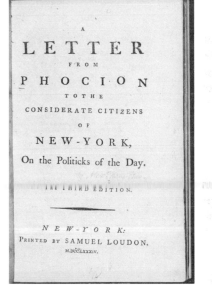

A

LETTER

FROM

PHOCION

TO THE

CONSIDERATE CITIZENS

OF

NEW-YORK,

On the Politicks of the Day.

THE THIRD EDITION.

NEW-YORK:

PRINTED BY SAMUEL LOUDON.
M.DCCLXXXIV.

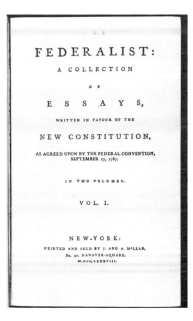

FEDERALIST:

A COLLECTION

OF

ESSAYS,

WRITTEN IN FAVOUR OF THE

NEW CONSTITUTION,

AS AGREED UPON BY THE FEDERAL CONVENTION,
SEPTEMBER 17, 1787.

IN TWO VOLUMES.

VOL. I.

NEW-YORK:

PRINTED AND SOLD BY J. AND A. M'LEAN,
No. 41, HANOVER-SQUARE.
M.DCC.LXXXVIII.

23. Title page of *The Federalist.* From the McLean first edition.

24. James Madison. Portrait by James Sharpless, Sr., painted c. 1796–97 (Independence National Historical Park Collection)

25. Mann's Tavern c. 1786. Site of the Annapolis Convention. Drawing by Polli Rodriquez (Courtesy of the Maryland Humanities Council and Maryland State Archives)

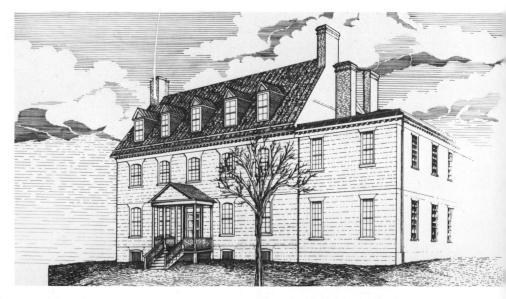

26. Women Voting in Late Eighteenth-Century New Jersey (Courtesy of *this Constitution* and Project '87)

27. Pennsylvania State House (Independence Hall). Site of the Federal Convention. From an engraving by W. Birch, 1799

28. Fort Stanwix. Council grounds for the Treaty of 1785 with the Six Nations and site of the successful stand of the Patriots against Barry St. Leger's advance toward the Mohawk Valley in 1777. Photograph of a model, 1897 (Gansevoor-Lansing Collection, New York Public Library)

29. Edmund Randolph. Fresco by Constantini Brumidi (Library of Congress)

31. James Wilson. Sepia on artist board by Longacre (National Portrait Gallery, Smithsonian Institution, Washington, D.C.)

30. Roger Sherman. Unidentified artist after Ralph Earle (National Portrait Gallery, Smithsonian Institution, Washington, D.C.)

32. William Paterson. Copy after a portrait by Mrs. B. S. Church (Supreme Court Historical Society)

33. George Mason. Painted in 1811 by Dominic W. Boudet, after the lost portrait by John Hesselius. (Independence National Historical Park Collection)

34. George Clinton. Portrait by T. B. Valenuit (Courtesy of the Oneida Historical Society)

35. Elbridge Gerry. From an engraving by J. H. Daniels (Library of Congress)

36. Richard Henry Lee. Portrait by Charles Willson Peale (National Archives and Records Administration)

37. George Washington. Plaster plaque by Joseph Wright (1756–93) (Courtesy of the estate of Robert W. Weir)

38. Washington's copy of the Constitution, with his notes. These sections concern the President's veto power (National Archives and Records Administration)

39. The federal ship *Hamilton,* centerpiece of New York City's grand procession celebrating the ratification of the Constitution by the necessary nine states. Three days later, July 26, 1788, New York ratified the Constitution (Martha Lamb, *History of New York City*)

"it follows of course, that the Confederated compact is no more than a rope of sand, and if a more efficient Government is not obtained a dissolution of the Union must take place."[76]

Winding down the talks with Gardoqui took time, however. Jay had to furnish Congress with the documentation regarding France's past attitude toward the issue of the Mississippi and the boundaries which, as Jay viewed it, provided little ground for optimism from the American point of view.[77] Further conferences with Gardoqui "produced nothing but debate," without advancing "one single step nearer to each other," as Jay reported to Congress.[78] "The Spanish project sleeps," Madison wrote Jefferson in March of 1787. Even though Madison, who had only just returned to Congress after a hiatus of more than three years, was convinced that "Mr. Jay's caution would revolt" at attempting to make a new treaty with the support of only seven states—"so irregular a sanction"[79]—the Virginian sought to persuade Congress to take the negotiations with Spain out of Jay's hands and transfer them to Jefferson's.[80] Jay rejoined quickly, pointing to the advantages of continuing talks near the seat of Congress, and Congress killed Madison's proposal.[81] The next day, Georgia moved that the repeal did not authorize the Secretary to permit the impairment or abandonment of the free right of navigation. As amended, the resolve asserted that Congress did not authorize Jay to enter into any stipulation with the Spanish envoy.[82]

Alert to evidence of rising sectional tensions[83] and louder talk of Western secession plots, Jay conceded that "a treaty disagreeable to one-half of the nation had better not be made, for it would be violated."[84] The Secretary took two additional steps. After carefully reconsidering the issues, he conceded in September 1788 that a forbearance of the use of the Mississippi was "more questioned than it then appeared to be," and recommended that Congress reassert the nation's right to the river's navigation and its intention never to cede it.[85] By these remarks, Jay, a foremost continentalist and spokesman for enlarging the powers of the central government, should have set to rest all rumors, no matter how fanciful, that he was spearheading a move to break up the Union.

Amid a polite exchange of letters, Don Diego de Gardoqui finally took his departure, but not before President Washington had examined the papers relating to the negotiations that Jay turned over to him, and decided not to press the Senate on the issue at that time. A resolution of the outstanding issues would be deferred for some years more until Thomas Pinckney was dispatched to Spain as envoy extraordinary following the Jay treaty with Great Britain in 1794.[86] By the Pinckney treaty, Spain recognized the boundary claims of the United States under the treaty with Britain of 1783 (the Mississippi to the west, the 31st parallel to the south) and accepted the American claim to the free navigation of the Mississippi, with the right of deposits at New Orleans for a limited period, and thereafter, if insisted upon, at another point to be designated. The winning of the West had begun.

CHAPTER 10

Effective Union or Dismembered States?

Early Nationalist Efforts

W HEN the Articles of Confederation were about to go into effect, it was clear to a few dedicated young nationalists that the Congress would be operating in a straitjacket. Unable to levy and collect taxes or regulate commerce, further limited in its powers by Article II, Congress from a practical point of view would find the Articles impossible to amend.

What to do? Hamilton, among the very first to stake out an advanced position, held no doubts. In his now famous letter to fellow nationalist James Duane, believed to have been penned from army headquarters at Liberty Pole, New Jersey, around September 3, 1780, Hamilton drew up a scathing indictment of the Articles, summed up in the statement: "The fundamental defect is a want of power in Congress." Arguing that the Confederation was "defective" and necessitated alteration, Hamilton declared that "the idea of an uncontrollable sovereignty in each state over its internal police," would "defeat the other powers given to Congress, and make our union feeble and precarious." Hamilton's alternative remedies: "Give Congress powers competent to the public exigencies," either by exercising the "discretionary powers" that Hamilton presumed to have been originally vested in that body "for the safety of the states," or by calling "immediately a convention of all the states with full authority to conclude finally upon a general confederation."

The second, which "should give Congress complete sovereignty," except as to "internal police, property rights, and internal taxes," was the one Hamilton preferred.[1]

Suffice to say that Hamilton was seven years ahead of his time, but fellow nationalists by a series of creeping steps nudged closer and closer to the movement to scrap the Articles and adopt a new Constitution. Foremost among the newer members of Congress to be found in this camp was young James Madison. His initial tack toward energizing the powers of Congress was to formulate a program based on his conception of Congress's "implied" powers, which he deduced from Article XIII of the Articles of Confederation requiring the states to abide by the determination of Congress and to observe "inviolable" the "Articles of this Confederation."

Believed to be the first occasion when Madison used a phrase so pregnant with meaning for later constitutional history, the proposals of the committee on which he served, along with James Varnum of Rhode Island as chairman and James Duane of New York,[2] deserve more than passing mention. Congress was asked to propose a new amendment to the Articles authorizing Congress "to compel the states to fulfill their federal engagements." Congress would be empowered to seize the vessels and merchandise of the citizens of the offending states and to prohibit their trade and intercourse both with other states and with foreign countries. This was indeed a revolutionary proposal because, with few exceptions, powers delegated to "the United States in Congress Assembled" were to be made effective only through the "instrumentality of the state governments." Such distraint or prohibition was to be in effect until the respective state or states complied with the requisitions of Congress. Herein Madison's committee anticipated a striking difference between the Articles and the instrument of government which was to supplant them. Congress referred the proposed amendment to a "grand committee" made up of one delegate from each state.[3] Thereafter the proposal died.

An undaunted Madison kept proposing amendments which would facilitate procedures or clarify the powers of Congress.[4] Two years later he moved for a permanent fund to be collected under the authority of Congress, a proposal reflecting earlier propositions of Hamilton and Robert Morris. The phraseology did not seem clear enough to satisfy his uninhibited fellow delegate Hamilton, who remarked in the course of the debate that the collectors should be appointed by Congress. As was noted earlier, Madison was forced ruefully to enter a note in his "Minutes" to the effect that Hamilton's "imprudent remark" "had let out the secret."[5]

If Hamilton's disclosure was meant to be a secret, the New Yorker did not think so. His remarks conformed to a public position he had taken six months earlier. In his "Continentalist" No. VI, he had stated: "The reason of allowing Congress to appoint its own officers of the customs, collectors of taxes, and military officers of every rank, is to create in the interior of each state a mass of influence in favour of the Fœderal Constitution."[6] Hamilton did not seem to calculate the extent of state jealousy and particularism existent at this time.

Still the nationalists pressed ahead for some kind of indefinite grant of revenue from the states, a resolution having special pertinence to the relationship between the holders of public loan certificates and the military officers, a connection of special concern during the winter of 1783.[7] Madison found it necessary to refute the argument that granting Congress a permanent fund would place "the purse and the sword" in the same hands, an oft-repeated remark especially attributed to Arthur Lee and John Francis Mercer.[8] Proposals to strengthen the powers of Congress continued to be made in 1784.[9] If the old Congress could not achieve powers to tax and to regulate interstate commerce, two states, recognizing the need for common action, would take the initial steps. An unusual convergence of issues drawn from history, geography, and technology linked the chain of events that would draw twelve of the thirteen states to Philadelphia in May of 1787.

The Mount Vernon Conference

It all started on a small scale, a localized conflict between Maryland and Virginia over the jurisdiction and navigation rights of waters they shared in common. For reasons quite obscure, the Virginia Constitution of 1776—in the writing of which both Thomas Jefferson and James Madison had had a hand—recognized the claims of Maryland to the southern, i.e., the Virginia, shore of the Potomac River under the Baltimore Charter of 1632, though the Virginia Constitution also asserted Virginia's rights to the free navigation of the Potomac and Pocomoke* rivers.[10] In 1784, Madison had visited Alexandria, a port on the Virginia side of the Potomac. Shippers, foreign or domestic, were a canny breed, quick to find out which port of call offered the best deal. Madison was shocked to observe "several flagrant evasions" practiced with "impunity and success" by foreign vessels that had loaded at the port, presumably free from duty or customs supervision by the state of Virginia. On March 16, 1784, he expressed his dismay in a letter to his friend and political ally Thomas Jefferson, then sitting in Congress prior to his departure to take over the American ministry in France. Indubitably, Madison complained, Virginia should in its Constitution have expressly reserved the jurisdiction of its half of the two rivers. What better moment to approach Maryland than now and correct this maladroit piece of drafting, he asked.[11] The latter state was in particularly "good humor," having ratified the Articles of Confederation following Virginia's cession of its Western lands to Congress. Hence, it seemed timely to resolve the issue by appointing commissioners from the two states. Jefferson agreed, as he himself was disenchanted with some of the restraints of his state's constitution under which he had struggled to function as governor.

The idea met with general favor and both states designated representatives to meet, Virginia as early as June of 1784, and Maryland in January 1785. Virginia, however, kept fumbling the ball. That legislature's instructions to its delegates addressed only the rectification of the claims over the Potomac; they neglected to mention the Pocomoke River or the need to survey and divide jurisdiction over the Chesapeake Bay. Thus, the Virginia legislature in a careless moment failed to cover many issues that had plagued relations between the two colonies and states in these waters—shore rights, customs duties, disagreements over navigation, coastal defense, and lighthouses. Maryland's instructions, on the other hand, covered all the points at issue.[12]

Moreover, the muddle in Virginia continued. The state named George Mason, Edmund Randolph, Alexander Henderson, and James Madison as commissioners, but someone placed these appointments in a pigeonhole, with the result that Governor Patrick Henry neglected to notify his commissioners either of their appoint-

*The Pocomoke rises in southern Delaware, flows south across the Maryland border, emptying into Pocomoke Sound, an inlet of the Chesapeake Bay.

ment or of the time and place set for the meeting. Maryland, scrupulous in its instructions, conscientiously notified its commissioners to attend the conference at Alexandria the week of March 21, 1785. Thus, the Marylanders—Daniel of St. Thomas Jenifer, Thomas Stone, and Samuel Chase—arrived at Alexandria to find not a single Virginia commissioner awaiting them. They descended upon Alexander Henderson, an Alexandria resident, informing him that they were present and ready to proceed. News reached Mason at Gunston Hall, and that gout-ridden delegate, obviously embarrassed, decided that the meeting should proceed without delay, even though Randolph and Madison had failed to make an appearance (not receiving notification in time) and in spite of the fact that the Virginia authorizing resolution empowered *"any three"* of the commissioners to "frame such liberal and equitable regulations concerning the said river, as may be mutually advantageous to the two states."[13]

The conference, however, was not destined to remain at Alexandria. The delegates were quickly honored by an invitation from General George Washington to adjourn a few miles south to Mount Vernon, where he offered the hospitality of his estate.[14] There the conference convened on March 25. Washington acted as host but did not participate. However, it could not be said that his hospitality was entirely disinterested. Shortly to be elected president of the recently formed Potomac Company, initiated in January 1785 by acts of the Virginia and Maryland assemblies, Washington, with the collaboration of his friend and political ally "Light-Horse" Harry Lee, was already engaged in an ambitious engineering and navigation program. His objective was to bring the Potomac to the Shenandoah and Ohio valleys by a series of locks. Such a plan would make possible a successful penetration of the interior by a waterway system, at least as far west as Cumberland and the Allegheny Mountains, thereby joining East and West to the advantage of the Potomac and Chesapeake regions. Washington's company was about to embark on the construction of an initial series of locks to bypass a formidable obstacle to his long-range program—the Great Falls of the Potomac, a surging, roaring cataract some thirty-five feet high in the Potomac, which forms a series of rapids about fifteen miles above the present city of Washington where the river descends some ninety feet. Steamboating on the Potomac was being seriously considered (although its execution was held up by the fiercely contested rival claims of "inventors" James Rumsey and John Fitch), and the navigation of the interior waterways was now gaining national attention.

In the warm atmosphere of Mount Vernon and with the obvious encouragement and expert knowledge of General Washington, all the chief issues were amicably settled and an interstate compact quickly drawn up. The meeting concluded on March 28, 1785. The commissioners' report went beyond tidewater navigation to consider a multitude of problems related to navigation and commerce. It provided for entrance and clearance of vessels at naval offices and established the proportion of duties to be paid where entry was made in both states. It declared the Potomac River "a common High Way," not only to the citizens of Virginia and Maryland but to those of the United States and to all other persons "in amity with the said states" trading to or from Virginia or Maryland. It provided for common fishing rights, for erecting lighthouses, beacons, and buoys in Chesapeake Bay to be charged jointly to both states. It dealt with jurisdiction over piracy and other crimes committed on the waters off the Potomac, Pocomoke, or Chesapeake Bay; it included a provision for attachment for debt of vessels entering the Pocomoke. As regards naval security, the commissioners urged that Congress authorize the two states to make due provision, if and when needed. The commissioners further recommended equality in the valuation accorded the current money of the two states as well as foreign gold and silver coin, along with a uniform treatment of protested bills of exchange. Finally, they recommended that duties on imports and exports be the same for both states.

Indeed, the sweeping, if sensible, recommendations of the Mount Vernon Conference liberally interpreted the instructions that the respective legislatures had given to them. The five commissioners wrote to the president of the Executive Council of Pennsylvania on March 28, 1785, outlining the plans for expanding the navigation of the Potomac as far as practicable to open a convenient route from the head of such navigation to the waters running into the Ohio. Since much, if not all, of this route ran through Pennsylvania, they urged the legislature of that state to allow vessels from Maryland and Virginia passing through Pennsylvania to be exempted from duties or tolls other than those necessary to help defray Pennsylvania's share of expenditures on its portion of the project. Significantly, the commissioners further asserted the principle that the same rights of navigation be accorded the citizens of the United States, thereby stressing the notion that transportation on navigable or inland waters was a national concern.[15]

In truth, the commissioners had raised questions of great national import, timed to express a general consensus of the needs of a nation still in deep depression. Currency, commerce, navigation, debt collection, and discriminatory duties—all these were problems that could only be resolved by individual states on a stopgap basis or through interstate compacts. In fact, they compelled national attention and regulation.

Both states ratified the compact, the Maryland legislature even going so far as to propose the inclusion of Delaware in the agreement. As floor manager, James Madison, the ardent nationalist, steered the agreement through the Virginia legislature.[16] Had it been his choice, the compact would have been submitted to Congress for ratification in deference to the sixth article of the Articles of Confederation barring "two or more states" from entering into "any treaty, confederation, or alliance" without the consent of the United States in Congress assembled. His nationalist proposal was voted down, however. Instead, the Virginia House adopted a resolution, which Madison initiated and John Tyler, not then identified as an extreme nationalist, sponsored. It authorized a meeting of Virginia delegates with other state commissioners at Annapolis in 1786 to discuss "such commercial regulations [as] may be necessary to their common interest and their permanent harmony."

One example of how the ghost of the Mount Vernon Conference would haunt the Federal Convention at Philadelphia two years later has been uncovered in the recently studied notes on debates of Pierce Butler, the Irish-born South Carolina Federalist. That delegate has left us a motion made by the Maryland delegates that "no regulation of commerce or revenue shall extend to giving the ports of one state any preference to those of another state nor to require vessels bound to or from one state to pay any toll or duty in any other but the state they may have cleared for, or suffer stoppage, molestation or hindrance from the ports of any other state."[17] Thus, despite the agreement at Mount Vernon, Marylanders still felt that, with a Convention dominated by larger states such as Virginia, vessels bound for Baltimore or other Chesapeake Bay ports might be required to enter and clear first at Norfolk at the mouth of the Bay. "A tender point in Maryland," as Charles Carroll remarked; the Maryland delegation had introduced a resolution on August 25 restricting the federal government's rights over the destination of merchantmen and over ports of entry. The motion, referred to a committee of one member from each state, had led to a resolution adopted by the Convention and ultimately incorporated in part into Article I, section 9, of the Constitution, barring preferential treatment "by any Regulation of Commerce or Revenue" to the ports of one state over those of another, and providing that vessels bound to or from one state should not be obliged to enter, clear, or pay duties in another.[18] By this stroke Maryland protected the privileges it had won in its earlier compact with Virginia while further curbing continued interference with commerce and navigation by the states.

The Pinckney Plan

If the action of the Mount Vernon commissioners set the stage for the Annapolis Convention of September 1786, and buoyed the hopes of men like Madison and Hamilton that states rather than Congress offered a more feasible route to radical constitutional revision, there were others who felt that Congress should be given one last chance. At this time the chief proponent of initiating change through Congress was Charles Pinckney of South Carolina, who would later stake out a large, if inflated, claim as a principal author of the Constitution. Early in 1786, as a member of a three-man delegation dispatched to New Jersey to convince its legislators of the necessity of honoring the requisitions of Congress,[19] he had urged the legislators to issue a call for a national convention. Then in May of '86 Pinckney turned back to Congress, urging his colleagues to call a general convention and moving for a grand committee to be appointed to review national affairs. The committee did not make its report until early August, when it proposed seven additional Articles of Confederation, six of which were concerned with the regulation of trade and the collection of federal revenues and requisitions. Not only would these amendments have given Congress exclusive power over foreign and interstate commerce, but they would have set up a seven-member court to try cases against federal officials and hear cases on appeals from state courts pertaining to foreign relations and congressional regulations on commerce and revenue.[20]

This new initiative sounded bolder than it was in fact, for it was calculated to enable Congress to discharge its traditional duties, while adding thereto the regulation of trade. Its cumbersome judicial remedies for nonenforcement stopped short of the coercive power earlier proposed by Madison. Issued at the time of the great debate over the Mississippi question, the proposals were buried amidst rising sectional tensions.[21]

The Annapolis Convention

What permanently interred the Pinckney proposal was the conviction of the nationalists that the road to constitutional reform lay toward Annapolis—toward cooperative state initiative, rather than in New York where a timid and disunited Congress lacked the prestige and even the will to reform itself.

Whether Madison deserves the credit for the Annapolis plan as he later claimed, despite admitted misgivings on his own part, or whether it resulted from his backstairs initiatives, are questions which probably will never be settled. We know that at the time the proposition was adopted Madison entertained doubts as to its feasibility, while claiming credit for it some twenty years later.[22]

This we do know: the proposition for the Annapolis Convention was presented to the Virginia legislature on January 21, 1786, by John Tyler, Revolutionary Patriot, later governor, and father of a later President. Not prominently identified with the nationalist cause, Tyler's credentials for sponsoring the move would make him less suspect with the state's particularists than would Madison's, now regarded as the state's foremost advocate of enlarging the powers of the national government. Madison had only just been on the losing side of a strenuous debate over a proposal to the legislature to give Congress direct power over commerce.[23] Tyler's bill for an interstate convention lay on the table. As a ninety-seven-day session was about to conclude, an exhausted legislature took it up and adopted it with only two dissenters. The bill as amended in the Senate named an eight-man delegation, a number so large, in Madison's opinion, that it would "stifle the thing in its birth."[24] The bill called for an interstate convention "for the purpose of forming such regulations of trade as may be judged necessary to promote the general interest,"[25] and it was accompanied by a circular letter addressed to the other twelve states proposing a time and place for the meeting. The Virginia commissioners, in the absence of Madison (one of its named members), picked centrally located Annapolis and set the first Monday in September as the date for holding the Convention.[26]

Few assemblages as memorable ever accomplished so much against so many obstacles. One might have thought, first of all, that the choice of Annapolis would have been considered a compliment to its neighbor. Quite the contrary, Maryland, the host state, declined to appoint commissioners on the ground that such a meeting transcended the powers of Congress and would weaken its authority.[27] Not only did Maryland refrain from participating, but its government did not even proffer the State House for a meeting place. Then, an even more insurmountable item proved to be the convening of a majority of delegates from the thirteen states. Delayed for one reason or another, not a single commissioner from New England put in an appearance, nor did the states of the lower South participate. Should one half the states fail to participate, asked Jacob Broome, a Delaware commissioner, "how ridiculous will all this parade appear?"[28]

Dispirited as Madison had seemed at the time of the adoption of the original Annapolis resolves, he appeared to have made up his mind to ensure its success, come what may. In the spring of '86 he had prepared, with the Annapolis meeting in mind, a set of "Notes of Ancient and Modern Confederacies,"[29] and his correspondence from time to time until the meeting at Annapolis varied with his own moods from constructive to cautious pessimism.[30] On a late summer visit to Philadelphia, he informed Jefferson that "many Gentlemen both within and without Congress wish to make this Meeting subservient to a Plenipotentiary Convention for amending the Confederation." For his own part, Madison was nonetheless still committed to proceeding cautiously. "Though many are in favor of such an event," he confessed, "yet I despair so much of its accomplishment at the present crisis that I do not extend my views beyond a Commercial Reform. To speak the truth, I almost despair even of this."

When Madison reached Annapolis on September 6 and took up lodgings at Mann's Inn, which seems to have served as the site of the subsequent conference, he found that other delegates were tardy in arriving. He might very well have agreed with the logic of the suggestion of some disheartened delegates that, since only five of the thirteen states were to be finally represented at the Convention, the rump group should call off the meeting and try for a different site; but it was the presence of a few delegates that made the difference in the character of the summons that was ultimately issued. From New Jersey, Abraham Clark informed Madison that his delegation was authorized not only to consider commercial arrangements but to enter into important matters—matters that might be necessary to the "common interest and permanent harmony of the several states." Then Tench Coxe, a Pennsylvania delegate, informed the group that his state had recommended a broad consideration of the commercial laws of the individual states to achieve a "blending of interests" to "cement the union."

Perhaps the biggest difference was made by the presence of New York's ardent nationalist Alexander Hamilton. Back in 1780, Hamilton had called for a constitutional convention. In 1782, he had persuaded the New York Assembly to approve such a resolution.[31] The following year he joined Madison in proposing in Congress a general convention and then drew up a lengthy resolution to the purport, a proposal that, in Hamilton's words, was abandoned "for want of support."[32] He had never abandoned the goal. The winter of '86 saw him draft a petition on behalf of the inhabitants of New York City urging the state legislature to comply with the requisitions of Congress and declaring that "Congress without revenue cannot subsist."[33]

It was to Hamilton that Madison turned after looking over a wishy-washy resolution that Edmund Randolph, a member of a five-man committee, had drafted, seemingly striking the wrong note. Hamilton complied. His resolution was toned down somewhat, apparently in deference to Randolph's sensibilities. Although the very brief minutes do not attribute authorship to Hamilton, both Madison and the Convention's secretary, Egbert Benson, were emphatic in crediting him with the "Address of the Annapolis Convention," which was unanimously adopted. The "Address" begins by stating that the delegates did not "conceive it advisable to proceed on the business of their mission, under the Circumstances of so partial and defective a representation." It then lays the groundwork for the historic summons.

Deeply impressed however with the magnitude and importance of the object confided to them on this occasion, your Commissioners cannot forbear to indulge an expression of their earnest and unanimous wish, that speedy measures may be taken, to effect a general meeting, of the States, in a future Convention, for the same and such other purposes, as the situation of public affairs may be found to require.

Indeed, Hamilton goes further, endorsing the New Jersey proposition while insisting that the power of the delegates to the proposed convention be enlarged. "The power of regulating trade is of such comprehensive extent," he argued, "and will enter so far into the general System of the fœderal government, that to give it efficacy, and to obviate questions and doubts concerning its precise nature and limits, may require a correspondent adjustment of other parts of the Fœderal System." The "Address" then asserts:

That there are important defects in the system of the Fœderal Government is acknowledged by the Acts of all those States, which have concurred in the present Meeting; That the defects, upon a closer examination, may be found greater and more numerous, that even these acts imply, is at least so far probable, from the embarrassments which characterise the present State of our national affairs—foreign and domestic, as may reasonably be supposed to merit a deliberate and candid discussion, in some mode, which will unite the Sentiments and Councils of all the States. In the choice of the mode your Commissioners are of opinion, that a Convention of Deputies from the different States, for the special and sole purpose of entering into this investigation, and digesting a plan for supplying such defects as may be discovered to exist, will be entitled to a preference from consideration, which will occur, without being particularised.

While not seeking to enumerate the circumstances which would support "the propriety of a future Convention with more enlarged powers," the resolution points out that "the Situation of the United States" is "delicate and critical," and then follows with the formal summons:

Under this impression, Your Commissioners, with the most respectful deference, beg leave to suggest their unanimous conviction, that it may essentially tend to advance the interests of the union, if the States, by whom they have been respectively delegated, would themselves concur, and use their endeavours to procure the concurrence of the other States, in the appointment of Commissioners, to meet at Philadelphia on the second Monday in May next, to take into consideration the situation of the United States, to devise such further provisions as shall appear to them necessary to render the constitution of the Fœderal Government adequate to the exigencies of the Union; and to report such an Act for that purpose to the United States in Congress Assembled, as when agreed to, by them, and afterwards confirmed by the Legislatures of every State will effectually provide the same.

Though your Commissioners could not with propriety address these observations and sentiments to any but the States they have the honor to Represent, they have nevertheless concluded from motives of respect, to transmit Copies of this report to the United States in Congress assembled, and to the executives of the other States.[34]

Congress, which understandably showed no great warmth to a proposal that set up a mechanism to bypass that body, referred the invitation to a committee on October 11, but not until February 21, 1787, and after Virginia requested favorable action, did it adopt a cautiously phrased endorsement of the proposal. On that day, Congress described as "expedient" a convention *"for the sole and express purpose of revising the Articles of Confederation* and reporting to Congress and the several legislatures such alterations and provisions therein."[35] Without awaiting Congress's call, five states—Virginia, New Jersey, Pennsylvania, Delaware, and North Carolina—had already named delegates to the Philadelphia Convention. Significantly, eight of the twelve states to send delegations to Philadelphia instructed their delegates to operate under the broad Hamiltonian formula, while the remaining four restricted them to revising the Articles as authorized by Congress. Rhode Island, the thirteenth, mired down in bitter conflicts over paper money and debtor-creditor relations, refused to name a delegation.

How the issue of apparently irreconcilable instructions would be resolved seemed insignificant to a nation confronted with a possible dismemberment over the Mississippi question raised by the proposed Spanish treaty, and even closer to home with the prospects of a rebellion spreading from some rural counties of Massachusetts and enveloping the entire nation.

Rebellion in Massachusetts

The deepening and spreading impact of the postwar depression cast a long shadow over the efforts of the nationalists to forge a union and imbued its leadership with a sense of crisis. The civil disorder that erupted in Massachusetts and spread to other states was so deeply rooted in the frontier counties that its outbreak should not have caught conservatives by surprise. Yet, as early as February 1786 so well informed a lawyer as Nathan Dane, who had only recently served in the Massachusetts legislature and was to distinguish himself by his constructive role as a delegate to the Continental Congress, would remark: "The deliberate and firm manner in which she [Massachusetts] had conducted her policy, formed her laws, regulated her finances, and administered justice since the peace . . . have given her a degree of respectability that every other state acknowledged."[36]

Perhaps "every other state," but indubitably Dane's smug observation might have been refuted point by point by the inhabitants of the western counties of Massachusetts. No one could remember a time since the outbreak of the contest against Great Britain when that region was not boiling over in protest. Even the wartime prosperity shared by many farmers passed them by, as their products were too remote from Eastern markets. These counties had been the core of a convention movement which began as early as 1774, in vocal opposition to the high-handed actions of the British government. Shortly the movement would resume in defiance of creditors and their debt collection machinery—the courts with their excessive fees and the "mercenary lawyers," the creditors' tool. Under the initial leadership of a Congregational pastor named the Reverend Thomas Allen, the "Berkshire Constitutionalists," as they were called, sought the creation of a responsive constitutional government, including popularly elected judges. What they got was the Constitution of 1780, a conservative instrument which retained property qualifications for voting, gave judges tenure for good behavior, and conferred upon the governor broad appointive powers.

As early as 1775, the "Constitutionalists" had initiated a movement to close down the courts and prevented the judges from sitting in Hampshire until 1778 and in Berkshire until 1781.[37] Compounding the problems of the debtor farmer were the fiscal policies of the state, which seemed to discriminate against the yeoman farmer and favor the Eastern businessman. Like other states, Massachusetts issued paper money in 1780 payable later in specie and acceptable as legal tender. But since the emission money continued to depreciate, the government left it to the courts to determine its value, and in 1781 made the emissions no longer legal tender at any value. Desperately short of specie, the frontier towns found it difficult to pay taxes, and by 1783 over sixty towns in the two westernmost counties were listed as delinquent. Many of the inhabitants of these towns petitioned to do roadwork in lieu of taxes. On top of this, the state levied an excise tax on spirits distilled from one's own orchard, a tax which was especially burdensome to the poor yeoman.[38]

Confirming the conviction of the agrarian interests that the tax burden was being disproportionately shifted upon their shoulders by the commercial interests was the evidence from the assessment roles. While in 1781 the seaport towns were assessed for the same kinds of property as ten years earlier, the assessors now reached out to the farming centers for new sources of revenue, listing barns, neat cattle under two years, and swine under one year, none of which had been itemized in previous returns. Before the Constitution of 1780 went into effect, one third of the state tax was levied on polls and two thirds on real estate. But the new legislature stepped up the proportion paid by polls, reaching a new high for this period in 1785 of one pound per poll. In 1778, polls amounted to 30 percent of the entire levy; in 1781, 32.1 percent; in 1784, 36.3 percent of the state tax; and by 1786, the proportion had been increased to 40 percent. This tax, payable in specie, struck hardest at the interior counties which were the least wealthy. Thus, in the 1784 levy, Worcester actually paid 32.3 percent on polls, and Suffolk, Boston's county, only 22.8 percent. These statistics, perhaps more convincingly than any amount of rhetoric, highlight the grievances of the central and western counties.[39]

The early leadership of the protest movement was drawn from the ranks of little men, often mouthing Revolutionary catchwords and leveling sentiments but hardly prepared to suffer martyrdom. In the early 'eighties the embers of discontent were kindled by a cast-off preacher named Samuel Ely. Forced out of his parish in Somers, Connecticut, by factional quarrels, he moved across the border and settled in Hampshire County. He first came to public notice by promoting the calling of a convention in 1782. Then he raised a mob to prevent the holding of the courts at Northampton in April of that year. Ely was arrested, tried for sedition, and accused of having insisted "the constitution is broke already, the governor has too much salary, the judges of the superior court have too much salary. We can get men that will ride the circuit for half the money." Finally, he warned that "the General Court should not sit. We will pay no more respect to them than to puppies." Condemned to a term in prison, he was released by action of a mob. Then, when the ringleaders in the prison break were captured and held as hostages, the commander of the militia agreed, under duress, to release them on their parole. Everyone but Ely was pardoned. He fled to Vermont, that refuge of Yankee malcontents. From the evidence at hand it appears that this uneducated, crude, frustrated leader of the premature insurgency was in fact more of a true revolutionary in temper than his successors who would don the mantle of leadership.

In the four years that followed Ely's flight, economic conditions worsened and the state government was intransigent about providing relief. As farm prices slowly declined and the wages of farm laborers shrank to a low of 40 cents a day by 1787,[40] farm mortgages were foreclosed in rapidly increasing numbers and debtors were imprisoned and even sold into servitude.[41] The figures tell the gruesome story. In the two-year period beginning with August 1784, the Court of Common Pleas of Hampshire County prosecuted 2,977 cases of debt, a 262 percent increase over the years 1770–72. Some 31.4 percent of the county's male inhabitants over sixteen had piled up debts they could not repay, almost three times as many as in the earlier period. Darker statistics can be unearthed from Worcester County, whose courts processed four thousand suits for debt in the year 1785–86. Debtors in the year 1786 made up 80 percent of the occupants of Worcester's jail. Without belaboring the point, from Berkshire County in the western part of the state to Essex along the coast, the courts were deluged with suits against debtors. Nor was this condition confined to Massachusetts; the contagion of debt had spread its symptoms throughout New England from Connecticut to New Hampshire and Vermont.[42]

These jails rivaled any that Dickens described. The one in Worcester was a small three-story building. The lower story was assigned to serious criminals, the second story to minor offenders and debtors who had liberty of the yard. It was in this jail that Colonel Timothy Bigelow, Worcester's most famous soldier of the Revolution, spent his declining years, while war profiteers like Stephen Salisbury, who had kept far from the sound of cannon, waxed fat on mortgage foreclosures. One of the memorable passages in Edward Bellamy's *The Duke of Stockbridge* is his picture of the tavern-jail at Great Barrington, small, cramped, its walls and floors mildewed and stained with mold—a dark, noisome spot where Perez Hamlin, the veteran returned from the wars, first laid eyes upon his debtor brother, the emaciated Reuben—a fictional account faithful to contemporary eyewitness stories, the court records, and newspaper reports.

The rapid amortization of the state debt, a policy advocated by fiscal conservatives, not only helped initiate a sharp deflationary thrust but appeared to its opponents to shift the tax burden disproportionately upon the agrarian as opposed to the commercial interests. A study of petitions and votes shows the clear-cut character of sectional alignments in the critical years of 1785–86. On file in the state archives for the three-week period ending February 6, 1786, are petitions for paper money from fourteen towns, chiefly from the interior part of the state. While support was found in the coastal areas, too, the seaboard interests in the legislature (notably Suffolk) strongly opposed altering the laws for the collection of private debts. Even in seafaring Essex the representatives were about evenly divided on this question, but when one examines the votes of legislators coming from merely thirty miles west of Boston—from Worcester, for example—one finds a total opposition to Suffolk on virtually all the social and economic issues that came before the General Court.[43]

Had Samuel Ely been executed back in 1782 instead of being permitted to escape, one writer in the Boston press suggested, the insurgency that broke out four years later might have never occurred.[44] This ill-tempered speculation failed to account for the new leadership of the so-called Regulator movement. True, none possessed the fiery and magnetic qualities of a Samuel Adams or the precise intellect of his cousin John or the iron will of a Robespierre. Daniel Shays has earned a certain tarnished immortality by having the revolt named for him, but he cannot be credited with launching the movement of insurgency—a claim that Ely had already staked out—nor does he appear at any stage to outdistance measurably some of his co-leaders. In the vicinity of Springfield the military direction of the insurgency was assumed by Luke Day, a demagogue and declaimer, in bad economic straits, a veteran who had been breveted a major, Shays' senior in years by four and roughly equal in military ability. Day raised his own men, drilled and paraded them, and in lieu of uniforms had them wear a sprig of hemlock in their hats. In the absence of enough guns, they carried hickory clubs. Once sufficient arms were procured, Day talked of opposing the state militia at Springfield, and, if necessary, of spilling "the last drop of blood that ran in his veins." This extreme sacrifice, however, he forbore at a critical moment in the revolt.

At the time of the outbreak of the rebellion, Shays, its titular leader, was thirty-nine years old. Born into poverty in eastern Massachusetts, he had worked as a farm laborer, then finally settled at Pelham, where he had a farm of his own. An early enlistee, he quickly won a promotion to sergeant for bravery at Bunker's Hill. He fought with Arnold and Gates at Saratoga and with Anthony Wayne stormed Stony Point. Mustered out in 1780, he bore at least one wound to remind him of his five years of war service. "I served in the company of Shays," commented one who later fought against him. "I knew him to be a brave and a good soldier."[45]

On quitting the service Shays returned to Pelham, served as a delegate to various conventions, and managed just barely to keep out of debtors' jail. Captured by the oratory of radical associates who met and harangued at Conkey's Tavern, not far from his farm, Shays was soon recognized as an exceptional drillmaster and was thrust into the forefront of the Regulator movement. By October '86 he appears to have been in supreme command of the insurgent troops.

Behind the demagogues and the discontented veterans were a host of others—small farmers, mechanics, and respected figures—undeserving the characterization of "rabble." Out of the twenty-one prominent figures who were to be indicted for treason in Worcester County at the April term, 1787, of the Supreme Judicial Court, fifteen are described in the indictments as "Gentlemen" and only six as "Yeomen."[46] At the start of the rioting Joseph Hawley, a prominent conservative figure in western Massachusetts, warned a like-minded associate: "You would be astonished to know with what amazing rapidity the spirit of the insurgents propagates. Many are infected with it of whom you would never have the least suspicion. We are not certain who besides the Devil sprang Ely at first. But we are not at a loss who ventilates the flame, for the fire is now become such a flame as I cannot describe it to you. The General Court have not had any affair of greater magnitude before them since the Revolution."[47]

Dark suspicions that devious-minded conservatives seeking a highly centralized, even a monarchical system, had secretly fomented the rebellion were nurtured by Antifederalist figures for many years after the uprising had been stifled. At the height of the insurrection, Mercy Otis Warren predicted to John Adams: "Time will make curious disclosures, and you, Sir, may be astonished to find the incendiaries who have fomented the discontents among the miserable insurgents . . . in a class of men least suspected."[48] Her views were supported by the contemporary statement of a conservative who identified one element among the insurgents as consisting of persons "who wished to carry popular measures to such extremes as to shew their absurdity, and demonstrate the necessity of lessening the democratick principles of the constitution."[49] If there was some undercover encouragement of the radicals by conservatives in order to create a backlash in favor of stronger national measures, the sinister conspirators have never been disclosed. Neither British money nor Loyalist connections seem to have been uncovered. True, the erratic protomonarchist Baron von Steuben had expressed sympathy with the rioters,[50] but the insurrectionists had little need for outside agitators to set them in motion.

With the armed overthrow of the state government as their apparent objective, the Shaysites set off a quick counterreaction on the part of the Eastern propertied class with the encouragement of Governor Bowdoin. Seeing that the federal government was cautious and irresolute about the use of federal troops, adequate funding for which Secretary at War Henry Knox was unable to procure, men of property raised and recruited their own military force, responding to General Benjamin Lincoln's call to subscribe to a large loan to support the state troops, a special army of 4,400 troops which Lincoln commanded. The state dispatched General Rufus Putnam, Shays' old commanding officer, to hold a series of conversations with the rebel leader, but the latter, while disavowing any treasonable intent, refused to risk his neck by throwing himself on the mercy of the governor.

The rebels' military debacle is too well known for detailed narration. Poorly organized, poorly led, their inflamed rhetoric outdistanced their military capacity. Shays, assuming that he was going to be reinforced by Luke Day, marched his men up to the Springfield arsenal, a federal property. A message from Day asking for an extra day was intercepted, and unknowing, Shays went ahead with his attack, only to be routed by a determined General William Shepherd's salvos of artillery. The rest was anticlimax. Lincoln's forces cut off Day's retreat, while Shays, rejecting surrender, marched to Petersham. In a memorable march through subzero temperature, Lincoln advanced his forces some thirty miles in thirteen hours. Their front reached Petersham at nine in the morning, and the complacent insurgents were thrown into complete confusion by the seemingly impossible feat. The body of the insurgents was captured; their leaders fled to adjacent states.

The insurrection was over, but it had a profound effect on two fronts. The voters repudiated their conservative state government in an election held in the spring of '87. John Hancock, a moderate, running on the popular program of amnesty for the rebels, defeated Governor James Bowdoin, the inflexible foe of the Shaysites. A pro-Shaysites House of Representatives supplanted its conservative predecessor, and many of the Shaysite recommendations were carried out by the new legislature. Clothing, household goods, and tools of trade were exempted by law from debt process; personal property as well as real estate was now acceptable in payment of debts. Imprisoned debtors might now secure their freedom by taking the pauper's oath. A new fee bill was passed reducing court charges. No direct tax whatsoever was enacted in 1787, and the years following saw a lightened tax burden. As a gesture to the changed order John Hancock voluntarily cut his own salary.[51]

If Shays' Rebellion had been a purely localized affair, its national significance would have been minor, but in fact it touched off a wave of backcountry resistance to debt recovery and tax collection that spread from New England to pockets of defiance flaring up from New Jersey to South Carolina. At York, Pennsylvania, debtors forcefully prevented the sale of cattle seized for taxes in November of '86. The previous summer Maryland's Charles County Courthouse was closed down by a "tumultuous assemblage of the people." In South Carolina, farmers attacked the Camden Courthouse and sent the judges scurrying home. So serious did the situation seem in his home state that Judge Aedanus Burke warned somewhat hysterically that not even "five thousand troops, the best in America or Europe, could enforce obedience to the Common Pleas."[52] In April of 1787 the people of Virginia's Caroline County entered into an association to purchase no property sold at auction, and as the delegates were convening in Philadelphia, a mob burned down Virginia's King William County Courthouse, destroying all the records. Later that summer Madison reported to Jefferson that "the prisons and Court Houses and clerks' offices have been willfully burnt."[53]

Thus, the spread of the Shays' contagion conveyed a sense of urgency to the nationalists, who now recognized that in addition to setting up a more efficient government with powers over taxation and commerce, there was a need for a central government that could maintain civil order in the states. "The only thing at this critical moment that can rescue the states from civil disorder," observed Pierce Butler, arguing in support of the new Constitution, is a strengthened national government.[54]

At the Philadelphia Convention, Shaysism bolstered the conviction of delegates that the regulation of the militia must be a national concern. Madison warned that "without such a power to suppress insurrections, our liberties might be destroyed by domestic faction." Charles Pinckney argued that little faith can be put in the militia's doing the job. Hence, what was needed was "a real military force." We had been experimenting without it, he reminded his fellow delegates, and now "we see the consequences in their rapid approaches to anarchy."[55] The result was the incorporation of the guaranty clause providing for federal intervention at a state's request to prevent "domestic violence" (Article I, section 8).[56] Although the Philadelphia delegates did not create a standing army, they empowered Congress "to raise and support armies" for a maximum of two years (Article I, section 8). Still other provisions of the Constitution, such as the prohibition of states from emitting currency or impairing the obligation of contracts, were an obvious response to the debtor relief measures so damaging to creditors and propertied interests generally in the Confederation years, and indubitably to Shays' Rebellion.

In sum, Shays' Rebellion and its spillover to other states created a crisis atmosphere shared by the nationalists and effectively exploited by them. So sober and objective a private citizen as George Washington was bestirred to write a friend in late October of '86, asking for the facts. "For God's sake, tell me what is the cause of all these commotions? Do they proceed from licentiousness, British-influence disseminated by the tories, or real grievances which admit of redress? If the latter, why were they delayed 'till the public mind has been so much agitated? If the former why are not the powers of Government tried at once?" He followed up with a letter to Henry Lee, instructing his correspondent: "Know precisely what the insurgents aim at. If they have *real* grievances, redress them if possible," but "if they have not, employ the force of government against them at once."[57] The momentum of insurrection increased Washington's agitation. "We are fast verging to anarchy and confusion," he wrote Madison soon after, following up this alarming prediction with a quotation from a communication only just received from Secretary at War Knox concerning the Shaysites: "Their creed is that the property of the United States has been protected from confiscation by the joint exertion of *all*, and therefore ought to be the *common property* of all."[58] With Shays' Rebellion "nearly extinct," Madison shared Washington's concern that the punitive measures taken against the insurgents might bring on "a new crisis."[59]

CHAPTER 11

Creating a New Constitution

Theory versus Practice

W HEN that eminent senior statesman John Dickinson, formerly Pennsylvania's president of the Executive Council but now representing the state of Delaware at the Philadelphia Convention, listened to fellow delegates spin out arguments drawn from political theories, both ancient and modern, he was prompted to issue a rebuke: *"Experience* must be our only guide," he observed. *"Reason* may mislead us." Dickinson was talking common sense, for so very much of the Constitution was crafted on lessons drawn from the operations of the states as colonies, on the precedents provided by the state constitutions, and on the obvious examples of the inadequacies of the Articles of Confederation.

Dickinson's rebuke, however sensible, failed to stem the flow of oratory in which delegates and later ratifiers revealed their familiarity with republics and confederacies, ancient and contemporary, and their reading in a wide range of literature by political theoreticians. The more sophisticated delegates had read their Machiavelli, their Harrington and their Hobbes, their Montesquieu, their Locke, and their Hume. Therefrom they had derived variant notions about a republican system rooted in civic virtue, community, and benevolence, about the desirability of mixed government and rotation in office, about the connection between power and corruption, and the necessity of incorporating in their proposed model a system of checks and balances and separation of powers. In the great debates that the final draft of the Constitution would precipitate, both critics and defenders of the new charter discoursed on the diverse views of Bolingbroke and Locke, would draw upon the Commonwealthmen, and Gordon and Trenchard, and some leaned heavily on the venerated figures of the Scottish Enlightenment. Their debates, too, would reflect the antithetical principles of the English court and country parties. From these ingredients would be brewed a variety of theoretical concoctions dealing with the relation between liberty and power, bearing on the tensions between virtue and commerce, on interest politics and the protection of minority rights.[1]

Theory and history aside, however, Dickinson's point was well made. What the delegates were crafting in Philadelphia was an entirely new system of governance for an extended republic, a system without precedent, and one whose innovations were carefully attuned to the need to achieve consensus.[2]

The Delegates: A Collective Portrait

The signal was almost muted when it was reluctantly sounded by Congress. On February 21, 1787, that body, after considerable delay, responded to the request of the Annapolis Convention and that of a number of states by issuing a formal resolution expressing "the opinion of Congress" that "it is expedient that on the second Monday in May next, a convention of delegates, who shall have been appointed by the several states, be held at Philadelphia . . . for the sole and express purpose of revising the Articles of Confederation and reporting to Congress and the several legislatures such alterations and provisions therein as shall when agreed to in Congress and confirmed by the states render the federal constitution adequate to the exigencies of Government and the preservation of the Union."[3]

May 14, the date Congress had set for the start of the Convention, found only two state delegations in Philadelphia, those of Pennsylvania and Virginia. Heavy rains had mired roads deep in mud, and it was not until May 25 that a quorum of seven states could be formed.

In retrospect, Americans now see the year 1787 as an explosion of political genius. One scholar has called it "a classic perhaps even unparalleled example of the power of political leadership by intellectuals in a situation where their understanding of human nature was firm and realistic, their grasp of earlier thinking broad and acute, their capacity to learn from their own and others' experiences discriminating," and the time ripe for resolution of "the problem of curbing power and protecting people's liberties."[4]

"If all the delegates named for this Convention at Philadelphia are present," commented the French chargé d'affaires, "we will never have seen, even in Europe, an assembly more respectable for the talents, knowledge, disinterestedness, and patriotism of those who compose it." On the whole these men were not neophytes as political leaders. Three had been in the Stamp Act Congress, seven in the First Continental Congress. Eight had signed the Declaration of Independence, and two, the Articles. Two would become President, one Vice President, and two Chief Justices of the Supreme Court. Sixteen had been or would later hold state governorships. Forty-two at one time or another had sat in one or another of the Continental Congresses, while at least thirty were Revolutionary War veterans. Many had served their states with distinction, drafting constitutions and codifying their laws.

A composite portrait shows the Framers to have been mature native-born Americans, many college-trained, and although only about a dozen were practicing lawyers, three times that number had studied law. Many were cosmopolitan in outlook, at least eighteen having worked or studied abroad, while eight of the Framers were born outside of the United States, all, however, in what was the British Empire. In fact the Philadelphia Convention might be considered a rally of nationalists with different gradations of attachment to their own states. Although the delegates felt no sense of alienation from the people, the constituency for which they spoke lived in the cities and commercial areas or on the large plantations dependent on a world market for their products, while the backcountry was not well represented. Indeed, most Antifederalists refused to attend. Patrick Henry perhaps summed up their attitude when he declined, saying he "smelt a rat." In absenting themselves or quitting the Convention, the Antifederalists permitted that body to achieve a consensus by avoidance of certain controversial issues and the settlement of others by compromise. At the Convention the differences between the large and small states and between North

and South proved far more serious than did divergencies over protecting property. The delegates did not have to be persuaded about
the evils of cheap money and even agreed at the end to curbing state
laws impairing the obligation of contracts. On such issues they
stood in basic agreement.

Save for Jefferson who was on duty in Paris, Adams, still representing America at a frigid St. James's Court, and Jay, still trying to
direct the nation's foreign affairs, most of the nation's leading
statesmen could be counted among the fifty-five men who eventually assembled in Philadelphia. Not that leadership qualities were
equally distributed among the twelve states that participated, Rhode
Island, torn by factional strife, choosing not to attend.[5] Virginia and
Pennsylvania boasted the most prestigious delegations, although
South Carolina sent some of its leading statesmen, and Connecticut,
Delaware, and New Jersey were ably represented.

If there was any single person who made the difference in building a consensus at the Constitutional Convention—in the delegates
investing the chief executive with broad powers, and, finally, on
winning ratification in divided states—it was George Washington. It
was his presence and known support for the nationalists rather than
his sparse remarks at the Convention that counted heavily. Retired
from public life and with a declared intention to stay out of "public
business," Washington was, regardless of his private wishes, chosen
by Virginia to head its state delegation to the Convention. Personal
and business interests provided compelling reasons to stay at
Mount Vernon, not to speak of political considerations. Should the
Convention fail, his reputation could well be damaged. During the
month of March 1787 Washington was bombarded by letters from
friends, not least among them Henry Knox and James Madison.[6]
Concerned, as he wrote Madison, that the "defects of the Articles"
must be "probe[d] to the bottom,"[7] he did not rush headlong into
the fray. "My name is in the delegation to the Convention," he
wrote John Jay on March 10, "but it was put there contrary to my
desire, and remains contrary to my request."[8] At length he yielded
to the pleas of his friends, and on March 28 wrote Governor Randolph agreeing to lead the Virginia delegation. "To see this country
happy," he wrote, "is so much the wish of my soul."[9] As a national
leader he felt obliged to assume the risks.

In the intervening period prior to the Convention, Washington sought advice as to what role he should assume if he decided to participate. He solicited suggestions from John Jay, General Knox, and James Madison. Jay came out flatly for a separation of powers. "Let Congress Legislate, let others execute, let others judge." He also proposed a chief executive and a bicameral legislature and recommended that the Constitution should be "confirmed by the people . . . the only source of Just authority." Knox proposed a bicameral legislature, with the lower house serving for two or three years and a Senate for five or six. He wanted a "Governor General" to have the power to appoint judges to serve for good behavior, "but impeachable by the lower house and triable by the Senate."

Madison's proposal, which seems to have reached Washington after he had decided to attend the Convention, was for a system of federalism while emphasizing the subordination of the states to the national government. He would have a National Executive, but its shape was not yet formed in Madison's mind, along with a Council of Revision, and a national judiciary which would hear all cases of foreigners or inhabitants of other states, along with admiralty and maritime jurisdiction. His proposals for a bicameral legislature were not unlike the propositions found in the Virginia Plan when formulated. Finally, he confirmed Jay's notion that ratification by the people was necessary, and went so far as to declare that "inroads on the existing Constitution of the States will be unavoidable."[10] With many variations the suggestions of the three statesmen could be found in the final charter hammered out in Philadelphia.

No delegate, however, came better prepared than Madison. During the past year he had delved deeply into the history of ancient republics and confederacies. Only a month before the sitting of the Convention he had prepared a memorandum on "Vices of the Political System of the United States," in which he denounced the state legislatures for failing to honor the requisitions of Congress and for such derelictions as moratory laws and paper money, while focusing his attention on the American people and their divisions into factions according to economic interests, regional loyalties, and "the different kinds of property" they possessed. What made a government republican, he observed, was that decisions were made by a majority, and unless there were adequate checks, the interests of individuals or minorities might well be threatened—a theme which resonates in Madison's later contributions to *The Federalist*. Madison did something more than prepare the basic nationalist blueprint of the Virginia delegation. Of all the delegates he kept the most careful, minute-by-minute accounting of what transpired at the Federal Convention—his own shorthand system, which he would then transcribe each evening. In later years, particularly after the publication of the Journal of the Convention in 1819 and the abbreviated and unreliable Convention minutes of Robert Yates, a New York delegate, Madison made additions and alterations in the interest of accuracy, tinkered with his own prose to soften aspersions applied to prominent delegates, and even tampered with his own text—it has been charged—when earlier versions might later prove embarrassing. Nonetheless, of the various versions, mostly excerpts which have been unearthed, Madison's minutes, while still the fullest and most authoritative, cover only a relatively small portion of the total discussion and debate.

In addition to the prestige of Washington and the formidable talents of Madison, Virginia's delegation included George Mason, renowned as the author of the state's bill of rights as well as its constitution, and Edmund J. Randolph, then the state's governor and previously attorney general, who brought the prestigious family name of Randolph to the nationalist cause.

Pennsylvania's delegation matched Virginia's in prestige and talent. Its senior member was the legendary Benjamin Franklin. Serving at the time as president of the state's Executive Council, the eighty-one-year-old sage brought to the assemblage not only his unrivaled experience in the service of Empire, colonies, state, and nation, but international renown as diplomat, scientist, and humanitarian. His disarmingly candid manner masked a very complex personality, but his accommodating nature would time after time conciliate jarring interests.

James Wilson, able lawyer and noted Revolutionary pamphleteer, was to join persuasive argument, oratorical gifts, and democratic passion on behalf of the nationalist cause. Probably second only to Madison in influence at the Convention, he was a figure to be reckoned with in debate and as a constructive draftsman. In financial prestige, Robert Morris stood preeminent. A large, good-humored man, whose handsome residence provided hospitality for General Washington during his Philadelphia stay and frequent receptions for the other delegates, Morris surprised his colleagues by the paucity of his remarks. Except to nominate the Convention's president, to support proportional representation for the legislature, and confer upon Congress the power to incorporate a national bank, Morris—the record suggests—was more effective behind the scenes than in public debate, doubtless counting on his views being voiced by his brilliant young associate Gouverneur Morris, a native New Yorker but now a Pennsylvania resident, who added wit and dash to a relatively sober company and spoke as frequently as any in a very verbal conclave. A worldly bachelor, not famous for discretion, this Morris had an important hand in drafting the final text of the Constitution and is accepted as the author of the inspired Preamble.

South Carolina dispatched to Philadelphia John Rutledge, a first-class legal mind with firm credentials as a Revolutionary War leader. A moderate nationalist, he guided the labors of the important Committee of Detail. He was ably supported by the two Pinckneys, Charles Cotesworth, whose devotion to his state and section did not hamper him from espousing the cause of strong government, and his twenty-nine-year-old cousin Charles, who spoke frequently and contributed at critical places to the grand design being shaped on the floor of the Convention. A man of supreme vanity, he would later claim that the "Pinckney draught," which he submitted to the Convention immediately after the Randolph Plan but which was ignored, provided the foundation of the Constitution. When, as late as 1818, Pinckney submitted the text of his plan to John Quincy Adams, it seemed to be a variant of the first draft of the Constitution reported by the Committee of Detail on August 8 (a committee on which he did not serve but where his original draft was evidently examined). Either Pinckney's memory was faulty or his claim was bogus, although some recent writers give to the plan a serious weight that tested scholarship rejects.[11]

Massachusetts was represented by an able but hardly prestigious delegation, which numbered Nathaniel Gorham, a former president of Congress, who acted as presiding officer when the Convention sat as a committee of the whole; Caleb Strong, lawyer, legislator, and fair-minded Federalist; and Elbridge Gerry of Marblehead, a Signer of both the Declaration and the Articles. A tried-and-true republican, the maverick Gerry was a committed antinationalist, who at the same time happened to be the largest holder of Continental securities of any person at the Convention as well as a major investor in Western Lands. Rufus King, barely thirty-two, had served in Congress, where he imbibed nationalist notions from such friends as Alexander Hamilton. A principled Federalist, he had already won a reputation as vigilant observer and critic of Southern expansionist aspirations. He kept a set of useful notes of the business at hand.

The small states, notably Connecticut, New Jersey, and Delaware, boasted talented delegations. Delaware's Dickinson may have been the most prestigious, and certainly a sober counterbalance to his colleague Gunning Bedford, whose intemperate defense of states' rights called forth a rebuke from Rufus King.[12] Connecticut's delegation proved not only accomplished but unusually effective. William Samuel Johnson, a lawyer and jurist, now thoroughly rehabilitated from any taint of Loyalism, had just been named president of Columbia College, while the rustic manners of Roger Sherman, a Signer of the Declaration, belied his political shrewdness, common sense, and committed nationalism, and Oliver Ellsworth, an able jurist and, with Sherman, a major figure in the Connecticut Compromise. Ellsworth would later draft the Judiciary Act implementing the Constitution he would effectively support.

Maryland had the unusual distinction of dispatching to the Convention the most intemperate and insufferably voluble antinationalist, Luther Martin, who quit the Convention before it ended, leaving the signing to his fellow delegates, James McHenry, Daniel of St. Thomas Jenifer, Daniel Carroll, and John Francis Mercer, physician and soldier, none of whom played significant roles at the Convention, and the last of whom has left us a partial report of its transactions, while signing the Constitution with some reluctance but out of respect for the opinions of the majority.[13]

The New Jersey delegation was as distinguished in attainments as any coming from the smaller states. It was headed by their perpetual governor, William Livingston, a Whig intellectual, a committed nationalist, and a man of sardonic wit, who happened to be the father-in-law of John Jay. He was ably seconded by William Paterson, Irish-born Princetonian, the state's wartime attorney general and author of the "New Jersey Plan," as well as by two other lawyers, David Brearly, the jurist who earlier had upheld the principle of judicial review of unconstitutional legislation, and Jonathan Dayton, not quite twenty-seven, whose chief distinction was that he was the youngest delegate among the fifty-five, with a reputation tarnished in later years by his suspected involvement in Aaron Burr's dubious schemes.

While there was a scattering of criticism of the nationalist shape which the Constitution assumed despite its compromises, every state but one among the twelve represented signed the Constitution. The exception was New York, where the legislature under prodding from the state's leading Antifederalist, Governor George Clinton, sent a three-man delegation including two Antifederalists, Robert Yates and John Lansing, Jr., both upstate lawyers, to the Convention to curb the lone committed nationalist Alexander Hamilton. As Madison correctly predicted, they were "likely" to be "a clog on their Colleague."[14] The first two quit the Convention early in July, discontented with its course, and Hamilton, who also took a leave for some weeks, returned in time not only to sign the Constitution but personally to insert next to the signatures the states which the Signers represented. Alexander Hamilton's signature, representing a minority of his own delegation, had no legal standing, and he had in fact been humiliated by his state's being deprived of a vote by the departure of his New York colleagues, leaving him a minority of one. A man of immense talents and consuming ambition, a centralist who, save possibly for Madison, had more to do in bringing the Convention about than any single person, Hamilton at Philadelphia did not live up to the high expectation of his friends and, if anything, seemed to confirm the worst suspicions of his foes.

The Nationalist Initiative

The eleven days prior to the convening of the Convention, which the Virginia delegates spent either at Mrs. House's lodgings, where Madison settled in early, or at the more spacious and pretentious *Indian Queen* (save for Washington, who was whisked away to the more elegant residence of Robert Morris), were devoted to deliberations over a plan whose essentials James Madison had previously outlined in letters to Jefferson, Randolph, and Washington. It was this plan which was the basis of the so-called Virginia Plan, and the delegation was prepared to have Governor Randolph spring it on the Convention just as quickly as that body was organized for deliberations.

May 25 saw a quorum of seven state delegations seated in the East Room of the State House. Here the Declaration of Independence was signed and the old Congress had mainly deliberated over the years until driven out by an insubordinate state militia. The chamber, some forty by forty feet, with a twenty-foot-high plaster ceiling, proved adequate for the great business at hand. The delegates seated themselves at tables covered with green baize, three or four delegates to a table.

Organization was the first order of business. The Pennsylvania delegation had planned the initial gesture to come from its most venerable member, but Franklin was indisposed, and Robert Morris moved that General Washington be the presiding officer, a motion seconded by John Rutledge. Unanimously elected, Washington was escorted to his chair by his two co-sponsors, and in a brief speech asked the delegates for their indulgence for any errors he might commit in the execution of his post. James Wilson then nominated Benjamin Franklin's grandson, Temple Franklin, as secretary, but Hamilton's nominee, William Jackson, a former army officer, prevailed.

Then came the rules, which were adopted on the following session, May 29. Possibly in deference to restrictions embodied in the instructions to the state of Delaware, it was decided that the Convention follow the voting rules of the Continental Congress, by which each state had an equal vote, a majority of the states present to decide any question. Two other rules were adopted which indubitably facilitated decision making and flexibility: a rule of secrecy and a rule of "mutability," the latter giving the Convention the right to reconsider votes already taken by a majority.[15] In the main, the rule of secrecy, which allowed delegates to talk more freely and modify declared initial positions with more readiness if word of their remarks and votes did not leak back home, was vigilantly guarded by the presiding officer. The wide, lofty windows were nailed shut and guards posted outside the doors. It was inevitable, however, that gossipy delegates did leak information, including old Doctor Franklin, a great anecdotalist who had to be cautioned.[16] Secret disclosures on crucial issues did not show up in the correspondence of the delegates, however, save that of Madison. On September 6, he disclosed the basic "outline" of the Constitution in a letter to Jefferson, who did not receive it until October 13.[17] After he had left the Convention, William Paterson described the assemblage to a fellow delegate from Connecticut: "Full of Disposition and noisy as the Wind, it is said, that you are afraid of the very Windows, and have a Man planted under them to prevent Secrets and Doings from flying out."[18] What came out of Philadelphia has been called "an open covenant secretly arrived at." And years later Madison would insist that "no Constitution would ever have been adopted by the convention if the debates had been public."[19]

The Virginia delegation wasted no time in spreading its plan on the record. On May 29, Governor Randolph presented for the consideration of the Convention "sundry propositions in writing, concerning the American confederation, and the establishment of the national government." These began on a conciliatory note, characteristic of Randolph, who wished to avoid alarming delegates still attached to the old Articles. After reviewing the recognized weaknesses of the Confederation government under the Articles, he proposed a series of resolutions, the first of which might have been calculated to put the delegates off guard. It read:

> Resolved that the Articles of Confederation ought to be so corrected and enlarged as to accomplish the objects proposed by their institution, namely "common defense, security of liberty, and general welfare."

When the delegates listened further, they would be hearing a Madisonian proposal radically new and enormously variant from the existent system. The fourteen resolutions that followed proposed in essence to demolish the Articles of Confederation and erect in their stead a strong national government on a popular foundation. To start with, the government was to have three branches. The first to be proposed was a bicameral legislature, in which the first house was to be popularly elected, while the second house was to be picked by the lower from candidates named by the state legislatures. This "National Legislature" would have authority to make laws "in all cases in which the separate states are incompetent" and to nullify any state laws contrary to the "articles of Union." In each house representation was to be proportionate "to the quotas of contributions or to the number of free inhabitants."

Randolph then proposed the creation of a National Executive, who was to have all the executive powers granted Congress under the Articles. With the concurrence of a number of federal judges, the National Executive would have a qualified veto over the acts of Congress. Whether the National Executive was to be singular or plural remained unspecified, nor was the term of office or eligibility for reelection specified.

Thirdly, there was to be a National Judiciary, consisting of one or more supreme tribunals and inferior courts to be chosen by the National Legislature, to hold office during good behavior. The jurisdiction of such courts extended to piracies and felonies on the high seas, prize cases, foreigners and citizens of other states, impeachment of national officers, and "questions which may involve the national peace and harmony."

Resolutions also provided for the admission of new states, guarantees of a republican government in each state, a flexible amendment procedure, and ratification of "the amendments which shall be offered to the Confederation," to be by special assemblies recommended by the state legislatures but expressly chosen by the people.

An audacious plan, despite the transparent subterfuge that it was presented as a series of amendments to the Articles of Confederation. It was obvious to every listener that what was submitted was a national government, with checks and balances, and supreme over the states. In essence, this was the basic outline, with numerous significant refinements and modifications, of the final Constitution signed on September 17 after almost four months of study and debate.

After the house resolved itself into a "Committee of the Whole House to consider the state of the American Union," to which the Randolph Plan was to be referred, Charles Pinckney laid before the house his own draft of a federal government which, according to Yates's records, he confessed "was grounded on the same principle as the above resolution." This, too, was referred to the same committee, but never seems to have been discussed by the full Convention.[20]

The next day, pursuing a procedure to be followed throughout its sessions, the Convention resolved itself into a Committee of the Whole, the president left the chair, and Nathaniel Gorham by ballot of the house took the chair of the committee, a procedure that was followed again on May 30. For a few moments the response to the Randolph Plan seemed auspicious. On motion of Governor Randolph, the Convention voted six to one "that a *national* government ought to be established consisting of a *supreme* Legislative, Executive, and Judiciary."[21] The dissenting state was Connecticut, while New York was divided, Hamilton aye, Yates no. Once taken and never reversed, the vote on the Randolph resolution was perhaps the most significant taken by the Convention. It was a commitment to set up a supreme central government.[22]

While so much of the Virginia scheme remained to be filled out, and on each point opinion often widely diverged, it does seem odd that the issue of representation should initiate the great debate and consume so much of the delegates' time for another month and a half. The composition and method of election of each branch of the bicameral legislature split the delegates down the middle, not only in terms of large states against the smaller ones, but democratic nationalists against republicans who had doubts about the virtue of the people. In the latter category could be found two old Patriots with long-established radical credentials. Opposing the resolution that members of the first branch of the legislature be elected by the people, Roger Sherman argued that the people "should have as little to do as may be possible about the Government. They wanted information and are constantly liable to be misled." Elbridge Gerry bolstered Sherman's dissenting voice. With Shays' Rebellion very much in his mind, he declared: "The evils we experience flow from the excess of democracy. The people do not want virtue; but are the dupes of pretended patriots." Gerry still defended his republican credentials, but conceded that experience had tempered his republicanism and shown him "the danger of the levelling spirit."[23]

George Mason eloquently argued the case for representative democracy. Viewing the first house as "the grand depository of the democratic principle of the Government," he insisted that it ought to have first-hand knowledge "and sympathize with every part of the community." James Wilson sustained Mason's contention, declaring that he was "for raising the federal pyramid to a Considerable altitude," and for giving it as broad a base as possible. Madison, in turn, considered the "popular election of one branch of the national

Legislature as essential to every plan of free Government." By a vote of six to two, with two divided, the election of the first branch of the national legislature by the people carried the day.[24]

The Virginia Plan continued to enjoy a string of successes, although it was to be somewhat altered in the report of the Committee of the Whole of June 13. Now the National Executive was to consist of a single person who was given a qualified veto not to be shared with the National Judiciary. The national legislature was authorized to veto state laws contravening treaties entered into by the United States. Representation in the first branch of the national legislature was to be "in proportion to the whole number of white and other free citizens of every age, sex and condition, including those bound to servitude for a term of years, and three fifths of all other persons not comprehended in the foregoing description, except Indians, not paying taxes." The right of suffrage in the second house would follow that of the first, and that second branch would be elected by the legislatures of the separate states.[25]

A combination of successive nationalist victories, notably the direct election of the first house by the people and the June 13 alteration of representation according to an old formula, provoked the small states to come up with an alternative plan to head off what their delegates considered an unstoppable trend toward centralization and control by the large states. By June 15, within two days of the report to the Committee of the Whole, it was clear just what shape the small states' plan would take. Generally called the New Jersey Plan, as it was sponsored by William Paterson, it seems to have drawn upon David Brearly of Paterson's own state, Luther Martin, Roger Sherman, and possibly John Lansing, Jr. It proposed a one-house legislature elected by states regardless of population, an apparently plural executive elected by Congress, and a Supreme Court chosen by the executive with curtailed jurisdiction. Paterson made one further obeisance to the national system. He would have declared the acts of Congress and all treaties "the supreme law of the respective states," binding upon the state courts. Otherwise, and save for the granting to Congress the crucial rights to tax and regulate commerce, Paterson's Plan would have amounted to a reconstitution of the government under the Articles of Confederation, with a unicameral legislature in which each state had an equal vote.[26]

Up to this point Hamilton had been virtually silent, but when on

June 18 John Dickinson successfully moved to postpone consideration of the New Jersey Plan and instead took up his proposal to revise and amend the Articles of Confederation in accordance with Congress's instructions, the New Yorker took the floor and held it for some six hours. The "sketch," as Hamilton would call it, would have reduced the states to mere subdivisions, with an executive in each state to be appointed by the national government, a chief executive elected for life by electors chosen in turn by electors popularly chosen. Compounding these horrors was Hamilton's notion of a Senate chosen for life and his investment of the executive with an absolute veto power. While Hamilton criticized the Virginia and New Jersey plans as being too democratic, it is likely that his extremist proposals were calculated to offset both Dickinson's plan to revise and amend the Articles and the New Jersey Plan, especially distasteful to the New Yorker. What Hamilton had in mind was too high-toned, centralized, and even monarchical for the delegates, as Charles Pinckney's brilliant oration some seven days later would reveal, with its defense of America's exceptionalism and its egalitarian climate. When Hamilton gathered up his papers, his auditors sat stunned and silent. Then the Committee of the Whole rose and the house adjourned.[27]

If Hamilton's speech was a calculated plan to undercut any idea of revising and amending the old Articles but was designed instead to bolster the national powers under the Randolph Plan, it could be credited with one success. On the very next day Paterson's proposals were defeated by seven to three,[28] a decisive vote which amounted to a complete rejection of the Confederation form of government.

The Great Compromise

Although discarded, the Paterson Plan had disclosed a bitter rift between the small and large states over the issues of proportional representation versus state equality. After days of animated debate, the first great compromise of the Convention was reached. Roger Sherman proposed that each state be given an equal vote in the Senate and that representation in the lower house be made proportional to population. The solid support given this plan by Sherman's fellow delegates from Connecticut, Oliver Ellsworth and William

Samuel Johnson, led it to be called the Connecticut Compromise. The United States, Dr. Johnson eloquently reminded his fellow delegates, was for many purposes "one political society" composed of individuals, while for other purposes, the states also were political societies with interests of their own. These notions did not seem contradictory to him. Instead, "they were halves of a unique whole," and as such, "ought to be combined" to the end that "in *one branch* the *people* ought to be represented, in the *other* the *states.*"[29]

Having decided in principle that the rule of suffrage in the first branch should not be equal as in the Articles of Confederation, the Convention then considered the Ellsworth motion that "equality be the rule in the second branch." Ellsworth warned that the Eastern states, save perhaps Massachusetts, "would risk every consequence rather than part with so dear a right" as equality.[30] While decisions were being made on refining, amending, and adapting a number of aspects of the Virginia Plan, the Great Compromise was not reached until July 16 when, on the recommendation of a committee of eleven delegates, the Convention voted to give each state an equal vote in the second branch of the national legislature while distributing seats in the first branch on the basis of one member for every forty thousand inhabitants (which house would also have the sole right to initiate money bills), while in the Senate each state should have an equal vote. The motion passed five to four, with all the large states voting in the negative except Massachusetts, which was divided.[31] Embraced in the Great Compromise was the adoption of the proposal advanced by James Wilson some weeks before to have representation and direct taxes proportioned to "the whole number of white and other free citizens and inhabitants of every age, sex, and condition, including those bound to service for a term of years, and three-fifths of all other persons, except Indians not paying taxes."[32] In essence, this clause became Article I, section 2, of the final Constitution. The draftsmen, to avoid spelling out distinctions of color, substituted the phrase "the whole number of free persons" for white and other free citizens, while continuing to abstain from mentioning slavery by referring to the enslaved blacks as "all other Persons." In this form the rule of representation survived until the Civil War and the ratification in 1868 of the Fourteenth Amendment.

Despite the apprehension of Madison, Randolph, and Wilson that equality in the second house would "destroy the proper foundation of Government,"[33] and an adjournment until the next morning to give the large states a chance to caucus on the question, no common ground could be found, and it was decided with reluctance to accept the compromise.[34]

The Great Compromise in fact as well as in law embodied the principle of federalism in the Constitution, a principle reinforced by the Electoral College and the grant of merely enumerated powers to Congress, and reinforced by the Ninth and Tenth Amendments. Indeed, four days after the adoption of the compromise Oliver Ellsworth persuaded the Convention to drop the word *"national"* and retain the proper title "the United States" wherever appropriate, a motion unanimously passed.[35] However its title, the new government could act directly on the people and retained a hybrid national character without precedent in the previous history of republics.[36]

The Great Confrontation

More than a fortnight before the so-called Great Compromise was reached, James Madison, who would resist to the bitter end the concessions secured by the small states, perceived little harm to them from the national plan he had endorsed. Rather did he see "the great danger to our general government" arising from the opposing interests of North and South. "Look to the votes of Congress," he asserted, *"and most of them stand divided by the geography of the country, not according to the size of the states."* He elaborated on this point the very next day, in a speech in which he explained the difference between the sections as arising only "partly from climate," but "principally from the effects of their having or not having slaves." At that time his solution was to have one branch represent only the free inhabitants, the other represent everyone, "counting the slaves as [if] free."[37]

While Madison's plan was ignored, like a number of his other proposals, he was on target in predicting that the next major issue to divide the Convention would be a North-South confrontation indirectly over slavery. That confrontation resulted from the report of a Committee of Detail appointed on July 23, and chaired by John Rutledge. For that committee, Edmund Randolph turned out a proposed draft of the Constitution which, as he explained it, was "to insert essential principles only" to make it possible to accommodate the Constitution "to times and events" and "to use simple and precise language and general propositions." Randolph's notion of confining a Constitution to broad principles rather than cluttering up the document with unnecessary details was a master stroke which accounts for that document's enduring adaptability and relevance. James Wilson then put the Randolph draft into smoother language and the printers were ordered to print just enough copies for each of the delegates.

The most important contribution of the Committee of Detail was to list eighteen specific powers of Congress, to which it added the crowning power "to make all laws" that appeared "necessary and proper" to carry "into execution" these and "all other powers vested" in the government. Alexander Hamilton would find in this clause the basis of his doctrine of "implied powers" set forth in a classic state paper supporting the chartering of a national bank and penned as Washington's Secretary of the Treasury. Secondly, the Committee of Detail included a list of prohibitions upon the states, who were forbidden to coin money, to make treaties, or grant titles of nobility, among other curbs.

The delegates debated the committee's draft clause by clause from August 6 to September 10, and although many other recommendations of the committee stirred debate, the most bitter division would occur over the inclusion among the enumerated powers of Congress of the grant of "the exclusive power of regulating Trade and levying Imposts."[38]

Since the principal grounds for calling the Convention were to enlarge the powers of the central government over commerce as well as to give it the right to levy and collect taxes, and since every plan presented at the Convention gave Congress the right to regulate foreign and domestic commerce, the fact that such a grant of power should now precipitate a serious dispute might well have come as a surprise to many delegates. The fact is, though, that the lower South saw this power over commerce as in effect granting a monopoly to Northern shippers and correspondingly increasing the prices paid by Southern importers.

Accordingly, the states of the lower South found it appropriate to introduce some curbs on that unrestricted power. Charles Cotesworth Pinckney sought to require commercial legislation to win a two-thirds vote of each house rather than be adopted by a simple majority. Supporting Pinckney's position, George Mason declared:

The southern states are the *minority* in both houses. Is it to be expected that they will deliver themselves bound hand and foot to the eastern states, and enable them to exclaim in the words of Cromwell—"The Lord hath delivered them into our hands!"[39]

For James Madison, a long-time proponent of conferring upon the national legislature broad powers over commerce, this issue was crucial to the success of the Convention. He exhorted his fellow delegates that, "as we are laying the foundation of a great empire, we ought to take a permanent view of the subject." The great issue, he reminded his listeners, was "the necessity of securing the West India trade to the country."[40] Madison prevailed, and Congress won the power to regulate commerce by majority vote.

A victory, true, but every regional concession brought a price and begot a compromise. Thus the great slavery issue, hitherto handled tangentially or ignored, came to the fore when the delegates took up the recommendations of the Committee of Detail on import and export duties. Defeated on the commerce clause, the South was determined to support the recommendation of the Committee of Detail barring Congress from taxing exports from any state or prohibiting the migration or importation of such persons "as the several States shall think proper to admit."[41]

What has subsequently persuaded some scholars that a deal had been reached over this issue between Connecticut and the South were the surprising remarks of Roger Sherman. While disapproving of the slave trade, he now felt it expedient to offer as few impediments to the general constitutional scheme as possible. Why quibble, he asked in a vein of uncritical optimism, when "the abolition of slavery seemed to be proceeding throughout the United States?" If Sherman spoke for some Northerners, George Mason in response spoke for few Southerners. Certainly his tirade against slavery shocked the delegates from the lower South. While placing the blame for the original slave traffic on British merchants as well as the British government, which had disallowed every effort of the colonies to prohibit the traffic, he would not exculpate his fellow Southerners of guilt. Painting an ugly picture on a broad canvas, Mason's blast against slavery stands out as one of the Convention's most stirring speeches. Emphasizing the point that the "present question" not only concerned the importing states "but the whole Union," Mason pointed out that the states in the upper South had prohibited the importation of slaves, but that such action would be in vain if South Carolina and Georgia "remained at liberty to import them," and as a consequence would spread slavery to the West, a region already calling for slaves. Reminding the delegates that the poor despised labor performed by slaves and that the institution blocked white immigration into the South, Mason in an eloquent peroration asserted that slavery had a "pernicious" effect on manners. Then his powerful and prophetic peroration:

> Every master of slaves is born a petty tyrant. They bring the judgment of heaven upon a country. As nations cannot be rewarded or punished in the next world they must be in this. By an inevitable chain of causes and effects providence punished national sins by national calamities, I hold it essential to every point of view that the General Government have power to prevent the increase of slavery.[42]

In rejoinder, General Pinckney pointed out that Virginia would gain by stopping the importation of slaves as their value would rise, while South Carolina and Georgia could not "do without slaves." Rutledge warned that the people of the lower South would never "be such fools as to agree to a plan of union" unless "the right to import slaves were untouched."[43]

Here was an impasse which divided North and South and each of the two sections in turn. The North was not united. Differing from Connecticut were delegates like John Dickinson and John Langdon who placed the issue on the high moral ground of honor and conscience as well as safety. Could "some middle ground" be found, Randolph inquired. In response, New Jersey's Governor Livingston recommended that no prohibition of the slave trade be permitted before the year 1800. Mollified by the concession from a Northerner, Charles C. Pinckney proposed substituting "the year 1808" for Livingston's 1800.[44] James Madison objected that such a permissible twenty-year period for slave importation was "dishonorable to the American character," but the Virginian was overruled once again. With minor modifications of phraseology, the Convention voted to bar the prohibition of the slave trade before 1808. Even the

North divided on this crucial vote, nor was there a solid South, as Virginia voted "nay."[45]

What the delegates did thereby was to validate the system of slavery by this and two other compromises: the three-fifths rule for representation and direct taxes (Article I, section 2), and the provision for the return to their owners of "persons held to Service or Labour" crossing state lines (Article IV, section 2). True, the compromises contributed to the forging of the Union, but at a terrible price. Slavery, within a very few years, would prove a smoldering source of contention between the sections, some day to erupt in a tragic conflagration.

Shaping the Presidency

From the opening gun fired at the Convention by Edmund Randolph to almost the final days of the assemblage, the "National Executive" proved a subject of innumerable proposals and debate. The Virginia Plan had recommended instituting a national executive "with power to carry into effect the national laws." When the proposal came up for discussion on June 1, both Charles Pinckney and James Wilson argued for a "vigorous executive," one who could execute his duties with "energy, dispatch, and responsibility."[46]

Over the weeks a singular collection of nationalists and state's righters were identified as supporters of a single chief executive. They numbered Washington and Madison, Wilson and Gouverneur Morris, Alexander Hamilton, Elbridge Gerry and Rufus King, John Dickinson, and Pierce Butler—a range of viewpoints covering all regions of the country and varying opinions on other issues. Contrariwise, a group including George Mason, Roger Sherman, Benjamin Franklin, Edmund Randolph, and Hugh Williamson of North Carolina favored a plural executive chosen by Congress, a proposal comparable to the British parliamentary system.

Again the delegates displayed their talent for settling sharply divergent views by a series of compromises. First, beginning on June 1, James Wilson and Edmund Randolph crossed swords on the need for a single person to serve as chief executive. Wilson argued that a single person would provide effective leadership without becoming a tyrant; Randolph, in response, supported a three-man executive chosen from different parts of the country to avoid the appearance of monarchy, a fear that George Mason also reflected.[47]

James Wilson persisted in battling for a single chief executive. A plural office, he held, would lead to nothing but "uncontrolled, continued and violent animosities." His views prevailed, and the single chief executive was carried by a majority, with the states of Delaware, New York, and Maryland voting against the motion. What persuaded the majority above all else was the widely accepted view that George Washington would be the first holder of the office, and it was the image of Washington as the nation's leader that shaped their ideas of the powers to be given a president.

The manner of electing the President provided another divisive issue. The original Virginia Plan would have had the chief executive elected by the national legislature, a proposal that in time was dropped. The Framers were torn by considerations that would make the head of state responsible directly to the people rather than to the states and by fears that so democratic a system would be too extreme for the time. Those committed nationalists James Wilson and Gouverneur Morris eloquently argued the case for having the President elected directly by the people. George Mason retorted that "it would be as unnatural" to permit the people to elect a president "as it would, to refer a trial of colours to a blind man."[48] Roger Sherman stated his preference for having the President chosen by the national legislature, a proposal Morris ridiculed as "like the election of a pope by a conclave of cardinals." In retrospect it is understandable that Morris's proposal for direct election by the people should have been voted down with only his own state of Pennsylvania supporting the proposition. Most of the delegates were not accustomed to seeing their state's governor elected popularly since at that time only four of the thirteen states allowed eligible voters to elect their governor; in eight he was chosen by the legislature.

For a moment it almost seemed as though Roger Sherman's adopted motion to have Congress elect the President would stand, but Madison came to the rescue. He reminded the delegates that such an arrangement would violate the principle of the separation of powers. After countless proposals and reconsiderations, the ultimate decision resulted in another compromise. The Convention decided to have the President elected by an "Electoral College," comprising electors who would be chosen in each state "in such manner" as its legislature might "direct." Each state would have the same number of electors as it would send senators and representatives to Congress. The electors would vote by ballot for two persons, of whom one could not be an inhabitant of the state. The person having the greatest number of votes would become President; the second highest, Vice President. Pursuing a Roger Sherman proposal, the delegates provided that in the event that no person gained a majority of the electors, the House of Representatives would choose the candidate from the top five, each state's delegation casting one vote. The plan, another crucial compromise, proved a victory—first for the small states, then for the slave states, who had an advantage in the lower house through the three-fifths rule, and ultimately for both federalism and democracy, since very shortly after 1789 the state legislatures provided for the election of each state's presidential electors by popular vote.[49]

How long should a president's term be and should he be eligible for reelection? Hamilton, in his June 18 speech, seemed to indicate his preference for a life term, a view he later denied having endorsed except as an "experimental proposition," insisting that his final opinion at the Convention favored a three-year term.[50] Proposals ranged from Hamilton's three-year term permitting eligibility to run again to a seven-year term without such eligibility. Over the eligibility of the President for reelection Gouverneur Morris and George Mason clashed. The former argued that ineligibility would "destroy the great motive for good behavior, the hope of being rewarded by reappointment," while Mason warned that such eligibility might well result in the nation being governed by a president serving for life. This spirited exchange was concluded by the adoption of a provision providing for the impeachment of the President, a decision tied to another providing for a four-year term for both President and Vice President without imposing a limitation on the right of either to reelection.[51]

As to the various powers to be granted the President, the most intense and lengthiest wrangling occurred over his power to veto laws passed by Congress. The Virginia Plan had called for entrusting such power to a council of revision comprising the President and members of the national judiciary. For a time, Franklin's views against entrusting such powers solely to the President prevailed, with ten states voting against giving the President an absolute veto. Thereupon the Virginia proposal, for which Madison fought so long and hard, was revived by James Wilson, only to be opposed by Elbridge Gerry and John Rutledge on grounds that it would violate the principle of separation of powers and involve the judges in improperly giving extrajudicial opinions. By a narrow margin the Council of Revision was rejected and instead a compromise proposal conferring a veto power on the President which two-thirds of Congress could override was finally accepted by a closely divided vote.[52]

The share of power to be granted the President in making war raised significant issues and required definitions and parameters. Many of the delegates wished to see the war powers lodged in the legislative branch, wherein they had previously been vested. Charles Pinckney would have given them to the Senate exclusively, but his fellow delegate Pierce Butler favored instead vesting the power in the President, "who would have all the requisite qualities and will not make war but when the Nation will support it." A more prudent James Madison, with Gerry as seconder, moved to insert "declare," striking out "make" war, but "leaving to the Executive the power to repel sudden attacks." Mason, who declared that the executive was "not safely to be trusted" with the war power, was for "clogging rather than facilitating war, but for facilitating peace." Gerry declared that he "never expected to hear in a republic a motion to empower the executive alone to declare war." The motion to insert "declare" in place of "make" carried by seven states to two.[53]

As finally adopted, the Constitution takes an ambivalent stand. Article I, section 2, vests in Congress the right to declare war and to raise and support armies, while limiting appropriations to their use to a maximum of two years. Article II, section 2, describes the President as commander-in-chief. From this apparent division of powers one might infer that the Convention intended to distinguish between declaring war and supporting it, on the one hand, and conducting its operations, on the other. However, the Convention's action failed to remove the specter among Antifederalists, notably Patrick Henry at the Virginia Ratifying Convention, of a president "in the field, at the head of his army, prescribing the terms on which he shall reign master."[54] To allay such criticism, Hamilton in the 75th *Federalist* stated that he was not prepared to place at the "sole disposal" of the President "interests of so delicate and momentous a kind which concern the intercourse with the rest of the world." From these words the reader might reasonably infer that, regardless of how Hamilton would feel in the coming years, when he urged President Washington to take the field against the Whisky rebels, or when later he served as second-in-command of the army, Hamilton in 1788 was not prepared to interpret the President's powers as commander-in-chief as extending beyond the defense against invasion absent legislative sanction. Over the years the Constitutional Convention's caution in the matter of warmaking has proven well founded. As declarations of war have become old-fashioned if not obsolete, presidents have seized upon the ambivalent treatment of the subject in the Constitution to embark upon a variety of overseas military ventures on their own. Congress, in defense, has sought by resolution to define more precisely the parameters of the President's warmaking powers.[55]

For the Judicial Branch: A Bare Outline

Perhaps out of prudence, perhaps because the conception of the judicial branch differed substantially in the various plans, beginning with Virginia's, that were set before the Convention, the Framers treated the role of the federal judiciary with a remarkable economy of words. Aside from vesting the judicial power of the United States in one Supreme Court and such inferior courts as Congress might establish, the Framers in their final draft briefly described the jurisdiction of the federal judiciary as extending "in all Cases, in Law and Equity, arising under this Constitution, the Laws of the United States, and Treaties made under their authority." The courts were given jurisdiction over maritime and admiralty law, over foreign ambassadors, ministers, and consuls, to hear controversies to which the United States was a party, to controversies between two or more states, and to a variety of diversity of jurisdiction cases, notably "between a State and Citizens of another State," and between citizens of different states. *Chisholm* v. *Georgia* to the contrary notwithstanding, the debates suggested that the Framers did not believe the federal courts should have jurisdiction over cases in which a citizen was suing a state.[56]

A vexing issue at the Convention was where to locate the power to declare state laws unconstitutional. Even ardent nationalists shied away from granting the power to Congress. In the end it was a bitter states'-rights delegate who hit upon a satisfactory resolution of the problem. Luther Martin had a clause inserted making the Constitution and the laws and treaties of the United States "binding upon the judiciary of each State."[57] The supremacy clause, as it is called, became the cornerstone of national sovereignty when Congress in 1789 enacted the Judiciary Act providing for appeals from state courts to the federal judiciary. The Convention prudently abstained from spelling out just what body would have the right to declare acts of Congress unconstitutional, but from the sense of the debates it was implied that the federal judiciary would exercise that power.

In his concluding letters in *The Federalist,* Hamilton was at pains both to reassure his readers that the judicial branch would be "the weakest of the three departments of power," and to insist that the federal courts had the right to declare invalid laws contrary to the Constitution. Significantly, he assumed that judicial review would encompass all legislation, whether by state legislatures or by the federal Congress. Refusing to concede that the legislative branch was the constitutional judge of its own powers, he insisted that to deny to the judiciary the power to invalidate unconstitutional laws "would be to affirm that the deputy is greater than his principal; that the servant is above his master; that the representatives of the people are superior to the people themselves; that men acting by virtue of powers may do not only what their powers do not authorise, but what they forbid."[58]

The Committee of Style

Within ten days the Committee of Detail had hammered out the basic charter of government. The delegates debated the committee's draft clause by clause from August 6 to September 10, when the Constitution was approved and referred to a Committee of Style. Again, the Convention selected some of the most talented penmen among the delegates. William Samuel Johnson chaired the committee, with Gouverneur Morris, Madison, Rufus King, and Alexander Hamilton serving under him. It was Morris, however, whom Madison credited with being largely responsible for the Constitution's final phraseology. In a mere two days he produced a document distinguished for its precision of language and clarity of style. Morris's most noteworthy contribution was in changing the wording of the Preamble. Since new governments would go into operation upon ratification of nine states and no one could be certain which states would ratify, Morris very sensibly reworded the Preamble as drafted earlier by the Committee of Detail. Instead of "We the people of the United States of New Hampshire," etc., "do ordain, declare and establishing the following Constitution for the government of ourselves and our posterity," Morris's Preamble designated the people as the source of authority, thereby elevating the sights of government and couching its purposes in incomparable language. As he reported it, the Preamble read:

WE THE PEOPLE *of the United States, in Order to form a more perfect Union, establish Justice, insure domestic Tranquility, provide for the common defence, promote the general Welfare, and secure the Blessings of Liberty to ourselves and our Posterity, DO ordain and establish this* Constitution *for the United States of America.*

One other and very significant point. During the Convention debates various attempts had been unsuccessfully made on the initiative of Rufus King, with Madison's support, to insert a prohibition on states impairing the obligation of contracts. The Convention seemed to prefer "retrospective laws," but dropped the idea when Dickinson pointed out that in Blackstone ex post facto legislation applied only to criminal cases.[59] Elbridge Gerry would have extended the prohibition to Congress, but could find no seconder to his motion.[60] Nonetheless, the final draft reported by the Committee of Style included a clause forbidding any *state* from passing any "law impairing the obligation of contracts."[61] Probably the handiwork of either Hamilton or King, the insertion caused not even a ripple of comment on the floor when it was read.

The Final Day

On the last day of the Convention, September 17, 1787, Benjamin Franklin's good humor and conciliatory comments contributed much to achieving unanimous agreement on an acceptable formula for the Constitution's adoption. After the engrossed Constitution (a fair copy in the hand of Jacob Shallus, a clerk) was read, Franklin,

Preamble of the Constitution

Signatures to the Constitution

as Madison records it, "rose with a speech in his hand, which he had reduced to writing for his own conveniency," and which James Wilson read for him. Franklin confessed that there were several parts of the Constitution which he did not "at present" approve, but conceded that he was not sure that he should "never approve them," for, the older he grew, the more he came to doubt the infallibility of his own judgment. As example of people who regarded themselves as "in possession of all truth," he cited the case of "a certain French lady, who in a dispute with her sister said, 'I don't know how it happens, Sister, but I meet with nobody but myself, that's always in the right'—*Il n'y a que moi qui a toujours raison.*" Hoping for unanimous approval, Franklin then moved that the Constitution be signed by the members and offered a formula that would make the occasion possible: "Done in Convention, by the unanimous consent of *the States* present the 17th of September etc. —In Witness whereof we have hereunto subscribed our names," a deliberately ambiguous formula drafted by Gouverneur Morris to win over the dissenting members.

Just before the final vote Nathaniel Gorham proposed, to "lessen the objections to the Constitution," that the number of representatives be changed from one for every forty thousand to one for every thirty thousand. After King and Daniel Carroll, the latter from Maryland, seconded the motion, Washington, in one of the very few occasions when he formally spoke, endorsed the proposed change on the ground that it would remove the fears of "many" delegates about "the smallness of the proportion of Representatives." With no dissenting voice, this last-minute amendment was unanimously adopted.

The dissenters then spoke up. Randolph, the nominal originator of the basic plan the Convention adopted, apologized for declining to sign on the weak ground that he wished to maintain freedom of action. Gerry, warning that a civil war might result from the "present crisis of the United States," declared he would withhold his signature on the ground that the Constitution would not "abate the heat and opposition of parties." Hamilton, who alone among the New York delegation had returned to Philadelphia after the departure of all three many weeks before, conceded that "no man's ideas were more remote from the plan than his were known to be," but, while declaring that there was no real choice "between anarchy and

Convulsion on one side, and the chance of good to be expected from the plan on the other," Hamilton urged every member to sign.

Franklin's motion was then adopted by a vote of ten states to none, South Carolina divided and New York not voting (although that did not prevent Hamilton from affixing his signature to the document). After thirty-nine delegates had signed, all those present except Randolph, Mason, and Gerry, Madison tells us that "the Convention dissolved itself by an Adjournment sine die."[62]

It was now for the people to decide.

CHAPTER 12

Ratification and Union

The Role of the Convention and Congress

THE delegates to the Constitutional Convention were sober realists. They recognized that in the main their work had been the result of an overriding consensus on the part of its membership on the need to infuse the central government with energy. On the other hand, some among those who walked out before the closing, along with the relatively few who declined to sign the Constitution, did in fact represent a broad spectrum of opinion rooted in isolated pockets of rural areas remote from arteries of easy communication and held by state-centered politicians who would resist the loss of their power, by localists who feared the Leviathan state, and by rural libertarians who were dismayed by the absence of a bill of rights. Furthermore, the Convention had overstepped its instructions from Congress, if not from most of the states. Instead of recommending amendments to the Articles, the delegates were in actuality proposing an entirely new government.

It is noteworthy that the Convention did not include in its draft covering the mechanics for ratification a provision for the submission of the Constitution to Congress or requiring the approval of that body. Having exceeded the authority granted them by Congress, the Convention delegates decided to pursue what amounted to a revolutionary course by declaring ratification of nine states sufficient "for the establishment of this Constitution between the

States so ratifying the same." Above all states, all factions, and all interest groups stood the people, as the Preamble felicitously reminded the country.

During the closing days of the Federal Convention a proposal by Charles Carroll to prepare an address to the people to accompany the Constitution was voted down by six states to four. Rutledge pointed out the impropriety of such an address if the people did not know whether Congress "would approve and support the plan."[1] The ambiguous formula of signing, prepared by Gouverneur Morris and formally offered by Franklin, had been adopted, as previously noted, in the misguided hope that all those present would sign. Had not Franklin himself conceded that "it is too soon to pledge ourselves before Congress and our Constituents shall have approved the plan."?[2]

Thus, despite any provision in the text of the Constitution for requiring the approval of Congress, it seemed to have been the sense of the Convention that shrewd politics, if not common courtesy, required that the document be transmitted to Congress with an accompanying letter.[3] Major Jackson did so at once, and the Constitution reached Congress in New York on September 20. Its arrival and reading precipitated three days of debate, during the course of which nearly one third of the members had also participated in the Philadelphia Convention. Richard Henry Lee of Virginia and Nathan Dane of Massachusetts denounced the Convention for exceeding its mandate; Madison, supported by Abraham Clark and William Bingham, stoutly defended the Convention's action and sought a favorable congressional resolution to accompany the Constitution's transmittal to the states. Congress yielded to the Federalists and in substance adopted the Convention's unanimous resolution of September 17 that was appended to the Constitution with Washington's conciliatory covering letter of that date to Congress. With the unanimous vote of twelve states present, Congress resolved on September 28 that the Constitution "be transmitted to the several legislatures in Order to be submitted to a convention of Delegates chosen in each state by the people thereof."[4]

It is obvious that the hands of pro-Constitution delegates were seen in the wording of the message of transmittal virtually identical with that recommended by the Convention. In utilizing an institution innovated by the Massachusetts ratifiers in 1780, Congress carefully chose to bypass the state governors and legislatures, with their known attachment to states' rights. In most cases approval by legislative bodies would have required passage by two houses. As speedy ratification was the objective of the pro-Constitution forces, then the single-chambered, specially elected state ratifying conventions seemed to offer the greatest promise of agreement. It was the lack of such ratifying conventions to approve the Articles of Confederation that, in the judgment of Charles Pinckney, with due recognition of wartime conditions, had resulted in the subordination of the Confederacy to the state legislatures, and it was the requirement of unanimity for adoption of the Articles which had so long delayed its operation and prevented any augmentation of its powers.[5]

First Returns

Some states moved rapidly. The small states, having won a handsome victory in the Connecticut Compromise, offered little, if any objection. Between December 7, 1787, and January 9, 1788, Delaware, New Jersey, Georgia, and Connecticut ratified the Constitution, the first three states unanimously. On the other hand, Pennsylvania was the earliest to initiate the mechanism for ratification. In that state, the Federalists sought a quick affirmative vote before their opponents in the interior could get mobilized. They were determined to call a state convention whether or not Congress acted, and they controlled the assembly. On the morning of September 28 George Clymer, a Federalist Signer of the Constitution, successfully pushed through a resolution calling for a convention. The assembly then adjourned until the afternoon when, on reassembling, it was discovered that enough opponents had stayed away to prevent a quorum, which under the Pennsylvania constitution was defined as two thirds of the elected members.[6]

Meantime the Federalists in Congress had acted fast. William Bingham, a Pennsylvania delegate in Congress, sent a copy of the congressional resolution transmitting the Constitution to the states by express rider and it reached Philadelphia very early Saturday morning, the 29th. But when the members convened, they still lacked a quorum. The members present then ordered the sergeant at arms and the assistant clerk to bring in the absent members. With the assistance of a mob, two Antifederalists were dragged out of

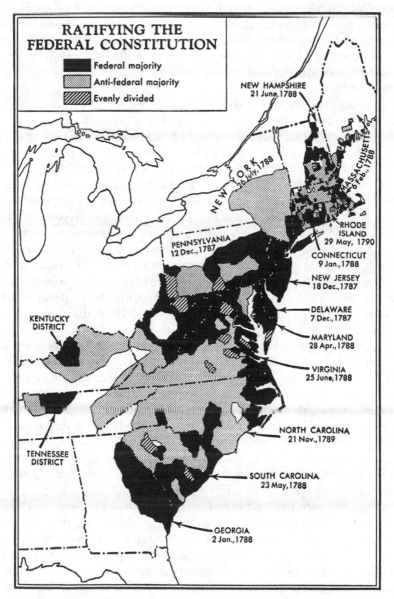

RATIFYING THE FEDERAL CONSTITUTION

- ■ Federal majority
- ▨ Anti-federal majority
- ▧ Evenly divided

NEW HAMPSHIRE
21 June, 1788

NEW YORK
26 July, 1788

MASSACHUSETTS
6 Feb., 1788

RHODE ISLAND
29 May, 1790

PENNSYLVANIA
12 Dec., 1787

CONNECTICUT
9 Jan., 1788

NEW JERSEY
18 Dec., 1787

KENTUCKY DISTRICT

DELAWARE
7 Dec., 1787

MARYLAND
28 Apr., 1788

VIRGINIA
25 June, 1788

NORTH CAROLINA
21 Nov., 1789

TENNESSEE DISTRICT

SOUTH CAROLINA
23 May, 1788

GEORGIA
2 Jan., 1788

Ratifying the Federal Constitution (From Richard B. Morris, ed., *Encyclopedia of American History*, 6th ed., Harper & Row) their lodgings and forcibly returned to the assembly. A quorum was then declared present and the delegates voted that afternoon for the election of delegates for the convention to meet in Philadelphia on November 20. Thus, the first call for a ratifying convention disclosed the crude tactics to which both sides might resort to achieve their ends.[7]

This was not the last of the violence, however. On election night a mob attacked the homes or boarding houses where some Philadelphia and Western assemblymen and councilors were lodged. Antifederalists blamed James Wilson for fomenting it, but despite a posted reward no rioters were apprehended.[8]

In the November election the Federalists gained a sweeping victory, by forty-four to twenty-four, although Antifederalists claimed that the lop-sided result did not fairly reflect the division of the electorate.[9] Accordingly, when the ratifying convention assembled, the Antifederalists lost all their preliminary procedural motions. Their argument that the new government would be "consolidated" rather than "federal" and lead to the virtual annihilation of state governments was ably refuted by James Wilson, who contended that the power of the Constitution was derived from the people and provided for a federal government with limited powers. While the Constitution was adopted, as expected, by a vote of forty-six to twenty-three, what was especially significant was the proposal of one of the Antifederalist leaders, Robert Whitehill, that the Convention adjourn to consider a list of fifteen amendments which he presented. Although this motion was defeated overwhelmingly, it presaged a post-Convention campaign of Pennsylvania Antifederalists for amending the Constitution. That the Constitution would continue to be belabored in the western part of the state was evident from the behavior of a crowd in Carlisle that greeted the report of ratification by burning in effigy "James the Caledonian."

The campaign to amend the Constitution was preceded in Pennsylvania by the presentation of petitions, chiefly from the Western countries, bearing some six thousand signatures, requesting the assembly to censure the Pennsylvania delegates to the Constitutional Convention for exceeding their authority, to rescind the state's ratification, and to so instruct the Pennsylvania delegates to Congress. Most of these positions were "tabled" by the assembly, which adjourned before others reached it. Frustrated and defied, the opponents did not give up. On July 3, 1788, after news of ratification by the ninth and tenth states reached Carlisle, the Antifederalists of Cumberland County sent out a circular letter calling a convention to meet at Harrisburg in September to nominate candidates for the House of Representatives in the first federal elections and to draft amendments to the Constitution.[10]

Pennsylvania now stood out as a glaring example of how not to win friends for the Constitution. Ahead lay the next big test in the important state of Massachusetts. Meeting so shortly after the disorders and dissension of Shays' Rebellion, the Federalists, including the state's Signers of the Constitution, Gorham, King, and Strong, acted with caution, treating with respectful consideration the substantial opposition by delegates from Shaysite country and from the Maine counties, the latter feeling that a vote for the Constitution would doom their chances for separate statehood. While at the outset a probable majority seemed arrayed against the Constitution, the Federalists counted on the prestige and learning of their leadership to turn the tide. Perhaps their trump card was the holdout John Hancock, elected president of the convention, who was converted to the cause of ratification by the prospects proffered him by Federalists exploiting his notorious vanity and ambition of winning the presidency of the United States, if Virginia, with its obvious candidate for that high office, failed to ratify.

The unlettered rural delegates offered more homespun rhetoric perhaps than at any other convention. Once it was agreed to take up the Constitution paragraph by paragraph before trying for a vote, the advantage obviously lay with the informed Federalists. The Antis fought bravely, with more passion than reason. "These lawyers and men of learning and money men," declared Amos Singletary, a delegate from Sutton, "that talk so finely, and gloss over matters so smoothly, to make us poor illiterate people swallow down the pill, expect to get into Congress themselves; they expect to be the managers of the Constitution, and get all the power and all the money into their own hands, and then they will swallow up all us little folks, like the great *Leviathan.*" "Yes," he added, "just as the whale swallowed up *Jonah.*"

A more conciliatory note was injected by one spokesman from Shays' country, Jonathan Smith of Lanesboro in Berkshire County. "I am a plain man," he said, "and get my living by the plough. I am not used to speak in public, but I beg you leave to say a few words to my brother ploughjoggers in this house." Describing "the black cloud" that spread over the state the last winter, he adverted to its "dreadful effect," bringing on "a state of anarchy and that led to tyranny." And what were the effects of that anarchy? "People, I say, took up arms, and then if you went to speak to them, you had the musket of death presented to your breast. They would rob you of your property, threaten to burn your houses, oblige you to be on your own day and night." Indeed, so great was the distress, Smith observed, that "had any person that was able to protect it, come and set up his standard, we should all have flocked to it, even if it had been a monarch." Contrariwise, Smith saw the Constitution as "a cure for these disorders. It was just such a thing as we wanted. I got a copy of it and read it over and over. I had been a member of the convention to form our own state constitution, and had learnt something of the checks and balances of power, and I found them all here. I did not go to any lawyer, to ask his opinion—we have no lawyer in our town, and we do well enough without. I formed my own opinion, and was pleased enough with it." Smith did not share Singletary's suspicion of upper-class Federalists. "These men of learning are all embarked on the same cause with us, and we must all sink or swim together, and shall we throw the Constitution overboard because it does not please us alike?" Urging action, Smith concluded: "There is a time to sow and a time to reap; we sowed our seed when we sent men to the federal convention. Now is the harvest, now is the time to reap the fruit of our labor, and if we wont do it now, I am afraid we never shall have another opportunity."

The most significant action of the Massachusetts Convention and the step that, rustic oratory aside, did most to win over enough dissenters, was the series of recommendatory amendments offered by John Hancock, amendments that "would remove the fears and quiet the apprehensions of many of the good people of the commonwealth . . . and more effectually guard against an undue administration of the federal government." These proposed amendments removed the apprehensions of a sufficient number of Antifederalists to secure ratification on February 6 by the close vote of 187 to 168. As the first convention to propose recommendatory amendments, Massachusetts established a pattern. Of the seven states which had yet to ratify, only one, Maryland, failed to take such action.[11]

As an aftermath no Massachusetts Federalist was burned in effigy as in western Pennsylvania. Instead, once the votes had been counted, William Widgery of New Gloucester in Maine took the floor to declare that "he should return to his constituents, and inform them, that he had been overruled, and that it had been carried by a majority of wise and understanding men; that he should endeavour to sow the seeds of union and peace among the people he represented"; and concluded by pledging his support to the new Constitution.[12]

The Great Debate

The publication of the Constitution precipitated one of the great political and ideological debates in American history. Antifederalists had, even prior to the Convention, begun to mount a formidable campaign against the Constitution. The strength of the opposition was now demonstrated in such populous states as Pennsylvania and Massachusetts, whose ratifying conventions as we have seen, disclosed the country as being far less united over the merits of the new national charter than were the delegates who had signed it.

The pro-Constitution forces, who had shrewdly styled themselves "Federalists" rather than nationalists, drew their strength from the commercial and manufacturing interests, from both entrepreneurs and artisans, from people residing in or accessible to the main arteries of commerce both along the seaboard and in the interior, from creditors, Revolutionary officers, and the bulk of the professional men—but by no means all. In contrast, the Antis won the allegiance of states' righters parochial in their vision, agrarians with limited access to markets, paper money advocates, debtors in various categories, and other particularists and special interests not represented at the Convention.

Unlike the Federalists, who proffered a blueprint of government, the Antis failed to counter with an alternative constitution. Except for a bill of rights, the key amendments they proposed to the Articles of Confederation had been sponsored unavailingly by the nationalists for more than half a decade.[13] They did score points against various sections of the Constitution and one signal omission, guarantees of civil liberties, but much of their argument was ad hominem in character. They targeted the elitist tone of the Constitution's sponsorship and exploited popular fears of a government controlled from the top by a highly ambitious sector of the establishment with conservative inclinations. They claimed to be spokesmen for the great mass of the people, but the touchstone of their democratic credentials was their insistence on the inclusion in the Constitution of more explicit guarantees of personal liberties, their advocacy of a unicameral legislature, a popularly elected judiciary, and a weak executive.

In retrospect one is entitled to question whether the Antifederalists' faith in democracy was more solidly grounded than their adversaries'. Evidence both from private correspondence and from the debates at the federal and ratifying conventions reveals the Antis' leaders of the stature of Richard Henry Lee of Virginia and New York's Governor George Clinton to have been as distrustful of the judgment of the masses as were their opponents. "Experience seems to have proven that our governments have not Tone enough for the unruly passions of men," wrote Lee while the Federal Convention was in session.[14] Clinton, despite his popularity with his state's masses, criticized the people for their fickleness and their tendency to "vibrate from one extreme to another," obviously with Shays' Rebellion which he had condemned very much in mind. At the Federal Convention Gerry had charged that "the evils we experience flow from an excess of democracy," and Maryland's impetuous John F. Mercer, whose brief notes on the Convention have only recently been unearthed, professed little faith in his neighbors as voters, for "the people cannot know and judge the character of candidates. The worst possible choice will be made."

If the Antis shared with their opponents a fear of the people's judgment, it was doubtless qualified by an abiding concern over the ease of organizing and controlling votes in towns and cities (advantages for the Federalists) and the difficulties confronting those who wished to organize a diffuse rural majority in opposition. As one reads the literature two centuries later, one is struck by the excessive compulsion of the Antis to express their fears, as one writer describes it, "in melodramatically picturesque terms."[15] Richard Henry Lee immediately comes to mind. While conceding that the

Constitution had "a great many excellent regulations in it," Lee warned that were it to be adopted unamended, "either a tyranny will result from it, or it will be prevented by a civil war."[16] The latter did occur some generations later, but the Union survived.

What distinguished the Antifederalists from their opponents was their deep concern about the threat posed to individual liberties by a powerful central authority. By concentrating their heaviest fire on the absence in the proposed Constitution of adequate safeguards for civil liberties—as distinguished from their scattershots at the shape of the national legislature, the presidency, and the judiciary—the Antifederalists contributed significantly to the final product, the Constitution with its initial ten amendments.

Nor were the Antifederalists slow in bombarding the public with pamphlets and newspaper letters. In his widely read *Letters From the Federal Farmer*, Richard Henry Lee charged that the change now proposed amounted to a transfer of power from the many to the few. From Massachusetts, James Winthrop's "Agrippa" letters attacked on two fronts: the Constitution gave too much power to the central government, left too little to the states, and would create a *permanent aristocracy*. Melancton Smith, in an *Address to the People of the State of New York*, warned that the Constitution would create an "aristocratic tyranny" that must soon terminate in "despotism." The Antifederalists challenged the practicality of the notion that a federal republic could exercise authority over so vast an extent of territory as the United States and found fault with the kind of dual sovereignty the Constitution envisioned. The omission of a bill of rights became a special target for George Mason's broadside, *Objections to the Proposed Federal Constitution*, a hard-hitting piece of polemics emanating from the pen of the renowned author of Virginia's Declaration of Rights. If federal law were paramount, the state bills of rights would be rendered nugatory, Mason contended.

More extreme critics made more extravagant accusations. The Constitution, they charged, had been framed by a *"dark conclave"* of "monarchy-men," "bold conspirators" who sought not only an elective king and a standing army but an "aristocratical Congress of the *well-born.*" Examples of such jaundiced rhetoric were to be found in a series of letters called *The Genuine Information*, which were run in the Baltimore papers. Authored by Luther Martin, the Maryland delegate who had quit the Convention before it completed its work, his main target was Article III, concerning the judiciary. Martin insisted that the states were better judges of the construction of tax laws than the federal judiciary, and as for an inferior federal court system, that would be superogatory, giving rise to an army of federal officials at enormous expense. In the course of time each of the three branches of the federal government would raise its own bureaucratic army, but none of the three could have envisioned the scope of that bureaucracy two centuries later.[17]

In contrast to the Antifederalists, their opponents had a concrete plan which was endorsed by public figures of commanding prestige and experience, the latter a point that would score heavily in a society still deferential to elitist governance. Despite such advantages and the known support of Washington, the Federalists observed a rising tide of criticism and were concerned that, having won the battle, they now might lose the war. To the Antifederalist barrage they responded vigorously and effectively, most notably in a series of letters to the New York newspapers published between October 27, 1787, and May 28, 1788, and then brought out in book form in June of 1788 to influence the ratification in New York. Writing under the pseudonym of "Publius," the three contributors to *The Federalist* were: Alexander Hamilton, initiator of the plan and author of fifty-one letters; James Madison, credited with twenty-nine; and John Jay who wrote five, along with his persuasive *An Address to the People of the State of New York*.[18]

The principal task of *The Federalist* was to demonstrate that rejecting the Constitution would create a vacuum of power, a return to the irresolute and impotent Confederation. Its authors felt obliged to reassure their readers that a republican federalism would provide energetic government while preserving personal liberties and taking into account the separate and different interests of the thirteen states. Such devices as checks and balances, courts composed of judges holding office during good behavior, and representation of the people in the national legislatures by deputies of their own election would "tend to the amelioration of popular systems of civil government."

"Publius" assured his readers that the government they were debating was *federal* rather than national, although such offices as the presidency combined both federal and national features, as was true of the amending process. Madison sought to reassure the country that the federal principle would guarantee to the people of an extended republic that "a coalition of interests, parties, and sects which it embraces, a coalition of a majority of the whole society, could seldom take place on any other principle than those of justice and the general good," while safeguarding minority rights.

How effective *The Federalist* may have been in winning votes for the Constitution outside of New York and Virginia may well be a matter of debate, but it has since come to be accepted as an incomparable exposition of the Constitution, a classic in political science unsurpassed in both breadth and depth by the product of any later American writer.[19]

With Maryland voting for the Constitution by an overwhelming margin of sixty-three to eleven, over the vehement protests of Samuel Chase and Luther Martin,[20] and South Carolina some weeks later approving the Constitution by a two-to-one vote despite the slave trade provision in the Constitution,[21] battle-lines were now drawn in what would prove the fiercest contests of the first eleven states to ratify—Virginia and New York.

For twenty sweltering days the Virginia ratifiers debated the pros and cons of the Constitution in Richmond's New Academy on Shockoe Hill. Dominating the great debate were that incomparable spellbinder Patrick Henry leading the Antifederalists, and the scholarly James Madison on behalf of the Constitution. The task of Madison, who made up in his mastery of the subject and debating skills what he lacked in oratorical ability, was indeed formidable, for it was believed that three fourths of the people of Virginia were opposed to the Constitution.[22] From the start both sides were feverishly active. Arrangements were made for express riders to carry reports of the course of the balloting in New Hampshire, expected to ratify as the ninth state, ahead of Virginia and New York, while Madison and Hamilton used special couriers to keep posted on their respective conventions. An agitated Patrick Henry had the effrontery to warn the Westerners that the Mississippi would be lost if the new plan were adopted and threatened the dissenting sects that under the Constitution a religious establishment would be set up.[23]

Despite the support of so prestigious a figure as George Mason, Henry's forces when finally assembled were outmaneuvered and poorly organized. The Federalists pushed through the elections of Edmund Pendleton as chairman of the convention and Chancellor

George Wythe as chairman of the Committee of the Whole. Madison could also count upon Attorney General James Inniss, whose oratorical skills were considered a match for Patrick Henry's and John Marshall, who made up for his carelessness in dress by his close attention to the needs of the clients he served in his growing Richmond law practice. Quick to capitalize on the mistakes of his opponents, Madison would find that errors in both tactics and substance were not slow in emerging. The first was committed by Mason when he proposed that the Constitution be debated "clause by clause," for it was in the command of each article, section, and clause of the Constitution that the advocates of the Constitution would quickly prove their superiority. No one, however, could confine Patrick Henry to such a logical procedure. In the course of his harangues he ran the gamut from attacking the Constitution as a whole to picking out at random objectionable clauses.

True, Henry launched his remarks with an attack on the Preamble. Why "We the People" instead of "We the States," he queried. The reason for the phraseology was obvious. It was to trap a confederation and replace it with a great consolidated government, destroying the rights of the states. And other rights, too—the rights of conscience, liberty of the press, "all your communities and franchises, all pretensions to human rights and privileges, are rendered insecure, if not lost, by this change." Already eight states had accepted the plan, Henry had heard, but as for him, he would reject it even if "twelve and a half have adopted it."

Save perhaps for Washington, who, while refraining from attendance, had made persuasive efforts to win Randolph over to supporting the Constitution, the governor's stand was unknown. Now he hurled his thunderbolt. He would support the Constitution and oppose any amendments prior to ratification.

The surprise announcement only stirred Henry to more tempestuous efforts. He castigated the Constitution for the military powers it gave the President and for its new power to tax. "Stay out, stay out!" he implored.

Patiently Madison replied point by point, expounding paragraphs from *The Federalist,* describing the government as partly consolidated, partly federal, its legislative powers as being strictly defined and limited. "Either we grant these powers or let the Union be dissolved," he warned. His hat in his hands, his notes in his hat, his voice barely audible in the large hall, Madison dragged body and mind through the debates. His reasoned and systematic analysis of the powers of taxation contributed to a physical exhaustion that kept Madison away from the convention for several days.

Patrick Henry never relented. He warned Kentuckians that they would lose the Mississippi, that the North would surrender this great waterway, and ridiculed Madison's distinctions between the federal and national attributes of the new government. "The brain is national," he declaimed, "the stamina federal, this limb national, that limb federal—but what it really signified was that a great consolidated government would be pressing on the necks of the people."

The great debate first projected a tall ungainly young man of thirty-two onto a national stage. The Constitution would guarantee "a well regulated democracy" and the preservation of liberty, John Marshall exhorted his fellow delegates. Only a strong government could retain the Mississippi, he insisted. Defending the concept of an extended republic, he pointed out that the objection to the concept came from writers "where representation did not exist." Closing with a defense of direct taxation and a praise of the Constitution as a protection of the nation in time of war, Marshall had concluded his first recorded utterance on the Constitution of which he was to become the greatest interpreter. Marshall had still another chance in the debate on the judiciary. Sounding a mournful note, Henry declaimed, "The purse is gone; the sword is gone," and now the scales of justice were to be given away. In rebuttal, Marshall contended that the national courts would provide trials as fair as the state courts. And then he advanced a prophetic assertion. Should Congress "make a law not warranted by any of the powers enumerated," the national courts "would declare it void." Nowhere else but the judiciary would provide such protection.[24] Who among the prescient delegates hearing this claim could have realized that Marshall himself would one day give reality to this prediction?

The Antis now smelled defeat. Their only hope was a ratification of the Constitution conditional upon the adoption of amendments, and they proposed some twenty amendments and a Bill of Rights of twenty articles. Madison's insistence on ratification without prior amendments was put forward as a proposition by Attorney General James Inness. By a vote of eighty-nine to seventy-nine the convention ratified the Constitution unconditionally, with amendments recommended to the consideration of Congress.[25]

Although New Hampshire, the ninth state, ratified the Constitution four days ahead of Virginia, thus putting the charter into effect, a key battle remained to be waged to attach New York to the Union. Without New York the nation would remain split asunder, and the significance of New York City, both as the nation's temporary capital and a major center of commerce, was not lost on either side. Hints that the city might secede from the rest of the state and join the Union were voiced behind the scenes during the convention, and the specter of a state cut off from the sea and the tax resources of its major city could not fail to disturb the upstate Antifederalists.

When, on June 17, 1788, the New York ratifying convention assembled in Poughkeepsie's old courthouse, the Antifederalist delegates outnumbered their opponents by more than two to one. In terms of the political pulse of the state these figures carried special significance, for the delegates had been elected by the most democratic suffrage of any of those attending ratifying conventions in the other twelve states, with every free male citizen over twenty-one being eligible to vote; the liberal franchise was supported by the Federalists to the bafflement of the Antis. Significant also was the geographical split on the Constitution. New York City had dispatched a slate of Federalist delegates to the convention by a vote of ten to one. Most of the state north of Westchester, which also chose Federalists, was captured by the Clintonian Antis.[26]

While Governor Clinton had assumed the leadership in organizing the opposition and was elected the convention chairman, he left the operations on the convention floor largely to John Lansing, Jr. and Melancton Smith. The Federalists counted principally on Hamilton and Jay. The Antis, while conceding Hamilton's eloquence and ability to secure debating points, privately joked about his speeches as a warmed-over version of "Publius," with Clinton acknowledging that this "second edition" of *The Federalist* was well delivered. If Hamilton scored debating points, it is not clear that he won votes. To the Antis, despite Hamilton's republican cloak, he was "known" and feared, while Jay's friendly, moderate, and conciliatory approach, especially backstage, seemed to be more telling with his opponents.[27]

The Federalist strategy, as disclosed in the opening motion by Chancellor Robert R. Livingston, whose patronizing manner ruffled the feathers of his opponents, was to consider the Constitution "clause by clause." The prompt adoption of this motion by the convention would ensure ultimate victory, for not only did it give the Federalists needed time to learn the decisive news of New Hampshire's ratification as the ninth state, but also the result, more crushing to the Clintonian opposition, of the Federalist victory in Patrick Henry's Virginia. It was now obviously futile to oppose a Constitution already in being. Accordingly, the Antifederalists focused on loading any adoption with conditional amendments of a crucial character and insisting on a second convention to rectify defects in the Constitution they were reviewing.

In turn, the Federalists conceded the need for amendments, but insisted that they must be recommendatory. Hamilton proffered a list of thirteen (none of which dealt with civil liberties) that were acceptable to the Federalist side. John Jay, serving on a subcommittee with the two floor leaders of the opposition, Lansing and Smith, drafted a circular letter for Governor Clinton to transmit to the other states under his signature. The letter struck a conciliatory note. It called for a "Convention to meet at a Period not far remote" to consider amendments proposed by several state ratifying conventions as well as New York's. For Jay this had been a tremendous concession, for earlier that spring he had denounced the whole idea of a second convention in his *Address to the People.* His apparent sponsorship of the move evoked a vehement reaction from James Madison.[28]

Unanimously agreed to, the circular letter failed to halt a last-ditch stand by the Antifederalists. The convention still had to vote down a new motion by Lansing reserving the right of the state to secede if the amendments were not adopted. Lansing's motion was defeated by the perilously close vote of thirty to twenty-eight (Clinton abstaining), and by almost the same slim margin of thirty to twenty-seven, the convention ratified the Constitution. A number of Antifederalists, including Gilbert Livingston, Melancton Smith, and Samuel Jones, had switched to the Federalist side, while seven Antis abstained.[29]

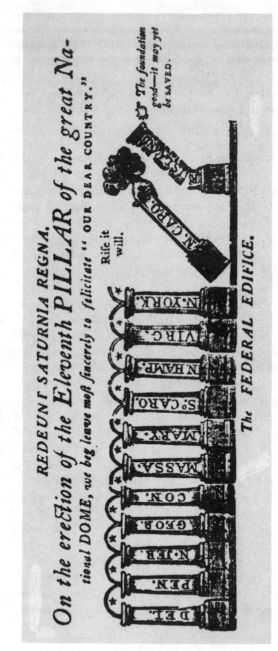

The Federal Edifice: New York, the Eleventh Pillar

The Hold-outs

In each of the major cities of the nation great parades and public banquets were staged to celebrate their respective state's ratification, although in New York City—since the Union was a fait accompli as a result of New Hampshire's ratification, followed quickly by Virginia—that colorful salute, in which all ranks, professions, and crafts joined, actually occurred three days before the Poughkeepsie delegates took final action. A union of eleven states now existed, and it was that number that organized the first Congress without waiting for North Carolina and Rhode Island, both still hold-outs.

In North Carolina the determined stand of the Antis was directed by an Eton-educated landed aristocrat named Willie Jones, who gathered around him a handful of self-made backcountrymen, paper money enthusiasts, and Western Land speculators, whom the Federalists underrated as "a set of fools and knaves."[31] The Antis' lack of technical knowledge was more than compensated for by their belligerency. Willie Jones came into the North Carolina ratifying convention with a two-to-one majority against the Constitution. In addition, he could also exploit a letter from Thomas Jefferson in Paris in which the American minister let it be known that he favored a second convention "to adopt the improvements generally acceptable and omit those found disagreeable." Among the latter was the omission of a bill of rights, which to Jefferson appeared to be "a degeneracy in the principles of liberty to which I had given four centuries instead of four years."[32] Jefferson subsequently modified his position when he learned that conventions had proposed various amendments, including a bill of rights, but his later stand was not widely circulated in North Carolina. The Antis allowed Federalist leaders like James Iredell to expound the Constitution clause by clause. Then they jolted the pro-Constitution forces with the introduction of a series of amendments, which in addition to those offered by Virginia, denied the federal government control over paper money emitted by the states "or in liquidating and discharging the public securities of any one of the states."[33] On August 2 an avalanche of votes buried the Federalists' motion to ratify.

North Carolina now moved for a second convention, and when that move seemed to get nowhere, Congress pressed ahead with its formulation of a bill of rights. Finally, the state ratified the Constitution at Fayetteville by the convincing majority of 194 to 77.[34]

Now Rhode Island stood alone. Its legislature refused even to call a ratifying convention, an intransigency that prompted the towns of Providence and Newport to consider seceding from the state and joining the Union. President Washington warned the General Assembly of the possible consequences of its obduracy,[35] and Congress initiated steps to impose duties on Rhode Island's shippers and exclude the state's products from United States ports.[36] Even a total embargo was in contemplation.

In the end the assembly yielded to calling a ratifying convention, the lower house by a substantial margin, but in the upper house the tie vote was broken by a deciding ballot cast by Governor John Collins. The convention met only to adjourn to attend to a state election and set up a coalition government. A spangle rather than a star, Rhode Island had demonstrated exceptional talent at exasperating the rest of the country. When the convention met again, it did ratify the Constitution, but by the ungraciously minuscule majority of thirty-four to thirty-two. It had joined the Union not out of affection but from necessity.[37]

The Demise of the Initial Second Convention Movement

The circular letter drafted by Jay for the New York ratifying convention and circulated to the states by Governor Clinton proved a fillip to Antifederalists not only in New York but in Virginia and Pennsylvania as well, while heartening the opposition in hold-out states like North Carolina and Rhode Island to delay ratification.[38] Even in the short run Madison's fears of the ill effects of New York's Circular Letter proved unfounded. In Jay's own state, despite the campaign launched at the end of October '88 by a group of "Federal Republicans" headed by Customs Collector John Lamb and including Melancton Smith,[39] sentiment was already moving in a contrary direction. A fortnight earlier Jay had been able to report to Edward Rutledge that the temper of the opposition, once "violent," had "daily become more moderate," while the proposal for a second convention should, in the writer's judgment, "terminate all questions on the subject." "If immediately carried," he observed, "its friends will be satisfied, and if convened three years hence, little danger, perhaps some good will attend it."[40]

The proposal for a second convention, earlier advanced by the outvoted Antifederalists of Pennsylvania and called in Harrisburg in 1788 and by the Virginia legislature,[41] as well as in the hold-out states of North Carolina and Rhode Island, was rendered nugatory by the swift action of the First Congress in coming to terms with the principal issues raised by the Constitution's opponents. As for John Jay, we know from his own admission that he was not displeased that the country did not rush into a second convention.[42] Soon to be Chief Justice, he would have a Constitution to interpret, and uncertainty and instability were the last things that he and his Federalist colleagues on the bench would have desired.

"The Great Rights of Mankind"

The most significant action taken by the First Congress under the Constitution when it convened in New York's old City Hall in 1789 was to honor the pledge made by the Federalists in some five states to add to the Constitution a set of guarantees of the rights of individuals and to confirm the people and the states in the possession of all powers not delegated to the federal government or prohibited to them. True, the proponents of the Constitution, notably Hamilton in *Federalist* No. 84, had consistently argued that a declaration of rights was irrelevant to a constitution of enumerated powers. Even James Madison had long adhered to this position. Whether due to the persuasive letters of Jefferson or in response to public opinion as expressed in the debates in the ratifying conventions and in Antifederalist writings, Madison came to recognize the need for a change of course. He would soon reassure a critical Jefferson that such a declaration would enhance the legitimacy of the new government "without weakening its frame or abridging its usefulness in the judgment of those who are attached to it."[43] When, on a later celebratory occasion, John Quincy Adams declared that the Constitution "had been extorted from the grinding necessity of a reluctant nation,"[44] he might well have added that without the general understanding that a pledge of guarantees of individual liberties would be forthcoming, the Constitution might never have become a fait accompli.

The initiative was Madison's. On June 8, 1789, he rose in the House of Representatives, to which office he had recently been elected despite the opposition of Patrick Henry, and moved that the

House consider the subject of amendments. He informed the House that it was "bound by every motive of prudence, not to let the first session pass over without proposing to the State Legislatures some things to be incorporated into the Constitution that will render it . . . acceptable to the whole people of the United States." Conceding that the great mass of the people who opposed the Constitution "disliked it because it did not contain effectual provisions against encroachments on particular rights," he argued that it was the duty of Congress "to provide those securities of liberty . . . and expressly declare the great rights of mankind secured under this Constitution."[45] While both the initiator and energizer of the movement to win congressional approval for the Bill of Rights, Madison needs share authorship with others for the first ten amendments as they appear in their final form. Madison's propositions were drawn for the most part from the Virginia Declaration of Rights of 1776 and the amendments proposed by Virginia in 1788, but he followed New York rather than the Virginia precedent of substituting "due process of law" for "the law of the land."[46] He also had at hand a pamphlet including the several hundred amendments proposed in seven states.[47]

Although Madison was normally attuned to good writing, he fell from grace on this occasion when he would have inserted a declaratory prefix to be put before the words "We the People" in the Preamble. He would have introduced the Preamble with the declaration that government was created "for the benefit of the people and was derived from their authority alone." This wordy redundancy was fortunately rejected out of hand by the House. Again, Madison wished to have his amendments incorporated within the Constitution itself, a notion that Roger Sherman successfully thwarted. The logic of Madison's insistence on such incorporation is difficult to comprehend. As one congressman pointed out, "if the amendments are incorporated in the body of the work, it will appear, unless we refer to the archives . . . that George Washington and the other worthy characters who composed the convention, signed an instrument which they never had in contemplation."[48] The decision not to incorporate the Bill of Rights but to treat it as a set of separate amendments was crucial, for it is difficult to imagine that a bill of rights dispersed throughout the body of the Constitution would command the position it would later attain as the vital center of American constitutional law.

As the twelve amendments drafted by Madison from the many times that number submitted by the states made their course through a select committee of eleven and then through the House and Senate and a Conference Committee, further changes followed.[49] Most shortsighted of these was the elimination of Madison's provision prohibiting the *states* from infringing on freedom of conscience, speech, press, and trial by jury in criminal cases, a provision which Madison deemed the most important amendment in the entire list. As a result, the Bill of Rights as adopted, contrary to Madison's intent, imposed restrictions only upon the federal government. It was not until the Fourteenth Amendment that the Constitution would impose significant limits upon state power to infringe individual liberties.

Madison was also to find his proposed amendment incorporating the doctrine of separation of powers consigned to the scrapheap. Its wording deserves inclusion herein as a reminder of the importance some of the Framers attached to this principle of governance:

The powers delegated by this Constitution are appropriated to the departments to which they are respectively distributed: so that the Legislative Department shall never exercise the powers vested in the Executive or Judicial, nor the Executive exercise the powers vested in the Legislative or Judicial, nor the Judicial exercise the powers vested in the Legislative or Executive Departments.

Undaunted by setbacks, Madison would score two significant victories. It was his version of the first guaranty of the First Amendment—the nonestablishment clause—that survived in its final form. Furthermore, when the provision on reserved powers in what is now the Tenth Amendment was taken up, a member of the House moved to add "expressly" so that the text would read "the powers not expressly delegated to the federal government would be reserved to the states." Madison remembered the fateful consequences of Burke's insertion of "expressly" in the second article of the Articles of Confederation and vigorously argued that "it was impossible to confine a Government to the exercise of express powers. There must necessarily be admitted powers by implication, unless the Constitution descended to recount every minutiæ."[50] Ironically, Madison's insistence on the exclusion of "expressly" laid the basis for Hamilton's implied powers argument in defending the constitutionality of Congress's establishing the Bank of the United States, and that Hamiltonian interpretation was upheld by Chief Justice Marshall in the landmark case of *McCulloch* v. *Maryland.*[51] Madison would soon retreat from so bold an application of the "elastic clause," but over time his earlier interpretation would prevail.

On September 25, 1789, the date celebrated as the anniversary of the Bill of Rights, the Senate concurred in the twelve amendments voted in the House. Apart from the first two—dealing with re-enumeration in the House of Representatives and changing the compensation of senators and representatives, both of which failed of ratification, the remaining ten amendments, appropriately renumbered, survived to be ratified. Before the ratification process was completed, the number of states in the Union had increased from eleven to fourteen as a result of ratification of the Constitution by North Carolina and Rhode Island and the admission of Vermont to the Union in 1791. Ratification of the Bill of Rights now required by eleven states occurred with Virginia's approval on December 15, 1791. Three of the original thirteen states that did not ratify at that time—Connecticut, Georgia, and Massachusetts—did so as a symbolic gesture in 1939.

Spelling Out Article III

Of the three branches of the federal government, the Constitution devotes the briefest space to describing the judiciary and enumerating its powers. Whether pressures of time or political caution explain the short shrift given by the Framers to the judiciary, there is no question that the Convention placed much reliance on the judicial branch for upholding the supremacy of treaties and the laws of Congress. Since fears of a federal judiciary's intrusion on the state court system were so commonly voiced by Antifederalist critics of the Constitution, Hamilton felt obliged to add several more "Publius" letters to the seventy-seven published in the newspapers, and to incorporate this addenda in the two-volume edition of *The Federalist,* issued in the late spring of 1788. First, he went out of his way in the 78th *Federalist* to reassure his readers that the judicial branch would always be the "least dangerous to the political rights of the Constituents," for, unlike the other two branches, "it had no influence over the sword or the purse." Nevertheless, he had no hesitancy in asserting that the federal courts had the right to declare invalid laws contrary to the Constitution, and that judicial review would encompass all legislation, whether by state legislatures or by the federal Congress. Such power would not make the judicial superior to the legislative branch, he argued, since in fact under the Constitution all three branches were co-equal. However, to deny the judiciary the power to invalidate unconstitutional laws "would be to affirm that the deputy is greater than his principal; that the servant is above his master; that the representatives of the people are superior to the people themselves, that men acting by virtue of powers may do not only what their powers do not authorise, but what they forbid." Hence, Hamilton refused to concede that the legislative branch was the constitutional judge of its own powers, and that the construction it put on them was conclusive upon the other departments.[52]

The Federal Judiciary

It remained, however, for the Judiciary Act of September 24, 1789, to incorporate the principle of judicial supremacy into the federal judicial system. That act, largely the work of Oliver Ellsworth of Connecticut and fellow Federalists on a Senate committee, spelled out the mechanisms by which the judicial branch would perform its duties and underpinned the principle that federal laws and treaties were to be "the supreme Law of the Land." A scrupulously detailed statute of some thirty-five sections, it provided for a Supreme Court consisting of a chief justice and five associate justices, for thirteen federal district courts of one judge each—one district for each of the eleven existing states and two additional districts in Virginia and Massachusetts for Kentucky and Maine—and for three circuit courts, each composed of two justices of the Supreme Court sitting in conjunction with one district court judge. The jurisdiction, organization, and procedures were set forth in detail, while concurrent jurisdiction was given to the state courts in certain cases involving federal law.

Perhaps most significant, the Judiciary Act provided for appeals in certain instances from state courts to the federal judiciary, specifically in rulings on a federal treaty or law; on state laws which had been challenged as contrary to the Constitution, treaties, or laws of the United States; or in rulings against rights or privileges claimed under the Constitution or federal law. By this means the federal judiciary would be enabled to uphold Article VI of the Constitution embracing the supremacy clause (section 25).[53] Nowhere in the Judiciary Act do we find an explicit power granted to the Supreme Court to rule on the constitutionality of acts of Congress, although such power could be inferred from the act's authorizing appeals to the Supreme Court from the decisions of state courts involving the constitutional construction of acts of Congress. Beyond that line draftsmen felt it either unnecessary or imprudent to venture.

If the Bill of Rights appeased most critics of the Constitution and the Judiciary Act provided a mechanism for upholding its supremacy, the first national administration under the presidency of George Washington provided a series of precedents which became embodied in the constitutional structure: the Cabinet system, the role of the Senate to "advise and consent" to treaties, the unilateral power of the executive to proclaim neutrality, and toward the end of Washington's first term in office, the roots of a party system. The Framers of the Constitution and the first federal administration had forged a Union. No one could foresee how "posterity" would respect it.

In his opening *Federalist* letter Alexander Hamilton had raised a profound question. "It seems to have been reserved to the people of this country, by their conduct and example," he declared, "to decide the important question, whether societies of men are really capable of establishing good government from reflection or choice, or whether they are forever destined to depend for their political constitutions on accident and force."

"We the people" have decided the question in the affirmative without abdicating our right to exercise eternal vigilance.[54]

Notes

Chapter 1. A People, Independent and at Peace

1. Richard B. Morris, *The Peacemakers: The Great Powers and American Independence* (repr. 1965 ed., Boston, 1983), pp. 447–48.
2. According to the report of Brook Watson, British Commissary-General, dated November 24, 1783, the total number of men, women, and children who left New York during the year was 29,244, but these include a large proportion of discharged soldiers with their families and an estimated 3,000 blacks claimed as personal property. Henry P. Johnston, "Evacuation of New York by the British," *Harper's New Monthly Magazine*, LXVII (1883), 909–23.
3. James Riker, *Evacuation Day, 1783* (New York, 1883), p. 21.
4. William Bayard to General Frederick Haldimand, New York, August 8, 1783, Haldimand Papers, British Museum, London.
5. Of the regiments sent to the West Indies as reinforcements from the British Isles, from October 1776 to February 1780, 8,437 embarked, 932 died in passage, for an 11 percent average loss. Piers Mackesy, *The War for America* (Cambridge, Mass., 1964), p. 526.
6. It is estimated that forty-four officers were present, including Generals James Clinton, Greene, Hand, Huntington, Knox, Kosciuszko, Lincoln, McDougall, Patterson, Schuyler, Stark, and von Steuben, and such lower-ranking officers as Humphreys, Jackson, Lamb, Tallmadge, along with Governor Clinton, James Duane (then on the Governor's Council and soon to be the city's mayor), and Alexander Hamilton.
7. William Alexander Duer, *Reminiscences of an Old Yorker* (New York, 1867), pp. 96–103.
8. On conditions in New York after the evacuation, see Sidney I. Pomerantz, *New York An American City, 1783–1803* (New York, 1938); Raymond A. Mohl, *Poverty in New York, 1783–1825* (New York, 1971); *Minutes of the Common Council of the City of New York, 1784–1831* (19 vols., New York, 1917), I, passim.

9. Jean P. Brissot de Warville, *New Travels in the United States* (2 vols., London, 1792), I, 138. The pillaging on Long Island and Westchester, where in the latter county lawless banditti on both sides operated, see Thomas Jones, *History of New York in the Revolutionary War* (2 vols., New York, 1879), I, 336–410; Otto Hufeland, *Westchester County During the American Revolution* (New York, 1926), chs. vii–viii; *JJ*, II, 10, 168.

10. Lt. Col. Stephen Kemble, "Papers," New-York Historical Society *Collections*, XVI (1883); Johann D. Schoepf, *Travels in the Confederation, 1783–1784*, ed. by A. J. Morison (2 vols., Philadelphia, 1911), I, 23; *Pennsylvania Evening Post*, April 24, 26, May 10, 1777; *New Jersey Archives*, 2d ser., I, 347–50, 362–67.

11. Charles Royster, *The Continental Army and American Character, 1775–1783* (Chapel Hill, 1979), p. 456; Sung Bok Kim, "The Continental Army and the American People," *New York History*, LXIII (1982), 465–66. For looting by American troops in the West Florida campaign, see James Alton James, *Oliver Pollock* (New York, 1937), pp. 117–30.

12. For Elizabethtown, see *JJ*, I, 573n; II, 172n., 185–187.

13. David D. Wallace, *The Life of Henry Laurens* (New York, 1915), pp. 240, 424, 526.

14. See Charles Stedman, *History of the Origin, Progress, and Termination of the American War* (2 vols., London, 1794), II, 193; Joseph W. Barnwell, ed., "Letters of John Rutledge," *South Carolina Historical Magazine*, XVIII (1917), 44; Eliza Wilkinson, *Letters of Eliza Wilkinson During the Invasion and Possession of Charleston, S.C. by the British in the Revolutionary War* (repr. 1839 ed., New York, 1960). The slow and tedious mass evacuation of Loyalists, slaves, and British soldiery from Charleston is described in Edward McCrady, *The History of South Carolina in the Revolution, 1780–1783* (repr. 1902 ed., New York, 1960), pp. 475, 674.

15. Mary Beth Norton, *Liberty's Daughters: The Revolutionary Experience of American Women, 1750–1800* (Boston, 1980), pp. 203–04.

16. Franklin to Oswald, *BFS*, VIII, 620–23, 632n.; Charles R. King, ed., *The Life and Correspondence of Rufus King* (6 vols., New York, 1894–1900), IV, 94; Morris, *Peacemakers*, p. 379.

17. Bradford Torrey and Francis H. Allen, eds., *The Journal of Henry D. Thoreau* (14 vols. in 2; repr. 1906 ed., New York, 1962), VII, 132–37; VIII, 220–21.

18. Shoepf, *Travels*, p. 37; Arthur C. Bining, *Pennsylvania Iron Manufacture in the Eighteenth Century* (Harrisburg, Pa., 1938), p. 75; Richard P. McCormick, *Experiment in Independence* (New Brunswick, N.J., 1950), pp. 129–30.

19. Carl O. Sauer, *Land and Life* (Berkeley, 1963), p. 154, and particularly useful on this subject has been the perceptive analysis by William Cronon, *Changes in the Land: Indians, Colonists, and the Ecology of New England* (New York, 1983); also A. P. Usher, "Soil Fertility, Soil Exhaustion, and Their Historical Significance," *Quarterly Journal of Economics*, XXXVII (1923), 385–411; Avery Craven, *Soil Exhaustion as a Factor in the Agricultural History of Virginia and Maryland, 1606–1860* (Urbana, Ill., 1926); Philip T. Coolidge, *History of the Maine Woods* (Bangor, Me., 1963); Roland M. Harper, "Changes in the Forest Areas of New England in Three Centuries," *Journal of Forestry*, XVI (1918), 442–52.

20. Benjamin Franklin, "Information to Those Who Would Remove to America," [September, 1782], *BFS*, VIII, 604–05.

21. Bernard Bailyn, *Lines of Force in Recent Writing on the American Revolution* (San Francisco, 1978).

22. S. H. Sutherland, *Population Distribution in Colonial America* (New York, 1936), pp. 68, 158, 222; Curtis P. Nettels, *The Emergence of a National Economy, 1775–1815* (New York, 1962). For the unprecedented dynamics of U. S. continental expansion, see D. W. Meinig, *The Shaping of America: Atlantic America, 1492–1800* (New Haven, 1986), pp. 416–17.

23. [Vergennes, Rayneval, or Montmorin], "Reflections on the Peace," AHN:E 4203; Goltz to Frederick II, December 13, 1782, Frederick II to Thulemeier, May 26, 1783, Marvin L. Brown, *American Independence Through Prussian Eyes* (Durham, N.C., 1959), pp. 127, 128, 201. Turgot to Richard Price, *JAW*, IV, 273, et seq.

24. Alexis de Tocqueville, *Democracy in America*, trans. by Henry Reeve, ed. by Henry Steele Commager (London, 1946), p. 103. Philosophers like the Abbé Morellet, on the other hand, recognized the revolutionary impact of America and its peculiar advantages stemming from the absence of a feudal structure. Morellet to Shelburne, April 22, 1782, *Lettres de l'Abbé Morellet à Lord Shelburne, 1772–1803* (Paris, 1898), pp. 190–92.

25. L'Abbé Ferdinand Galiani to Mme. D'Epinay, May 18, 1776, *Lettres de L'Abbé Galiani . . .* (2 vols., Paris, 1905), II, 225–26. Bernard Bailyn's multivolume investigation of immigration in the prewar years has been initiated by *The Peopling of British North America* and *Voyages to the West* (New York, 1986), the latter devoted to an analysis of the origins and destination of some 10,000 British emigrants in the years just preceding the American Revolution.

26. Richard B. Morris, ed., *Encyclopedia of American History* (6th ed., New York, 1982), p. 648; Congress poll, 3,011,000.

27. *Historical Statistics of the United States*, 1960, Ser. Z, 1–19; Ser. A, 1–3.

28. Morris, ed., *Encyclopedia*, p. 648; W. S. Rossiter, *A Century of Population Growth* (Washington, D.C., 1909), pp. 96–103.

29. Morris, ed., *Encyclopedia*, p. 649. On the point of greater longevity of Americans than Europeans, see Brissot, *Travels*, I, 364, 368. Even though demographics point to a fertility decline in America, particularly in the Northeast, beginning in the Revolutionary years and continuing into the decades ahead, mortality rates were lower than in Europe. Recent historical demographers have painstakingly sought to discern patterns from the available census figures and to ascertain the relationship between premarital pregnancy (a not uncommon phenomenon) and church membership and family wealth. Maris A. Vinovskis, ed., *Studies in American Historical Demography* (New York, 1979), pp. 122, 123; See also Vinovskis, *Fertility in Massachusetts from the Revolution to the Civil War* (New York, 1981), who stresses cultural differences as against socioeconomic determinants. For methodology, see Daniel S. Smith, "A Perspective on Demographic Methods and Effects in Social History," *WMQ*, XXXIX (1982), 442–69. See also Philip J. Greven, *Four Generations; Population, Land, and Family in Colonial Andover, Massachusetts* (Ithaca, N.Y., 1970); John Demos, *The Little Commonwealth: Family Life in Plymouth Colony* (New York, 1973). For the survival of

bundling in the Confederation years, see H. R. Stiles, *Bundling: Origin, Progress, and Decline* (Albany, N.Y., 1869), pp. 81–82.

30. M. L. Hansen, *The Atlantic Migration, 1607–1860* (Cambridge, 1941), pp. 69–70; Carl Wittke, ed., *We Who Built America* (New York, 1940), pp. 95–96.

31. Hansen, *Atlantic Migration*, pp. 56, 69–70; John A. Krout and Dixon Ryan Fox, *The Completion of Independence, 1790–1830* (New York, 1944), p. 6.

32. Morris, *Peacemakers*, p. 382; W. A. S. Hewins, comp., *Whitefoord Papers* (Oxford, 1898), p. 187.

33. See Clifford Geertz, *The Interpretation of Cultures: Selected Essays* (New York, 1973), pp. 234, et seq.

34. Hector St. John de Crèvecoeur, *Letters From an American Farmer* (London, 1782), Letter III. Crèvecoeur, who went into voluntary Tory exile during the war, offered a much less sympathetic account in his *Sketches of Eighteenth-Century Americans*, first published in 1925, ed. by H. L. Bourden, R. H. Gabriel, and S. T. Williams (New Haven). The work abounds in generalities and lacks specificity about people, places, and time.

35. Crèvecoeur, *Letters*, Letter III.

36. American Council of Learned Societies, "Report of the Committee on National and Linguistic Stocks in the Population of the United States," American Historical Association, *Annual Report, 1931*, I (Washington, D.C., 1932), 107–441.

37. See Donald H. Akerson, "Why the Accepted Estimates of the Ethnicity of the American People, 1790, Are Unacceptable," *WMQ*, XLI (1984), 102–19. See also Forrest and Helen Shapiro McDonald, "The Ethnic Origins of the American People, 1790," *ibid.*, XXXVII (1980), 179–99. For the view that the McDonalds overweight the Irish, Scots, and Welsh proportions, see Thomas I. Purvis, "The European Ancestors of the United States Population, 1790," *ibid.*, XLI (1984), 92. See also Thomas J. Archdeacon, *Becoming American: An Ethnic History* (New York, 1983), p. 25.

38. Shoepf, I, 108–09.

39. Jefferson to George Flower (1812) in Paul L. Ford, ed., *Writings of Thomas Jefferson* (10 vols., New York, 1892–99), VII, 83.

40. Quoted in L. M. Miner, *Our Rude Forefathers: America's Political Verse, 1783–1788* (Cedar Rapids, Iowa, 1937), pp. 61–62.

41. John Jay to John Trumbull, October 27, 1797, *HPJ*, IV, 232. The term "Americanism" is first attributed to the Reverend John Witherspoon in 1781. See Mitford M. Mathews, *Dictionary of American English* (Chicago, 1951). Jay, however, placed the term in a broader than linguistic context. To him it was a political duty to create a truly "independent nation."

42. Since Jay frequently boasted that he had not a drop of English blood in his veins (just French Huguenot and Dutch), he must have had tongue in cheek when he wrote these lines. For a criticism of this as a viable longer-range explanation, see Elise Marienstras, *Les mythes fondateurs de la nation américaine* (Paris, 1976), pp. 280–83.

43. "The Continentalist," No. 6, *New-York Packet*, July 4, 1782.

44. John Jay to John Lowell, May 10, 1785, in *WJ*, I, 190.

45. Washington to Theodorick Bland, April 4, 1783, *GWF*, XXVII, 294.
46. Noah Webster, "The Reforming of Spelling," 1789, *Old South Leaflets*, No. 196 (Boston, n.d.), VIII, 389–90.
47. John S. Morgan, *Noah Webster* (New York, 1975); Richard M. Rollins, *The Long Journey of Noah Webster* (Philadelphia, 1980); Daniel J. Boorstin, *The Americans: The Colonial Experience* (New York, 1958), pp. 271–90, 409–12. See also H. R. Warfel, *Noah Webster: Schoolmaster to America* (New York, 1967); E. Jenifer Monaghan, *A Common Heritage: Noah Webster's Blue-Back Speller* (Boston, 1983); M. M. Mathews, *Dictionary of Americanism on Historical Principles* (Chicago, 1951); and H. L. Mencken, *The American Language:* (3 vols., 4th ed., New York, 1936–48), Vol. II: *The American Language, Supplement One*, chs. 1–6; Vol. III: *The American Language, Supplement Two*, chs. 7–11.
48. *Massachusetts Centinel*, January 12, 1785.
49. See Clarence S. Brigham, *American Newspapers, 1690–1820* (2 vols., Worcester, Mass., 1947).
50. Matthew Carey, *Autobiography* (Brooklyn, N.Y., 1942); *GWF*, XXX, 8.
51. John Adams to Timothy Dwight, April 4, 1786, Massachusetts Historical Society: Adams Papers, reel 113.
52. For a perceptive analysis, see Kenneth Silverman, *A Cultural History of the American Revolution* (New York, 1976), pp. 519–36. For the rewriting of Barlow's *Vision*, emphasizing his new republican and deistic opinion and published in 1807 as *The Columbiad*, see John Bidwell, "The Publication of Joel Barlow's *Columbiad*," American Antiquarian Society, *Proceedings*, XCIII (1984), 337–80.
53. *The Autobiography of Colonel John Trumbull*, ed. by Theodore Sizer (New Haven, 1953), p. 82.
54. John Trumbull to Jonathan Trumbull, Jr., February 27, 1787, Trumbull Papers, Yale University Library. For Stuart, see the recent study of Richard McLenathan, *Gilbert Stuart* (New York, 1986). For Peale, see Edgar P. Richardson, Brooke Hindle, and Lillian B. Miller, *Charles Willson Peale and His World* (New York, 1982) and Charles Coleman Sellers, *Mr. Peale's Museum* (New York, 1900).
55. Silverman, *Cultural History*, pp. 558–63. See G. C. D. Odell, *Annals of the New York Stage* (7 vols., New York, 1927–31), I, 249–63.
56. Cited in Silverman, *Cultural History*, p. 673.
57. Robert R. Drummond, "Alexander Reinagle and His Connection with the Musical Life of Philadelphia," *German-American Annals*, n.s., V (1907), 294–306.
58. Irving Lowens, *Bibliography of Songsters Printed in America before 1821* (Worcester, Mass., 1976); Gilbert Chase, *America's Music* (New York, 1955), pp. 117–18.
59. Henry Steele Commager, *The Empire of Reason* (Garden City, N.Y., 1977), pp. 242–43.
60. For the variety of scientific interests, see Raymond P. Stearns, *Science in the British Colonies of America* (Urbana, Ill., 1970); Brooke Hindle, *The Pursuit of Science in Revolutionary America* (Chapel Hill, N.C., 1956); and John C. Greene, *American Science in the Age of Jefferson* (Ames, Iowa, 1984).
61. For a revisionist treatment of Jefferson as a statesman caught up in the moder-

nity of individual effort, commercial activity, and economic expansion, see Joyce Appleby, *Capitalism and the New Social Order: The Republican Vision of the 1790s* (New York, 1984).

Chapter 2. The Military-Fiscal Complex: The Army, the Creditors, and the Nation

1. John Shy, *Toward Lexington: The Role of the British Army in the Coming of the American Revolution* (Princeton, 1965), pp. 418, et seq., argues that it was reasonable to keep an army in America after the Seven Years' War.
2. *TJP*, I, 133–34.
3. As to those who would read into the Second Amendment the right of an ordinary person to carry a gun for self-protection, see *Sozinsky v. U.S.*, 300 U.S. 506 (1937); *U.S. v. Miller*, 307 U.S. 174 (1939), holding that the state's police power could regulate the carrying of guns for criminal purposes. More recently, *Lewis v. U.S.*, 445 U.S. 55 (1980). Cf. also dicta of Douglas, J. in dissent in *Adams v. Williams*, 407 U.S. 143 (1972).
4. Washington to President of Congress, December 20, 1776, *GWF*, VI, 403. The issue of year-to-year enlistments proved troublesome in the conduct of the war and by 1777 special bounties had to be offered to induce three-year terms. New England states added their own bounties to the Continental's. While the total enlistments in the Continental Army exceeded the militia, the latter was never completely supplanted.
5. Because of the factor of multiple enlistments, statistics on enrollments are suspect. Heitman suggests that total enlistments of all troops, Continental and state militia, approximated 250,000, while the largest numbers in the Continental Army seem to have been attained in November 1778 and amounted then to 35,000. See Francis B. Heitman, *Historical Register of Officers of the Continental Army During the War of the Revolution, April, 1775, to December, 1783* (Washington, D.C., 1914), p. 691.
6. Cf. Royster, *Continental Army*, who discounts some of the composite portraits of the army that have been drawn by such scholars as Edward C. Papenfuse, Gregory A. Stiverson, Mark F. Lender, John R. Sellers, and Robert A. Gross (whose *The Minutemen and Their World* [New York, 1976], pp. 146–53, gives a case-by-case analysis).
7. Charles J. Bullock, *The Finances of the United States from 1775 to 1780* (Madison, Wisc., 1895), p. 133; W. G. Anders, *The Price of Liberty: The Public Debt of the American Revolution* (Charlottesville, Va., 1983).
8. In fact, the language of the king of France made it clear that he considered his subsidy a gift. Henri Doniol, *Histoire de la Participation de la France à l'établissement des États-Unis d'Amérique* (5 vols., Paris, 1886–92), II, 713; cf. *RDC*, I, 376–84. This was one of the issues in the bitter but oft-told Lee-Deane controversy.
9. R. A. Bayley, *The National Loan of the United States of America from July 4, 1776 to June 30, 1880* (Washington, D.C., 1882), pp. 11–14.
10. E. James Ferguson, *The Power of the Purse: A History of American Public Finance, 1776–1794* (Chapel Hill, N.C., 1961), p. 36.

11. *JCC,* VII, 724. See *JJ,* II, 130–32.
12. Allan Nevins, *American States During and After the American Revolution, 1775–1789* (New York, 1924), p. 506.
13. *HPJ,* I, 208. By April 1779 the exchange rate of currency for specie was 16:1. Anne Bezanson, *Prices and Inflation During the American Revolution* (Philadelphia, 1951), p. 65.
14. *JCC,* XV, 1018.
15. *JJ,* I, 513; *JCC,* XV, 1036.
16. *JJ,* II, 130–33.
17. *BFS,* IX, 234.
18. Four fifths of the domestic debt was held in states from Pennsylvania northward. Pennsylvania alone had over one third. *JCC,* XXV, 915 (February 26, 1783); *ASP, Finance,* I, 239. Cf. Hamilton's 1790 estimate, *HP,* VI, 111.
19. For the system after 1779, see Ferguson, *Power of the Purse,* pp. 48–51.
20. John Adams to Vergennes, June 22, 1780, *RDC,* III, 809–19; Morris, *Peacemakers,* pp. 196–98.
21. Ferguson, *Power of the Purse,* p. 52.
22. *Connecticut State Records,* II, 566–69; *JCC,* XV, 1289.
23. Doings of the Committee of the States of New Hampshire, Massachusetts, and Connecticut assembled at Boston, August 1780, to consider the "Affairs relating to the War," Force transcripts, XIV, Library of Congress; *Rhode Island Colonial Records,* IX, 153, 161. For the Hartford meeting of November 1780, see *Connecticut State Archives, Revolutionary War,* XIX, folios 13, 250, 282, 285.
24. *MP,* I, 429; W. G. Sumner, *The Financier and the Finances of the American Revolution* (2 vols., New York, 1891), I, 93; *HP,* III, 314 (April 1, 1783).
25. This movement for price regulation on a state and local convention level is traced in detail in Richard B. Morris, *Government and Labor in Early America* (repr.1946 ed; new ed., Boston, 1981), pp. 92–125.
26. Hamilton to James Duane, Liberty Pole, September 3, 1780, *HP,* II, 400–18.
27. Article VIII provided for a "common treasury," out of which would be defrayed expenses incurred "for the common defense or the general welfare," and paid by the states "in proportion to the value of all land within each state," estimated according to "such mode as the united states in congress assembled, shall from time to time direct and appoint." However, the taxes for paying that proportion were to be "laid and levied by the authority and direction of the legislatures of the several states within the time agreed upon by the united states in congress assembled," a vague and varying method that never worked effectively. Robert Morris to Franklin, November 27, 1781, *RMP,* III, 267, et seq.
28. *JCC,* XII, 436.
29. Ferguson, *Power of the Purse,* pp. 140–41, 180.
30. Josiah Quincy, Jr., ed., *The Journals of Major Samuel Shaw, the First American Consul at Canton* (Boston, 1847), p. 100.
31. Jared Sparks, *The Diplomatic Correspondence of the American Revolution* (12 vols., Boston, 1829–30), XII, 236.
32. For varying appraisals of Morris, see Clarence L. Ver Steeg, *Robert Morris,*

Revolutionary Financier (Philadelphia, 1954); Ferguson, *Power of the Purse,* wherein one finds a more critical treatment of his subject than in the same editor's introduction to vol. 1 of the *Robert Morris Papers.* Earlier appraisals are provided by Emil P. Oberholtzer, *Robert Morris, Patriot and Financier* (repr. 1903 ed., New York, 1968), and Sumner, *The Financier.*

33. For a perceptive treatment of the Newburgh affair, pointing the finger at General Horatio Gates, see Douglas Southall Freeman, *George Washington* (7 vols., New York, 1949–57), V; Ferguson, *Power of the Purse;* and more recently, Richard Kohn, *The Eagle and Sword* (New York, 1975), as well as his article in *WMQ,* XXVII (1970), 187–220. For a defense of Gates's role, see C. Edward Skeen, "The Newburgh Conspiracy Reconsidered," *WMQ,* XXXI (1974), 273–90.

34. James Madison, "Notes of Debates," January 24–25, 1783, in *MP,* VI, 117–32; *JCC,* XXIV, 9–95, 862–66. See also Roger J. Champagne, *Alexander McDougall and the Revolution in New York* (Schenectady, N.Y., 1975), pp. 189, et seq.

35. Compare the instructions from the Committee of the Army, December 7, 1782 (McDougall Papers, New-York Historical Society) with William Henry Smith, ed., *The St. Clair Papers* (2 vols., Cincinnati, 1882), I, 575, the latter distinctly less moderate in tone.

36. This memorandum to the committee was presented on January 6, 1783. *JCC,* XXXIV, 95n., 291–92. See also *LMCC,* III, 570.

37. *JCC,* XXIV, 94–95.

38. Gouverneur Morris to Henry Knox, February 7, 1783, *LMCC,* VII, 34n.–35n.

39. Madison, "Notes of Debates," January 6, 7, 1783, *MP,* VI, 16, 18.

40. *HP,* III, 246–47; Madison, "Notes of Debates," January 28, 1783, *MP,* VI, 143n.

41. "Notes of Debates," March 17, 1783, *MP,* VI, 348.

42. Hamilton to Washington, February 13, 1783 (dated by Lodge February 7), *HP,* III, 153–55. Knox was also contacted, but his response was cautious, if not negative. Knox to Alexander McDougall, February 21, 1783, Knox Papers, Massachusetts Historical Society.

43. *HP,* III, 277–79.

44. Gouverneur Morris to John Jay, January 1, 1783, *JJ,* II, 485–86. The cipher passages appear in the Gouverneur Morris Papers, Columbia University. They were later obliterated in the copy that reached Jay and bore his endorsement: "Recd. 17 Feb. 1783." It appears "with deletions and corrections" in Jared Sparks, ed., *The Life of Gouverneur Morris with Selections from His Correspondence and Miscellaneous Papers* (3 vols., Boston, 1832), I, 248–49.

45. *JCC,* XXIV, 295–97 (March 11, 1783).

46. Washington to Hamilton, March 4, 1783, *HP,* III, 277–79.

47. *JCC,* XXIV, 298–99.

48. *GWF,* XXVI, 222–37.

49. Henry Steele Commager and Richard B. Morris, eds., *The Spirit of '76* (New York, 1983), pp. 1283–85.

50. Quincy, ed., *Samuel Shaw Journals,* pp. 103–04.

51. *JCC,* XXIV, 310–16. The maverick Timothy Pickering, the only dissenting

voice, condemned the officers for their hypocrisy in denouncing an address they "had read with admiration" and discussed "with rapture." Kohn, *Eagle and Sword*, p. 316n.; Ferguson, *Power of the Purse*, p. 163n.

52. Kohn, *Eagle and Sword*, p. 316n.
53. Quincy, ed., *Samuel Shaw Journals*, p. 103–04.
54. Madison, "Notes of Debates," March 22, 1783, *MP*, VI, 375–78; *JCC*, XXIV, 202–03, 206–10.
55. *Ibid.*, pp. 206–10; Ferguson, *Power of the Purse*, p. 164.
56. *JCC*, XXV, 901–02 (February 19, 1783).
57. Robert Morris to Washington, June 20, 1783, *RMP*, cited in Ferguson, *Power of the Purse*, p. 104n.
58. See Hamilton to Washington, correspondence of March–April 1783, in *HP*, III, 290, et seq.
59. Hamilton to George Clinton, Princeton, June 29, 1783, *HP*, III, 407–08.
60. *HP*, III, 99; *JCC*, XXIV, 413–16; Burnett, *Congress*, pp. 576–84; Varnum L. Collins, *The Continental Congress at Princeton* (Princeton, 1908). Marbois to Castries, Philadelphia, July 9, 1783, wherein he indicated a certain public sympathy for the unpaid soldiers. AN:CC. For Secretary Charles Thomson's account of the Princeton experience, see Eugene R Sheridan and John M. Murrin, eds., *Congress at Princeton* (Princeton, 1985).
61. See Rufus King to Elbridge Gerry, July 4, 1786, in Charles C. King, ed., *Life and Correspondence of Rufus King* (6 vols., New York, 1894–1900), I, 186.
62. Jay to Elbridge Gerry, Paris, February 19, 1784, in *JJ*, II, 694–95n.; Rufus King to Gerry, July 4, 1786, in King, ed., *King Correspondence*, I, 186. Lafayette at Washington's request had superintended the organization of the French branch of the Society and received royal permission on December 18, 1783. Edgar F. Hume, *Lafayette and the Society of the Cincinnati* (Baltimore, 1934), pp. 10–11.
63. Aedanus Burke, *Considerations on the Society of the Order of the Cincinnati* (Philadelphia, 1783).
64. Leading Massachusetts politicians like Samuel Adams, Samuel Osgood, and Stephen Higginson took their cue from the popular reaction and denounced the creation of a "race of hereditary patricians." See particularly the citations in Van Beck Hall, *Politics Without Parties: Massachusetts 1780–1791* (Pittsburgh, 1972), p. 157n.
65. H. G. R. de Mirabeau, *Considérations sur l'ordre de Cincinnatus, ou imitation d'un pamphlet Anglo-Américaine* (London, 1784); Wallace E. Davies, "The Society of Cincinnati in New England, 1783–1800," *WMQ*, V (1948), 3–25; Merrill Jensen, *The New Nation* (New York, 1950), pp. 261–65; and, more recently, Minor Myers, Jr., *Liberty Without Anarchy: A History of the Society of the Cincinnati* (Charlottesville, Va., 1983), who stresses the pro-monarchist and centralizing views of many of the Society's members.
66. Benjamin Rush to Richard Price, June 2, 1787, "Richard Price Letters," Massachusetts Historical Society *Proceedings*, 2d ser., XVII (1903), 367–68.
67. John Armstrong to Horatio Gates, April 29, 1783, in Louis C. Hatch, *The Administration of the American Revolutionary Army* (New York, 1904), pp. 208–09.

68. Royster, *Continental Army*, p. 335.
69. *JCC*, XXV, 703 (October 18, 1783).
70. "Report on a Military Peace Establishment," Philadelphia, June 18, 1783, *HP*, III, 378–83; *JCC*, XXV, 222–44. For the attempts to adjust ingrained republican mistrust of a standing army to the needs for an effective system of national defense, see Lawrence D. Cress, "Republican Liberty and National Security," *WMQ* XXXVIII (1981), 73–96.
71. *JCC*, XXIV, 284, 325, 806.
72. Friederich Kapp, *The Life of Friedrich Wilhelm von Steuben* (New York, 1859), p. 187.
73. See Royster, *Continental Army*, pp. 350–60. For the touching account of the plight of the impoverished ex-soldiers, see Quincy, ed., *Samuel Shaw Journals*, p. 107.

Chapter 3. Congress and the People

1. Gordon S. Wood, *The Creation of the American Republic* (Chapel Hill, N.C., 1969). Thus, compare Claude H. Van Tyne, "Sovereignty in the American Revolution," *American Historical Review*, XII (1906–07), 538, with Curtis P. Nettels, "The Origins of the Union and of the States," Massachusetts Historical Society *Proceedings*, LXXII (1957–70), 68–83. The present writer has developed this argument for the precedence of Congress in "The Forging of the Union Reconsidered: A Historical Refutation of State Sovereignty Over Seabeds," *Columbia Law Review*, LXXIV (1974), 1056–93, and in his American Historical Association Presidential Address, "We The People: The Bicentennial of a People's Revolution," *American Historical Review*, LXXXII (1977), 1–19.
2. Jack N. Rakove, *The Beginnings of National Politics: An Interpretive History of the Continental Congress* (New York, 1979), p. 52.
3. Burnett, *Congress*, pp. 34, 502–03.
4. *JCC*, I, 66 (October 14, 1774), emphasis in the original. In his classic work, Kent quotes from the proposed draft, "the good people of these colonies," rather than from the version actually adopted. See James Kent, *Commentaries on American Law*, ed. by Oliver Wendell Holmes, Jr. (4 vols., 12th ed., Boston, 1873).
5. Joseph Story, *Commentaries on the Constitution of the United States* (Boston, 1833), I, 138, following Nathan Dane, *Abridgment and Digest of American Law* (Boston, 1823–24, 1829), IX, 211.
6. *JCC*, I, 102 (October 22, 1774).
7. *Ibid.* An appeal was also addressed "to the Inhabitants of the Province of Quebec," urging them "to unite with us in the social compact." *Ibid.* at 105 (October 26, 1774).
8. *Ibid.*, 112 (October 26, 1774).
9. Only the delegates from Connecticut, Delaware, New Jersey, Pennsylvania, and Rhode Island were chosen by the legal assemblies (see chart at end of chapter). For a criticism of the rump character of some of the extralegal elections, see

"The Censor," in an unidentified Philadelphia newspaper, March 5, 1776, *FAA*, V, 71–72.

10. For a useful review of this transitional period of governmental authority at the colony level, see Merrill Jensen, *The Founding of a Nation* (New York, 1968), pp. 508–34.

11. *JCC*, II, 187–90.

12. See Agnes Hunt, *The Provincial Committees of Safety of the American Revolution* (Cleveland, 1904), pp. 159–65.

13. William Whipple to John Sullivan and John Langdon, July 8, 1775, and Meshech Weare to Continental Congress, July 8, 1775, in *New Hampshire State Papers*, ed. by N. Bouton (33 vols., Concord, N.H., 1867–1915), V, 1560–61.

14. JA, *Diary*, II, 247. Jere R. Daniell, *Experiment in Republicanism: New Hampshire Politics and the American Revolution, 1741–1794* (Cambridge, Mass., 1970), pp. 106–12.

15. *JCC*, III, 319, 326–27.

16. B. P. Poore, comp., *The Federal and State Constitutions, Colonial Charters, and Other Organic Laws of the United States* (2 vols., 2d ed., Washington, D.C., 1878). F. N. Thorpe, ed., *The Federal and State Constitutions* (7 vols., Washington, D.C., 1909), IV, 2451. The term "state" was not employed to characterize New Hampshire's government until it adopted a resolution authorizing independence on June 11, 1776. On September 12, 1776, the New Hampshire Representatives appointed delegates to Congress to represent the "State." *JCC*, VI, 920.

17. Edward McCrady, *The History of South Carolina in the Revolution 1775–1783* (New York, 1901), pp. 110, 115, 235.

18. *JCC*, IV, 342. The resolve was voted May 10; the Preamble, written by John Adams, was adopted five days later, *ibid.*, at 357–58. See JA, *Diary*, III, 335, 382–86.

19. Duane is the only person mentioned by Adams, along with Dickinson, as regarding the resolution as too precipitate. JA, *Diary*, III, p. 335.

20. See chart at end of chapter.

21. 2 Dallas (U.S.) 419, 470–71 (1793).

22. *Chisholm* v. *Georgia, supra.*, n. 21.

23. See *Ware* v. *Hylton*, 3 U.S. (3 Dall.), 199, 232 (1796), (per Chase, *J.*). See also *Penhallow* v. *Doane*, 3 U.S. (3 Dall.), 54, 80, 90–94, 109–12, 117 (1795) (per Paterson, *J.*).

24. Pennsylvania, Maryland, and North Carolina claimed only the exclusive right to regulate their own internal government and police. Thorpe, ed., *Federal and State Constitutions*, III, 1686; V, 2787, 3082.

25. See Nettels, "Origins," *loc. cit.*, pp. 68, 76–77.

26. Von Holst saw these powers as inherently those of Congress, which was in the process of forming itself into a sovereign state exercising external sovereignty. If Congress became a national state de facto, argues Von Holst, the success of the Revolution it had declared retrospectively conferred upon its acts the necessary binding legal authority. See Hermann von Holst, *The Constitution and Political History of the United States*, trans. by J. J. Lalor (8 vols., Chicago, 1881–92), pp. 8, 9.

27. See Julius Goebel, Jr., *History of the Supreme Court of the United States; Volume I, Antecedents and Beginnings to 1801* (New York, 1971), p. 146n.
28. *JCC*, I, 67–73 (October 14, 1774).
29. *Ibid.*, I, 75–81 (October 20, 1774). The nonimportation and nonexportation resolves were left to local enforcement.
30. "Petition to the King," *JCC*, I, 104 (October 24, 1774); "Address to the People of Great-Britain," *ibid.*, pp. 81–90 (October 21, 1774); "Memorial to the Inhabitants of the British Colonies," *ibid.*, pp. 90–101 (October 27, 1774).
31. *JCC*, II, 81. Congress warned, however, that "any North American colony failing to accede to, or violating the Association would be cut off from trade or intercourse with the rest," *ibid.*, 79.
32. *Ibid.*, 97.
33. *Ibid.*, 103.
34. *Ibid.*, 128.
35. *Ibid.*, 163 (July 8, 1775).
36. *Ibid.*, 178 (July 13, 1775).
37. *Ibid.*, 212 (July 28, 1775).
38. JA, *Diary*, II, 132–34 (September 5, 1774).
39. *JCC*, I, 25 (September 6, 1774); *LMCC*, II, 12–15.
40. *JCC*, VI, 1081 (August 1, 1776).
41. *JCC*, XV, 1036.
42. *Ibid.*, 1051–62.
43. *MP*, I, 302–10 (September 1779–March 1780).
44. *JCC*, XXXI, at p. 902 (October 13, 1786).
45. Story, *Commentaries*, p. 145n., citing *American Museum*, I, 8, 9 (1787).
46. For the views of Chief Justice Jay, see, e.g., *Chisholm* v. *Georgia, op. cit.;* for those of Justice Blair, see *Penhallow* v. *Doane, op. cit.;* for those of Justice Paterson, *ibid.*, at pp. 53, 54, 80–81, 90; for those of Justice Iredell, see James Iredell, *Answers to Mr. Mason's Objections to the New Constitution,* in Paul Leicester Ford, ed., *Pamphlets on the Constitution* (Brooklyn, N.Y., 1888), p. 333, wherein he cited with approval an opinion of Jay's delivered when the latter was Secretary for Foreign Affairs, that "a treaty once made, pursuant to the sovereign authority . . . became immediately the law of the land"—*ibid.*, at p. 355. Iredell considered it "unquestionable" that prior to the Articles of Confederation, Congress exercised "with propriety" the "high powers" of external sovereignty, even though it did so, and here he departed from Paterson, "with the acquiescence of the states." *Penhallow* v. *Doane,* pp. 54, 80, 81, 90. But see *ibid.* at pp. 93–94.
47. See, e.g., Convention on Rights and Duties of States, December 26, 1933, Article I, 29 Stat. 3097, T.S. No. 881; Edvard Hambro, *The Case Law of the International Court* (Leyden, 1961), p. 83 (covering cases until 1951); and L. F. L. Oppenheim, *International Law; A Treatise* (8th ed., New York, 1955), ed. by H. Lauterpacht, § 494. A state is no less sovereign for having imposed limitations on its own foreign relations powers. With respect to the United States, see Samuel B. Crandall, *Treaties: Their Making and Enforcement* (2d ed., Washington, D.C., 1916), § 1–67; Charles C. Hyde, *International Law* (3 vols., 2d rev. ed., Boston, 1945), § 495–509, and sources cited at § 495 n. 5. See generally

Louis Henkin, *Foreign Affairs and the Constitution* (New York, 1975), the best and most comprehensive recent guide to the subject.

48. *JCC*, IX, 915–16.

49. *JCC*, IX, 915–23 (comparison of drafts of Article IX of the Articles of Confederation, final version adopted on November 5, 1777). For a fairly recent work on the war and foreign affairs power of Congress during the period of the Articles of Confederation, see Arthur Bestor, "Separation of Powers in the Domain of Foreign Affairs: The Intent of the Constitution Historically Examined," *Seton Hall Law Review* (1974), pp. 527, 565–69. Also Abraham D. Sofaer, *War, Foreign Affairs, and Constitutional Power* (Cambridge, Mass., 1976).

50. Article II of the Treaty of Paris of 1783 with Great Britain speaks to the alteration of the northern, southern, and western boundaries of the former colonies.

51. Nettels, "Origins," *loc. cit.*, pp. 77–79. Since the delegates from only nine of the thirteen states in Congress were required for ratification of the treaty, it could be argued that as many as four states could have had their boundaries determined without their formal consent. *Ibid.*, pp. 78–79.

52. *JCC*, II, 54 (May 17, 1775).

53. *Ibid.*, at p. 65 (May 26, 1775).

54. *Ibid.*, at pp. 83–84 (June 9, 1775). This particular directive antedates by almost a year the call to the colonies to set up state governments.

55. See *ibid.*, at pp. 89–105 (June 14–23, 1775).

56. See *ibid.*, at p. 106 (June 24, 1775), pp. 187–90 (July 18, 1775).

57. In effect, the devalued currency operated as a form of taxation, *ibid.*, at p. 103 (June 22, 1775). See also H. James Henderson, *Party Politics and the Continental Congress* (New York, 1974).

58. *JCC*, II, 111–22 (June 30, 1775), 209–10 (July 27, 1775).

59. *Ibid.*, III, 378–87.

60. *Ibid.*, VII, 268–69 (April 15, 1777).

61. *Ibid.*, III, 392.

62. *Ibid.*, V, 922.

63. See, e.g., the French Treaty of Amity and Commerce, February 6, 1778, *JCC*, IX, 421 (May 4, 1778); draft of a commission to negotiate a Dutch Treaty, *ibid.*, XV, 1235 (November 1, 1779); final Dutch Treaty, October 8, 1782, in *ibid.*, XXIV, 68 (January 23, 1783); Treaty with Sweden, April 3, 1783, *ibid.*, XXIV, 458, 468, 470 (July 29, 1783).

64. *Ware* v. *Hylton*, *loc. cit.*, pp. 199, 232.

65. See *JCC*, V, 833 (September 28, 1776); VIII, 520–51 (July 1, 1777); XI, 546, 547 (May 28, 1778); XV, 1121 (September 28, 1779); XVIII, 1168, 1171 (December 19, 1780). Letters of credence were addressed to foreign sovereigns naming and identifying the commissioners authorized to negotiate on Congress's behalf.

66. *JCC*, XV, 1121 (September 28, 1779).

67. *RDC*, VI, 402.

68. David Hunter Miller, ed., *Treaties and Other International Acts of the United States of America, 1776–1863* (8 vols., Washington, D.C., 1931–48), II, 151–56.

69. Richard B. Morris, ed., *Select Cases of the Mayor's Court of New York City, 1674–1784* (New York, 1935), p. 322.
70. *Ibid.*
71. *HP*, III, 489.
72. *JCC*, XXXII, 178 (April 13, 1787). This injunction was later embodied in the supremacy clause of the Constitution.
73. The eight treaties were as follows: two agreements relative to loans with France of July 16, 1782, and February 25, 1783; treaties of commerce with the Netherlands and Sweden of October 8, 1782, and April 3, 1783; the provisional treaty with Great Britain, November 30, 1782, and the Definitive Treaty, September 3, 1783; the Treaty of Amity with Prussia, September 10, 1785, and the treaty with Morocco, July 18, 1787.
74. For a strained interpretation of Virginia's illegal action, see James Brown Scott, *Sovereign States and Suits Before Arbitral Tribunals and Courts of Justice* (New York, 1925), pp. 55–57; see also pp. 35–40, 46–47, 54, 63.
75. See Crandall, *Treaties*, ss. 1–67.
76. Vérac, French Ambassador to Russia, to Vergennes, September 1, 1780, MAE: CP: Russie, vol. 96, pp. 337–46; Vérac to Vergennes, November 14, 1780, *ibid.*, vol. 105, pp. 324, 331; audience of Sir James Harris, British Ambassador to Russia, with Empress Catherine II, December 19, 1780, in James Harris, 3d Earl of Malmesbury, ed., *Earl of Malmesbury, Diaries and Correspondence of James Harris, First Earl of Malmesbury* (2 vols., London, 1844), I, 357. Count Panin, the Russian chancellor, proposed a Peace Congress, in addition to separate polling of the states on the treaty with England. Each of the "United Colonies of America" would send delegates to the Peace Congress who would be accountable only to their respective assemblies. For a fuller discussion, see Morris, *Peacemakers*, pp. 147–72.
77. Vérac to Vergennes, two letters, February 18 and March 1, 1781, MAE: CP: Russie, vol. 156, pp. 163; Baron de Breteuil, French Ambassador to Austria, to Vergennes, February 11, 1781, *ibid.*, Autriche, vol. 56; Vergennes to Vérac, March 11, 1781, *ibid.*, Russie, vols. 177–79; Breteuil to Vergennes, April 19, 1781, *ibid.*, Autriche, vol. 237.
78. Vergennes to Vérac, two letters, October 8, 1780, and again in a dispatch of October 12, 1780, *ibid.*, Russie, vols. 241, 243, 368, 369; Vergennes to Breteuil, March 4, 1781, May 7, 1781, *ibid.*, Autriche, vol. 92, p. 300.
79. Vergennes to Breteuil, March 4, 1781, *ibid.*, vol. 342, p. 92.
80. John Adams to Vergennes, July 21, 1781, MAE: CP: États-Unis, vol. 441; *RDC*, IV, 595–96.
81. *JCC*, III, 371–75 (November 25, 1775).
82. *Ibid.*, VII, 13 (January 4, 1777). The decrees and papers are collected in National Archives Microcopy No. 162, The Revolutionary War Prize Cases; Records of the Court of Appeals in Cases of Capture, 1776–1787 (1954).
83. *Ibid.*, IX, 916; XIX, 354–56.
84. Henry J. Bourguignon, *The First Federal Court; The Federal Appellate Prize Courts of the American Revolution* (Philadelphia, 1977), pp. 48–50. Some of the Court's opinions are found in 2 U.S. (2 Dall.), 1–42.

85. W. W. Hening, ed., *The Statutes at Large: Being a Collection of All the Laws of Virginia, from the First Session of the Legislature in the Year 1619* [*to 1792*] (13 vols., Philadelphia and New York, 1823), *Virginia Laws*, 3d Sess., c. 26, X, 98. *TJP*, II, 572–75.

86. An Act for Establishing A Court of Admiralty, September 9, 1778, *Pennsylvania Statutes*, X, 277, c. 811, § 4; repealed, c. 887 (March 8, 1789), *ibid.*, X, 97.

87. *Houston* v. *Sloop Active*, Revolutionary War Prize Cases, no. 39 (1778), *loc.cit.*

88. *JCC*, XIII, 86, 87 (January 19, 1779).

89. *Ibid.*, 136–37 (February 2, 1779).

90. *Ibid.*, 281–86 (March 6, 1779).

91. *Ibid.*, 283–84 (March 6, 1779).

92. *Ibid.*, 284.

93. See below, notes 103–106.

94. *JCC*, XIII, 285 (March 6, 1779).

95. *Ibid.*, XVI, 61–64.

96. *Ibid.*, XVII, 457–59 (May 24, 1780). For the activities of the new court, see Goebel, *Supreme Court*, pp. 172–82.

97. *JCC*, XIX, 315 (March 27, 1781).

98. For a discussion of the initial litigation, *Penhallow* v. *The Lausanna*, see the learned note by L. Kinvin Wroth, in *Legal Papers of John Adams* (3 vols., Cambridge, Mass., 1965), II, 352–95, ed. by L. Kinvin Wroth and Hiller B. Zobel. For the trial in the New Hampshire Maritime Court (December 16, 1777), see *ibid.*, p. 368; for the case before Congress's Court of Appeal (June 1779) and the Confederation Court of Appeals (September 1783), see *Revolutionary War Prize Cases*, no. 130.

99. The first appeal was argued by John Adams. See JA, *Legal Papers*, II, 367–69.

100. *JCC*, XVI, 61; XVII, 459 (May 24, 1780).

101. National Archives microfilm, record group 214, case 6 (1794); *Penhallow* v. *Doane*, 3 U.S. (3 Dall.) pp. 53, 63–64, 108–13.

102. *Ibid.*, pp. 53, 64. For the minutes of this case, see Edwin Surrency, ed., "The Minutes of the Supreme Court of the United States, 1790–1806," *American Journal of Legal History*, V (1961), 369, 375–78.

103. 3 U.S. (3 Dall.), 53, 109–12.

104. *Ibid.*, 80.

105. *Ibid.*, 90.

106. *Ibid.*, 93–94. Justice Cushing did not reach this issue.

107. See Peter S. Onuf, *The Origin of the Federal Republic; Jurisdictional Controversies in the United States, 1775–1787* (Philadelphia, 1983), p. 57.

108. See *Report of the Delegates of the U.S.A. to the 7th International Congress of American States* (Washington, D.C., 1933), pp. 136, 137; Marjorie Millace Whiteman, ed., *Digest of International Law* (15 vols., Washington, D.C., 1963–73), VIII, 13–14, 104, 348, 355, 574, 575.

109. Article 28 of the Articles of War provided for "such punishment" as a general court martial would impose on members of the Continental Army convicted "of holding correspondence with, or giving intelligence to the enemy." *JCC*, II, 116 (June 30, 1775).

110. Washington to Congress, October 2, 1775, in Washington Papers, Ser. 8, Library of Congress; *GWF*, IV, 9–11.
111. Massachusetts Historical Society, *Collections*, "Warren-Adams Letters," Vol. 72 (1925), 152–53, 180.
112. *JCC*, III, 334.
113. *GWF*, VIII, 185; *American Archives*, 4th ser., III, 1158.
114. *JCC*, III, 331 (November 7, 1775).
115. "Proceedings of a General Court Martial of the Line held at Headquarters in the City of New York by a Warrant from his Excellency George Washington, Esq.," June 26, 1776, Washington Papers, Vol. XIX, Library of Congress. Washington to Provost of the Army, June 28, 1776, *GWF*, V, 182; Bradley Chapin, *The American Law of Treason: Revolutionary and Early National Origins* (Seattle, Wash., 1964), p. 55.
116. *JCC*, V, 475–76 (June 24, 1776).
117. *Ibid.*
118. Chapin, *Law of Treason*, p. 57. See also W. Hurst, "Treason in the United States, Part I," *Harvard Law Review*, LVIII (1944), 226; Goebel, *Supreme Court*, I, 107.
119. *JCC*, V, 475–76 (June 24, 1776).
120. Chapin, *Law of Treason*, pp. 38–54.
121. *JCC*, IX, 784–85 (October 8, 1777); 1068 (December 30, 1777); X, 384 (April 23, 1778).
122. Chapin, *Law of Treason*, p. 56; Brunhouse, *Counter-Revolution in Pennsylvania*, p. 47.
123. In upholding a Pennsylvania treason conviction, one judge declared that governments functioning prior to independence derived their power to enforce treason statutes from the sovereign authority of Congress. See *Pennsylvania v. Chapman*, 1 U.S. (1 Dall.) 51, 54 (1781) (per McKean, *C.J.*); *Pennsylvania Archives*, I, 644–46. In the debates at the Constitutional Convention, William Samuel Johnson of Connecticut went so far as to deny that there could be treason against a particular state even under the existing Confederation, "the Sovereignty being in the Union." *Documents Illustrative of the Formation of the Union . . .* (Washington, 1927), p. 577.
124. *GWF*, VII, 61–62.
125. *JCC*, IV, 195 (March 9, 1776). For John Jay's comment on military oaths, see his letter to Alexander McDougall, March 13, 1776, *JJ*, I, 235–36. See also Harold M. Hyman, *To Try Men's Souls: Loyalty Tests in American History* (Berkeley and Los Angeles, 1959); Jensen, *New Nation*, p. 173; Max Savelle, "Nationalism and Other Loyalties in the American Revolution," *American Historical Review*, LXVII (1962), 901.
126. *JCC*, VII, 95 (February 6, 1777). In a letter to Speaker John Hart of the New Jersey Assembly, Clark urged the legislature to take "proper Notice of it," and "not tamely Submit their Authority to the Controul of a power unknown in our Constitution." Abraham Clark to John Hart, February 8, 1777, Emmet Collection, New York Public Library; *LMCC*, II, 242–43.
127. *JCC*, VII, 165–66 (February 27, 1777).
128. *Ibid.*, 166 (February 27, 1777).

129. Abraham Clark to Elias Dayton, March 7, 1777, *LMCC*, II, 291–92.

130. *JCC*, VII, 258 (April 12, 1777); X, 114–15 (February 3, 1778). See, e.g., oath of John Bancroft, et al., as Commissioners to Examine Claims against the United States, April 12, 1777; oath of Joseph Pierson, as Assistant Commissary of Forage, May 14, 1778; oaths of Francis Hopkinson, as one of the Commissioners of the Navy, William Shippen, Jr., as Director General of the Hospitals of the United States, and John Benezet, as Commissioner of Claims; all taken February 21, 1778, PCC 201, Oaths of Allegiance, 1776–1789, p. 195.

131. For example, the Committee for Detecting Conspiracies in New York tendered the following oath to former Loyalists within the state:

> . . . we do accordingly disclaim and renounce all Allegiance to the said King and Crown, and we do further solemny [sic] swear that we consider ourselves as Subjects of the State of New York. . . . And we do further most solemnly swear, that as good Subjects of the State of New York we will do our Duty in supporting the Measures of the General Congress of the United States of America for the Establishment of the Liberties and Independence of the said State in opposition to the Arbitrary Claims, wicked usurpations, and hostile Invasion of the King and parliament of Great Britain their Agents and adherents, and that we will make known and as good subjects of the said State of New York do our Duty in suppressing all Treasonable Plotts or conspiracies against the said American States in General, or the State of New York in particular which may come to our knowledge.

> Loyalists Transcripts, Vol. XLIII, 219–20, New York Public Library; "Minutes of the Committee and of the First Commission for Detecting and Defeating Conspiracies in the State of New York," New-York Historical Society *Collections*, LVIII (1925), 427.

132. See, e.g., Passport issued by John Jay, president of Congress, to Captain Joseph Deane, June 1779, PCC 49, pp. 501–02. Congress proffered Dr. Richard Price citizenship "of the United States" on October 16, 1778 (*JCC*, XII, 984–85). Price respectfully declined. Price to Franklin, Arthur Lee, and Adams, January 18, 1779, Historical Society of Pennsylvania. For an instance when Congress requested the state of New York to grant citizenship to "officers" and "men" who were refugees from Canada, while undertaking itself to provide subsistence for the whole party of eighty, along with women and children, see *JCC*, XXIV, 496–98 (Aug. 9, 1783).

133. Numerous examples are found in the Franklin Papers, American Philosophical Society, Philadelphia.

134. John Jay to Benjamin Franklin, Aranjuez, May 31, 1781; Franklin to Jay, Passy, August 20, 1781; *JJ*, II, 80–82, *BFS*, V, 156–62.

135. Henry Laurens, *A Narrative of the Capture of Henry Laurens, of his Confinement in the Tower of London, etc., 1780, 1781, 1782*, South Carolina Historical Society, *Collections*, I (1857), 18–19.

136. The Treaty with Great Britain should have settled all doubts on this question, but if any doubts did remain about the powers of the federal government to confer citizenship in the collectivity, they were removed by the adoption of the Constitution. The power to "establish an uniform rule of naturalization" was

among the enumerated grants to Congress. U.S. Constitution, Article I, sect. 8, clause 4. Congress promptly exercised this power by enacting a statute in 1790 which prescribed the rules for the acquisition of U.S. citizenship by persons of foreign birth. Act of March 26, 1790, 1 Stat. 103. Five years later, the Supreme Court held that state expatriation statutes could not constitutionally affect U.S. citizenship, for state jurisdiction over such matters was merely local. See *Talbot* v. *Jensen*, 3 U.S. (3 Dall.), 133 (1795).

137. 1 Martin (N.C.) 5 at p. 7 (1787). As a result of the comity clause in the Articles citizenship conferred by a single state, as one authority points out, seemed "to acquire a necessary national dimension." James T. Kettner, *The Development of American Citizenship, 1608–1870* (Chapel Hill, 1978), pp. 220–21, 224. See also C. J. Anteau, "Paul's Perverted Privileges, or the True Meaning of the Privileges and Immunities Clause of Article Four," *WMQ,* IX (1967–68), 2–5.

Chapter 4. Congress and the States: Operating Under the Articles of Confederation

1. *JCC,* II, 195, et seq. A copy in the Library of Congress contains some comments or amendments by George Wythe of Virginia, with a comparison of the proposals on representation between Franklin's Albany Plan of Union and his present "Sketch."
2. *BFS,* VI, 420–26. Cf., *JCC,* II, 194–202 (July 21, 1775).
3. See Burnett, *Congress,* pp. 216–18.
4. For the variations in the dating of this draft, see Paul H. Smith, et al., *LDC,* I, 291, 347; Rakove, *National Politics,* pp. 137n.–138n.
5. Rakove, *National Politics,* p. 145.
6. Joseph Hawley to John Adams, Watertown, December 18, 1775, Massachusetts Historical Society: Adams Family Papers, reel 345. "Hints for the consideration of Mr. Gerry," *ibid.:* Gerry Papers. Hawley to Samuel Adams, April 1, 1776, and to Elbridge Gerry, October 13, 1776, New York Public Library: Samuel Adams Papers, boxes 2 and 3. Rakove, *National Politics,* p. 428, n. 17.
7. According to H. James Henderson's head-count of "radicals" and "conservatives," the former had the edge by seven to six, "although the conservatives had the edge in talent and influence." *Party Politics,* pp. 136, 137.
8. Edward Rutledge to John Jay, June 29, 1776, *JJ,* I, 280–81.
9. Dickinson's draft, with its interlineations, deletions, and marginalia, attests to his willingness to make concessions. See John Dickinson, "Arguments against the Independence of these Colonies in Congress," Pennsylvania Historical Society: Dickinson Mss. We also have a draft, with only minor variations, in the hand of Josiah Bartlett of New Hampshire, *LDCC,* IV, 235–55. Bartlett recorded notes of the discussions of the Dickinson committee, including comments, probably on the Franklin Plan, passed on to him by George Wythe, not a member of the Dickinson committee. *Ibid.,* IV, 199–201.
10. Josiah Bartlett's draft omits this religious section entirely. *LDCC,* IV, 234.
11. *JAW,* IX, 401–02.
12. *JCC,* V, 554.

13. See Merrill Jensen, *The Articles of Confederation: An Interpretation of the Social-Constitutional History of the American Revolution, 1774–1781* (Madison, Wisc., 1940), chs. 4, 5; and his *Fundamental Testaments of the American Revolution* (Washington, D.C., 1973), pp. 67–69.

14. See Thomas Burke to the Governor of North Carolina, March 11, April 29, November 4, 1777, *LMCC*, II, 542; *LDCC*, VI, 167–73.

15. See Thomas Burke's "Remarks on the Articles of Confederation" [ante December 16, 1777], *LDCC*, III, 419–21; [c. December 18, 1777], pp. 433–37.

16. Thomas Burke to Richard Caswell, April 29, 1777, *ibid.*, VI, 671–74.

17. *Ibid.* Burke put together notes of these debates only after returning to North Carolina in November 1777.

18. For a close discussion of the impact of this article, see Jensen, *Articles of Confederation*, pp. 129–39, 161–76.

19. *McCulloch* v. *Maryland*, 4 Wheat. 316 (1819). Marshall's opinion drew heavily upon Hamilton's argument for implied powers in his exposition of the constitutionality of the Bank of the United States. *HP*, VIII, 63–135 (February 23, 1791).

20. These and other objections of Burke, which were overridden, are recorded in notes which may have been written between October 25 and November 15, 1777. *LMCC*, II, 552–58.

21. Rakove, *National Politics*, p. 176, citing Eliphalet Dyer.

22. Thomas Burke, "Notes on the Articles of Confederation," *LMCC*, II, 554.

23. This point is made by Irving Brant, *James Madison: The Virginian Revolutionary* (Indianapolis, 1941), p. 384. By the end of the war, when Burke served as governor of North Carolina, one historian has viewed him as "a hopeless reactionary." Elisha P. Douglass, "Thomas Burke, Disillusioned Democrat," *North Carolina Historical Review*, XXVI (1941), 152.

24. *JCC*, V, 547n.; *LDCC*, IV, 253n.

25. Cf. *JCC*, V, 547–48; X, 826–27 (October 21, 1777).

26. Delegates were subject to annual elections, to recall at any time by their respective state legislatures, and were ineligible to serve more than three years in any six-year period (Article V).

27. John Adams to James Warren, February 17, 1777, *LMCC*, II, 260.

28. Twelve states were present as late as October 21, despite Laurens's prediction, and the end of the month saw a relatively full representation. *JCC*, XII, 1036–38 (October 21); ten states were present on October 29, *ibid.* 1076.

29. On January 2, 1779, thirteen states were present at the Thomas Paine hearing. *JCC*, XII, 35.

30. Thomas Jefferson to Edward Pendleton, Annapolis, December 16, 1783, *TJP*, VI, 337.

31. See Morris, *Peacemakers*, pp. 447–48.

32. Thomas Jefferson to Governor Benjamin Harrison, January 16, 1784, *TJP*, VI, 468–69.

33. Burnett, *Congress*, p. 595.

34. Jefferson to Madison, February 20, 1784, *TJP*, VI, 546.

35. Charles Thomson to Jefferson, May 19, 1774, *ibid.*, VII, 273.

36. Richard Henry Lee to Madison, November 26, 1784, *MP,* VIII, 151.
37. Chairman David Ramsay to Governors of the States, January 31, 1786, *LMCC,* VIII, 290–91.
38. Chairman David Ramsay to Benjamin Rush, February 11, 1786, *LMCC,* VIII, 301.
39. Burnett, *Congress,* pp. 646–47.
40. Samuel Alleyne Otis to James Warren, November 27, 1787, *LMCC,* VIII, 684.
41. Jennings B. Sanders, *Evolution of Executive Departments of the Continental Congress, 1774–1789* (Chapel Hill, N.C., 1935), p. 4n.
42. Jefferson to James Monroe, April 12, 1785, *TJP,* VIII, 79.
43. Nathan Dane to Samuel Holten, March 15, 1788, *LMCC,* VIII, 707; Abraham Baldwin to Joseph Clay, March 31, 1788, *ibid.,* p. 712.
44. Sanders, *Evolution of Executive Departments,* pp. 128–52.
45. Jay C. Guggenheimer, "The Development of the Executive Department, 1775–1789," in J. F. Jameson, ed., *Essays in the Constitutional History of the United States in the Formative Period* (Boston, 1889); Wesley E. Rich, *The History of the United States Post Office to the Year 1829* (Cambridge, Mass., 1924), pp. 49–50, 53–56, 59–64, 67.
46. *JCC,* II, 197.
47. *Ibid.,* V, 431, 433.
48. Cf. Jensen, *Articles of Confederation,* p. 178, with Rakove, *National Politics,* p. 431n.
49. See *TJP,* VII, 140, et seq. (April–May 1784).
50. *JCC,* XXVII, 474–77 (May 29, 1784).
51. Jefferson to Madison, April 25, 1784, *TJP,* VII, 119.
52. John Francis Mercer to Jacob Read, September 23, 1784, *LMCC,* VII, 591.
53. Samuel Hardy to Charles Thomson, August 16, 1784, *ibid.,* p. 585.
54. Charles Thomson to Jacob Read, September 27, 1784, *ibid.,* p. 593.
55. Thomas Mifflin of Pennsylvania, who served from November 3, 1783, to November 30, 1784, marked the first breach in the custom which had been established of giving each state the presidency before bestowing it a second time upon the same state, Thomas McKean having served briefly in 1781. On the office of the presidency, see Jennings B. Sanders, *The Presidency of the Continental Congress, 1775–1789* (Chicago, 1930); Charles C. Thach, *The Creation of the Presidency, 1775–1789* (Baltimore, 1922).
56. Brissot disapproved of the "naked bosoms" and pretentious headdresses of the lady guests at a dinner given by President Griffin, but informs the reader that the annual rotation of office is a reminder to our incumbent that "he is a simple citizen, and will soon return to the station of one." Brissot, *Travels,* I, 169–70.
57. John H. Hazelton, *The Declaration of Independence: Its History* (rev. ed., New York, 1970), p. 209.
58. *LDCC,* XI, 440–41.
59. Laurens to John Houstoun, President of Georgia (Aug. 27, 1778). *LDCC,* X, 509–11.
60. For the anti-Morris innuendoes of "a certain great man" (meaning Laurens), see *RDC,* II, 607, 608. On Laurens's unsent note, see Thomson to Committee of Congress, September 6, 1779, *LMCC,* IV, 401–408.

61. David D. Wallace, *The Life of Henry Laurens* (New York, 1915), pp. 243–45.
62. Henderson, *Party Politics*, pp. 187–96.
63. *RDC*, II, 858.
64. Henderson, *Party Politics*, pp. 232–34.
65. *JJ*, I, 507–08, 521–26.
66. *Ibid.*, 510.
67. *JCC*, XIII, 58–61; *JJ*, I, 512.
68. *JJ*, I, 512.
69. Jay to Washington, April 26, 1779, *JJ*, I, 588.
70. Elias Boudinot to George Washington, June 11, 21, 1785, *LMCC*, VII, 193–94; Madison, "Notes of Debates," June 21, 1783, *MP*, VII, 176–78; Elias Boudinot to Elisha Boudinot, June 23, 1783, *LMCC*, VII, 195.
71. See Henderson, *Party Politics*, p. 358.
72. Louise B. Dunbar, *A Study of "Monarchical" Tendencies on the United States from 1776 to 1801*, University of Illinois Studies in the Social Sciences, X, 1 (Urbana, Ill., 1923), ch. IV.
73. For the role of the Ohio Company lobbyist, the Reverend Manasseh Cutler, in the picking of St. Clair as the first territorial governor, see Jensen, *New Nation*, p. 356; Staughton Lynd, *Class Conflict, Slavery, and the United States Constitution* (Indianapolis, 1967).
74. *JCC*, XX, 55–57; Sanders, *Executive Departments*, p. 179.
75. Jay to Charles Thomson, July 10, 1782, *JJ*, II, 2–3.
76. Benjamin Rush, *Autobiography*, ed. by George W. Corner (Princeton, 1948), p. 155. See also J. Edwin Hendricks, *Charles Thomson and the Making of the Nation* (Rutherford, N.J., 1979).

Chapter 5. The People and the States: Constitution-making and Constituent Power

1. Henry Laurens, "A Narrative of the Capture of Henry Laurens, of his Confinement in the Tower of London, 1780, 1781, 1782," South Carolina Historical Society, *Collections*, I (1857), 53–54. The pamphlet in question was Sir William Meredith's *Account of Some Proceedings on the Writ of Habeas Corpus* (London, 1782?), a letter addressed to a member of the Irish Parliament.
2. In fact, the whole issue of the applicability of English law to the colonies was confused by Calvin's Case, 7 Coke Rep. 1 (1608), which distinguished acquisition of territory by conquest from a Christian king, where the laws remained unaltered subject to the will of the king, and conquest from an infidel, where the laws were abrogated and the inhabitants governed by the king; but once he introduced them, they could not be altered without express reference to Parliament. The courts could not refrain from further refinements. Holt, *C. J.*, is reputed to have said that in the case of an uninhabited country newly discovered by English subjects, all the laws in England were in force there. Earl of Derby's Case, 2 And. 116; Holt 3; 2 Salk. 411; 4 Modern 222; Comerback 228. While confusion over this issue reigned throughout the colonial period, there was little dispute that in the dominions of the Crown no act not specifically

mentioning them would apply. Joseph H. Smith, *Appeals to the Privy Council from the American Plantations* (New York, 1950), pp. 466–71; William F. Duker, *A Constitutional History of Habeas Corpus* (Westport, Conn., 1980).

3. Smith, *Appeals to the Privy Council*, p. 475n.

4. Julius Goebel, Jr., and T. Raymond Naughton, *Law Enforcement in Colonial New York* (New York, 1944), p. 506.

5. A. H. Carpenter, "Habeas Corpus in the Colonies," *AHR*, VIII (1902), 18–27. Thus, while royal instructions to the governors directed that no acts passed by a colonial legislature providing for habeas corpus were to be approved, the governor in turn was to proceed by specified instructions to provide the equivalent relief "for any criminal matters (unless for treason or felony)"; those committed for treason or felony were to have the right to petition in open court for prompt trials. Leonard W. Labaree, ed., *Royal Instructions to British Colonial Governors, 1670–1776* (2 vols., New York, 1935), nos. 463, 464, 466.

6. See table in Bernard Schwartz, *The Great Rights of Mankind: A History of the American Bill of Rights* (New York, 1977), pp. 86–88, contrasting the "ought not" in the first six state Declarations of Rights with John Adams's more precise substitute of "shall" for "ought" in the Massachusetts Constitution of 1780, p. 91. *Eight* Revolutionary state constitutions were prefaced by bills of rights, while *four* contained guarantees of individual rights in the body of their texts. Despite explicit instructions to draw up a bill of rights, the New York drafting committee inexplicably ignored this part of their instructions, but some specific rights were protected by clauses inserted directly in the text, such as jury trial and the free exercise of religion. Acts of attainder were prohibited "other than those committed before the present war," such acts not to work "a corruption of blood," and no new courts were to be instituted, "but such as shall proceed according to the course of the common law." William A. Polf, *The Political Revolution and New York's First Constitution* (Albany, N.Y., 1977).

7. Samuel E. Thorne, "Dr. Bonham's Case," *Law Quarterly Review*, LIV (1938), 543.

8. For the inconsistencies of James Otis on this issue, see "The Rights of the British Colonies Asserted and Proved," in Bernard Bailyn, ed., *Pamphlets of the American Revolution* (Cambridge, Mass., 1965), I, 178–81, 412–17, 447.

9. *Our Revolutionary Forefathers: The Letters of François, Marquis de Barbé-Marbois, 1779–1785*, trans. and ed. by Eugene P. Chase (repr. 1929 ed., Freeport, N.Y., 1969), p. 100.

10. For a scholarly analysis in depth, see M. H. Smith, *The Writs of Assistance Case* (Berkeley, 1978); also Richard B. Morris, "Then and There the Child Independence Was Born," American Heritage, *A Sense of History* (New York, 1985), pp. 72–83.

11. Bernard Bailyn, *Ideological Origins of the American Revolution* (Cambridge, Mass., 1967); Richard B. Morris, *The American Revolution Reconsidered* (New York, 1967), p. 39; Donald S. Lutz, *Popular Consent and Popular Control: Whig Political Theory in State Constitutions* (Baton Rouge, La., 1980). See also chapter XI, note 1.

12. Samuel Cooper, *Sermon Preached before His Excellency John Hancock . . . October 25, 1780* (Boston, 1780), p. 27.

13. See R. R. Palmer, *The Age of the Democratic Revolution: The Challenge* (2 vols., Princeton, 1959–64), I, 216.

14. *FAA*, VI, 1351–52.

15. Italics mine. W. L. Saunders, ed., *Colonial Records of North Carolina* (10 vols., Raleigh, N.C., 1886–90), IX, 1268–71.

16. R. G. Thwaites and L. P. Kellogg, eds., *Documentary History of Dunmore's War* (Madison, Wisc., 1905), pp. 368, 371; Francis S. Philbrick, *The Rise of the New West* (New York, 1965), pp. 83–84.

17. Robert Y. Taylor, *Massachusetts, Colony to Commonwealth: Documents on the Formation of Its Constitution, 1775–1780* (New York, 1961), pp. 26–29.

18. *FAA*, 4th ser., VI, 895.

19. Thorpe, ed., *Constitutions*, VII, 3813.

20. *Ibid.*, V, 3082, 3083.

21. *JAW*, IV, 184–87.

22. Adams to Gates, March 23, 1776, *LDCC*, III, 431.

23. "Common Sense," in Philip S. Foner, ed., *The Complete Writings of Thomas Paine* (2 vols., New York, 1945), I, 27, 28, 37.

24. For a critique of John Adams's failure to explain why republicans had a monopoly on virtue, see Willi Paul Adams, *The First American Constitutions: Republican Ideology and the Making of the State Constitutions of the Revolutionary Era*, tr. by Rita and Robert Kimber (Chapel Hill, N.C., 1980), p. 124.

25. Thorpe, ed., *Constitutions*, V, 2628.

26. Oscar and Mary F. Handlin, eds., *The Popular Sources of Political Authority* (Cambridge, Mass., 1966), p. 153.

27. The specially elected fourth Congress, which convened in White Plains on July 9, 1776, adopted the Declaration of Independence unanimously (lacking instructions, New York's delegates at Philadelphia refused to vote on that issue) and changed its name the following day to "the Convention of the Representatives of the State of New York." *JJ*, I, 287.

28. Nevins, *American States*, pp. 132, 133.

29. Howard C. Rice, Jr., ed., *Travels in North America in the Years 1780, 1781, and 1782*, by the Marquis de Chastellux (2 vols., Williamsburg, 1963), I, 161–62. See also Samuel Eliot Morison, "The Struggle Over the Adoption of the Constitution of Massachusetts, 1780," Massachusetts Historical Society *Proceedings*, L (1910–17), 241–49; Handlin, eds., *Popular Sources*, pp. 475–930.

30. *JCC*, I, 110.

31. Poore, ed., *Federal and State Constitutions*, II, 1908–09.

32. Adams, *First American Constitutions*, p. 207, citing M. J. C. Vile, *Constitutionalism and the Separation of Powers* (Oxford, 1967), p. 119.

33. See Margaret B. Macmillan, *The War Governors of the American Revolution* (New York, 1943), chs. IV, V; Wood, *American Republic*, pp. 127–61.

34. James Duane to Robert R. Livingston, John Jay, Gouverneur Morris, and Robert Yates, April 19, 1777, *JJ*, I, 386–88.

35. *Journal of the House of Representatives of the Commonwealth of Pennsylvania, 1776–*

1781 (1 vol., Philadelphia, 1782), I, 56; Richard B. Morris, "The Forging of the Union Reconsidered," *Columbia Law Review,* LXXIV (1974), 1076.

36. *JJ,* I, 389–47.

37. Nevins, *American States,* pp. 150, 151.

38. William C. Bruce, *Benjamin Franklin Self Revealed* (2 vols., New York, 1917), II, 249n.

39. See Brunhouse, *Counter-Revolution;* J. Paul Selsam, *The Pennsylvania Constitution of 1776: A Study in Revolutionary Democracy* (Philadelphia, 1936).

40. *Commonwealth of Virginia* v. *Caton et al.,* 4 Call, 8, 17–18. Previously, as early as 1780, a New Jersey court refused to accept the validity of an unconstitutional act of the legislature. *Holmes* v. *Walton,* for which see Austin Scott, "Holmes vs. Walton: The New Jersey Precedent" *AHR,* IV (1898–99), 456–69.

41. Section 25. On the other hand, the federal courts' power to pass on the constitutionality of *federal* legislation was established by decisions of the Court itself, with sparing use prior to the Civil War. See Edward S. Corwin, *The Doctrine of Judicial Review* (Princeton, 1914), p. 17, who questions whether that power was to be implied from either Articles III or VI of the Constitution, while conceding that it conformed to views shared by most of the Framers.

42. G. J. McRee, *Life and Correspondence of James Iredell* (2 vols., New York, 1857–58), II, 148, 169–70, 172–76.

43. *New York Laws,* 6 Sess. 1783, c. 31. That statute was enacted just before the New York legislature learned the terms of the Preliminary Peace of November 30, 1782, barring such legislation. For postwar efforts to punish the Loyalists in New York, see Philip Ranlet, *The New York Loyalists* (Knoxville, Tenn., 1986), pp. 169–74.

44. "Letter from Phocion," *HP,* III, 483–97.

45. Similarly, in the South Carolina case of *Ham* v. *McClaws and Wife* (1 Bay's Rep. 93) (1789), where the court felt bound to give a construction to a state statute, in effect invalidating it, but defending its position on the ground that the legislature never "had it in their contemplation to make forfeiture of negroes. . . ." Corwin lists *Rutgers* v. *Waddington* under "alleged precedents," and hails it as "a marked triumph of legislative sovereignty," while conceding that the court managed to evade the operation of the statute in the case at hand —Corwin, *Judicial Review,* p. 73. Boudin regards the holding as merely an application of the common-law rules applying to the construction of statutes. L. B. Boudin, *Government by Judiciary* (2 vols., New York, 1932), I, 56–58.

46. For the record of the case, see Richard B. Morris, ed., *Select Cases of the Mayor's Court of New York City, 1674–1784* (Washington, D.C., 1935), pp. 57–59, 302–27; Julius Goebel, Jr., *The Law Practice of Alexander Hamilton* (4 vols., New York, 1964), I, 282–543.

47. First published in J. and A. McLean, *The Federalist* (2 vols., New York, 1788); later in *The Independent Journal* (June 17) and in *The New-York Packet* three days later.

48. See Brissot de Warville, *Travels,* I, 118.

49. James M. Varnum, *The Case, Trevett against Weeden . . . Tried Before the Honorable Superior Court in the County of Newport, September Term, 1786* (Providence, R.I.,

1787), pp. 21–33 passim.; also in 4 *Am. State Trials* 548, ed. by John D. Lawson (New York, 1915); Brinton Coxe, *An Essay on Judicial Power and Unconstitutional Legislation* (Philadelphia, 1893), pp. 236, 242.
50. *Bayard* v. *Singleton,* 1 Martin (N.C. 5), (1787).
51. *JAW,* IV, 216.
52. Simeon Howard, "Sermon Preached Before the Honorable Council and Honorable House of Representatives . . . May 31, 1780," in J. W. Thornton, *Pulpit of the American Revolution* (Boston, 1860), pp. 390, et seq.

Chapter 6. The New Nation's First Depression

1. Despite partial, incomplete, and inaccurate data, there were identifiable recessions and periods of depressed economy in the colonial period. The earliest recorded depression in the Thirteen Colonies occurred in New England in 1640, but the population was still restricted and the impact geographically confined. Later punitive acts of Parliament, like the Boston Port Bill and the New England Restraining Act, were damaging to port and fishing activities in New England on the eve of the Revolution. See Willard L. Thorp, *Business Annals* (New York, 1926), p. 112. For three recorded pre-Revolutionary depressions, see Morris, ed., *Encyclopedia of American History,* p. 746.
2. Margaret G. Myers, *New York Money Market* (2 vols., New York, 1931), I, 17.
3. Morris, *Government and Labor,* pp. 117, 118, 152, 153. See also Edward G. Bourne, "Alexander Hamilton and Adam Smith," *Quarterly Journal of Economics,* VIII (1894), 328–44; and for the earlier influence of Adam Smith by way of Bernard Mandeville, see Forrest McDonald, *Novus Ordo Seclorum* (Lawrence, Kans., 1985), pp. 120–25. John Adams, for example, had in his model treaty supported the freest possible trade. See below and chapter VIII, In Diplomacy: Friction and Frustration.
4. See John D. R. Platt, *Jeremiah Wadsworth: Federalist Entrepreneur* (New York, 1982).
5. Jan W. Schulte Nordholt, *The Dutch Republic and American Independence* (Chapel Hill, N.C., 1982), p. 255.
6. Glenn Porter, ed., *Encyclopedia of American Economic History* (New York, 1980), p. 240 (1910–14 = 100). Massachusetts Bureau of Labor Statistics, *16th Annual Report* (Boston, 1885), pp. 160–449.
7. In August 1784 five large London firms in the American trade had to close their doors, and as remittances from America precipitously declined, so did the British export trade. Platt, *Jeremiah Wadsworth;* Robert East, *Business Enterprise in the American Revolutionary Era* (New York, 1938). For the rash of bankruptcies of Philadelphia importing firms (of which some sixty-eight have been identified), see Thomas M. Doerflinger, *A Vigorous Spirit of Enterprise: Merchants and Economic Development in Revolutionary Philadelphia* (Chapel Hill, 1986), p. 262.
8. Timothy Pitkin, *A Statistical View of the Commerce of the United States of America* (repr., New Haven, 1935), p. 30. British exports to the United States in fact averaged £1,300,000 for the years 1783–89 less than comparable export figures for the years 1770–75, and 25% lower in 1791–92 than in 1768–72. James B.

Hedges, *The Browns of Providence Plantation* (Cambridge, Mass., 1952), pp. 292–93. James F. Shepherd, Jr. and Gary M. Walton, "Economic Changes After the American Revolution," *Explorations in Economic History*, XIII (1976), 397–422, at p. 411.

9. U.S. Bureau of the Census, *Historical Statistics of the United States: Colonial Times to 1970, Part 2* (Washington, D.C., 1975), p. 1176. For the same years the U.S. trade balance with Scotland was also invariably unfavorable to the U.S., although the amounts are less than a quarter of the English trade. *Ibid.*, p. 1177. *WMQ*, XXXII (1975), 307–25; XXXIV (1977), 577.

10. One estimate puts exports of specie for the three years at £1,260,000. Roy A. Foulke, *The Sinews of American Commerce* (New York, 1941), p. 102.

11. R. G. Adams, ed., *Selected Political Essays of James Wilson* (New York, 1930), pp. 145, 146.

12. Ronald Hoffman, *A Spirit of Dissension: Economics, Politics, and the Revolution in Maryland* (Baltimore, 1973), pp. 268–72.

13. See, e.g., Mercy Otis Warren, "History of the Rise, Progress and Termination of the American Revolution," in Herbert J. Storing, ed., *The Complete Anti-Federalist* (6 vols., Chicago, 1981), VI, 203. Warren speaks of "discontents artificially wrought up, by men who wished for a more strong and splendid government."

14. See, for example, Dawson's attempted refutation of John Lothrop Motley, who had described the Confederation era as a period of "chaos." "The Motley Letters," *Historical Magazine*, 2d ser., IX (1871), 157, et seq.

15. Others who spread the notion of Constitution by conspiracy include J. Allen Smith, *The Spirit of American Government* (Chautauqua, N.Y., 1911), p. 37; Arthur F. Bentley, *The Process of Government* (Chicago, 1908); and in a more naked form, A. M. Simons's *Social Forces in American History* (New York, 1912).

16. Charles A. Beard, *An Economic Interpretation of the Constitution of the United States* (New York, 1949), pp. 47–48.

17. (New York, 1950), pp. 423–24.

18. Edward Channing, *History of the United States* (6 vols., New York, 1905–25), III, 481.

19. Andrew C. McLaughlin, *The Confederation and Constitution, 1783–1789* (New York, 1905), p. 71.

20. Jay to Jefferson, December 14, 1786, *HPJ*, III, 223.

21. McLaughlin, *Confederation and Constitution*, p. 107. To compound the confusion, McLaughlin proceeds to give his readers a gloomy picture of economic distress in Rhode Island at the height of the paper money controversy, reporting the unemployed "wandering aimlessly about with no hope of employment," using Brissot de Warville's account of Newport—idlers on the street corners, houses falling in ruins, shops offering only the most mediocre articles, and bad food, "grass growing in the streets, everything announcing misery," *ibid.*, pp. 150–51, citing Brissot, *Travels*, I, 118, and John Quincy Adams' "Diary," in Massachusetts Historical Society *Proceedings*, 2d ser., XVI, 450.

22. Tench Coxe, *A View of the United States of America . . .* (Philadelphia, 1794), pp.

3–4. Recent investigations point to a "severe contraction" in these years, something "truly disastrous." John J. McCusker and Russell R. Menard, *The Economy of British America, 1607–1789* (Chapel Hill, N.C., 1985), pp. 366, 373.
23. Pitkin, *Commerce*, pp. 84–85.
24. See Curtis P. Nettels, *The Emergence of a National Economy, 1775–1815* (New York, 1962); Douglass C. North, *The Economic Growth of the United States, 1790–1860* (New York, 1961), pp. 18, 19; Gordon C. Bjork, "The Weaning of the American Economy," *Journal of Economic History*, XXIV (1964), 541–60. For the economy on a state and local basis during these years, see the unpublished dissertations listed in McCusker and Menard, *Economy of British America*, pp 367–68n.
25. Jefferson to Madison, July 1, 1784, *TJP*, VII, 356.
26. *Ibid.*, X, 14, et seq.
27. *BFS*, IX, 300–01.
28. Robert R. Livingston Papers, New York Public Library: Bancroft transcripts.
29. See, e.g., Le Tombe to Castries, "Mémoire du Consulat de France à Boston" [n.d., 1784]; Oster to Castries, Williamsburg, July 27 and December 4, 1785; Oster to D'Annemours, Williamsburg, December 7, 1784; Crèvecoeur to Castries, New London, Connecticut, July 15 and August 8, 1784, AN:CC.
30. Anne Bezanson, Robert D. Gray, and Miriam Hussey, *Wholesale Prices in Philadelphia, 1784–1861* (Philadelphia, 1937), pp. 16, 212, 228, 242.
31. George Rogers Taylor, "Wholesale Commodity Prices at Charleston, South Carolina, 1732–1791," *Journal of Economic and Business History*, IV (1932), 356–69.
32. *Ibid.*, 368, 369n.
33. Pierce Butler to Thomas FitzSimons, Philadelphia, February 15, 1788, in Pierce Butler MSS, Library of the Historical Society of Pennsylvania; Harry Grant to Christopher Champlin, Charleston, South Carolina, March 14, April 16, 1788, in Massachusetts Historical Society: Wetmore Collection. Both items are cited by Taylor, *loc. cit.*, p. 369.
34. Morris, *Peacemakers*, p. 559n; Miller, *Treaties*, II, 96–107.
35. Shelburne to Morellet, March 13, 1783, Lord Edmond Fitzmaurice, *Life of William, Earl of Shelburne* (3 vols., London, 1876), III, 323.
36. *JJ*, II, 390, 401.
37. Cabinet Minute, October 17, 1782, *Correspondence of King George III, 1760–1783*, ed. by Sir John Fortescue (6 vols., London, 1928), VI, 144.
38. Morris, *Peacemakers*, pp. 429–30.
39. *Parliamentary History*, XIII, 602–14, debate March 7, 1783.
40. Fernand Braudel, *The Wheels of Commerce* (New York, 1982), p. 65.
41. Congress had Adam Smith's *Wealth of Nations* on a list of books ordered for its library, both the first edition of 1776 and the second of 1778. See "Report of Books for the Use of Commerce," January 23, 1783, *MP*, VI, 65, 86. Both James Madison and James Monroe were familiar with Adam Smith and were in favor of discarding mercantilist policies for freedom of trade. See Monroe to Madison, May 31, 1786, *MP*, IX, 84n.; Madison to Jefferson, April 27, 1785,

ibid., VIII, 265–70; Monroe to Jefferson, June 16, 1785, *TJP*, VIII, 216. Although he did not quote Smith, as early as 1776–77 Gouverneur Morris had voiced the conviction that unimpeded commerce was the spring of civilization and progress, and that "Prosperity is the principal Cause and Object of Society." See Gouverneur Morris, "On Government," n.d., Columbia University: Gouverneur Morris Papers.

42. In April an act had been passed vesting in the King in Commons temporary authority to regulate American commerce, 23 Geo. III, c. 39.

43. *Extra-Official State Papers*, III, Appendix xiii, pp. 56–57.

44. See citations in Morris, *Peacemakers*, p. 126, and Robert L. Schuyler, *The Fall of the Old Colonial System* (New York, 1945); L. J. Ragatz, *The Fall of the Planter Class in the British Caribbean, 1763–1833* (New York and London, 1928); and Vincent T. Harlow, *The Founding of the Second British Empire* (2 vols., London, 1952–63), II, 254–55, 266–67. For a balanced, if nontraditional treatment, see Charles T. Ritcheson, "Anglo-American Relations, 1783–1794," *South Atlantic Quarterly*, LVIII (1959), 364–80; and in his *Aftermath of Revolution: British Policy Toward the United States 1783–1795* (Dallas, Tex., 1969), pp. 3–146, the author stresses the expansion of postwar Anglo-American trade after the Revolution, is generally supportive of British trade policies toward the United States, and cites widespread evidence of smuggling. Cf. Herbert C. Bell, "West Indian Trade and British Commercial Policy, 1783–93," *English Historical Review*, XXXI (1916), 429–41. For the failure of Nova Scotia to capitalize on this prohibition of New England fish shipments, see "Memoir of the Cod Fishery, Nova Scotia, 31 December 1817," Canadian Public Archives: Nova Scotia, CCCV, 113, cited in Gerald Graham, *Sea Power and British North America, 1783–1820: A Study in British Colonial Policy* (repr. 1941 ed., Westport, Conn., 1969), pp. 52–55.

45. East, *Business Enterprise*, pp. 246, 247. For smuggling out of Rhode Island with French boats carrying two flags and two lists of crew members, see Le Tombe to Castries, Boston, December 2, 1786, AN:CC. See also Tench Coxe, *Brief Examination of Lord Sheffield's Observations* (Philadelphia, 1791), p. 16. Nelson's strong-arm methods to break up the complicity of the West Indian planters and customs officials with American ship captains in the systematic smuggling operations conducted by the latter are treated in Sir Nicholas Harris Nicolas, ed., *The Dispatches and Letters of Vice Admiral Lord Nelson* (7 vols., London, 1845–46), I, 174–86; Ragatz, *Fall of Planter Class*, pp. 183–94.

46. These figures are found in Weeden, *Economic and Social History of New England*, I, 832; Nettels, *National Economy*, p. 55.

47. Lorenzo Sabine, *Report on the Principal Fisheries of the American Seas* (Washington, D.C., 1853), p. 174. See also James D. Phillips, *Salem in the Eighteenth Century* (Boston, 1937); Hedges, *Browns of Providence*, pp. 279–85.

48. Dorchester to Grenville, September 26, 1790, PRO: CO 42/69, f. 14. For further confirmation, see New England fisheries reports and memorials cited in *TJP*, XIX, 145n., 153.

49. *TJP*, XIX, 206–36, at pp. 209, 211, 214.

50. See Jefferson to Adams, November 27, 1783, May 11 and 30, 1786; Adams to

Jefferson, June 6, 1786, *TJP*, IX, 64, 594–95, 605; and chapter VIII below, In Diplomacy: Friction and Frustration.

51. *Historical Statistics of the U.S., Part 2.* See also Petition to Congress of the Inhabitants of Nantucket, January 6, 1790, cited in *TJP*, XIX, 146–47.

52. Elmo P. Hohman, *The American Whaleman* (New York, 1928), pp. 35, 36; Hedges, *Browns of Providence*, pp. 295–96; Gerald S. Graham, "The Migrations of the Nantucket Whale Fishery: An Episode in British Colonial Policy," *New England Quarterly*, VIII (1935), 179–202. Van Beck Hall, *Politics Without Parties*, pp. 1–28; Alexander Starbuck, *The History of Nantucket County, and Town* (Boston, 1926), pp. 393–400.

53. See below, chapter VIII.

54. Victor S. Clark, *History of Manufactures in the United States, 1607–1860* (Washington, D.C., 1916), pp. 95, 145; Weeden, *Economic and Social History of New England*, II, 764–65, 776–77, 806.

55. Brissot, *New Travels*, I, 450.

56. *Ibid.*, pp. 450–51.

57. Minutes of the Chamber of Commerce of New York City, March 3, 1785, New York Public Library; Staughton Lynd, "The Revolution and the Common Man" (Ann Arbor, Mich., University Microfilms, 1963), pp. 223–37, mobilizes a convincing case for the depression, contra Forrest McDonald, *We the People*, p. 296, n. 139. See also E. Wilder Spaulding, *New York in the Critical Period* (New York, 1932), ch. 1; Pomerantz, *New York, an American City* (New York, 1938), pp. 147–56.

58. See Richard B. Morris, "Criminal Conspiracy and Early Labor Combinations in New York City," *PSQ*, LII (1937), 51–85.

59. General Account of the Treasurer's receipts and payments, January 1, 1784–December 31, 1787, January 1–December 31, 1788, *Votes and Proceedings of the Assembly*, 11 Sess., January 16, 1788, at p. 23; 12 Sess., January 13, 1789, at p. 56.

60. "AZ," *Political Intelligencer*, September 20, 1786, and sources cited in Richard P. McCormick, *Experiment in Independence: New Jersey in the Critical Period* (New Brunswick, N.J., 1950), p. 108.

61. Bezanson, *Prices and Inflation*, pp. 86, 127, 160, 179.

62. The depletion of nearby woods as a result of the failure to introduce conservation measures essential to the iron industry, competition of farmers for labor, and high interest costs were among the reasons assigned for the languishing state of the industry. Schoepf, I, 36–38, 86–87, 116–19. Arthur C. Bining, *British Regulation of the Colonial Iron Industry* (Philadelphia, 1933), pp. 71–72; *Pennsylvania Iron Manufacture*, pp. 177–78, 182–83.

64. Lawrence Kinnaird, *Spain in the Mississippi Valley, 1765–1794* (3 vols., Washington, D.C., 1949), III, 31–32, 112–13, 295; John W. Caughey, *McGillivray of the Creeks* (Norman, Okla., 1938), pp. 23–24.

65. Justin Williams, "English Mercantilism and Carolina Naval Stores, 1705–1776," *Journal of Southern History*, I (1935), p. 8.

66. *Historical Statistics of the U.S., Part 2*, p. 1192.

67. *Ibid.*, p. 1189.

68. Morris, ed., *Encyclopedia*, pp. 702–03. See also Nettels, *Emergence*, pp. 50–51; Lewis C. Gray, *History of Agriculture in the Southern United States* (2 vols., Gloucester, Mass., 1958), II, 593, 610, 1030.
69. Wallace, *Henry Laurens*, p. 429.
70. Consular records, AN:BAE B, 1:927, f. 234; also Jacob M. Price, *France and the Chesapeake* (2 vols., Ann Arbor, Mich., 1973), II, 728, et seq. For the relationship of American planters to Scottish merchants, see T. M. Devine, *The Tobacco Lords: A Study of the Tobacco Merchants of Glasgow and Their Trading Activities, c. 1740–1790* (Edinburgh, 1975).
71. Price, *France and the Chesapeake*, II, 728, et seq.
72. *Historical Statistics of the U.S., Part 2*, pp. 1190.
73. F. L. Nussbaum, "French Colonial *Arrêt* of 1784," *South Atlantic Quarterly* (1928), pp. 62–78.
74. See, e.g., Vice Consul de La Forest to Castries, New York, November 25, 1785; Oster to Castries, Williamsburg, December 24, 1785, December 31, 1786, December 31, 1787, AN: CC.
75. See, e.g., *TJP*, VIII, 385–91; IX, 139–40.
76. Price, *France and the Chesapeake*, II, 786.
77. *Ibid.*, 788.
78. Gray, *History of Agriculture*, II, 596, 603–05.
79. See, e.g., Spaulding, *New York*, p. 15; Nettels, *National Economy*, pp. 69–70; McDonald, *Novus Ordo Seclorum*, pp. 102–05.
80. *DC*, IV, 216–17, 220, 258.
81. Arthur H. Cole, ed., *Industrial and Commercial Correspondence of Alexander Hamilton Anticipating His Report on Manufactures* (Chicago, 1928), pp. 20, 30, 39, 50; Weeden, *Economic and Social History of New England*, II, 832; George Bancroft, *History of the Formation of the Constitution of the United States* (New York, 1896), pp. 138–39.
82. See Le Tombe to Castries, Boston, August 19, 1785; Toscan to Castries, Boston, October 18, 1785; La Forest to Luzerne, October 22, 1785, to Castries, December 12, 1785, AN: CC. For complaints of consular agents to John Jay, see Jay's report to Congress, March 14, 1787, enclosing the protest of the Dutch consul of February 20, 1787 on a Virginia tariff, PCC 81, 124; *DC*, VI, 492–97; "JJ, III"; see also *JCC*, XXXII, 83; XXXIII, 676. On Massachusetts, see *LMCC*, VIII, 189n.–90n.
83. AN:Colonies, C8B:18.
84. Albert S. Gieseke, *American Commercial Legislation Before 1789* (Philadelphia, 1910), pp. 128–29, 131, 137–38.
85. *Ibid.*, pp. 128–34, passim. Emory R. Johnson, et al., *History of Domestic and Foreign Commerce of the United States* (2 vols., Washington, D.C., 1915), I, 135–39; Nettels, *National Economy*, pp. 69, et seq.
86. Marbois to Luzerne, January 29, 1788, MAE:CP EU.
87. Blanche E. Hazard, *Organization of the Boot and Shoe Industry in Massachusetts Before 1875* (Cambridge, Mass., 1923), p. 29.
88. For statistics on use of water power in this era, see Louis C. Hunter, *A History*

of Industrial Power in the United States, 1780–1930 (2 vols., Charlottesville, Va., 1979), I, 46, 94, 101, passim.

89. For the thesis that American technology in the 1780s set the stage for the industrialization in the century ahead, see Neil L. York, *Mechanical Metamorphosis: Technological Change in the Revolutionary Era* (Westport, Conn., 1985), p. 175. See also Victor S. Clark, *History of Manufactures in the United States, 1607–1860* (3 vols., New York, 1929), I, 180–81; W. Winterbotham, *An Historical, Geographical, Commercial, and Philosophical View of the American United States* (4 vols., London, 1795), II, 367, 404, et seq.

90. See John Jay, Circuit Court Diary, April 29 and May 16, 1790, with uneven progress reported in wool and cotton cards. Document in Columbia University: Jay Papers. By 1786 Massachusetts had 2,397 factory establishments, exclusive of spermaceti oil works, distilleries, and shipbuilding, often encouraged by government. McDonald, *Novus Ordo Seclorum*, p. 102. On pro- and anti-manufacturing sentiment in the crisis of the eighties, see Drew R. McCoy, *The Elusive Republic: Political Economy in Jeffersonian America* (New York, 1980), pp. 105–19.

91. For Madison's assertion that Connecticut taxed imports from Massachusetts, see Gaillard Hunt, ed., *The Writings of James Madison* (9 vols., New York, 1900–10), II, 395.

92. Virginia was an exception. Regulations and imposts levied by Virginia not only ran counter to the U.S. Treaty of Amity and Commerce with France, but diverted to Georgetown, then in the state of Maryland, a considerable part of the commerce from Alexandria. Brissot, *New Travels*, I, 426.

93. Morris, *Government and Labor*, p. 203; Charles Pettit to Joseph Reed, February 13, 1784, New-York Historical Society: Joseph Reed MSS. Cole, *Hamilton Industrial Correspondence*, pp. 6, 10, 30, 39, 50, passim; S. Rezneck, "The Rise and Early Development of Industrial Consciousness, 1760–1830," *Journal of Economic and Business History*, IV (1932), 788, 789. Charles G. Steffen, *The Mechanics of Baltimore: Workers and Politics in the Age of Revolution, 1763–1812* (Urbana, Ill., 1984), pp. 83–120.

94. See Jensen, *New Nation*, p. 300, citing Vernon G. Setser, *Commercial Reciprocity Policy of the United States 1774–1829* (Philadelphia, 1937), p. 65.

95. *Report of the Privy Council, 1791*, pp. 29, 37, 44–45.

96. A sketch of "Origins of the Constitutional Convention" (unfinished), is in Hunt, ed., *Madison Writings*, II, 395.

97. *JCC*, XXVI, 321–22 (April 30, 1784).

98. Rufus King to Elbridge Gerry, May 19, 1785, King, *Life*, I, 97–98.

99. *JCC*, XXVIII, 202–06 (March 28, 1785).

100. Monroe to Jefferson, July 15, 1785, *TJP*, VIII, 296.

101. Jensen, *New Nation*, pp. 402–05.

102. The result was the Tariff of 1789, transferring the drama of tariffs from the states. See *American Museum*, I (1790), 19; IV (1788), 347–48; *ASP, Financial.*

103. Eric Foner, *Tom Paine and Revolutionary America* (New York, 1976), pp. 26, 27;

Thomas Paine, *Life and Writings of Thomas Paine*, ed. by M. C. Conway (4 vols., New York, 1894–96), I, 102.

104. Bray Hammond, *Banks and Politics in America from the Revolution to the Civil War* (Princeton, 1957), pp. 42–43; Marbois to Castries, Philadelphia, March 24, 1784, AN:CC. For the constructive wartime role of the Pennsylvania Bank, see Jerry Grundfest, *George Clymer, Philadelphia Revolutionary* (New York, 1982), pp. 156–57.

105. Hamilton to James Duane, September 3, 1780, *HP*, II, 416.

106. Hamilton to Robert Morris, April 30, 1781, *HP*, II, 604–05.

107. James Wilson insisted that Congress possessed such powers. *Considerations on the Bank of North America* (Philadelphia, 1785).

108. *LMCC*, V, 220; *JCC*, XX, 519, 545–46, 1186–90 (1781); Pelatiah Webster, *Political Essays* (Philadelphia, 1791), p. 447; Lawrence Lewis, Jr., *A History of the Bank of North America* (Philadelphia, 1882); Margaret G. Myers, *A Financial History of the United States* (New York, 1970), pp. 40–43. Marbois to Castries, Philadelphia, March 24, 1784, AN:CC. For agrarian opposition to the Bank's issuance of notes as an "aristocratical idea," an opposition voiced by William Findley and John Smilie, see Mathew Carey, ed., *Debates and Proceedings of the General Assembly of Pennsylvania on the Memorials Praying a Repeal or Suspension of the Law Annulling the Charter of the Bank* (Philadelphia, 1786).

109. For the "Constitution and Outline of a Charter," see *HP*, III, 514–20. Syrett finds no evidence that these documents, although in Hamilton's hand, were authored by him.

110. See Oscar and Mary Handlin, *Commonwealth: Massachusetts, 1774–1861* (New York, 1947), pp. 107–08.

111. Resolution of July 6, 1785, *JCC*, XX, 499–500.

112. A. B. Hepburn, *A History of Coinage and Currency in the United States* (New York, 1915), pp. 11–12. Schoepf, who traveled in the States in the years 1783–84, cites similar variations on the eve of the postwar period. *Travels in the Confederation*, II, 9.

113. Hall, *Politics Without Parties*, p. 36. On the general issue, see also Kenneth Coleman, *Debtor and Creditor in America* (Madison, Wisc., 1970).

114. Bray Hammond, *Banks and Politics in America: From the Revolution to the Civil War* (Princeton, 1957), p. ix. The "myth" is perpetuated in Harold F. Williamson, ed., *The Growth of the American Economy* (New York, 1951), p. 87.

115. See Ronald Hoffman, *A Spirit of Dissension: Economics, Politics, and the Revolution in Maryland* (Baltimore, 1973), p. 268.

116. See also Schoepf, *Travels in the Confederation*, II, 130–32.

117. Paine, *Works*, II, 178.

118. Hoffman, *Dissension*, pp. 271–72.

119. Hunt, *Madison Writings*, I, 244; McCormick, *Experience*, pp. 186–206.

120. *New York State Laws*, 9 Sess., April 18, 1786; for bankruptcy statutes, see *ibid.*, 9 Sess., especially February 13, 1786; March 31, 1786, c. 228; 10 Sess., April 20, 1787, c. 94. See also "Minutes of the Chamber of Commerce," I, 380, et seq., in Chamber of Commerce, New York City; Warville, *New Travels*, I, 158,

159; *New-York Packet,* March 9, 1786, January 8, 1787; *New York Daily Advertiser,* February 23, 1786, Suppl., January 8, 1787. See also Spaulding, *New York in the Critical Period,* pp. 113–49.

121. Brant, *Madison,* II, 317–18, 361–63.

122. Madison to Jefferson, August 12, 1786, *MP,* IX, 95; Jay to Adams, November 1, 1786, *HPJ,* III, 215.

123. Frank G. Bates, *Rhode Island in the Formation of the Union* (New York, 1898), pp. 123–31. McLaughlin, *Confederation and Constitution,* pp. 151–53; Boudin, *Government by Judiciary,* I; Coxe, *Judicial Power and Unconstitutional Legislation,* p. 242; Charles Warren, *The Supreme Court in United States History* (2 vols., Boston, 1922), I, 68n. Rhode Island's old charter, still governing, had no provision directly pertinent to obligation of contracts. Irwin H. Polishook, *Rhode Island and the Union* (Evanston, Ill., 1969), pp. 133–42.

124. *Providence Gazette,* July 8, 1791, cited by Warren, *Supreme Court,* I, 68n.

125. *RFC,* II, 439–40, 597, 619. Clinton Rossiter, *1787: The Grand Convention* (New York, 1966), p. 230. While Congress was authorized to coin money and regulate its value, it was not explicitly given the power to issue paper money, establish legal tender, or impair contracts. In fact, the power to issue bills of credit was struck out of the draft by a vote of nine to two. Under the doctrine of implied powers, however, Hamilton assumed such power before the Constitution was two years old. Hammond, *Banks and Politics,* p. 89.

126. See Tyler Dennett, *Americans in Eastern Asia* (New York, 1941), pp. 4–7; Foster Rhea Dulles, *The Old China Trade* (Boston, 1930), pp. 4–12; East, *Business Enterprise,* pp. 255–56; Clarence L. Ver Steeg, "Financing and Outfitting the First U.S. Ship to China," *Pacific Historical Review,* XXII (1953), 1–12; Jonathan Goldstein, *Philadelphia and the China Trade, 1682–1846* (University Park, Pa., 1978); Magdalen Coughlin, "The Entrance of the Massachusetts Merchant Into the Pacific," *Southern Historical Quarterly,* XLVIII (1966), 327–52.

127. Dennett, *Eastern Asia,* pp. 20–27. For further correspondence on the opening up of India, Madras, and the trading possibilities of the Coromandel coast, see Stephen Popham to Sir Archibald Campbell, March 10, 12, 1787; Charles N. White to Stephen Popham, From St. George, March 9, 1787; Stephen Popham to Thomas Randolph, Madras, October 6, 1788; Thomas Randolph to Jay, Madras, October 7, 1788; John Pintard to Jay, October 24, 1787, DNA: PCC 78, XVIII, 647; XIX, 589–605, passim, 647.

128. Thomas Barclay in France proved the exception to the general practice of appointing consular agents. For a list of agents in French ports in 1788 (prior to the ratification of the French Consular Convention), see *TJP,* XIV, 56–62. For Jay's recommendation for the setting up of a regular consular system and the issue of whether consuls should be permitted to engage in trade, see *JCC,* XXIX, 722–24, 831–32, 846, 861.

129. *JCC,* XXIX, 855 (October 27–28, 1785); Wilbur J. Carr, "The American Consular Service," *American Journal of International Law,* I (1907), 894; Emory R.

Johnson, "The Early History of the United States Consular Service, 1776–1792," *PSQ*, XIII (1898), 19–40.

130. Cited by East, *Business Enterprise*, p. 250.

Chapter 7. A Cautiously Transforming Egalitarianism

1. See, e.g., *Chisholm* v. *Georgia*, 2 Dallas (U.S.) 419, 471 (1793).
2. J. R. Pole, *The Pursuit of Equality in American Society* (Berkeley, 1978), p. 13.
3. John Adams to Thomas Brand Hollis, June 11, 1790, and to Samuel Adams, February 4, 1794, in Charles Francis Adams, ed., *The Works of John Adams* (10 vols., Boston, 1856), IX, 569–71; I, 462.
4. James Wilson, "Lectures on Law," in Robert G. McCloskey, ed., *The Works of James Wilson* (2 vols., Cambridge, Mass., 1967), I, 240.
5. Staughton Lynd and Alfred F. Young, "After Carl Becker; The Mechanics in New York City Politics, 1774–1801," in *Labor History*, V (1964), 215–24; Robert J. Dinkin, *Voting in Revolutionary America* (Westport, Conn., 1982), pp. 27–43; Chilton Williamson, *American Suffrage from Property to Democracy* (Princeton, 1960).
6. Space does not permit inclusion of statistical data which some investigators have interpreted as supporting the thesis that a long-run inequality emerged during the eighteenth century. Admittedly, the rapid increase in the population would decrease the amount of freehold or unoccupied land in settled areas after several generations. Contrariwise, such inequalities may have been mitigated by the improvement in transportation, which would increase the number of markets where one would buy and sell while encouraging organized efforts to settle farther west. Even there, of course, great variations existed in the quality of land farmed. Caution also must be observed in the reliance on tax lists, since numerous propertyless members of families could look forward to inheriting land. Scholars have used National Archives and Records Service, U.S. Direct Tax of 1798, microcopy (Washington, D.C., 1965), among them Lee Saltow and Aubrey C. Land, "Housing and Social Standing in Georgia, 1798," *Georgia History Quarterly*, LXIV (1980), 450–51. As Bernard Bailyn points out, the Boston tax list covers neither all real property nor all owners of real property, and includes neither personal property nor actual income. Bernard Bailyn, *Lines of Force* (Washington, D.C., 1975), p. 14. These areas and issues have been probed by James T. Lemon and Gary B. Nash, by Kenneth A. Lockridge, Allan Kulikoff, G. B. Warden, Bruce M. Wilkenfeld, Billy B. Smith, Dirk Hoerder, Herman Wellenreuther, and John K. Alexander, among others. Noteworthy documentation is provided by Alice R. Jones, "Wealth Estimates for the New England Colonies about 1770," *Journal of Economic History*, XXXII (1972), 104, and in her massive three-volume statistical study, including *Wealth of a Nation-to-Be* (New York, 1980). Recently, Steffen (*Merchants of Baltimore*, p. 23) estimated that in one section of Baltimore in 1783 the bottom four-tenths of the inhabitants held zero percent of the total wealth; the top tenth, sixty-five percent.
7. Schulte Nordholt, *The Dutch Republic*, pp. 259–62.

8. Iredell, J., in *Chisholm* v. *Georgia,* 2 Dallas (U.S.) 419, 448 (1793).
9. Henry Steele Commager, *The Empire of Reason* (Garden City, N.J., 1977), p. xi.
10. See the note by Julian P. Boyd in *TJP,* II, 305-24, 495-607, 663-64; Dumas Malone, *Jefferson and His Time* (6 vols.), Boston, 1948-81), I, 261-63, 269-73; Merrill Peterson, *Thomas Jefferson and the New Nation* (New York, 1970), pp. 124-33.
11. Hening, *Statutes,* IX, 226, 227. For the treatment of the eldest son's double portion in Pennsylvania and Massachusetts, see Nevins, *American States,* pp. 442-43. For Connecticut, see Toby L. Ditz, *Property and Kinship: Inheritance in Early Connecticut, 1750-1820* (Princeton, 1986). A conspectus of the subject is provided by Stanley N. Katz, "Republicanism and the Law of Inheritance in the American Revolutionary Era," *Michigan Law Review,* LXXVI (1977), 1-29. In a family-oriented farm society, despite partible succession, male parents normally retained legal control of a sizable portion of the family estate during their lifetime. See Greven, *Four Generations;* Gross, *The Minutemen.* For Charles Pinckney's eloquent tribute to the pervasive influence of these egalitarian reforms in his speech at the federal Convention, see *RFC,* IV, 34-35.
12. Smaller entails, those under £200 could be broken by a writ of *ad quod damnum* from the Secretary's office. The cost for docking entails after 1767 was £2, along with an additional £2 for every £100 of value of an estate below £500, and £1 for each £100 above that amount. *Virginia House Journal, 1766-1769,* p. 113.
13. Robert E. and B. Katherine Brown, *Virginia, 1705-1786: Democracy or Aristocracy?* (East Lansing, Mich., 1964). See also Richard B. Morris, *Studies in the History of American Law* (repr. 1930 ed., Philadelphia, 1959), ch. 11; Clarence R. Keim, "The Influence of Primogeniture and Entail in the Development of Virginia" (Ph.D. dissertation, University of Chicago, 1926); and Elisha P. Douglass, *Rebels and Democrats* (Chapel Hill, N.C., 1955), pp. 300-02.
14. See Beverley Bond, Jr., *The Quit-Rent System in the American Colonies* (New Haven, 1919), p. 20; Nevins, *American States,* p. 444.
15. See Kent, *Commentaries,* p. 20.
16. See below, chapter IX, The West and the Mississippi.
17. *JCC,* XX, 429-47.
18. See, e.g., Beatrice G. Rubens, "Pre-Emptive Rights in the Disposition of Confiscated Estates," *WMQ,* XXII (1965), 435, et seq. Harry B. Yoshpe, *The Disposition of Loyalist Estates in the Southern District of New York* (New York, 1939), pp. 100, et seq.; Richard D. Brown, "The Confiscation and Disposition of Loyalists' Estates in Suffolk County, Massachusetts," *WMQ,* XXI (1964), 534-50; David Maas, "The Return of the Massachusetts Loyalists" (Ph.D. dissertation, University of Wisconsin, 1972).
19. For the general problem see William E. Nelson, "Emerging Notions of Modern Criminal Law in the Revolutionary Era: An Historical Perspective," *New York University Law Review,* XLII (1967), 450-58; Douglas Greenberg, *Crime and Law Enforcement in the Colony of New York, 1691-1776* (Ithaca, N.Y., 1976), p. 223; Kathryn Pryor, "Crime, the Criminal Law, and Reform in Post-Revolutionary Virginia," *Law and History,* I (1981), 53-85. For Beccaria in America, see Paul

M. Spurlin, "Beccaria's Essay on Crimes and Punishment in Eighteenth-Century America," *Studies on Voltaire in the Eighteenth Century*, XXVII (1961), 1489.

20. Caleb Patterson, *The Constitutional Principles of Thomas Jefferson* (Austin, Tex., 1953), p. 21.

21. *TJP*, II, 492–507, "A Bill for Proportioning Crimes and Punishments in Cases Heretofore Capital." Thomas Jefferson Randolph, ed., *Memoir, Correspondence, and Miscellanies, from the Papers of Thomas Jefferson* (2d ed., 4 vols., Boston, 1830), I, 120–33.

22. Pennsylvania Constitution of 1776, ch. 38, *The Statutes at Large of Pennsylvania, from 1682 to 1809*, in James T. Mitchell and Henry Flanders, comps. (17 vols., n.p., 1896–1915), XII, 280.

23. *Ibid.*

24. See Lyman Butterfield's introduction to his two-volume edition of Rush's *Letters* (Philadelphia, 1951); H. G. Good, *Benjamin Rush and His Services to American Education* (Berne, Ind., 1918); Commager, *Empire*, pp. 21–23.

25. Negley King Teeters, *They Were in Prison: A History of the Pennsylvania Prison Society, 1787–1937* (Philadelphia, 1937); Harry Elmer Barnes, *The Evolution of Penology in Pennsylvania* (Indianapolis, 1927), pp. 86–91. *Pennsylvania Stat. at Large*, XII, 245, 247.

26. Nevins, *American States*, pp. 454–55. For the experiment of Massachusetts with its first prison in 1785, see A. Hersh, "From Pillory to Prison: The Rise of Criminal Incarceration in Early Massachusetts," *Michigan Law Review*, LXXX (1982), 1179. For the implementation of hard labor in Boston's Castle Island by the legislation of 1785, see *Perpetual Laws of Massachusetts* (Worcester, 1788), I, 228–31. At least until 1785 one investigator finds that in Massachusetts servitude was imposed more frequently than was hard labor in the house of correction. Linda Kealey, "Patterns of Punishment: Massachusetts in the Eighteenth Century," *American Journal of Legal History*, XXX (1986), 171–76. For the Richmond, Virginia, penitentiary, authorized in 1796, see Paul W. Keve, *The History of Corrections in Virginia* (Charlottesville, 1986).

27. See Morton J. Horwitz, *The Transformation of American Law, 1780–1860* (Cambridge, Mass., 1977); William E. Nelson, *Americanization of the Common Law* (Cambridge, Mass., 1975); Lawrence M. Friedman, *A History of American Law* (New York, 1973), pp. 181, 182. For the liberalization of divorce law in Pennsylvania, see T. R. Meehan, "Not Made Out of Liberty: Evolution of Divorce in Early Pennsylvania," *PMHB*, XCII (1968), 441–64; in Massachusetts, Nancy F. Cott, "Divorce and the Changing Status of Women in 18th Century Massachusetts," *WMQ*, XXXIII (1976), 586, et seq.; *Massachusetts Acts and Resolves, 1784–86*, pp. 564–67; in Connecticut, Henry S. Cohen, "Connecticut's Divorce Mechanism, 1636–1969," *American Journal of Legal History*, XIV (1970), 43. For the use of referees under New York's Citation Act of 1782, see Goebel, *Hamilton Law Practice*, I, 199–200. Richard B. Morris, "Legalism *versus* Revolutionary Doctrine in New England," *New England Quarterly* IV (1931), 195–215, at p. 215; George Dargo, *Law in the New Republic: Private Law and the Public Estate* (New York, 1983), pp. 8–9.

28. The disqualification in the Maryland Constitution barring Jews from public

office was not removed until 1825; Rhode Island, not until the adoption of the state constitution in 1842, and North Carolina not until 1868. Richard Price was in error when he reported in his *Observations on the Importance of the American Revolution* that the new American states were "perfect strangers to such establishments." See Anthony Lincoln, *Some Political and Social Ideas of English Dissent* (repr., New York, 1971), pp. 101, et seq.

29. See Leonard W. Levy, *The Establishment Clause: Religion and the First Amendment* (New York, 1986); Thomas J. Curry, *The First Freedoms: Church and State in America to the Passage of the First Amendment* (New York, 1986). See also Wood, *American Republic*, pp. 427-29.

30. James Madison to James Monroe, May 29, 1785, *MP*, VIII, 286.

31. Illinois Historical Society, *Collections*, XXV, xxxii, ccclxiv-ccclxv, ccclxxi; B. H. Hibbard, *A History of the Public Land Policies* (New York, 1924), p. 58.

32. Curry, *First Freedoms*, pp. 221-22.

33. Zephaniah Swift, *A System of the Laws of the State of Connecticut* (2 vols., Windham, Conn., 1795-96), I, 219.

34. Morris, *Government and Labor*, pp. 324-25n.; A. Roger Ekirch, "Bound for America," *WMQ* (1985), 188; A. E. Smith, *Colonists in Bondage* (Chapel Hill, N.C., 1947); Kenneth Morgan, "The Organization of the Convict Trade in Maryland," *WMQ* (1985), 202.

35. Morris, *Government and Labor*, p. 336; Walter Galenson, *White Servitude in Colonial America*, pp. 124-25; *JJ*, II, 572-73n., 583.

36. See Morris, *Government and Labor*, pp. 345-54.

37. *South Carolina Stat.*, V, 279 (1795); *South Carolina Acts of 1847* (Columbia, S.C., 1848), pp. 436, 437; *North Carolina Code* (Durham, N.C., 1939), sect. 276. Contrariwise, Virginia in the Confederation and early national years subjected the putative father to a jail term unless he posted security or declared himself insolvent. *Virginia Calendar of Acts, 1776-1801* (Richmond, Va., 1792), p. 183.

38. Thus, cf. *Pennsylvania Packet*, January 3, 1798, with *Massachusetts Centinel*, September 22 and October 20, 1784, *North Carolina State Records*, XXIV, 898 (1787).

39. See Pole, *Pursuit of Equality*, pp. 112, 113.

40. Laurence H. Tribe, *American Constitutional Law: A Structure for Liberty* (Mineola, N.Y., 1978), p. 574.

41. See Benjamin J. Klebaner, "Pauper Auctions: The New England Method of Public Poor Relief," Essex Institute *Historical Collections*, XCI (1955), 1-16.

42. *South Carolina Stat.*, V, 43, sect. 6 (1787). See also Richard B. Morris, "White Bondage in Ante-Bellum South Carolina," *South Carolina Historical and Genealogical Review*, XLIX (October 1948), 191-207.

43. *Georgia Colonial Records*, XIX, Part 2 (1774), p. 805; (1782), pp. 165-66; (1786), p. 376.

44. *New York Colonial Laws*, III, 645 (writer's italics).

45. See Richard B. Morris, ed., *A Letter from Henry Laurens to His Son John Laurens, August 14, 1776* (New York, 1964).

46. *TJP*, I, 383.

47. Cf. Dumas Malone, *Jefferson the Virginian* (Boston, 1948), p. 141, with A. Leon Higginbotham, Jr., *In the Matter of Color* (New York, 1978).

48. *TJP*, I, 314–15.

49. See Francis S. Philbrick, *The Rise of the West* (New York, 1965), pp. 125–27.

50. See, e.g., Winthrop D. Jordan, *White Over Black* (Chapel Hill, N.C., 1968), pp. 130–36; Donald L. Robinson, *Slavery in the Structure of American Politics, 1765–1820* (New York, 1971), pp. 88–97 passim; David Brion Davis, *The Problem of Slavery in the Age of Revolution, 1770–1823* (Ithaca, N.Y., 1975), pp. 166–67, 174–85; Edmund S. Morgan, *American Slavery, American Freedom: The Ordeal of Colonial Virginia* (New York, 1974); William M. Wiecek, *The Sources of Antislavery Constitutionalism in America, 1760–1848* (Ithaca, N.Y., 1977); William W. Freehling, "The Founding Fathers and Slavery," *American Historical Review*, LXXVII (1972).

51. See Robert McColley, *Slavery and Jeffersonian Virginia* (Urbana, Ill., 1964), p. 3; Bernard Sheehan, *Seeds of Extinction: Jeffersonian Philanthropy and the American Indian* (Chapel Hill, N.C., 1977); Robert W. Fogel and Stanley Engerman, *Time On the Cross: The Economics of American Negro Slavery* (2 vols., Boston, 1974). On the quasi-freedom of slaves in the South, see Richard B. Morris, "The Measure of Bondage in the Slave States," *Mississippi Valley Historical Review*, XLI (1954), 219–40.

52. Fredrika T. Schmidt and Barbara R. Willhelm, "Early Pro-slavery Petitions in Virginia," *WMQ*, XXX (1973), 133–46; Allan Kulikoff, *Tobacco and Slaves: The Development of Southern Culture in the Chesapeake, 1680–1800* (Chapel Hill, 1986), pp. 433–34.

53. Richard B. Morris, "The Course of Peonage in a Slave State," *PSQ*, LXV (1950), 260–62.

54. See William O'Brien, "Did the Jennison Case Outlaw Slavery in Massachusetts?", *WMQ*, XXII (1960), 219–41; John D. Cushing, "The Cushing Court and the Abolition of Slavery in Massachusetts," *American Journal of Legal History*, V (1961), 118–43.

55. See Arthur Zilversmit, *The First Emancipation: The Abolition of Slavery in the North* (Chicago, 1967), pp. 146–50; Edgar J. McManus, *A History of Negro Slavery in New York* (Syracuse, N.Y., 1966), pp. 163–66, 175n.

56. Pennsylvania Abolitionist Society, ser. 1, reel 2, Minutes, July 2, 1787, Pennsylvania Historical Society.

57. See editorial note, John Jay, Anti-Slavery, and the New York Manumission Society, in "JJ, III."

58. Jacob E. Cooke, *Tench Coxe and the Early Republic* (Chapel Hill, N.C., 1978), p. 149; *Annals of Congress*, 1st Cong., 2d sess., 1197–1205, 1412–15, 1474.

59. On a possible deal over this issue, see Staughton Lynd, *Class Conflict, Slavery, and the United States Constitution* (Indianapolis, 1967).

60. Leon F. Litwack, *North of Slavery* (Chicago, 1961).

61. Michael Mullin, ed., *American Negro Slavery: A Documentary History* (Columbia, S.C., 1976), p. 126. Legislation in the Upper South in the Confederation years placed the free blacks in jeopardy by providing that they could be hired out or sold for default on tax payments. See, e.g., Virginia act of 1782, c. xxi. Such

laws were reenacted down to the Civil War, with the Richmond Hustings Court providing abundant examples of enforcement.

62. *RFC,* I, 316; II, 321. Madison had Georgia specifically in mind as a violator of treaties with the Indians in his "Preface to Debates," *ibid.,* III, 548. Indeed, Georgia's prompt ratification of the Constitution seemed to have been sparked by its recognition that an "effective Government" would give Georgians aid against the Creeks. Randolph C. Downey, "Creek-American Relations, 1782–1790," *Georgia Historical Quarterly,* XXI (1937), 172–73.

63. Marshall, *C. J.,* in *Worcester* v. *Georgia* (6 *Peters* 559). See also Felix S. Cohen, *Handbook of Indian Law* (Charlottesville, Va., 1982), pp. 209–28.

64. The exclusion of Indians and blacks from voting in the draft Constitution of 1778 was a target of criticism in Massachusetts towns and the provision was dropped from the 1780 document. See W. Paul Adams, *First American Constitutions,* pp. 81, 184–88; Handlin, ed., *Popular Sources of Political Authority,* pp. 192, 231–32, 248–49.

65. See Reginald Horsman, "American Indian Policy in the Old Northwest, 1783–1800," *WMQ,* XVIII (1961), 35–53.

66. For example, the Massachusetts Act of 1786 proscribing Indian-white marriages proved a model for later New England legislation. See Alden T. Vaughan, "From White Man to Redskin," *American Historical Review,* LXXXVII (1982); Horsman, "American Indian Policy," see n. 65, p. 49; Daniel J. Boorstin, *The Lost World of Thomas Jefferson* (New York, 1948), ch. 2; Bernard Sheehan, *Seeds of Distinction: Jeffersonian Philanthropy and the American Indian* (Chapel Hill, N.C., 1975).

67. Randolph C. Downes, *Council Fires on the Upper Ohio* (Pittsburgh, 1969), pp. 271–74; Milo M. Quaife, "The Ohio Company of 1782," *Mississippi Valley Historical Review,* XVII (1930–31), 519.

68. Knox's recommendation in '86, coincident with Shays' Rebellion, has been labeled disingenuous. A secret report, unanimously approved by Congress, advises that the troops be used "chiefly in the eastern states" in case they had to protect the Springfield Arsenal, a target of the Shaysites, before being "moved to the western country." *Secret Journals of the Acts and Proceedings of Congress, Domestic Affairs* (4 vols., Boston, 1821), I, 267–70. In fact, intervention of federal troops in Massachusetts was never needed. Joseph P. Warren, "The Confederation and Shays' Rebellion," *AHR,* XI (1901), 41–67; Richard B. Morris in Daniel Aaron, ed., *America in Crisis* (New York, 1952), pp. 40–41. For Knox's call in 1787, see *JCC,* XXXII, 65–69.

69. Morris, *Peacemakers,* pp. 462–63; Barbara Graymont, *The Iroquois in the American Revolution* (Syracuse, N.Y., 1972), p. 259; Wilcomb E. Washburn, *The Indian in America* (New York, 1975), pp. 146–65. On the controversial issue as to whether the cession was made to Congress or to the states, see Joseph Story, *Commentaries on the Constitution of the United States* (3 vols., Boston, 1833), secs. 198–217, 229–42; more recently, Francis S. Philbrick, *The Rise of the West, 1754–1830* (New York, 1965), p. 114.

70. *JCC,* XI, 174–77.

71. *Ibid.,* IX, 846. Article XIV of the Dickinson draft gave Congress the authority

to purchase any Indian lands "for the general benefit of the United colonies." Authority to determine colony boundaries was asserted in Dickinson's draft, Article XVIII. The latter proposition was opposed by the landed states, but Jefferson, a Virginia delegate, was prepared to grant Congress the right to purchase Indian lands "not within the boundaries of any Colony." *Ibid.*, VI, 1076.

72. *Ibid.*, XXV, 602.
73. Gaillard Hunt, ed., *The Writings of James Madison* (9 vols., New York, 1900–10), I, 109–10; Franklin B. Hough, *Proceedings of the Commissioners of Indian Affairs* (Albany, N.Y., 1861), pp. 21, 22. Later, in *The Federalist*, when Madison was anxious to emphasize the weaknesses of the Confederation government under the Articles, he took a more ambivalent position.
74. Graymont, *Iroquois in the American Revolution*, pp. 259, et seq. On the Treaty of Fort Stanwix and the Phelps–Gorham Purchase, see Anthony F.C. Wallace, *The Death and Birth of the Seneca* (New York, 1970), pp. 173–74.
75. See Francis P. Prucha, *American Indian Policy in the Formative Years: The Indian Trade and Intercourse Acts, 1790–1834* (Lincoln, Nebr., 1962). Indeed, prior to the formal adoption of the Articles of Confederation, Congress had entered into a treaty with the Delaware Nation in 1778, providing passage through their lands and securing soldiers for the Continental Army, in return for which Congress guaranteed the territorial rights of the Delaware Nation and promised to abide by the existing British treaties with the Indians.
76. *JCC*, XXI, 491; Prucha, *American Indian Policy*, p. 36; Horsman, *loc. cit.*, pp. 16–31.
77. *JCC*, XXXII, 176 (April 13, 1787).
78. Marshall, C. J., in *Worcester* v. *Georgia*, 31 U.S. at 559 (1832). It is the argument of claimants in current Indian litigation that the supremacy clause applied to the Confederation treaties and invalidated respectively state acts inconsistent with and passed subsequently to such treaties. See Chase, *J.* in *Ware* v. *Hylton* (3 Dall. U.S.) 199 (1976) at 236–37. See also *Joint Brief of Appellants, Oneida Indian Nation of Wisconsin, Oneida of the Thames Band, and Oneida Indian Nation of New York* v. *State of New York* et al., U.S. Court of Appeals 7616 (1985); 691 Fed. 2d 1070.
79. *JCC*, XXXII, 340–41.
80. 1 *U.S. Stat.*, 137.
81. Horsman, *loc. cit.*, pp. 35–53.
82. George Bryan, "Account of the Adoption of the Constitution," Bryan Mss., Historical Society of Pennsylvania, Philadelphia.
83. Thus, the Twenty-Fifth Amendment on the presidential succession, ratified as recently as 1967, employs the male pronoun throughout to describe the office of the presidency.
84. Thomas Jefferson to Martha Jefferson, November 28, 1783, and Thomas Jefferson to Nathaniel Burwell, March 14, 1818, *TJP*, VI, 359–61; and Paul Leicester Ford, ed., *The Writings of Thomas Jefferson* (10 vols., letterpress ed., New York, 1892–99), IX, 151, 193.

85. Thomas Jefferson to Albert Gallatin, January 13, 1807, Ford, ed., *Writings*, IX, 7.
86. Thomas Jefferson to Nathaniel Burwell, March 14, 1818, *ibid.*, X, 104–06.
87. "Warren-Adams Letters," Massachusetts Historical Society *Collections*, LXXII (1917), 361, et seq.; LXXIII (1925), 380. See also Abigail Adams to John Adams, March 31 and May 7, 1776, in Butterfield, et al., eds., *Adams Family Correspondence* I, 370, 402–03. Margaret Livingston to Catharine W. Livingston, October 20, 1776, Ridley Papers, Massachusetts Historical Society.
88. John Adams to James Sullivan, *JAW*, IX, 375–78.
89. Article I, section 2, provides that the representatives shall be chosen by the electors of each state having the qualifications of the electors of the most numerous branch of the state legislature.
90. See Joan Hoff-Wilson and Albert L. Sachs, *Sexism and the Law: A Study of Male Beliefs and Legal Bias in Britain and the United States* (New York, 1979), pp. 417–19. Examples may be cited from Samuel A. Bates, ed., *Records of the Town of Braintree, 1640 to 1793* (Randolph, Mass., 1886), p. 509; W. A. Davis, *The Old Records of the Town of Fitchburg* (6 vols., Fitchburg, Mass., 1898), I, 39, 115, 214, 280; A. A. Lowell, *Worcester in the War of the Revolution* (Worcester, Mass., 1876), p. 116; Worcester Society of Antiquity *Bulletin*, XVI (1898), 373–78, 451, 452. For women voting on church matters, see Edward J. Brandin, *The Records of the Town of Cambridge, Massachusetts, 1693–1702* (Cambridge, Mass., 1930), pp. 68, 69; Francis E. Blake, *History of the Town of Princeton, Massachusetts* (2 vols., Princeton, Mass., 1915), I, 136. See also Rosemary S. Keller, *Abigail Adams and the American Revolution* (New York, 1982), pp. 160, 161. Focusing on women's control over property in seven colonies and states, Marylynn Salmon in *Women and the Law of Property in Early America* (Chapel Hill, 1986) argues that the law prior to the Revolution assumed that women would remain dependent and subservient after marriage, while documenting the steady extension of women's property rights in the post-Revolutionary decades.
91. Examples from Virginia are found in C. Bayley, *Popular Influence on Public Policy: Petitioning in Eighteenth Century Virginia* (Westport, Conn., 1979), p. 44.
92. *Result of the Convention of Delegates Holden at Ipswich in the County of Essex* (Newburyport, Mass., 1778), pp. 28, 29. Of all the Massachusetts towns, Northampton alone considered it necessary to explain why "infants" and "women" were excluded, defending its position with a summary reference to Locke's treatment of "paternal power" and to the *Essex Result*. Handlin, ed., *Popular Sources*, p. 36. The 1780 Constitution retained the exclusion of women found in the rejected instrument of 1778. *Ibid.*, pp. 451, 455.
93. Mary Philbrick, "Women's Suffrage in Revolutionary New Jersey," New Jersey Historical Society *Proceedings*, LVII (1939), 87–98.
94. This merely conformed to colonial practice. See Albert E. McKinley, *The Suffrage Franchise in the Thirteen English Colonies in America* (Philadelphia, 1905), p. 473; Eleanor M. Boatwright, "The Role and Civil Status of Women in Georgia, 1783–1830," *Georgia Historical Quarterly*, XXX (1941), 301–24.
95. The issue has been probed in a number of recent studies on women's role in

the period, including Linda K. Kerber, *Women of the Republic: Intellect and Ideology in Revolutionary America* (Chapel Hill, N.C., 1980), chs. 7, 9; Nancy Cott, *Bonds of Womanhood: Women's Place in New England, 1786–1835* (New Haven, 1977); and Suzanne Lebsock, *The Free Women of Petersburg: Status and Culture in a Southern Town, 1784–1860* (New York, 1984). For the advance of the education of girls and women in these years, see Thomas Woody, *A History of Women's Education in the United States* (2 vols., New York 1929); Lawrence A. Cremin, *American Education: The Colonial Experience, 1607–1783* (New York, 1970), pp. 440, 507, 609.

96. See note 27 above.

Chapter 8. In Diplomacy: Friction and Frustration

1. Statement of Jay's election and his oath as Secretary for Foreign Affairs, May 7, 1784–December 21, 1784, is in PCC 195 and in "JJ, III."

2. The act, first limited to a period of one year, was renewed in 1786 without limit. Resolution of September 7, 1785, *JCC*, XXIX, 685; "JJ, III."

3. On April 4, 1785 Congress authorized a two-year lease for the Department of Foreign Affairs and the War Office at Fraunces' Tavern (*JCC*, XXVIII, 208, 228). Jay removed his office to Gilbert Livingston's on lower Broadway in May 1788. See Jay and Henry Knox to the Board of Treasury, February 1, 1788, in PCC 120, II and "JJ, III."

4. *JCC*, XXVII, 687 (December 15, 1784); XXVIII, 36–37, (February 2, 1785); 56–57 (February 11, 1785).

5. Since Congress lacked the power to enforce treaty obligations on the states, a point which the American negotiators made clear to their British counterparts, it has been argued that they entered into these provisions with "clear consciences." James B. Scott, in Samuel Flagg Bemis, ed., *American Secretaries of State and Their Diplomacy* (New York, 1927), I, 98–99. Some state courts did take cognizance of these provisions, as did the later United States Supreme Court.

6. See Emory Evans, "Private Indebtedness and the Coming of the Revolution in Virginia," *WMQ*, XIX (1962), 511–35; Isaac Harrell, *Loyalism in Virginia* (Durham, N.C., 1926), pp. 81–83; Philip A. Crowl, *Maryland During and After the Revolution* (Baltimore, 1943), p. 65. For a recent examination of the debt question, see Charles F. Hobson, "The Recovery of British Debts in the Federal Circuit Court of Virginia, 1790 to 1797," *Virginia Magazine of History and Biography*, XCII (1984), 176–200.

7. A veritable mine of information on these claims and their disposition is found in the Audit Office Papers in the Public Record Office, including the documentation provided by John Anstey on his trip to the States in 1787–88. Transcripts of these claims are in the New York Public Library. See New York Public Library *Bulletin*, III, 416; IV, 7, 388. See also J. Eardly-Wilmot, *Historical View of the Commission . . . for Enquiring into the Losses, Services, and Claims of the American Loyalists* (London, 1815). The claims are also examined in Wallace Brown, *The King's Friends* (Providence, R.I., 1966), the methodology of which has been

criticized by Eugene Fingerhut, "Uses and Abuses of the American Loyalists' Claims: A Critique of Quantitative Analysis," *WMQ*, XXV (1968), 245–58. A comprehensive and balanced treatment of the Loyalists during the war is found in Robert M. Calhoon, *The Loyalists in Revolutionary America, 1760–1781* (New York, 1965).

8. For legislation, see Claude H. Van Tyne, *The Loyalists in the American Revolution* (New York, 1902), Appendices B and C.

9. In Massachusetts, Loyalist estates were confiscated not in response to public clamor for redistribution of property but to permit the creditors of Loyalists to recover just debts. Richard H. Brown, "Confiscation and Disposition of Loyalist Estates in Suffolk County, Massachusetts," *WMQ*, XXI (1964), 549–50. See Oscar Zeichner, "The Rehabilitation of Loyalists in Connecticut," *New England Quarterly*, XI (1938), 308–30, where the laws against the Loyalists were repealed before the close of 1783 and all laws repugnant to the Treaty of Peace repealed in 1787. Similarly, Massachusetts two years earlier; *Massachusetts Centinel*, February 9, 1785. See also *Laws of New Hampshire* (10 vols., Durham, N.C., 1904–22), IV, 177–80.

10. Oscar Zeichner, "The Loyalist Problem in New York after the Revolution," *New York History*, XXII (1940), 284–302.

11. See *HP*, III, 483–97, 530–58.

12. Zeichner, *loc. cit.*, pp. 297–302.

13. Brunhouse, *Counter-Revolution in Pennsylvania*, pp. 40–41.

14. *Ibid.*, pp. 154–55, 179, 181, 197.

15. Isaac S. Harrell, *Loyalism in Virginia; Chapters in the Economic History of the Revolution* (Durham, N.C., 1926), pp. 136–40; W. W. Hening, *The Statutes at Large* (13 vols., New York, 1819–23) XI, 324–25.

16. Christopher Gadsden to Francis Marion, November 17, 1782, in Bancroft Collection, New York Public Library.

17. Jensen, *New Nation*, pp. 276, 277.

18. Richard Walsh, *Charleston's Sons of Liberty: A Study of the Artisans, 1763–1789* (Columbia, S.C., 1959), pp. 111–23.

19. On the difficulties confronting Loyalists in judicial proceedings to recover post-treaty confiscated property, see W. E. Niles, "The American Revolution and the Emergence of Modern Doctrines of Federalism and Conflict of Laws," Col. Soc. of Mass., *Publications*, LXII (1984), 445–48. See also Van Tyne, *Loyalists*, pp. 269–95.

20. Pomerantz, *New York*, p. 91.

21. See, e.g., John Adams to John Jay, June 6, 1785; *JAW*, VIII, 259–61; *DC*, IV, 203–07.

22. On differing interpretations of historians regarding British intentions in this area, whether a desire to hold on to the fur trade or to set up a buffer state, see Alfred L. Burt, *The United States, Great Britain and British North America from the Revolution to the Establishment of Peace After the War of 1812* (repr. 1940 ed., New York, 1961)

23. *JJ*, II, 432.

24. *JCC*, XXVI, 30–31. See, e.g., William Livingston to Jay, June 15, 1786, wherein

New Jersey's Governor advised his son-in-law: "I do not know of a single instance in which the state has not strictly complied with the said proclamation of Congress as well as with the said recommendation as far as by the said treaty the United States was bound to comply with such." *DC*, V, 287.

25. The full report, which includes Adams's correspondence with Jay on the subject of treaty enforcement and Jay's state–by–state analysis, will be found in *JCC*, XXXI, 781–884.

26. Jay's report to Congress, April 6, 1787, *JCC*, XXXII, 177–84; *DC*, V, 105–13, "JJ, III."

27. Endorsement on Jay's April 6, 1787 report: "April 13th, 1787, agreed to unanimously." PCC 81, 213–25.

28. See Richard B. Morris, *John Jay, the Nation, and the Court* (Boston, 1967), pp. 73–96.

29. *Ibid.*, pp. 73–102; Hobson, *loc cit.*, pp. 187–200. Justice Chase in *Ware* v. *Hylton,* 3 U.S. (Dall.) 199 (1976) at 236–37, would have applied the treaty retrospectively, while other Supreme Court cases inferentially held invalid post-1783 statutes contrary to the treaty. *Owings* v. *Howard's Lessee,* 5 Cranch (9 U.S.) 344 (1809) 348, in which the circuit court decision was revoked on the ground of lack of clear title by the plaintiff in 1794, the year of the Jay Treaty, which protected the rights of British subjects to lands held in America at that time.

30. Temple to Carmarthen, December 7, 1786, "JJ, III."

31. Douglas Brymner, ed., *Canadian Archives* (1890), B, 50, 142. See also Bemis, *Jay's Treaty,* pp. 5–10. For Haldemand's rationale for refusing to evacuate his troops from the frontier posts, see A. L. Burt, "A New Approach to the Problem of the Western Posts," Canadian Historical Association, *Annual Report* (1931).

32. *RDC*, VI, 751n.

33. See below, note 63.

34. Jay to John Adams, September 6, 1785, *DC*, IV, 228–30; *HPJ*, III, 164–67.

35. Jay to Jefferson, July 14, 1786, *DC*, III, 14–16; *TJP*, X, 134–36; *HPJ*, III, 206–07.

36. Arthur St. Clair to Jay, December 13, 1788; Jay to St. Clair, January 28, 1789, both in PCC 120, IV; "JJ, III."

37. See *TJP*, XIX, 469–78.

38. See Philbrick, *Rise of the West*, pp. 158, 159.

39. Morris, *Peacemakers,* pp. 363, 364; John Bassett Moore, *History and Digest of International Arbitrations* (6 vols., Washington, D.C., 1898), I, 19–22; Justin Winsor, ed., *Narrative and Critical History of America* (8 vols., Boston, 1889), VII, 173–74n.

40. *JCC*, XXIX, 828, Resolution of Congress.

41. Jay: Report to Congress, May 8, 1786, *DC*, IV, 475–76; *JCC*, XXX, 243–44; "JJ, III."

42. John Adams to Jay, June 26, 1785, *DC*, IV, 224–27; *JAW*, VIII, 273–76.

43. John Adams to Jay, n.d. December 1785, *DC*, IV, 467–74; "JJ, III."

44. John Adams to Jay, October 21, 25, 1785, both in *DC*, IV, 367–93; *JAW*, VIII, 325–33 (October 21).

45. John Adams to Jay, February 14, 1788, *DC*, V, 357–59; *JAW*, VIII, 475–77.

46. Julian P. Boyd, *Number 7: Alexander Hamilton's Secret Attempt to Control American Foreign Policy* (Princeton, 1964), pp. x, xl.

47. *JCC*, V, 269–87.

48. *BFS*, IX, 3–7.

49. The conventional most-favored-nation privileges were stipulated with an innovation of recent French origin, providing that when a concession to another nation had not been made freely but in return for compensation, such a concession would not extend to the most-favored party, save in return for similar compensation. When Vergennes, in 1783, proposed deleting this exception, he was reassured by Congress "that it will be our constant care to place no people on more advantageous ground than the subjects of his Majesty." In return, Vergennes gave assurances of "perfect reciprocity" on the part of France. Miller, *Treaties*, II, 158–61. See also Vernon G. Setzer, "Did Americans Originate the Conditional Most-favored-nation Clause?", *Journal of Modern History*, V (1933), 319–23.

50. Miller, *Treaties*, II, 123–49.

51. *TJP*, VII, 265–67.

52. Miller, *Treaties*, II, 61–62, 164–65. See also Setzer, *op cit.*, pp. 319–23.

53. J. S. Reeves, "The Prussian-American Treaties," *American Journal of International Law*, XI (1917), 475–89; John Brown Scott, *The Treaties of 1785, 1789, and 1828 Between the United States and Prussia, as Interpreted by Opinions of Attorneys-General, Decisions of Courts, and Diplomatic Correspondence* (New York, 1918). For the recognition of the innovating features of this treaty, see Henry M. Adams, *Prussian American Relations, 1775–1871* (Cleveland, 1960), pp. 20–24. Consular relations were also initiated between the United States and Bremen and Hamburg. Ludwig Beutins, *Bremen und Amerika* (Bremen, 1953), p. 16.

54. John Adams to President of Congress, March 9, 1784, *DC*, II, 101.

55. For the development of trade relations with Russia despite the failure of Catherine II to respond to a treaty proposal, see Nikolai N. Bolkhovitinov, *The Beginnings of Russian-American Foreign Relations, 1775–1815* (Cambridge, Mass., 1975), pp. 94–96.

56. See Baron de Beelen-Bertholff to Jay, September 14, 1785, PCC, 80, I, and see editorial note on non-treaty states in "JJ, III."

57. Jay to Congress, October 11, 1785, *JCC*, XXIX, 824–25.

58. Jay to Congress, May 11, 1786, warning that "the commercial privileges" the United States enjoyed in Portuguese ports could at any time be revoked. *JCC*, XXX, 259–62.

59. "Observations on the Proposed Changes in the Treaty between Your Most Faithful Majesty and the U.S.A," 1786. Colleccao Ministerio dos Negociós Estragueros in Arquivo Nacional de Torre do Tombo, Lisbon.

60. *ASP, Foreign Relations*, I, 127–28.

61. Richard Söderstrom to Jay, September 27, 1785, and Jay to Congress, October 20, 1785, both in PCC 81 and "JJ, III."

62. See Vergennes to Otto, August 25, 1786, *DC*, I, 337 (extract) and George Bancroft, *History of the Formation of the Constitution of the United States of America*

(2 vols., New York, 1882), II, 386–87. See Castries to Vergennes, April 21, 1785; to both Kerey and to Muse, October 23 and 31, 1785; to La Forest, January 7, 1786, AN:CC.

63. Jay to Nathaniel Gorham, August 10, 1786, *DC,* VI, 178–79. See also note 77, chapter IX.

64. See the analysis of Moustier's 300-page report in Richard W. Van Alstyne, *The Rising American Empire* (New York, 1960), pp. 73–74.

65. Montmorin to Moustier, October 10, 1787, CP:EU, 1777–89, I, 421, et seq.

66. Jay to Jefferson, January 19, 1786, *TJP,* IX, 185–86; "JJ, III."

67. Jefferson to Jay, May 23, 1786, *TJP,* IX, 567–69; *DC,* III, 48–52.

68. Jay to Richard Henry Lee, July 29, 1785, in PCC 80. As endorsed thereon, Congress delayed until November 12, 1787, before transmitting "the French papers" on this subject to Jay's office. PCC 120, I.

69. Jefferson to Jay, August 14, 1785, *TJP,* VIII, 374. The foreign officers were less patient than their government. See, e.g., Jefferson to Jay, February 1, 1787, *ibid.,* XI, 101. For a report on Jay's attitude on the payment of the debts, see La Forest to Bureau of Commerce, New York, October 20, 1785, MAE:CC.

70. See Jay to William Bingham, July 17, 1787, and Bingham's reply to Jay, July 19, 1787, in PCC 120, III.

71. See François André Isambert, ed., *Recueil général des anciennes lois françaises* (29 vols., Paris, 1821–33), XXVII, 459.

72. Vernon G. Setser, *The Commercial Reciprocity Policy of the United States, 1774–1829* (Philadelphia, 1937), pp. 88–89.

73. Jay to Jefferson, August 13, 1785, *TJP,* VIII, 369–71n., and X, 100; *DC,* II, 356–57. For Jay's response to a later French edict excluding foreign whale oil, see Jay to John Adams, January 23, 1789, in Massachusetts Historical Society: Adams Papers, XLV, 139.

74. Jefferson to Jay, December 31, 1787, with the enclosure from Claude-Guillaume Lambert, Controller-General, December 29, 1787, *TJP,* XII, 466–71; *New-York Journal,* June 11, 1788. The monopoly was ended in 1791. Jefferson's actions and opinions in intervening against Morris are subject to a critical examination in Jacob M. Price, *France and the Chesapeake: A History of the French Tobacco Monopoly, 1694–1791, and Its Relationship to the British and American Tobacco Trade* (2 vols., Ann Arbor, Mich., 1973), II, 728–88.

75. Jefferson to Jay, February 5, 1786, *TJP,* XII, 564.

76. Jefferson to Jay, April 24, 1788, *ibid.,* XIII, 106. Jay's realism was well founded. Jefferson soon reported that the French in practice were starting to pare down some of the trade privileges only recently granted. Jefferson to Jay, May 23, 1788, *TJP,* XII, 191–92.

77. Miller, *Treaties,* II, 26.

78. See *RDC,* II, 522–32; III, 35; also *JJ,* II, 42n., 467–70.

79. *JCC,* XXI, 792–810, 845; *DC,* I, 284–93.

80. *JCC,* XXV, 846.

81. *DC,* I, 294–304.

82. Jay to Jefferson, July 13, 1785, *TJP,* VIII, 292–93; "JJ, III."

83. *JCC,* XXVII, 685–86.

84. *Ibid.*, XXVIII, 7n., 158n.
85. Morris, *Peacemakers*, pp. 191–210.
86. Jay to Nathaniel Gorham, October 9, 1786, *DC*, I, 331; *JCC*, XXXI, 764–65.
87. Jay to Jefferson, October 27, 1786, *TJP*, X, 488–90; *DC*, III, 113–15. For the possible influence of French Vice-Consul Oster of the port of Philadelphia on clauses 14 and 16 of the Consular Convention, see Oster to la Luzerne, MAE :CC.
88. Jefferson to Jay, November 14, 1788, *DC*, III, 455–507; *TJP*, XIV, 56–62.
89. Moustier report, 1788, AN: AE B III, carton 440, cited in *TJP*, XIV, 63–66.
90. Among the items in AN:CC, Vol. 927, see, e.g., Oster to Castries, Richmond, March 30, 1784; Williamsburg, December 27, 1784; Oster to la Luzerne, Norfolk, November 8, 1787; to Castries, Norfolk, December 6, 1787; la Forest to Castries, New York, September 25, 1786; to la Luzerne, New York, August 16, 1788.
91. Toscan to Castries, Boston, February 5, 1786; Le Tombe to Castries, Boston, October 14, 1786, *ibid.*
92. Oster to Castries, Norfolk, June 7, 1784; also la Forest to Castries, New York, October 10, 1786, *ibid.*
93. Crèvecoeur to the duc d'Harcourt, New York, January 1788, *ibid.*
94. See Oliver Pollock to Jay, June 3, 1785, PCC 120; *DC*, VI, 79–81 (letter only).
95. That Jay had taken a critical position toward the Consular Convention was known to Vergennes fairly soon, and Vergennes hoped that he would be able to take up the proposed revisions of the Convention with Jefferson directly, thereby obviating much correspondence. Vergennes to Otto, December 20, 1785, CP : EU, vol. 30, pp. 461–63. Otto to Jay, October 9, 1786; Jay to Otto, October 12, 1786, PCC 120, II; *DC*, I, 333.
96. See Jay to Sir John Temple, July 5, 1786, *DC*, VI, 29–31; "JJ, III."
97. James Monroe to Jefferson, August 15, 1785, *TJP*, VIII, 383.
98. Jay to Jefferson, October 3, 1786, *DC*, III, 72–73; *TJP*, X, 430–31n.
99. Jefferson to Jay, January 9, 1787, *DC*, III, 197–202; *TJP*, XI, 31.
100. Jefferson to Jay, November 14, 1788, see note 88.
101. *ASP, Foreign Relations*, I, 89–90; II, June 25, 1789; Miller, *Treaties*, II, 228–41. This Convention, along with the two Franco-American treaties of 1778, was abrogated in 1798 by act of Congress. The Treaty of 1800 with France provided merely for the presence in each country of "commercial agents," and ended once and for all the threat posed to the American legal system and U.S. sovereignty by the system of extraterritoriality sanctioned by the Consular Convention. For denial of admiralty jurisdiction to the French consuls, which the latter asserted as having been authorized by the French Consular Convention, see *Glass* v. *the Sloop Betsey*, 3 Dallas 5 (1794); R. B. Morris, *John Jay, the Nation, and the Court* (Boston, 1967), p. 97.
102. See Jacques Godechot, "Les Relations Économiques entre la France et les États-Unis de 1778 à 1789," *French Historical Studies*, I (1958), 26–39; Emory R. Johnson, et al., *History of Domestic and Foreign Commerce of the United States* (2 vols., Washington, D.C., 1915), I, 126.
103. Morris, ed., *Encyclopedia*, p. 703. Imports from Britain, 1783–89, averaged only

10 percent less than the prewar level; exports, on the other hand, declined to 50 percent of the prewar figure. See also Price, *France and the Chesapeake*, II, 786.

104. See James G. Lydon, "Fish and Flour for Gold: Southern Europe and the Colonial American Balance of Payments," *Business History Review*, XXXIV (1965), 182.

105. See Stephen Higginson to John Adams, August 8, 1785, "The Letters of Stephen Higginson," American Historical Association, *Annual Report* (2 vols., Washington, D.C., 1896), I, 723.

106. Committee of Secret Correspondence to Franklin, Deane, Lee, December 21, 1776, *RDC*, II, 230; Miller, *Treaties*, II, 8, 78.

107. *JJ*, II, 578.

108. For reports that "some European powers were encouraging the Algerines to impede American shipping," see John Bondfield, commercial agent at Bordeaux, to Jay, July 28, 1785, PCC 92. See also Ray W. Irwin, *The Diplomatic Relations of the United States with the Barbary Powers, 1776–1816* (Chapel Hill, N.C., 1931), pp. 8–9.

109. For Carmichael's activites, see Samuel G. Coe, *The Mission of William Carmichael to Spain* (Baltimore, 1928), p. 57; also Luella G. Hall, *The United States and Morocco, 1776–1956* (Metuchen, N.J., 1971), pp. 44, et seq.

110. John Paul Jones to Jay, August 6, 1785, *DC*, VII, 317–18, "*JJ*, III." Jay to Congress, October 13, 1785, *HPJ*, III, 170–71; "*JJ*, III"; *JCC*, XXIX, 833–34.

111. Jay to American Commissioners, March 11, 1785, PCC 81 and 121; *TJP*, VII, 19–22.

112. American Commissioners to Jay, London, March 28, 1786, *TJP*, IX, 357–59; *DC*, II, 341–43.

113. Jay to Congress, May 29, 1786, *DC*, II, 343–46; *HPJ*, III, 196–99; "*JJ*, III."

114. Jay to Jefferson, December 14, 1786, *TJP*, X, 596–99; *DC*, III, 133–38.

115. Jay to Congress, August 2, 1787, *JCC*, XXXIII, 451–53; "*JJ*, III."

116. Miller, *Treaties*, II, 185–227.

Chapter 9. The West and the Mississippi

1. "Agrippa," IV (Winthrop), *Massachusetts Gazette*, December 3, 1787.

2. Nathaniel Gorham at the Federal Convention, August 8, 1787, *RFC*, II, 221.

3. Terms which Pennsylvania accepted. *Journal of the Virginia House of Delegates, 1780 Sess.* (Williamsburg, Va., 1780), pp. 60–61; *Pennsylvania Archives*, 1st ser. (12 vols., Philadelphia, 1852–56), VIII, 570–71. For patterns of geographical expansion and settlement in this era, see, most recently, D. W. Meinig, *The Shaping of America* (New Haven, Conn., 1986), I, 348–75.

4. Declaration and Petition, January 15, 1777, *JCC*, VII, 239.

5. Jay to Egbert Benson, August 26, 1782, *JJ*, II, 326 (underscoring Jay's). For a recent treatment of the role of Congress in the Vermont controversy, see Peter S. Onuf, *The Origins of the Federal Republic* (Philadelphia, 1983), pp. 127–45; *JJ*, I, 410–11, 655–56; II, 73–74, 326–27. See also Hiland Hall, *The History of Vermont* (New York, 1868), pp. 329–36.

6. For the Hamilton-Chittenden correspondence, see *HP*, V, 161–62, 186–87, 211–12, 218–20.

7. *Report of the Regents of the State of New York on the Boundaries of the State of New York*, prepared by Daniel J. Pratt (2 vols., Albany, N.Y., 1884), II, 100–44, 147–51, 212–13; Goebel, *Hamilton Law Practice*, I, 554, et seq.

8. J. D. Richardson, ed., *Compilation of Messages and Papers of the Presidents, 1789–1897* (10 vols., Washington, D.C., 1896–99), I, 9, et seq.

9. A tract east of the line was also awarded Massachusetts as compensation for land in the western area that New York had already sold. *JCC*, XXXIII, 617–29.

10. For the impact of Massachusetts on land settlement in western New York, see Manfred Jonas and Robert V. Wells, eds., *New Opportunities in a New Nation: The Development of New York After the Revolution* (Schenectady, N.Y., 1983), p. 44.

11. The Penn family estates were taken over, one correspondent reminded Lady Juliana Penn, "not in a way of confiscation, but upon principles of policy and expedience." The legislature thought the estate "two [sic] large for a subject to possess, supposing it dangerous to the public that so much property should rest in the hands of one family." James Tilghman to Lady Juliana Penn, Chester Town, Maryland, August 14, 1782, University of Michigan: William L. Clements Library, Shelburne Papers, 72:311.

12. *The Susquehannah Company Papers*, ed. Julian P. Boyd and R. J. Taylor (11 vols., Wilkes-Barre, Pa., 1930–71), VII, 257–58, 244–46. See also Robert J. Taylor, "Trial at Trenton," *WMQ*, XXVI (1969), 521–47.

13. The rights recognized under the Confirming Act were overturned by the federal courts in *Van Horne's Lessee* v. *Dorrance*, 2 Dall. 304 (1795); but the Connecticut settlers were never dispossessed, while Pennsylvanian titleholders were later compensated. Onuf, *Origins*, p. 231n.

14. Schoepf, *Travels*, I, 337.

15. Thomas P. Abernethy, *Western Lands and the American Revolution* (New York, 1937), pp. 346–52; Jensen, *New Nation*, pp. 334–35.

16. See Richard Henderson's address to the Transylvania delegates, May 23, 1775, W. L. Saunders, ed., *North Carolina Colonial Records*, IX (10 vols., Raleigh, N.C., 1886–90), 1268–71.

17. See Thomas P. Abernethy, *From Frontier to Plantation in Tennessee* (Chapel Hill, N.C., 1932), chs. iv–v; S. C. Williams, *History of the Lost State of Franklin* (Johnson City, Tenn., 1924).

18. See T. Donaldson, *The Public Domain* (Washington, D.C., 1884), pp. 82, 86–88.

19. Philbrick, *Rise of the West*, pp. 113, 114.

20. See Story, *Commentaries on the Constitution*, secs. 198–217, 229–42.

21. *JCC*, XVII, 808.

22. Philbrick, *Rise of the West*, p. 116.

23. *JCC*, XVII, 808.

24. Burnett, *Congress*, pp. 98–99. For Virginia's subsequent unrestricted cession (December 1783), see Merrill Jensen, "The Creation of the National Domain, 1781–1784," *Mississippi Valley Historical Review*, XXVI (1939), 323–42.

25. *JCC*, XXVI, 275–79 (April 25, 1784).

26. *Ibid.* For a balanced appraisal of the 1785 Ordinance, see Peter S. Onuf,

"Liberty, Development, and Union: Vision of the West in the 1780s," *WMQ*, XLIII (1986), 179–213.

27. *JCC*, XXXIII, 399–401.

28. For talk in the Northwest of taking action similar to the establishment of the "free state of Franklin," see Arthur B. Hurlburt, ed., *Ohio in the Time of the Confederation* (Marietta, Ohio, 1918), pp. 95–99.

30. King, ed., *Life*, I, 107.

29. See, e.g., Jensen, *New Nation*, pp. 358–59; Philbrick, *Rise of the West*, pp. 126–33, for a critical but balanced account by the preeminent scholar of the subject.

31. Nathan Dane to Rufus King, in King, ed., *Life*, I, 289.

32. Francis S. Philbrick, "The Laws of the Illinois Territory, 1809–1818," Illinois State Historical Society *Collections*, XXV (Law Series V), (1950), cccxi–cccxii.

33. Thorpe, *Constitutions*, II, 957, et seq.

34. Philbrick argues that Congress under the Constitution had no authority to make any compacts binding upon any of the parties mentioned, or to represent the states, "who, alone of the parties mentioned, could enter into compacts." "Laws of the Illinois Territory, 1809–1818," p. cxcvii.

35. *JJ*, II, 97.

36. *Ibid.*, pp. 268–83.

37. *DC*, VI, 65.

38. Article VII, Fred L. Israel, ed., *Major Peace Treaties of Modern History, 1648–1967* (New York, 1967), I, 310.

39. Instructions to Gardoqui, July 25, 1784, AHN Estado leg. 3457; Gardoqui dispatches, V, 205–13, University of Chicago.

40. Morris, *Peacemakers*, pp. 350, 363; retained as the eighth article of the Definitive Treaty, *ibid.*, p. 464.

41. Rendón to José de Gálvez, August 31 and September 30, 1783, AGI: 87/1/7, No. 87.

42. José de Gálvez to Governor ad interim of Louisiana, June 26, 1784, *DC*, I, 136. See also Samuel Flagg Bemis, *Pinckney's Treaty: America's Advantage from Europe's Distress, 1783–1800* (rev. ed., New Haven, 1960), pp. 42–45. *JCC*, XXVII, 688–90, for a copy of the proclamation. In enforcing the proclamation, the Spaniards seized American boats at Natchez and confiscated their cargoes. Late in 1787 the Spaniards replaced the embargo with a tax of 25 percent on American products.

43. See Arthur P. Whitaker, *The Spanish-American Frontier, 1783–95* (rep. Gloucester, Mass., 1962), pp. 90–107.

44. Charles J. Kappler, comp., *Indian Affairs: Laws and Treaties* (Washington, D.C., 1904), p. 12 (treaty with Choctaw), p. 17 (treaty with Shawnee, recognizing the boundaries defined in the Definitive Treaty of 1783).

45. Rendón to José de Gálvez, see note 41 above.

46. *JJ*, I, 717, et seq.

47. See *JJ*, II, 94–95.

48. Dated October 2, 1784, in Manuel Canrotte, *La intervención de España en la independencia de los Estados Unidos de la America del Norte* (Madrid, 1920), pp. 270–76. The instructions explicitly mention Article VI of Jay's draft treaty of

that date, for which see *JJ*, II, 97–98n. See also Whitaker, *Spanish-American Frontier*, pp. 69–72.

49. *JCC*, XXIX, 657–58. The committee recommendation of August 25, 1785, is in *ibid.*, 561–62. The report, in the hand of Monroe, is in PCC 25, II, 441.

50. *ASP, Indian Affairs*, I, 15–17.

51. Resolution of Congress, October 13, 1785, *JCC*, XXIX, 829–30; "*JJ*, III."

52. For Gardoqui's memorial re Georgia boundaries, see Gardoqui to Jay, September 23, 1785, *DC*, VI, 129–31.

53. Gardoqui to Floridablanca, September 3, 1785, AHN Estado leg. 3886.

54. Gardoqui, Notes of a Conference with Jay, [February 1786], AHN Estado leg. 3895; see also Floridablanca to Jay, September 1, 1786, AHN Estado leg. 3884, exp. 8, doc. 34. See also Jay to Gardoqui, October 4, 1785, Jay Papers; "*JJ*, III"; Jay to Charles Thomson, March 3, 1786, Jay Papers; "*JJ*, III"; see also *JCC*, XXX, 95 and note.

55. Jay Papers.

56. Bemis, *Pinckney's Treaty*, p. 79.

57. Gardoqui to Jay, [before May 25] and May 25, 1786, *DC*, VI, 153–57; *JCC*, XXXI, 467–72; "*JJ*, III."

58. Washington to Richard Henry Lee, August 22, 1785, and to William Grayson, *GWF*, XXVIII, 230–34; to David Humphreys, July 25, 1785, pp. 202–05; to Lafayette, July 25, 1785, pp. 205–11; to Rochambeau, September 7, 1785, pp. 255–56; to John de Neufville, September 8, 1785, pp. 258–60; and to Richard Henry Lee, June 18, 1786, pp. 459–61. Crosskey and Jeffrey in their *Politics and the Constitution* stress Washington's backing for Jay's willingness to forbear insisting on the immediate navigation of the Mississippi and attribute it to Washington's interest in developing a connection between the Ohio River and the Atlantic ports.

59. Richard Henry Lee to Washington, in *Lee*, II, 391, 425–27.

60. For Lee's supportive views, see *LMCC*, VIII, 400, 417, 481–82.

61. Edward Rutledge to Jay, November 12, 1786, *HPJ*, III, 216–19.

62. Rufus King to Elbridge Gerry, July 4, 1786, in King, ed., *Life*, I, 177; Robert Ernst, *Rufus King, American Federalist* (New York, 1968), pp. 58–63.

63. See James Monroe to Patrick Henry, August 12, 1786, Monroe, *Writings*, I, 144–51. Earlier, writing to Madison, May 31, 1786, Monroe implied that he had been "apprized upon my first arrival here in the winter" of Jay's plan, *ibid.*, p. 132.

64. Gardoqui to Jay, [before May 25] and May 25, 1786 (see note 57 above), in Jay's Report to Congress, August 3, 1786, *JCC*, XXXI, 467–84; *DC*, VI, 165–77; "*JJ*, III."

65. *JCC*, XXX, 323.

66. *Ibid.*, XXXI, 457 and n. For Monroe's account of the stalemate on the committee, see Monroe to Jefferson, July 16, 1786, in Monroe, *Writings*, I, 141; *TJP*, X, 143. "I have a conviction in my own mind that Jay has managed this negociation dishonestly."

67. Jay, Report to Congress, August 3, 1786, see note 64 above.

68. See William Samuel Johnson's Notes of Debates on the Spanish Treaty, *JCC*, XXXI, 951-53.

69. *Ibid.*, 935-48.

70. *LMCC*, VIII, 429-30; *JCC*, XXXI, 952.

71. Cf. James Monroe to Patrick Henry, August 12, 1786, in Monroe, *Writings*, I, 144-51. Crosskey and Jeffrey, *Politics and the Constitution*, III, 298.

72. Otto to Vergennes, September 10, 1786, in Bancroft, *Formation of the Constitution*, II, 389-93.

73. *LMCC*, VIII, 429; Monroe, *Writings*, I, 145-46.

74. *JCC*, XXXI, 595, 694-97; *LMCC*, VIII, 429-30.

75. *JCC*, XXX, 568-69.

76. Timothy Bloodworth to Richard Caswell, September 4, 1786, *LMCC*, VIII, 462.

77. Jay to President of Congress, August 17, 1786, *JCC*, XXX, 537-52; *DC*, VI, 179-95; "JJ, III."

78. Jay to Arthur St. Clair, April 11, 1787, *DC*, VI, 199-203; *HPJ*, III, 240-43; *JCC*, XXXII, 184-89; "JJ, III." For the North–South voting cleavage on the Jay instructions, see Henderson, *Party Politics*, p. 300 (Table 25).

79. Madison to Jefferson, March 19, 1787, *MP*, IX, 317-22; *TJP*, XI, 219-23. Earlier, Monroe had made the same prediction: Monroe to Madison, August 30, 1786, Monroe, *Writings*, I, 159; *MP*, IX, 109. As a member of the Virginia House of Delegates, Madison on November 29, 1786 had put forth resolutions reaffirming America's rights to the navigation of the Mississippi, which were unanimously adopted. *Ibid.*, 181-84n.

80. Madison's motion of April 18, 1787, *JCC*, XXXII, 204; XXXIII, 734-36; *MP*, IX, 388.

81. Jay, Report to Congress, April 20, 1787, *DC*, VI, 228-32; *JCC*, XXXII, 217-20; "JJ, III."

82. *JCC*, XXXII, 288-89. For Rufus King's role in supporting Jay, see Ernst, *King*, pp. 68-73.

83. For the newspaper clamor over the issue, see Kaminski, ed., *DHRC, Commentaries*, XIII, 152-58.

84. Jay, Report to Congress, April 12, 1787, *DC*, VI, 203-08; *JCC*, XXXII, 189-204; "JJ, III."

85. Resolution of Congress, September 16, 1788, *JCC*, XXXIV, 530-35; "JJ, III."

86. Washington to Jay, July 14, 1789, *GWF*, XXX, 355. Jay to Washington: two draft messages on Spanish negotiations for the U.S. Senate and resolution on suspension of negotiations, [n.d., after July 24, 1789], DLC: Washington. Jay to Gardoqui, July 27, 1789, *DC*, VI, 269-70. For trade with Spain in this period, see Fernando Barreda, *Comercio maritimo entre los Estados Unidos y Santander, 1778-1829* (Santander, Spain, 1950).

Chapter 10. Effective Union or Dismembered States?

1. Hamilton to James Duane, September 3, 1780, *HP*, II, 400-18.

2. *JCC*, III, 236 (March 12, 1781); *MP*, III, 17-20.

3. *JCC*, XIX, 236–73; XX, 469–71, 893–96; Brant, *Madison*, II, 105–09.
4. See "Motion to Amend Articles of Confederation and the Rules of Congress," *MP*, IV, 86, 87 (March 1782).
5. *MP*, VI, 141–54 (January 28, 1783).
6. *New-York Packet*, July 4, 1782; *HP*, III, 105.
7. *MP*, VI, 264–66.
8. *Ibid.*, 264–77.
9. See Henry Tazewell's seven resolutions of May 19, 1784, *MP*, VIII, 38; Madison's bill to grant Congress limited powers to regulate commerce, June 5, 1784, *ibid.*, 57.
10. William MacDonald, ed., *Select Charters and Other Documents Illustrating American History, 1606–1775* (New York, 1906), p. 54; cf. Hening, *Statutes of Virginia*, IX, 118.
11. Madison to Jefferson, March 16, 1784, *MP*, VIII, 12–13; *TJP*, VII, 36–37.
12. Resolution Authorizing an Interstate Compact on Navigation and Jurisdiction on the Potomac, December 28, 1784, *MP*, VIII, 206–07.
13. George Mason to James Madison, August 9, 1785, Robert R. Rutland, ed., *The Papers of George Mason* (3 vols., Chapel Hill, N.C., 1970), II, 826; *GWF, Diaries*, II, 354.
14. For Washington's active role in the Potomac Company, see *Journal of the Virginia House of Delegates*, November 11–18, 1785; Brant, *Madison*, II, 367–69. For Washington's support of Rumsey and Madison's of both inventors, see *ibid.*, 470–71.
15. *Mason Papers*, II, 818. The Virginia resolution of December 28, 1784, cited in note 12, authorized the commissioners to make a representation to the state of Pennsylvania to allow produce or merchandise from Maryland and Virginia to travel through either of the two rivers lying within the limits of Pennsylvania free of duties or tolls as a contribution to the costs of the proposed improvement of navigation. Nothing, however, was said in the instructions about the citizens of other states.
16. Journal of the Virginia House of Delegates, December 5–30, 1785. Hening, *Statutes of Virginia*, XII, 50.
17. James H. Hutson, "Pierce Butler's Records of the Federal Convention," Library of Congress, *Quarterly Journal* (Winter 1980), 64–73.
18. *Documents Illustrative of the Formation of the Union*, pp. 619–20, 626, 654.
19. Charles Pinckney's speech before the New Jersey Assembly, March 13, 1786, *LMCC*, VIII, 319, 321–30.
20. *JCC*, XXX, 387; XXXI, 494–98.
21. The criticisms of the committee's report by Abraham Yates, Jr., are cited in Rakove, *Beginnings*, p. 372.
22. See note by Julian P. Boyd in *TJP*, IX, 206–08.
23. "Notes for Debate on Commercial Regulations by Congress," [November 30–December 1, 1785], *MP*, VIII, 431–32.
24. Madison to Monroe, January 22, 1786, *ibid.*, VIII, 485.
25. *Ibid.*, 476.
26. *Ibid.*, 471; Madison to Jefferson, March 18, 1786, *ibid.*, 472n.; *TJP*, IX, 332–36.

27. The Maryland House of Delegates proposed commissioners, but its action was blocked by the Senate. Daniel Carroll to Madison, March 12, 1786, *MP*, VIII, 496.
28. Jacob Broome to Tench Coxe, September 4, 1786, *LMCC*, VIII, 430.
29. *MP*, IX, 3–24.
30. Thus, cf., Madison to Monroe, March 14–19, 1786, *MP*, VIII, 497–98, 505–06, with Madison to Jefferson, August 12, 1786, *ibid.*, IX, 95–97; *TJP*, X, 229–36.
31. *HP*, III, 110–15, 152–56.
32. *Ibid.*, 420–26.
33. *Ibid.*, 647–49.
34. *Ibid.*, 686–90. The proceedings, which were kept by Egbert Benson, are found in Thomas Addis Emmet, *Annapolis Convention Held in 1786 with the Report of the Proceedings Represented to the States by President John Dickinson* (New York, 1891). The copy of the resolution among the Hamilton Papers in the Library of Congress is signed by the Convention president John Dickinson of Delaware, but curiously, "Js. Madison Jr" is listed below the signature as one concurring in the report. The proceedings show twelve signatories from the five states as signing the resolution. Misc. PCC. The Annapolis Convention papers, now in the National Archives, were turned over by Dickinson in later years to President Jefferson. Dickinson to Jefferson, December 28, 1803, Historical Society of Pennsylvania. Howard H. Wehmann, "The 'Lost' Record of the Annapolis Convention, 1786–1986," *Manuscripts*, XXXVIII (1986) 101–04. It should be noted that the committee that reported the draft resolution included neither Hamilton nor Madison. Its membership comprised Egbert Benson (N.Y.), Abraham Clark (N.J.), Tench Coxe (Pa.), George Read (Del.), and Edmund Randolph (Va.). The attribution to Hamilton of the "Address" was made by James Madison in his preface to the "Notes of Debates of the Constitutional Convention," Madison Papers, Library of Congress, and in Madison to Noah Webster, Oct. 12, 1804, in Hunt, ed., *Writings*, VII, 164–65. An interleaved note in Egbert Benson's hand in his *Memoir, Read Before the Historical Society of the State of New–York, 31st December, 1816* (New York, 1817) ascribes the Annapolis resolution to Hamilton, "although not *formally* a member of the Committee," and notes it received "unanimous assent." For this citation the writer is indebted to John D. Gordan III, Esq. of the New York bar. For the argument that the majority of the delegates in Congress preferred a "national" to a "federal" solution in their response to the Annapolis resolution, and for the differing versions of the state commissions to the Philadelphia Convention, see Crosskey and Jeffrey, *Politics and the Constitution*, III, 376–85.
35. *JCC*, XXII, 71–72 (February 21, 1787).
36. Nathan Dane to Thomas Dwight, February 11, 1786, cited by Robert A. East, "The Massachusetts Conservatives in the Critical Period," in Morris, ed., *The Era of the American Revolution*, p. 349.
37. Taylor, *Western Massachusetts in the Revolution*, pp. 31, 86–91.
38. Handlin, *Commonwealth*, p. 35.
39. Morris, "Insurrection in Massachusetts," in Daniel Aaron, ed., *America in Crisis*, p. 27.

40. Massachusetts Bureau of Statistics and Labor, *16th Annual Report* (Boston, 1885), pp. 160–449.
41. Imprisonment for debt and debt servitude are treated above in chapter VIII.
42. See Morris, *loc. cit.,* note 39 above, p. 24; David P. Szatmary, *Shays' Rebellion: The Making of an Agrarian Insurrection* (Amherst, Mass., 1980), pp. 29–30.
43. Morris, *loc. cit.,* note 39 above, and pp. 27–28. The regional and occupational breakdown of issues like paper money, consolidation of the state debt, the excise system, and debtor relief measures are tabulated in Hall, *Politics Without Parties,* pp. 108–22.
44. Cited by Hall, *Politics Without Parties,* p. 231.
45. Park Holland, "Narrative of the Shays' Rebellion," MS transcribed as an appendix to Joseph P. Warren, "Shays' Rebellion, A Study in the History of Massachusetts" (Ph.D. dissertation, Harvard University, 1900).
46. Jonathan Smith, "The Depression of 1785 and Daniel Shays' Rebellion," *WMQ,* V (1948), 88.
47. Joseph Hawley to Caleb Strong, June 24, 1782, Hawley Papers, Box 2, New York Public Library.
48. Mercy Otis Warren to John Adams, December 1, 1786, cited in East, "The Massachusetts Conservatives," in Morris, ed., *The Era of the American Revolution,* p. 349. She reiterated the same charge many years later in her *History of the American Revolution* (3 vols., Boston, 1805), III, 346. For the problems over whether there was a plot of the military–commercial–political junto to destroy republicanism and crush the "little folks," see Hall, *Politics Without Parties,* pp. 254, 255.
49. George R. Minot, *History of the Insurrections in Massachusetts in the Year MDCCLXXXVI* (Worcester, Mass., 1788), p. 105.
50. See John M. Palmer, *General Von Steuben* (New Haven, 1937), pp. 338, 339, wherein the authorship is confirmed of von Steuben's "Bellisarius" article in the *New-York Daily Advertiser,* November 1, 1786, in which the assembling of federal troops in Massachusetts for use in the "Indian War" was unmasked— troops by the way that Secretary at War Knox had assembled but never used. Robert East seems to stress the connection between von Steuben and William North, the latter busily engaged in seeking funds for federal troops. While solid evidence of a conspiracy is lacking, it is incontestable that nationalists like Knox were exploiting the turmoil for political ends. East, *loc. cit.,* pp. 380–86.
51. See Hall, *Politics Without Parties,* pp. 235–55.
52. Quoted in Robert Becker, "*Salus Populi Supremum Lex:* Public Peace and South Carolina Debtor Relief Laws, 1783 and 1788," *South Carolina Historical Magazine* (1979), 71.
53. John Dawson to Madison, April 15, June 12, 1787, *MP,* IX, 381; X, 47; Madison to Jefferson, September 6, 1787, *MP,* X, 163–65; *TJP,* XII, 103–04.
54. Pierce Butler to Elbridge Gerry, March 3, 1788, Gerry Papers, Library of Congress.
55. Madison, "Notes of Debates," *MP,* II, 47–49; cf. for Madison's "Preface to Debates," *ibid.,* III, 547, for the impact of Shays' Rebellion.

56. William Wiecek, *The Guaranty Clause of the United States Constitution* (Ithaca, N.Y., 1972), pp. 22–42.
57. Washington to David Humphreys, October 22, 1786, *GWF*, XXXIX, 27; to Henry Lee, October 31, 1786, *ibid.*, p. 34. Cf. Madison to Washington, November 5, 1786, *MP*, IX, 161.
58. Washington to Madison, November 5, 1786, *MP*, IX, 161. For a similarly exaggerated description of the goals of the Shaysites, see Henry Lee to Madison, October 19, 1786, *ibid.*, 143. Washington felt, however, that the punitive measures taken by Massachusetts against the insurgents were excessive. Washington to Madison, March 31, 1787, *ibid.*, 342–43.
59. Madison to Washington, February 21, 1787, *MP*, IX, 286.

Chapter 11. Creating a New Constitution

1. The theoretical underpinnings of the Revolutionary generation have inspired a very considerable body of research, especially over the past two decades, including Bernard Bailyn, *The Ideological Origins of the American Revolution* (Cambridge, Mass., 1967); Gordon S. Wood, *The Creation of the American Republic, 1776–1787* (Chapel Hill, N.C., 1969); J. G. A. Pocock, *The Machiavellian Moment* (Princeton, 1975), *Virtue, Commerce, and History* (Cambridge, 1985); John G. Murrin, "The Great Inversion, or Court versus Country," in J. G. A. Pocock, ed., *Three British Revolutions, 1641, 1688, 1776* (Princeton, 1980); James H. Hutson, "Country, Court and Constitution: Anti-Federalism and the Historians," *WMQ*, XXXVIII (1981), 337–68; Robert Shallope, "Toward a Republican Synthesis: The Emergence of an Understanding of Republicanism in American Historiography," *ibid.*, XXIX (1972), 49–80; Isaac Kramnick, "Republican Revisionism Revisited," *AHR*, LXVII (1982), 629–44; Lance Banning, *The Jeffersonian Persuasion: Evolution of a Party Ideology* (Ithaca, N.Y., 1978); Drew R. McCoy, *The Elusive Republic: Political Economy in Jeffersonian America* (Chapel Hill, N.C., 1980); John Patrick Diggins, *The Lost Soul of American Politics: Virtue, Self-Interest, and the Foundations of Liberalism* (New York, 1984); Joyce Appleby, *Capitalism and a New Social Order: The Republican Vision of the 1790s* (New York, 1984); Sean Wilentz, "Artisan Republican Festivities and the Rise of Class Conflict in New York City, 1788–1837," in *Working-Class America*, ed. by M. N. Frish and D. J. Walowitz (Urbana, Ill., 1983), 37–77; and most recently, Forrest McDonald, *Novus Ordo Seclorum: The Intellectual Origins of the Constitution* (Lawrence, Kans., 1985).
2. See John Agresto, " 'A System Without a Precedent': James Madison and the Revolution in Republican Liberty," *South Atlantic Quarterly*, LXXXII (1983), 129–44.
3. *RFC*, III, 14, 15.
4. James McGregor Burns, *Leadership* (New York, 1978), pp. 156, 157.
5. For an illuminating account of the factional strife in that state between the country party—pro paper money—and the mercantilist group, see Irwin H. Polishook, *Rhode Island and the Union* (Evanston, Ill., 1969), pp. 184–89.

6. Henry Knox and James Madison were sending an incessant stream of letters to Washington. *LMCC*, VII, 505n., *MP*, IX, 155, 166, 198, et seq.
7. Washington to Madison, March 31, 1787, *GWF*, XXXIX, 188.
8. Washington to Jay, March 10, 1787, *GWF*, XXIX, 175–77.
9. Washington to Edmund Randolph, March 28, 1787, *GWF*, XXIX, 186–88.
10. Washington made abstracts of Jay to Washington, January 7, 1787 (*HPJ*, III, 226–29; "JJ, III"); Henry Knox to Washington, January 14, 1787 (DLC: Washington); Madison to Washington, April 16, 1787, enclosing Jay's Circular to the States, asserting the nationalistic interpretation of treaties (*MP*, IX, 382–87).
11. The original draft is not extant. A "Pinckney Plan" is found in *RFC*, III, 106–23. Internal evidence suggests that portions were obviously later insertions. For a supportive position on the influence of the Pinckney Plan, see S. Sidney Ulmer, "Charles Pinckney: Father of the Constitution?", *South Carolina Law Quarterly*, X (1958), 225–47; "James Madison and the Pinckney Plan," *ibid.*, IX (1957), 415–44; and most recently, James Lincoln Collier and Christopher Collier, *Decision in Philadelphia* (New York, 1986).
12. *RFC*, I, 493.
13. *Ibid.*, II, 406.
14. Madison to Washington, March 18, 1787, *MP*, IX, 315.
15. *RFC*, I, 17.
16. See *ibid.*, III, 48, 59, 66; IV, 64, 65, 71, 73.
17. Madison to Jefferson, September 6, 1787, *MP*, X, 163–65; *TJP*, XII, 102.
18. William Paterson to Oliver Ellsworth, August 23, 1787, *RFC*, IV, 73.
19. For Luther Martin's later published disclosures, see below, Chapter XII.
20. The Randolph Plan is found in *RFC*, I, 18–23. The Pinckney Plan is referred to in *ibid.*, 23, 24. The accuracy of Madison's copy of the judiciary resolution (*RFC*, I, 95) is scrutinized by Charles F. Hobson, "The Virginia Plan of 1787: A Note on the Original Text," Library of Congress, *Journal*, XXXVII (1980), 201–14.
21. *Ibid.*, 30, 35.
22. *Ibid.*
23. *Ibid.*, 48.
24. *Ibid.*, 48–50.
25. *Ibid.*, 224–39.
26. *Ibid.*, 242–45.
27. For variant versions, see *HP*, IV, 178–211; Pinckney's own version of his speech will be found in *RFC*, IV, 28–37.
28. *RFC*, I, 313, 322.
29. *Ibid.*, 461, 462.
30. *Ibid.*, 468–69. The intemperate Gunning Bedford, Jr. of Delaware went so far as to warn that, if the large states remained adamant, the small states would "find some foreign ally . . . who will take them by the hand and do them justice." Rebuked some days later, he backed away from this extreme posture. *Ibid.*, pp. 489–93, 500–02, 514, 519.
31. *Ibid.*, II, 15, 16.

32. *Ibid.*, I, 205–06. See also Howard A. Ohline, "Republicanism and Slavery: The Origins of the Three-fifths Clause in the United States Constitution," *WMQ*, XVIII (1971), 563–84.

33. *RFC*, II, 8.

34. *Ibid.*, 272. For Madison's explanation to Jefferson, see *ibid.*, III, 135. See also Calvin Jillson and Thornton Anderson, "Voting Bloc Analysis in the Constitutional Convention: Implications for an Interpretation of the Connecticut Compromise," *Western Political Quarterly*, XXXI (December 1978), 535–47.

35. *RFC*, I, 335, 344.

36. See Madison's *Federalist* No. 39 for his subtle distinctions between the federal and national powers of the central government.

37. *RFC*, I, 476 (June 29); 486 (June 30).

38. *Ibid.*, II, 135, cf. p. 157, where the power reads: "to pass Acts for the Regulation of Trade and Commerce as well with foreign Nations as with each other *to lay and collect Taxes.*"

39. *Ibid.*, II, 451.

40. *Ibid.*, 452. The two–thirds vote for navigation laws bounced up again in the first Congress, only to go down to defeat. Linda Grant DePauw *et al.*, eds. *Documentary History of the First Federal Congress, 1789–1791* (Baltimore, 1972–   ), I, 162.

41. *Ibid.*, 183.

42. *Ibid.*, 370.

43. *Ibid.*, 371–73.

44. *Ibid.*, 400, 409.

45. *Ibid.*, 409. For Madison's later view that this claim was confined to importation and not to interstate navigation, see *ibid.*, III, 436–37. For the vote, see James McHenry in *Documents Illustrative of the Formation of the Union of the American States* (Washington, D.C., 1927), p. 617. See also Calvin Jillson and Thornton Anderson, "Realignments in the Convention of 1787: The Slave Trade Compromise," *Journal of Politics*, XXXIX (1977), 712–29.

46. *RFC*, I, 64–65, 74.

47. *Ibid.*, 66, 68.

48. *Ibid.*, II, 31.

49. See the capital article by Shlomo Slonim, "The Electoral College at Philadelphia," *Journal of American History*, LXXIII (1986), 35–58.

50. Hamilton to Timothy Pickering, September 15–16, 1803, in Richard B. Morris., ed., *Alexander Hamilton and the Founding of the Nation* (New York, 1957), pp. 158–59.

51. *RFC*, II, 493.

52. *Ibid.*, 587.

53. *Ibid.*, 318–19.

54. David Robertson, *Debates and Other Proceedings of the Convention of Virginia* (3 vols., Petersburg, Va., 1788–89). Similarly, "Cato," *New-York Journal*, November 8, 1787; an "Old Whig," [Philadelphia] *Independent Gazetteer*, December 4, 1787.

55. See Hearings Before the Committee on Foreign Relations, *U.S. Senate, 92d Congress, 1st sess., War Powers Legislation* (Washington, D.C., 1972), pp. 75–85.

See also W. Taylor Reveley, III, *War Powers of President and Congress: Who Holds the Arrows and Olive Branch?* (Charlottesville, 1984).

56. 2 Dallas (U.S.) 419, 421–27 (1793), upholding the right of a citizen of another state to sue one of the United States. Overturned by the Eleventh Amendment, ratified January 23, 1795.

57. *RFC,* II, 28; III, 273, 286, for Martin's qualifying comments as to his intentions.

58. Hamilton, *Federalist* No. 78. The papers of Delaware delegate Gunning Bedford, recently examined by James H. Hutson, disclose the willingness of some framers to have the judiciary play an active role in framing national policy.

59. *RFC,* II, 439, 440, 449.

60. *Ibid.,* 619.

61. *Ibid.,* 657.

62. *Ibid.,* 641–50.

Chapter 12. Ratification and Union

1. *RFC,* II, 623.

2. *Ibid.,* 645, 647.

3. *Ibid.,* 582.

4. *JCC,* XXXIII, 487–503, 540–41, 548–49.

5. Charles Pinckney, "Observations on the Plan of Government Submitted to the Federal Convention" (1787), in *RFC,* III, 107. James Madison, "Preface to Debates of the Convention of 1787," *ibid.,* 540–42.

6. Most state constitutions defined a quorum as a majority.

7. For protests by the seceding assemblymen and the Federalist response, see *DHRC,* II, 112–27.

8. *Ibid.,* p. 225.

9. *Independent Gazetteer,* December 5, 1787. On the question of representation in state ratifying conventions generally, see Charles W. Roll, Jr., "We, Some of the People: Apportionment in the Thirteen State Conventions Ratifying the Constitution," *Journal of American History,* LVI (1969), 21–40.

10. Jensen, ed., *DHRC,* II, 709; Merrill Jensen and Robert A. Becker, eds., *The Documentary History of the First Federal Elections, 1788–1790* (Madison, Wisc., 1975–), I, 240–41. For the Convention proceedings, see J. B. McMaster and F. D. Stone, eds., *Pennsylvania and the Federal Constitution, 1787–1788* (Philadelphia, 1888).

11. Samuel H. Harding, *The Contest Over the Ratification of the Federal Constitution in the State of Massachusetts* (repr., New York, 1970), p. 116.

12. Elliot, *Debates,* I, 182. *Debates, Resolutions, and other Proceedings of Commissioners of Massachusetts Convened at Boston . . . for the purpose of Assenting to and Ratifying the Constitution* (Boston, 1788), pp. 203, 207.

13. Thus, Richard Henry Lee would, on the basis of Article IX of the Articles of Confederation, give Congress exclusive control of the currency. Lee to George Mason, May 18, 1787, in James C. Ballagh, ed., *The Letters of Richard Henry Lee* (repr. 1911–14 ed.; 2 vols., New York, 1970), II, 422.

14. Lee to Thomas Lee Shippen, July 22, 1787, *ibid.*, II, 427.
    By now the motives of the Federalists and Antifederalists have been scruti-
    nized, and oversimplified formulas have been advanced to explain voting be-
    havior. One of the initial scholarly efforts, and still remarkably persuasive, if
    by no means all inclusive, is Orin G. Libby's *The Geographical Distribution of the
    Vote of the Thirteen States on the Federal Constitution, 1787–88* (Madison, Wisc.,
    1894). Two decades later Charles A. Beard, while not rejecting Libby's thesis,
    distinguished between holders of real property (small farmers and manor
    lords) and holders of personal property (merchants and public creditors). This
    oversimplified, if tentative, judgment has been severely criticized by Robert E.
    Brown (*Charles Beard and the Constitution* [Princeton, 1950]) and Forrest McDon-
    ald (*We the People: The Economic Origins of the Constitution* [Chicago, 1958]) and
    his *E Pluribus Unum: The Formation of the American Republic, 1776–1790* (Boston,
    1965), and revised by Lee Benson, (*Turner and Beard: American Historical Writing
    Reconsidered* [Glencoe, Ill., 1960]) and Jackson Turner Main, *The Anti-Federalists:
    Critics of the Constitution, 1781–1788* (Chapel Hill, 1961) and *Political Parties
    Before the Constitution* (Chapel Hill, N.C., 1975), the last with its emphasis on
    divisions between "localists" and "Cosmopolitans." The present writer finds
    that no single formula will suffice, and that geographical location, property
    concerns, and psychological imperatives varied from delegate to delegate and
    from state to state.
15. Cecelia Kenyon, "Men of Little Faith," in John P. Roche, ed., *Origins of American
    Political Thought* (New York, 1967), p. 215.
16. Lee to George Mason, October 1, 1787, Ballagh, ed., *Letters*, II, 438.
17. The Antifederalist position is spelled out in the magisterial work of Wood, *The
    Creation of the American Republic*, and in numerous other studies of recent
    decades, including Main, *The Antifederalists: Critics of the Constitution, 1781–1788;*
    Robert A. Rutland, *The Ordeal of the Constitution; The Antifederalists and the Ratifica-
    tion Struggle of 1787–1788* (Norman, Okla., 1966); C. Harvey Gardiner, ed., *A
    Study in Dissent: The Warren-Gerry Correspondence, 1776–1792* (Carbondale, Ill.,
    1968), and extensively documented in Herbert J. Storing, *The Complete Anti-
    Federalist* (7 vols., Chicago, 1981). For a sympathetic treatment of Martin, see
    Paul S. Clarkson and R. Samuel Jett, *Luther Martin of Maryland* (Baltimore,
    1970). Martin's violation of the secrets of the Convention in his *The Genuine
    Information* prompted vehement attacks, notably from Oliver Ellsworth. Morris,
    Witnesses, pp. 226, 227.
18. For the initiation of the series, the mechanics of its production, and the individ-
    ual stamp of each of the contributors, see Morris, *Witnesses*. For the best news-
    paper texts of *The Federalist*, the reader should use the edition of Jacob E.
    Cooke, ed., *The Federalist* (Middletown, Conn., 1961). A useful listing of numer-
    ous editions published here and abroad is provided by Roy P. Fairfield, ed.,
    The Federalist Papers (2d ed., Baltimore, 1981), pp. 308–14, 321–22. That author
    has also provided a helpful bibliographic guide to the innumerable mono-
    graphs that *The Federalist* has spawned. The question of the disputed authorship
    of certain *Federalist* letters has been substantially resolved as a result of the
    efforts of Douglass Adair, "The Authorship of the Disputed Federalist Papers,"

WMQ, I (1944), 97–222, 235–64. Applying statistical analysis to the text to determine authorship, Frederick Mosteller and David I. Wallace, *Inference and Disputed Authorship: The Federalist* (Reading, Mass., 1964), arrived at Adair's principal conclusions. For a helpful guide, see Thomas S. Engerman, Edward J. Erler, and Thomas B. Hofeller, eds., *The Federalist Concordance* (Middletown, Conn., 1980).

19. The more recent monographs on *The Federalist* include Garry Wills, *Explaining America: The Federalist* (New York, 1981), emphasizing the influence of the Scottish Enlightenment on "Publius"; Albert Furtwangler, *The Authority of Publius* (Ithaca, N.Y., 1984), which tends to minimize the influence of *The Federalist* on the voting behavior of delegates to the ratifying conventions; and David C. Epstein, *The Political Theory of the Federalist* (Chicago, 1984), which argues that the authors favored a "strictly republican" system.

20. Elliot, *Debates*, II, 547–56; Philip A. Crowl, *Maryland During and After the Revolution* (Baltimore, 1943), pp. 117, et seq.

21. Elliot, *Debates*, IV, 318–41, wherein the Constitution was approved with four recommendatory amendments, of which the most important was a rough draft of the Tenth Amendment.

22. Hugh Blair Grigsby, *History of the Virginia Convention of 1788* (2 vols., Richmond, Va., 1890–91), I, 160n.

23. John Blair Smith to Madison, June 12, 1788, *MP*, XI, 119–21.

24. Elliot, *Debates*, V, 551–62, at p. 559.

25. *Ibid.*, 440–44, 466.

26. Linda Grant De Pauw, *The Eleventh Pillar: New York State and the Federal Constitution* (Ithaca, N.Y., 1966), p. 185. For the argument that the rural counties were underrepresented, see Charles A. Beard, *An Economic Interpretation of the Constitution of the United States* (New York, 1913), p. 244; Spaulding, *New York in the Critical Period*, pp. 201–04; and Stephen L. Schechter, ed., *The Reluctant Pillar: New York and the Adoption of the Federal Constitution* (Troy, N.Y., 1985). Hamilton's role is documented in *HP*, V, 11–196; Jay's in "JJ, III."

27. Charles Tillinghast to John Lamb, June 21, 1788, Lamb Papers, New-York Historical Society.

28. Madison to Jefferson, August 10, 1788, *TJP*, XIII, 497–98; to Washington, August 11, 1788, *MP*, XI, 228–30. "I should tremble for the result of a second [Convention] meeting in the present temper . . ." Madison to G.I. Turberville, November 2, 1788. *RFC*, III, 354.

29. Francis Childs's *Debates and Proceedings of the Convention of the State of New-York . . .* (New York, 1788), a stenographic record that does not go beyond June 26, thereafter merely summarizing motions introduced. To fill the gap, one has to examine the "Journal" of the Convention's secretary, John McKesson, in the New York State Library and his "Notes" in the New-York Historical Society. Other missing gaps were captured by McKesson's "Notes" in the same library. Melancton Smith's "Notes" in the State Library, and the notes of Gilbert Livingston, a delegate from Dutchess County, provide the most complete coverage for the period beginning July 11; they are in the New York Public Library. For other scattering sources, see Morris, *Witnesses*, p. 267. Jay's role

is documented in "JJ, III." In addition, there are five scattering letters, between June 21 and July 19, 1788, of DeWitt Clinton commenting on some of the Poughkeepsie convention proceedings. DeWitt Clinton Papers, Rare Book and Manuscript Library, Columbia University.

30. J. R. Daniell, *Experiment in Republicanism: New Hampshire's Politics and the American Revolution, 1741–1794* (Cambridge, Mass., 1970).

31. See Rutland, *Ordeal of the Constitution*, p. 269.

32. Jefferson to William Carmichael, December 15, 1787, *TJP*, XII, 425–26; to William Smith, February 2, 1788, *ibid.*, 158; to Washington, May 2, 1788, *ibid.*, XIII, 128.

33. Elliot, *Debates*, IV, 214–17.

34. L. I. Trenholme, *Ratification of the Federal Constitution in North Carolina* (New York, 1932), chs. 5–6.

35. Washington to Jabez Brown, December 27, 1787, Emmet Collection, New York Public Library.

36. *The Debates and Proceedings in the Congress of the United States* (42 vols., Washington, D.C., 1834–56), II, 2214, 2236. Usually cited as *Annals of Congress.*

37. For the division on the vote, see Polishook, *Rhode Island*, p. 230.

38. See Edward P. Smith, "The Movement for a Second Constitutional Convention in 1788," in J. Franklin Jameson, ed., *Essays in the Constitutional History of the United States in the Formative Period, 1775–1789* (Boston, 1889), pp. 98, et seq.

39. Isaac Q. Leake, *Memoir of the Life and Times of General John Lamb* (Albany, N.Y., 1857), p. 231.

40. Jay to Edward Rutledge, October 15, 1788, *HPJ*, III, 362.

41. *Journal of the House of Delegates of the Commonwealth of Virginia* (Richmond, Va., 1788), pp. 13, 31–32.

42. Jay to Washington, September 21, 1788, *HPJ*, III, 360–61, "JJ, III."

43. Madison to Jefferson, October 17, December 8, 1788, *MP*, V, 271–73, 311; *TJP*, XIV, 16–21, 339–42.

44. John Quincy Adams, *The Jubilee of the Constitution. A Discourse Delivered at the Request of The New-York Historical Society* (New York, 1839), p. 55.

45. *Annals of Congress*, I, 441, 448–50.

46. "Due process" appears in the New York act of 1787 "concerning the Rights of the Citizens of this State." *Laws of the State of New York*, II, 344–45. Hamilton defined the term as being applicable only "to the process and proceedings of courts of justice." *HP*, IV, 35.

47. Madison included this pamphlet in a letter to Jefferson of October 17, 1788, *MP*, XI, 295–300n.; *TJP*, XIV, 16–22n.

48. Quoted in Bernard Schwartz, *The Great Rights of Mankind: A History of the American Bill of Rights* (New York, 1977), p. 174.

49. For a comparison of Madison's proposed amendments of June 8, the amendments reported by the House Select Committee, July 28, the amendments passed by the House, August 24, and those passed by the Senate, September 9, with the final amendments passed by Conference, September 25, 1789, see the various texts in Schwartz, *Great Rights*, pp. 231–46; also *MP*, XII, 196–210,

332–40 passim; also Goebel, *Supreme Court*, I, 435–56; De Pauw, ed., *First Federal Congress*, I, 151 *passim*; V, 1–48.

50. *Congressional Register*, II, 234; *MP*, XII, 346. Madison's presentation and defense of the Bill of Rights is conveniently found in *MP*, XII, 57–59, 188, 201–07, 339–46.

51. *MP*, XII, 346; *HP*, VIII, 97; 4 Wheat. 316 (U.S.) (1819).

52. *The Federalist* No. 78.

53. *Statutes at Large of the United States of America*, I, 73–93 (1789). De Pauw, ed., *First Federal Congress*, I, 80–83, 176–80, 183, 190; V, 1150–1212; Felix Frankfurter and James M. Landis, *The Business of the Supreme Court: A Study in the Federal Judicial System* (New York, 1928). William Paterson and Caleb Strong were major collaborators with Ellsworth in drafting the bill. For the Process Acts which shortly followed the Judiciary Act, see Goebel, *Supreme Court*, I, 509–51.

54. On the American public's past lack of commitment to constitutional issues and its readiness to place veneration of the Constitution above comprehension, see Michael Kammen, *A Machine That Would Go of Itself* (New York, 1986).

Bibliography

Notes on the Sources

Central to the documentation of the activities of the federal government in the years 1774–89 is a collection of published records, notably *Journals of the Continental Congress, 1774–1789* (34 vols., Washington, D.C., 1904–37), edited by Worthington C. Ford, et al. The happenings in Congress are illuminated by Edmund C. Burnett's edition of *Letters of Members of the Continental Congress* (8 vols., Washington, D.C., 1821–36), a series which is now being recompiled from more complete sources and edited by Paul Smith, et al., *Letters of Delegates to Congress* (in progress, Washington, D.C., 1976–   ).

The principal depository of the papers of the Congress and of its subordinate committees and administrative agencies is available in microfilm publication: *Record Group 11: General Records of the United States Government: Papers of the Continental Congress, 1774–1789,* 204 rolls, by the National Archives, including the journals of Congress, reports of committees, memorials and petitions, papers submitted by state governments, diplomatic correspondence; papers relating to the Superintendent of Finance and the Board of Treasury, the Secretary for Foreign Affairs, and the Secretary at War, papers relating to expenditures under domestic and foreign loans; Indian affairs and treaties—collected and arranged by Charles Thomson, Secretary of Congress.

The state constitutions are published in Francis N. Thorpe, comp., *The Federal and State Constitutions . . .* (7 vols., Washington, D.C., 1909). Aside from the printed legislative proceedings, laws, and the relatively few law reports of the states for this period, a most helpful source is William

Sumner Jenkins, collector and compiler, *Records of the States of the U.S.A.: A Microfilm Compilation*, edited by Lillian A. Hamrick, prepared by the Library of Congress in association with the University of North Carolina (1,600 reels, Library of Congress, Photoduplication Service, Washington, D.C., 1950, 1951).

An invaluable but incomplete source of diplomatic writings of the Confederation years is the long out-of-print series, *The Diplomatic Correspondence of the United States of America from the Signing of the Definitive Treaty of Peace ... to the Adoption of the Constitution ...* (7 vols., Washington, D.C., 1833–34), published at the direction of the Secretary of State. That collection is supplemented by Francis Wharton, ed., *The Revolutionary Diplomatic Correspondence of the United States* (6 vols., Washington, D.C., 1889). The treaties negotiated by the United States in the years 1778 to 1789 will be found in David Hunter Miller, ed., *Treaties and Other International Acts of the United States of America, 1776–1863* (6 vols., Washington, D.C., 1931–48).

One of the signal contributions to the scholarship of the Revolutionary and early national periods has been the new series of letterpress editions of American statesmen, which in many cases have provided enlarged, corrected, and updated annotation of previous collected works. The notable pioneer in the area—which has been a beneficiary of the support of the National Historical Publications Commission, the National Endowment for the Humanities, and some private foundations—was Julian P. Boyd, whose edition of *The Papers of Thomas Jefferson*, with recent volumes under the editorship of Charles T. Cullen, presently covers the years through 1791 (21 vols., Princeton, 1952–   ). Other new and more complete editions include: Harold C. Syrett, et al., eds., *The Papers of Alexander Hamilton* (26 vols., New York, 1961–79), supplemented by Julius Goebel, Jr., and Joseph H. Smith, eds., *The Law Practice of Alexander Hamilton* (4 vols., New York, 1964–80); William T. Hutchinson, William M. E. Rachal, Robert A. Rutland, et al., eds., *The Papers of James Madison* (Chicago and Charlottesville, Va., 1962–   ); Robert A. Rutland, ed., *The Papers of George Mason, 1745–1792* (3 vols., Chapel Hill, N.C., 1970); Leonard W. Labaree, William B. Willcox, et al., eds., *The Papers of Benjamin Franklin* (New Haven, 1959–   ); for later years the editions of John Bigelow (12 vols., New York, 1904) and Albert H. Smyth (10 vols., New York, 1905–07) are still invaluable. E. James Ferguson, John Catanzariti, et al., eds., *The Papers of Robert Morris, 1781–1784* (Pittsburgh, 1973–   ). For John Adams, see Lyman H. Butterfield, et al., eds., *Diary and Autobiography of John Adams* (4 vols., Cambridge, Mass., 1961), The Adams Papers, Series I, Diaries; Lyman H. Butterfield, et al., eds., *Adams Family Correspondence* (Cambridge, Mass., 1963–   ), The Adams Papers, Series II, Adams Family Correspondence; L. Kinvin Wroth and Hiller B. Zobel, eds., *Legal Papers of John Adams* (3 vols., Cambridge, Mass.,

1965), The Adams Papers, Series III, General Correspondence and Other Papers of the Adams Statesmen; and Robert J. Taylor, et al., eds., *Papers of John Adams* (Cambridge, Mass., 1977–), The Adams Papers, Series III, General Correspondence and Other Papers of the Adams Statesmen, supplemented by a microfilm edition of 400 reels of papers in the collections of the Massachusetts Historical Society.

Other ongoing series include Richard B. Morris, et al., eds., *John Jay: The Making of a Revolutionary; Unpublished Papers, 1745–1780* (New York, 1975); *John Jay: The Winning of the Peace; Unpublished Papers, 1780–1784* (New York, 1980); "John Jay: Confederation and Union; State Papers and Private Correspondence, 1784–1789" (forthcoming, New York, 1988)—a planned four-volume series of largely unpublished papers supplementing the older and selected edition of Henry P. Johnston, ed., *The Correspondence and Public Papers of John Jay* (4 vols., New York, 1890–93). Other statesmen's series in progress include Carl E. Prince, et al., eds., *The Papers of William Livingston* (Trenton, N.J., 1979–); Herbert A. Johnson, Charles T. Cullen, Charles F. Hobson, et al., eds., *The Papers of John Marshall* (Williamsburg, Va., 1974–); Philip M. Hamer, David R. Chesnutt, et al., eds., *The Papers of Henry Laurens* (Columbia, S.C., 1968–); and Don Higginbotham, ed., *The Papers of James Iredell* (Raleigh, N.C., 1976–).

Finally, the most comprehensive current statesman project involves the publication of the papers of George Washington, currently under the editorship of Donald Jackson and Dorothy Twohig. The work comprises: *The Diaries of George Washington* (6 vols., Charlottesville, Va., 1976–79), and *The Papers of George Washington: Colonial Series; Revolutionary Series; Presidential Series*, which are being published concurrently. When completed, this edition will be both more comprehensive and more accurate than the older standard collection edited by John C. Fitzpatrick, *The Writings of George Washington from the Original Manuscript Sources, 1745–1799* (39 vols., Washington, D.C., 1931–44). The Fitzpatrick is confined to letters from Washington— whereas the modern edition includes letters to Washington as well and drawn from the letterbook copies rather than the addressee's originals. Until superseded, Fitzpatrick remains a major source for the period.

The standard guide to the newspapers of this period is Clarence S. Brigham, ed., *History and Bibliography of American Newspapers, 1690–1820* (2 vols., Worcester, Mass., 1947). The Readex Corporation, in cooperation with the American Antiquarian Society, included most of the books, pamphlets, newspapers, journals, broadsides, and other items published in Charles Evans, et al., comps., *American Bibliography . . . [1639–1800]* (14 vols., Chicago and Worcester, Mass., 1903–59) in its microprint edition of *Early American Imprints, 1st ser., 1639–1800.*

For the Constitutional Convention, the standard source is Max Farrand, ed., *The Records of the Federal Convention* (rev. ed., 4 vols., New Haven, 1937), for which a supplement, including recently uncovered additional notes on the Convention by participants, compiled by James H. Hutson, is now in press. While the fullest and most authoritative, Madison's minutes cover only a relatively small portion of the total discussion and debate, as Hutson's study reveals. The Convention records can also be found in a somewhat different arrangement in a compact one-volume edition selected and arranged by Charles C. Tansill, *Documents Illustrative of the Formation of the Union of the American States,* House Doc. 398, 69th Cong., 1st sess. (Washington, D.C., 1927). For significant selected documents bearing on the contents of the Constitution, see *The Founders' Constitution,* Philip B. Kurland and Ralph Lerner, eds. (5 vols., Chicago, 1987); a useful reference work on the Constitution is the recent *Encyclopedia of the American Constitution* (4 vols., New York, 1986), Leonard W. Levy, et al., eds.

The ratification debates have been compiled from private sources for each state convention by Jonathan Elliot, ed., *The Debates in the Several State Conventions on the Adoption of the Federal Constitution . . .* (2d ed., 5 vols., Philadelphia and Washington, D.C., 1866), a collection which is being superseded by the current series in progress by John F. Kaminski and Gaspare J. Saladino, et al., eds., *The Documentary History of the Ratification of the Constitution* (Madison, Wisc., 1976–). The original reports or manuscript sources consulted in the preparation of the present volume are cited in chapter XII.

The essential sources for the establishment of the federal government are: *The Documentary History of the First Federal Elections, 1788–1790,* ed. by Merrill Jensen and Robert Becker (Madison, Wisc., 1976–), and *Documentary History of the First Federal Congress of the United States of America, March 4, 1789–March 3, 1791,* ed. by Linda Grant De Pauw, et al. (18 vols. projected, Baltimore, 1972–).

Short Titles

AGI	Archivo General de Indías, Seville
AHN	Archivo Histórico Nacional, Estado series, Madrid
AHR	*American Historical Review*
AN:AE and CC	Archives Nationales, Paris: Affaires Étrangères and Correspondance Consulaire
ASP	Walter Lowrie, et al., eds., *American State Papers. Documents, Legislative and Executive, of the Congress of the United States . . .* (38 vols., Washington, D.C., 1832–61)
Bemis,	*Jay Treaty* Samuel Flagg Bemis, *Jay's Treaty: A Study in Commerce and Diplomacy* (rev. ed., New Haven, 1962)

BIBLIOGRAPHY 391

BFS   Albert H. Smyth, ed., *The Writings of Benjamin Franklin* (10
           vols., New York, 1905–07)
Burnett,   *Continental Congress* Edmund C. Burnett, *The Continental
           Congress* (New York, 1941)
DC   Published under the direction of the Secretary of State,
           *The Diplomatic Correspondence of the United States of America
           from the Signing of the Definitive Treaty of Peace . . . to the
           Adoption of the Constitution . . .* (7 vols., Washington, D.C.,
           1833–34)
DHRC   Merrill Jensen, John P. Kaminski, Gaspare J. Saladino, et
           al., eds., *The Documentary History of the Ratification of the
           Constitution* (Madison, Wisc., 1976–   )
DLC   Library of Congress, Washington, D.C.
Elliot,   *Debates* Jonathan Elliot, ed., *The Debates in the Several State
           Conventions on the Adoption of the Federal Constitution* (2d
           ed., 5 vols., Philadelphia, 1876)
FAA   Peter Force, ed., *American Archives: Fourth Series, Contain-
           ing a Documentary History of the English Colonies in North
           America, from the King's Message to Parliament, of March 7,
           1774, to the Declaration of Independence by the United States*
           (6 vols., Washington, D.C., 1837–46)
GWF   John C. Fitzpatrick, ed., *The Writings of George Washington
           from the Original Manuscript Sources, 1745–1799* (39 vols.,
           Washington, D.C., 1931–44)
HP   Harold C. Syrett, et al., eds., *The Papers of Alexander Hamil-
           ton* (26 vols., New York, 1961–79)
HPJ   Henry P. Johnston, ed., *The Correspondence and Public Pa-
           pers of John Jay* (4 vols., New York, 1890–93)
JA, Diary Lyman H. Butterfield, et al., eds., *Diary and Autobiography
           of John Adams,* The Adams Papers, Series I (4 vols., Cam-
           bridge, Mass., 1961)
JAW   Charles Francis Adams, ed., *The Works of John Adams,
           Second President of the United States: With a Life of the Author*
           (10 vols., Boston, 1850–56)
Jay Papers Rare Book and Manuscript Library, Columbia University
JCC   Worthington C. Ford, et al., eds., *Journals of the Continen-
           tal Congress, 1774–1789* (34 vols., Washington, D.C.,
           1904–37)
JJ   Richard B. Morris, et al., eds., *John Jay: The Making of a
           Revolutionary; Unpublished Papers, 1745–1780* (New York,
           1975), Vol. I; *John Jay: The Winning of the Peace; Unpublished
           Papers, 1780–1784* (New York, 1980), Vol. II; "John Jay:

　　　　　　　　Confederation and Union; State Papers and Private Cor-
　　　　　　　　respondence, 1784–1789" (New York, forthcoming),
　　　　　　　　Vol. III
LDCC　　　　　Paul H. Smith, ed., *Letters of Delegates to Congress* (Wash-
　　　　　　　　ington, D.C., 1976–　)
LMCC　　　　　Edmund C. Burnett, ed., *Letters of Members of the Continen-*
　　　　　　　　tal Congress (8 vols., Washington, D.C., 1821–36)
MAE:CC and CP　Ministère des Affaires Étrangères, Paris: Correspond-
　　　　　　　　ance Consulaire et Commerciale and Correspondance
　　　　　　　　politique
Morris,　　　　*Peacemakers* Richard B. Morris, *The Peacemakers: The Great*
　　　　　　　　Powers and American Independence (New York, 1965)
MP　　　　　　William T. Hutchinson, William M. E. Rachal, Robert A.
　　　　　　　　Rutland, et al., eds., *The Papers of James Madison* (Chicago
　　　　　　　　and Charlottesville, Va., 1962–　)
PCC　　　　　　Papers of the Continental Congress, 1774–1789 (Record
　　　　　　　　Group 11, National Archives, Washington, D.C.)
PMHB　　　　　*The Pennsylvania Magazine of History and Biography*
PRO:FO　　　　Public Record Office, London: Foreign Office Papers
PSQ　　　　　　*Political Science Quarterly*
RDC　　　　　　Francis Wharton, ed., *The Revolutionary Diplomatic Corre-*
　　　　　　　　spondence of the United States (6 vols., Washington, D.C.,
　　　　　　　　1889)
RFC　　　　　　Max Farrand, ed., *The Records of the Federal Convention* (4
　　　　　　　　vols., New Haven, 1937)
RMP　　　　　　E. James Ferguson, et al., eds., *The Papers of Robert Morris,*
　　　　　　　　1781–1784 (Pittsburgh, 1973–　)
TJP　　　　　　Julian P. Boyd, Charles T. Cullen, et al., eds., *The Papers*
　　　　　　　　of Thomas Jefferson (Princeton, 1952–　)
WMQ　　　　　*William and Mary Quarterly,* 3d series unless otherwise
　　　　　　　　indicated

Index